They kill for all kinds of reasons, [text obscured] [text obscured] ne from all walks of life. One after another they stalk their prey, leaving a trail of blood and shattered lives in their wake.

Here, from the files of *True Detective* magazine, are the case stories of twenty-four of the most brutal serial murderers in the annals of crime history. In America, England, and Europe, they've left their mark on the people, challenged law enforcement agencies, and — for most — ended their vicious sprees behind bars . . . or at the hand of the executioner.

But one is still loose, and the report of his slaughter is included here, too, with the question: Can you help the police find The Green River Killer?

NON-FICTION FROM PINNACLE BOOKS

ZONE THERAPY   (17-208, $3.95)
by Anika Bergson and Vladimir Tuchak
For the first time, here is a layman's guide that pulls together all the systems of direct-pressure therapy on key parts of the body, including acupuncture, foot-and-hand reflexology, finger message . . . and much more! Zone therapy is simple, easy to learn and use. And anyone can do it!

THE POPCORN PLUS DIET   (17-065, $3.50)
by Joel Herskowitz, M.D.
By sticking to Dr. Herskowitz's painless and nutritious 21-day meal plan and curbing those annoying pangs of hunger with hot, tasty popcorn, you can lose up to two pounds a week. The Popcorn-Plus Diet is doctor-devised, medically tested, and nutritionalist-approved.

THE RELATIVITY OF WRONG   (17-169, $3.95)
by Isaac Asimov
There is no scientific region too remote nor area inaccessible to the probing pen of Isaac Asimov. In this, his remarkable twenty-fourth collection of astonishing real-life wonders, the good doctor carries the reader on a breathtaking rollercoaster ride that races from the center of the human brain to the outer reaches of the universe.

SERIAL MURDERERS

Edited by
ART CROCKETT

PINNACLE BOOKS
WINDSOR PUBLISHING CORP.

PINNACLE BOOKS

are published by

Windsor Publishing Corp.
475 Park Avenue South
New York, NY 10016

First Pinnacle Books printing: September, 1990

Printed in the United States of America

The Worst Mass Murderer in History, *True Detective:* May, 1985
End of the Trail for the Hillside Strangler, *Master Detective:* March,
  1980
Snuffing Lives was His Fiendish Passion! *Official Detective:* August,
  1988

Reign of Terror of the Green River Killer! *Master Detective:* February, 1985

Terror Spree of the Rampaging Rambo! *True Detective:* April, 1988

Weird Case of the Satan-Loving Night Stalker! *Official Detective:* March, 1986

Illinois Homosexual Homicide Horror, *True Detective:* December, 1979

Flooded the Valley of the Moon With Gore! *Official Detective:* February, 1990

We've Captured the Most Dangerous Serial Killers! *True Detective:* February, 1987

The Yorkshire Ripper! *True Detective:* October, 1981

How He Butchered the New York Beauties! *True Detective:* February, 1975

Texas Homosexual Torture-Murder Horrors! *True Detective:* November, 1973

The Mistakes that Trapped "Son of Sam," *True Detective:* December, 1977

Sex Murder, *Official Detective:* November, 1979

Virginia's Rampaging Serial Rape-Slayer, *Official Detective:* June, 1989

Did One California Maniac Kill all 11 Victims? *True Detective:* July, 1973

Oklahoma's Infamous Osage Murders! *Master Detective:* March, 1990

The Boston Strangler! *True Detective:* April, 1967

6 Pretty Victims in Texas' "Killing Fields," *Master Detective:* April, 1989

Chained Beauties for the Prowling Sex Monster! *Official Detective:* July, 1989

Stop the Brutal Beast who Stalks Young Innocents! *Master Detective:* February, 1989

The Demon Brothers of L.A., *Official Detective:* May, 1989

El Bandito — The Mad Dog of Five Nations, *Official Detective:* December, 1989

Did Alligators Eat the Pretty Texas Waitresses? *Master Detective:* January, 1971

TABLE OF CONTENTS

The Worst Mass Murderer In History

by Bill G. Cox

Texas' Bisexual Moonlight Killer:
He got his kicks raping the women he killed. Nobody knows how many. Some say 157, others think the figure is 167. In any case, his name will go down in the annals of crime as the most horrendous executioner who ever lived. Here's his shocking story.

The killer was like something from a horror novel. His story was "Halloween," "Psycho," "Jack the Ripper" all thrown together. He had one glass eye, glazed and scummy-looking, according to those who knew him and lived to tell about it. They said he never bathed, "always seemed greasy, dirty." But there was a "Dr. Jekyll-Mr. Hyde" aspect, too. He could be quiet, well-mannered, even hard-working sometimes. Social workers and shrinks may think the cards were stacked against him. He claimed to have sexually attacked and killed a woman school teacher when he was 13. At age 24, he stabbed to death his 74-year-old mother.

But it wasn't until later that the mass murder spree began, which investigators say could be America's worst to date.

He became a drifter, moving from state to state, aimlessly like a tumbleweed in the wind. But he had a definite philosophy and goal. In his own words later to officers he said he fulfilled it at random. "If I saw a woman by herself, she was mine," he said. Or, as one investigator would sum it up, after the killing marathon was at an end, "The motive was murder itself."

The killer admitted to necrophilism, too. He said he liked to have sex with a woman after he killed her. He killed in various ways, according to his statement: Stabbing, decapitation, strangulation, beating, shooting, burning. He was bisexual, and this led to an attachment to a homosexual he met at a rescue mission, where both were seeking food and shelter. The two became lovers. The homo, who frequently dressed as a woman, said later he was with the AC-DC killer when some of the women were killed.

The homo was later to confess to a heinous child killing, himself. It was a child murder case that ultimately resulted in Congress passing the Missing Children Act and was the basis for a television movie called "Adam."

Investigators think the one-eyed drifter—with the help of his homo lover in some cases, may have killed up to 165 persons, mostly women, in 17 states. If he is indeed linked to even one-quarter that number, the confessed woman stalker will have surpassed any previous record set by mass murderers in America, such monstrous statistics as 36 young men or boys killed by John Wayne Gacy in Illinois, or Juan Corona who killed 25 farm laborers in California, or Don Coral and Elmer Wayne Henley who tortured and killed 27 teenage boys in Houston, Texas.

The Boston Strangler and Jack the Ripper would be mere minor leaguers in comparison.

The nightmarish story of the on-going women massacres first surfaced in a Texas hamlet in June, 1983. Montague County Sheriff W. F. Conway—one of two Texas officers destined to break wide open the tangled web of mass murder—started with a missing person report. The report was made to the officer on Sept. 17, 1982 by an Oklahoma woman who was worried about the disappearance of her 80-year-old mother, Mrs. Katherine Rich of Ringgold, Texas.

Ringgold is a community of just over 50 residents. It is about 30 miles east of Wichita Falls, and about 5 miles south of the Oklahoma line. Ringgold's only business is a combination grocery store-service station. The owners keep a few comfortable chairs around because the Ringgold residents, besides buying supplies there, like to sit and talk a spell.

The relative who contacted Sheriff Conway was worried because there was no reason for Mrs. Rich's absence. And there were some other disquieting circumstances that Sheriff Conway soon was to learn about.

Conway is a strapping, 6-feet-2 Old West type of sheriff. His broad face has a John Wayne set to it. Residents and fellow lawmen in North Texas and neighboring Oklahoma have a nickname for the big sheriff. They call him "Houn' Dog" Conway. The nickname is well-deserved, says one Montague County officer who works with Conway.

"That's the opinion of him," the officer says. "Once he gets on your trail, watch out. The impression you get of him is that of a gun-toting sheriff from way back in the Wild West days. His speech. His walk." Pretty soon the whole country would hear about "Houn' Dog" Conway, the 61-year-old Texas sheriff whose tenacious investigation would open a Pandora's box of horror.

Mrs. Rich was a long-time resident of Ringgold, living alone in her three-bedroom home. Relatives who lived just across the Oklahoma line came by to check on her regularly. It was from the relatives that Conway heard about a couple that had worked for the elderly woman briefly. They were a strange couple—an older man in his 40s and a plumpish, teenage girl. It had been the actions of the couple that led to their being ordered off Mrs. Rich's place by her relatives.

The couple had drifted into Ringgold in May, 1982, following up a job lead from another of Mrs. Rich's relatives who lived in California. It came about this way, according to the reports to Sheriff Conway.

The California relative, a 51-year-old man, had picked up the couple near Beaumont, California on a cold night in January, 1982. They were hitchhiking, and the California businessman felt sorry for them. He offered the man a job. The man, who said his name was Henry Lucas, accepted.

11

He introduced the teenaged girl as his wife, "Becky," and the pair moved in.

Lucas and his young wife stayed in a small apartment provided by their benefactor. They remained five months, during which Lucas talked about the tough boyhood he had. He said he had been raised "dirt poor." Lucas recalled that his father had earned money by skinning minks after having both legs amputated because of a mining accident.

The Californian liked the couple, and in May he mentioned they might be a big help to his elderly relative in Ringgold Texas. Lucas could help make some needed plumbing repairs, and the girl could assist with the housework. After making the arrangements, the Californian put the couple on a bus for Ringgold.

The drifter and his young wife seemed likeable enough to the townspeople after they arrived on their new job. Ringgold's people were trusting types, who never even locked their doors at night.

But when the couple started doing shopping at the local store with checks signed by "Katy" Rich, the store operators became suspicious. It was the items purchased by Lucas and his wife that raised the storekeepers' suspicions. As a result, they called one of Mrs. Rich's relatives, who lived only a short distance away in Oklahoma.

When the relative arrived and looked over the list of groceries bought by the couple, she knew something was amiss. The list included a cake mix, and the relative knew Mrs. Rich's oven didn't work. The list also included soft drinks and cigarettes, neither of which the elderly woman ever used.

The relative notified still another family member. Together they went to Mrs. Rich's home. There they found her eating breakfast by herself; the couple were still asleep. And the place was in filthy condition, showing no signs of any housekeeping. The relatives ordered the couple to get off the premises.

The relatives gave the couple a ride to the Ringgold store. The drifter and his young wife said they would catch a bus to Wichita Falls. But instead they started hitchhiking, and once again a friendly motorist stopped and gave them a ride.

The motorist was a 52-year-old roofing contractor, who also served as minister of a religious group that had established a commune at Stoneburg, just 10 miles south of Ringgold.

Lucas introduced himself and his wife. He told the roofing contractor they were headed for Wichita Falls to pick up a check being mailed to them there for some work in California.

Arriving in Wichita Falls, Lucas checked at the post office. He came back and said the check hadn't come. The contractor offered to let the couple stay on at the religious commune, formerly a 15-acre chicken farm the religious group had bought for setting up their commune. The two dozen or so members worked at various jobs, but held their services four times a week.

The commune residents accepted the newcomers, but one woman would recall later she had bad feelings the moment she first laid eyes on Lucas. As she would relate months later, "There was a look in his good eye that didn't belong in a normal man. I saw it once before, and the man was mean." She said after that first meeting, she kept a .38 pistol handy.

Outwardly, the couple seemed friendly enough. Lucas helped the roofing contractor on jobs. He also repaired old TV sets to be sold in the religious group's thrift shop.

The girl Lucas introduced as his wife didn't do much. Lucas bought and repaired a junk car, and she was happy to drive it around the chicken farm. She also liked to pick at the church piano.

The woman who had been apprehensive about Lucas later recalled she saw another side of him one night that conflicted with his quiet, friendly daytime manner. "Henry was working on a gasoline engine and Becky was trying to help him," she said. "He was eating her out, saying she couldn't hold things to suit him. I talked to her later and she claimed he cussed her every night."

It was during August, 1982, that the same woman over-

13

heard the teenager tell Lucas that she wanted to leave him, saying, "I don't think anyone would put up with what I have."

On Aug. 23, 1982, Lucas told the roofing contractor that Becky wanted to return to relatives in Florida and he was going with her. A resident of the commune drove the couple to a truck stop just south of Stoneburg. The couple hoped to catch a ride there and hitchhike to Florida. That's the last time anyone in Stoneburg saw Becky.

But the next day, Lucas came back. He was in tears and said his wife had gotten into a truck with a truckdriver and left him. For a while, Lucas resumed his life at the commune. In September, Lucas accompanied the roofing contractor to Altus, Oklahoma, to help on a job that took four days. They returned to the commune for a church camp meeting that started September 15th.

The following day, Lucas told the contractor of plans to go to Ringgold for a visit with his former employer, Mrs. Rich.

When Lucas returned, he said he hadn't found Mrs. Rich at home. The elderly woman was never seen again after that day. And on September 17th, Lucas mentioned he had to go into town to buy some clothes. He never returned.

Questioning Mrs. Rich's relatives and the residents of the religious commune, Sheriff Conway put together the known activities of Lucas and his wife while they were living in his county.

The sheriff was of the opinion at this point that he might be investigating a murder—maybe even two if the sudden disappearance of Lucas' wife was taken into account. He called Texas Ranger Phil Ryan, stationed at Decatur, and asked for some help in the case.

Ryan is a contrasting personality to Sheriff Conway. The 36-year-old Ranger was likened to an accountant when it came to discussing his investigations. The comparison was made by a newspaper reporter.

The sheriff and the Ranger make a good investigative team, and together they came to the conclusion that Henry

Lucas was the man they needed to talk to most about the disappearance of Katherine Rich and the sudden departure of "Becky" Lucas.

First, Conway and Ryan launched a background check on Lucas. It didn't take long to come up with some startling information after the suspect's name was fed to the National Crime Information Center in Washington, D.C.

Lucas, crime records disclosed, had been convicted of second degree murder for the stabbing death of his mother in Michigan. This had been in 1960.

Events leading up to the matricide started when Lucas and his 74-year-old mother traveled from their home in Blacksburg, Virginia, to the small farming community of Tecumseh, Michigan to spend the Christmas holidays of 1959 with the relatives. According to accounts by authorities, Lucas and his mother had planned to stay for a month's visit.

But on Jan. 12, 1960, Mrs. Viola Lucas decided they would return home. Lucas didn't want to go and he argued with his mother. That night, the woman's body, stabbed several times, was discovered in a bedroom of the relatives' house. Lucas was gone.

Later, officers learned the suspect stole a car from a gas station in Tecumseh and drove to Blacksburg. On January 16th, he was arrested while hitchhiking near Toledo, Ohio.

Convicted of second degree murder, Lucas was sentenced to a prison term of 20 to 40 years. But after three months, he was transferred to a state hospital for the criminally insane, where he spent five years.

In June, 1970, after being returned to state prison for nearly five years, Lucas was paroled. A year later he was arrested in Tecumseh for attempting to kidnap two teenage girls. This charge sent him back to prison, where he was confined about four years. He was released on Aug. 22, 1975.

What he was doing in the eight years after his prison release as he drifted from state to state wouldn't come to light until the persistence of a rural Texas sheriff and a Texas Ranger would disclose one of the most shocking sagas of

15

wanton murder in recent years.

After learning that Lucas had left Stoneburg in the old car that Becky had enjoyed driving around the religious commune, Sheriff Conway tried to dig up information on the car. He didn't have much to go on. He finally located the man who had sold the car to Lucas. The sheriff learned that the car previously belonged to a relative of the man. The relative had died recently in Wichita Falls.

The sheriff had a hunch there might not have been time for a transfer of title. He asked the man who had sold the car to Lucas to make a search of family papers for any possible information about the vehicle.

The idea resulted in a good lead. A letter that had been mailed to the deceased relative in Wichita Falls by the California State Police was found. The letter had been sent there apparently because the motor vehicle records showed the deceased Wichita Falls resident as the person to whom the car was registered.

The letter said the car had been found abandoned at Needles, California and impounded on Sept. 21, 1982.

Sheriff Conway obtained a search warrant, which he forwarded to California authorities with a request to search the car for possible evidence in a homicide. California crime technicians discovered human blood in the old car. Unfortunately, the Texas investigators were unable to come up immediately with the blood type of the missing Katherine Rich to determine if the bloodstains were linked to her disappearance.

But Sheriff Conway and Ranger Ryan did learn more about Lucas' teenage companion, whom he always introduced as "Becky." A check with Florida authorities revealed the girl, 15 years old, was a runaway from Jacksonville, Florida. Moreover, since last having been seen in Stoneburg, Texas, she had not returned to relatives living in Florida.

Her full name was Frieda "Becky" Powell.

As the sheriff and Ranger continued to try to untangle the mystery, feelings were growing strong in Ringgold and Stoneburg and Montague, the county seat. People kept asking about progress in the case.

Two important developments improved the sheriff's outlook in October, 1982. The first was official word he received that Henry Lucas was wanted on an outstanding warrant charging him with theft of a car in Maryland. That gave the Texas officers a legal reason to arrest Lucas if they could find him.

And in mid-October, the object of their search resurfaced. The roofing contractor who originally had brought Lucas and his young wife to the religious commune because he felt sorry for them received a phone call from the drifter. Lucas said he was in Indiana, was cold, hungry and in need of some money. The contractor declined to help.

A visit from Sheriff Conway changed the contractor's mind. Conway said he was looking for Lucas on a stolen car warrant, but mainly the wanted man was suspected of the murder of Mrs. Rich.

It was hard for the contractor to believe that Lucas was a murderer, he told the sheriff. But he added he knew where the man was. He promised to get in touch if Lucas called back. The suspect did call the next day, and the contractor agreed to send him $100. Lucas hitchhiked back. It was Sunday, October 17th, when he quietly returned to the commune and for the first time attended a prayer service.

The sheriff was notified, and the next day, Conway picked up Lucas on the Maryland warrant and brought him to his office for questioning.

The sheriff and Ranger grilled Lucas about the missing Katherine Rich. The drifter agreed to take a lie detector test. The results of the test convinced Conway and Ryan that Lucas knew something about the woman's disappearance, probably had killed her. But they had no proof, not even a body.

The suspect placed the blame on the absence of both Mrs. Rich and "Becky" elsewhere. He told a wild tale of how the California man who had originally sent him and Becky to Texas to work for Mrs. Rich had abducted both women. He said the women had been kept in a motel in San Antonio. He handed over a key, telling the lawmen it

17

would fit the door of the motel room in San Antonio.

During the quizzing, the officers noticed that Lucas seemed sincerely concerned about his missing teenage wife.

The sheriff had contacted Maryland authorities, informing them of Lucas' arrest on the stolen car warrant. But the officials in that state decided not to extradite Lucas.

The suspect had been in jail about a week. With the word from Maryland, Conway had no legal grounds to hold him any longer.

Lucas was released, and he returned to the religious commune. The sheriff kept after him, though. He used the excuse of Lucas' missing wife to visit the drifter frequently.

Meanwhile, Ranger Ryan sent the key turned over by Lucas to Rangers at San Antonio, where the officers spent two days checking motels trying to find a door the key would open. They had no luck. Because of Lucas' known nomadic life, Sheriff Conway drove to Oklahoma and Louisiana to confer with officers about murders and kidnappings in those states, seeking any trace of Lucas in the cases. But he turned up nothing.

As the members of the religious commune learned of Lucas' background from officers, their feelings about the drifter for whom they had felt pity changed. Friendliness turned to fear. And since his release from jail, Lucas was acting strange.

"There were times when he was normal," the contractor would say later. "There were times when you knew he was dangerous."

Two hatchets and a bayonet disappeared from the thrift shop. The contractor feared Lucas might have taken them. At night, Lucas was restless. Once they heard him walking around on the roof. The contractor became worried enough to get a pistol and keep it close at hand.

Yet, Lucas caused no trouble. Still, the sheriff and his deputies kept close watch on the camp. In October, 1982, a hunter found a purse in a creekbed near Stoneburg. It was identified by relatives as having belonged to Katherine Rich.

That same month, Mrs. Rich's house burned down.

Cause of the fire was a mystery.

Three months passed with no new leads in the disappearance of either Katherine Rich or "Becky" Powell. During February, 1982, Sheriff Conway asked Lucas to take another polygraph test. This one was administered in Fort Worth. During the grilling, Conway unfolded a road map and pointed to locations where he thought the suspect might have left the body. From Lucas' reactions to the possible sites, the sheriff returned to Stoneburg and started searching an area about six miles away, near a railroad track. Conway was accompanied by his wife as he searched for three hours.

But the search didn't turn up anything.

Meanwhile, Lucas stayed at the commune.

Pressing hard for leads in the case, Conway and Ryan made a trip to California in May to examine Lucas' car, still impounded at Needles. The officers took blood samples from the vehicle. But they found nothing to link Lucas to the murder.

On June 4th, Lucas decided to hit the road again. He told the commune residents he was going on a trip. Before he left, he gave the contractor-minister a .22-caliber pistol, asking him to keep it until he came back. There were some extra bullets with the gun.

After Lucas left, the contractor called the sheriff and told him about the gun, now locked up in the church office.

The information gave Conway grounds for obtaining a new warrant for Lucas' arrest on a charge of a convicted felon possessing firearms. Only three days later, the contractor received another call from Lucas, who claimed he had found both Becky and Kate Rich.

Lucas, who said he was calling from Demming, New Mexico, said he had the woman and girl with him after locating them in California. He said he was bringing them back to clear himself. But the next day Lucas called again. This time he said he was having car trouble. The contractor agreed to drive to Demming and return Lucas and Becky and Mrs. Rich to Stoneburg.

But upon arrival in the New Mexico town, he found Lucas alone. The contractor called the sheriff after returning from New Mexico with Lucas. Conway arrested Lucas on the firearms charge.

The drifter was back in jail, but officers were no closer to making a case of murder against him than they had been. The sheriff instructed his jailers to leave Lucas alone and let him stew.

"I expect a criminal element to lie to you until he's caught," the sheriff would tell reporters later. "And then, when you've got him caught, you've tracked him so long and know so much about him, he'll just confess."

Lucas asked to see the contractor-minister from the commune. The suspect said during the jail visit that he had waited too long to be saved. He said he had made a bad mistake, but he didn't elaborate.

After being in jail four days, Lucas sent word to Sheriff Conway that he wanted to talk to him. Conway called Ranger Ryan, and they both went to the jail. The first words Lucas said were, "Well, sheriff, I might as well. I've got to get my business straight. You've got me."

"Yes, I've got you," the sheriff answered.

Thus began an all-night talkathon by Lucas to the two officers. He told of his nomadic lifestyle, how he frequently drove or hitchhiked coast to coast in two days by going without sleep; how he bought and abandoned junk cars along the road. He said he never worked in one place for more than a few weeks at a time—just long enough to buy a couple of pair of pants and cigarette money.

Then he got down to the business of murder, and the story he related was one of the likes of which the two officers had never heard before or ever expected to again.

The one-eyed drifter quietly related an incredible odyssey of murder.

Lucas told the sheriff and Ranger that he had stabbed Kate Rich to death and dumped her body in a field. After the second lie detector test, said Lucas, he returned and retrieved the body. Under cover of night, he took it to his shack at the commune and burned it in an oven, he said in a statement.

When told where the body had been left in the field, the sheriff realized he had missed finding it by only about six-tenths of a mile the evening he made his search.

During his night-long statement, Lucas claimed to have killed as many as 50 women throughout the nation.

During the next day, he led officers to his shack at the commune. There in the oven the investigators found ashes and fragments of human bones.

Lucas also admitted that he had stabbed to death "Becky" Powell, the teenage girl he said was his common-law wife and who he had first met in Florida when she was 12 years old. He accompanied Ranger Ryan to a site near Denton, Texas where he said he had disposed of the body after dismembering it. Skeletal remains later identified as those of a teenage girl were found in a field near the intersection of Interstate 35 and State Highway 380, west of Denton.

Within a few days, Lucas was indicted by a Montague County grand jury for murder in the slaying of Katherine Rich. It was when he was brought before State District Judge Frank Douthitt for arraignment on the murder indictment that the suspect dropped a bombshell in open court.

When the judge asked Lucas if he understood he was indicted for murder, the drifter replied with an answer that shocked the officials in the courtroom.

"Yes, I know—I've got about a hundred of them," Lucas said quietly.

When asked by the judge if he thought he was mentally competent to stand trial, Lucas answered, "There's about a hundred women out there that says different. It ain't normal for a fellow to go out and kill girls just to have sex with them."

The judge ordered Lucas held in jail with bond denied.

Criminal investigators from throughout the United States began to contact Ranger Ryan and Sheriff Conway about murders that had occurred in their jurisdictions. In fact, Ryan said that Lucas—who continued to talk freely to Ryan and Conway—was a prime suspect in the killing of women elsewhere in Texas, plus New Mexico, Oklahoma,

Florida, Arizona, Utah, California, Oregon, South Dakota, Minnesota, Illinois, Michigan, New Jersey, West Virginia, Louisiana and Missouri.

"He's given us bits and pieces of information on different killings, but we've got to understand he's confused," Ryan said.

The Ranger said that Lucas had traveled all over the U.S. and had been in and out of Texas several times since 1975.

And the one-eyed drifter had added a new twist to his tale of death. As he sat in his jail cell, he sketched the faces of women he said he had killed and as he remembered them.

Hale County authorities at Plainview, Texas were among the Texas officers who wanted to grill Lucas. The drifter's method of operations fit the circumstances surrounding a decapitation murder case on their books since February, 1982.

The nude, headless body of a young woman, her hands tied behind her with a brassiere, was found in a ditch four miles east of Plainview. The body was so badly decomposed that no identifiable fingerprints could be taken.

But on February 24th, a woman's head was found near Scottsdale, Arizona. Subsequent investigation and laboratory tests led officers to think the head was from the body found near Plainview.

When Lucas started talking at Montague about his cross-country murder spree, Hale County Sheriff's Department Capt. Mansel Gilmer and Texas Ranger Jim Mull drove there to question the suspect. During their interview, the officers were startled by the similarity of a sketch that Lucas drew on a yellow legal pad and a photograph made of the murder victim's reconstructed head.

And Lucas gave the lawmen a statement allegedly admitting the decapitation killing, according to Hale County Sheriff Charles Tue.

The officers said that Lucas related he had picked up the young woman hitchhiking on Interstate 20 near Abilene, Texas sometime in December, 1981. He claimed he had traveled cross-country with the woman before stabbing her to death near Plainview. He told officers that he raped the victim before her death, decapitated her, and raped her again. He said he used a knife.

He said he was driving toward California after the slaying and had forgotten about the woman's head in his car until "it started smelling." He had thrown it out in the desert near Scottsdale, the suspect said.

Lucas told the Hale county officers that he "got his kicks raping dead women," an officer said.

A Hale County grand jury indicted Lucas for murder of the unidentified woman on June 23, 1983.

In the meantime, another Texas sheriff gained a confession from Lucas. Williamson County Sheriff Jim Boutwell of Georgetown talked to the suspect for about two hours in the Montague jail. Afterwards, he disclosed that Lucas had made a statement allegedly admitting the slaying of a young, unidentified woman. Her body had been found near Georgetown in 1979.

The sheriff quoted Lucas as saying that the woman was a hitchhiker he picked up in Oklahoma City. "Later, at a rest stop, he said he had sex with her, and then strangled her with his hands," Boutwell said. "He said he had sex with her again after she was dead."

According to the sheriff, Lucas told of keeping the woman's body in his car as he drove south through Oklahoma and into Texas. He dumped the body along Interstate 35, near Georgetown. The corpse had been found on Halloween night, 1979.

Although the victim was unidentified, Boutwell said that Lucas had told him he thought the victim's first name was "Joanie" or "Judy."

Boutwell added that Lucas had given him details about the homicide that only the investigators knew.

Sheriff Boutwell told newsmen that Lucas had claimed having killed over 100 women, starting when he was 13 years old. "He said it was a compulsion with him," said the sheriff.

According to Sheriff Boutwell, Lucas said he shot, stabbed or strangled his victims; sometimes he buried them; sometimes he burned their bodies. Sometimes he carried pieces of the dismembered bodies in his car, the suspect was alleged to have told Boutwell.

Meanwhile, the talkative drifter's bond was set at $1 million in a hearing June 23rd before District Judge Southitt. The judge also appointed three psychiatrists to examine Lucas to determine if he were mentally competent to stand trial on the charges stacking up against him.

Lucas laughed when the judge set his bail at the high amount—even objected when his court-appointed attorney protested the bail was too high. He vowed to continue to help officers clear up the women killings he had admitted.

"I will finish what I have started," Lucas testified from the witness chair. "I will finish giving back the dead what I have taken."

He kept his word about talking the murder spree. Within a few days, the suspect gave statements to investigators regarding other slayings that had baffled Texas lawmen for months, even years in some cases.

One case involved the shooting death of Kevan Key, 19, of Austin, whose bullet-riddled body was found in Sheriff Boutwell's county. The body was found on a farm-to-market road north of Georgetown, just off Interstate 35, on November 6, 1978. That same day, the body of Key's girlfriend, Rita Salazar, 18, of Georgetown, also bearing multiple gunshot wounds, was found 59 miles north of Georgetown, near Waco in McLennan County.

The teenagers had gone to a movie, "Midnight Cowboy" in Austin the night of November 5th.

While driving to Georgetown afterward, their car ran out of gas near Round Rock. They left the car and started hitchhiking.

Somewhere along the way the luckless teenagers were picked up by Lucas and a companion, identified by Lucas as Ottis Elwood Toole of Jacksonville, Florida. Toole, as officers would learn, was an uncle of "Becky" Powell, Lucas' slain "common law" wife. All three had lived together for a time in Jacksonville and traveled together throughout the country, the probe would reveal.

The investigation that included lengthy grilling of both

Lucas and Toole would link the two men in several slayings in different states.

Although Toole later told officers that Lucas was with him when Key and Miss Salazar were killed, Lucas denied actually taking part in the killings, Boutwell said.

Sheriff Boutwell went to Jacksonville in October, 1983, and quizzed Toole at length. As a result of the investigation, Toole was indicted by a Williamson County grand jury for capital murder — committing murder during the course of another felony, robbery — in the slaying of Kevan Key. He also was indicted for aggravated kidnapping of Rita Salazar. District Attorney Ed Walsh of Georgetown said Toole was not indicted in the girl's death because she was killed in McLennan County. However, ballistics tests showed the same .22 pistol killed both victims, Boutwell said.

McLennan County officials said the suspect would not be charged in that county in the shooting death of the girl, pending further investigation. As the massive probe continued, Lucas and Toole were implicated in five other murders in two Texas counties.

Charges were filed against the two suspects in two slayings in the Odessa, Texas area. Lucas was indicted for murder on Aug. 11, 1983 in the strangulation slaying of Beverly Joyce Luttrull, 46. She was found nude and face up in a bedroom of her Odessa residence on March 13, 1981.

She had been strangled with a phone cord that was still wrapped around her neck, officers said.

Toole was indicted for capital murder on Nov. 9, 1983, in the bludgeon killing of 66-year-old "Happy" Howry, an Odessa shoe salesman, last seen alive on April 25, 1982. On May 6th of that year his body was found in a vacant lot in Big Spring, Texas, about 50 miles northeast of Odessa.

Meanwhile, based on information he had given to officers during his continuing talkfest, Lucas was taken to Conroe, Texas, about 40 miles north of Houston. There he led investigators to sites where he had disposed of three women he admitted killing.

Conroe Detective Jim Wiggins told newsmen that Lucas "had a regular habit of driving from Montague County to

25

Houston."

In written confessions made to the Montgomgery County officers at Conroe, Lucas told of killing Glorie Stephan, 28, of Houston, whose body was found near Magnolia, Texas on Oct. 2, 1981; an unidentified woman whose burning body was discovered in the area on April 16, 1983; and Laura J. Donez, a 16-year-old Houston student, whose corpse was found on March 17, 1983.

The sites to which Lucas led the officers were those where the bodies had been discovered earlier, officers said.

Lucas provided information about the three murders that only the killer could have known, said Montgomery County Sheriff Joe Corley.

The indictment against Lucas charged that he kidnapped, sexually assaulted and killed the women.

On Sept. 7, 1983, Lucas was indicted by a grand jury in Fort Bend County, Texas—the county that adjoins on the south of Harris County, in which Houston is located. The indictment charged Lucas in the stabbing death of Deion Marie Wilkinson, 22, of Houston.

Louisiana authorities also brought murder charges against Lucas and Toole in the April 4, 1981 abduction and shooting death of a 19-year-old Bastrop, Louisiana coed, Kathy Whorton. Both men were indicted for capital murder and kidnaping of the Northeast Louisiana University student.

With Lucas still telling investigators about his trail of woman killing, he faced his first trial for murder in late September, 1983. The one-eyed drifter had been found mentally competent to stand trial by the three psychiatrists appointed by Judge Douthitt in Montague County. Acting on a defense motion for a change of venue in the Kathryn Rich murder case, the judge moved Lucas' trial to Henrietta, Texas.

But before the murder defendant was transferred to the Henrietta jail, he made a crude attempt at suicide in the county jail at Montague. Sheriff Conway said deputies found Lucas bleeding in his cell shortly before the noon meal was served.

The sheriff said that Lucas had cut himself on his left wrist and hand with pieces of broken light bulb. The suspect was given first aid at a hospital in Bowie and returned to his cell.

During a pretrial hearing at Henrietta on Sept. 30, 1983, Lucas pulled a surprise and entered a plea of guilty to the murder of Kathryn Rich of Ringgold.

Originally, the defendant had pleaded not guilty to the indictment, and his trial had been set for October 18th. After consulting with both the prosecutor and defense attorney, Judge Douthitt accepted the guilty plea and sentenced Lucas to 75 years in prison.

It remained for a 15-year veteran with the homicide division of the Duval County Sheriff's Department to focus the investigative spotlight on Lucas's sordid years in Jacksonville, Fla., where the drifter had met Toole in 1976.

The results of County Detective J.T. Terry's trip to Texas to grill Lucas were shocking indeed. Terry came to Montague in September, 1983, primarily to talk to Lucas about the background of "Becky" Powell.

There also were some dozen or so murder cases in Duval County, involving women and stretching over a period of about three years, that had the marks of the confessed killer who had been talking so freely to Texas officers.

In all his years as a homicide investigator, Detective Terry had never heard such a story of random, relentless and cold-blooded murder as spun to him by Henry Lucas, who sometimes referred to himself in talks with officers as the "moonlight killer."

In all, Lucas calmly related to the Jacksonville sleuth, eight Jacksonville women had died at his hands; Toole, Lucas's homosexual lover, had helped haul some of the bodies, according to the story Terry listened to.

And it soon became apparent to the detective that Lucas was detailing facts about the Jacksonville woman killings that only the killer could know, because the details had never been made public.

"That was the most depressing day I ever spent with anybody," Detective Terry told a reporter later. "It was depress-

27

ing to sit there and listen to him talk about murders, the murder of his mother, and just show no remorse at all.

"I asked him on one case here, 'Why did you kill the woman?' He said, 'Hell, she was there.' Henry's theory was: 'If I saw a woman by herself, she was mine.' He didn't just go around looking for a woman, but, he said if he was driving around and saw a woman alone, she belonged to him."

Lucas' years in Jacksonville when he met and lived with Toole and "Becky" Powell and allegedly ravished and killed women at random were pieced together by Detective Terry. The confessed killer's lifestyle in Jacksonville was put together also by newspaper reporters who backtracked in the neighborhoods where he had lived.

Lucas came to Jacksonville from Maryland in 1976. At a mission that catered to the street people he met Ottis Toole. The two men became not only friends but also lovers, police said.

"Ottis is homosexual," Detective Terry said. "Henry is bisexual."

Lucas moved in with Toole's family, a family that was dominated by an elderly woman relative, according to investigators. It was then that the drifter met Toole's niece, Becky. She was about 12 years old at the time.

"When he first met Frieda, he took up a lot of time with her, fixing her bicycle, her wagon," Terry told newsmen. "They didn't have a lot of money, and I guess she just became dependent on him."

After his arrest in Montague, Texas and his confession that he had killed Becky Powell, Lucas repeatedly expressed remorse about the death of his teenage lover, the officer said. Investigators said it was the only one of his murders that seemed to prey on his mind.

He told Detective Terry, "She was the only woman I ever loved." When the detective asked Lucas why he had killed the girl, the suspect replied, "I just had to."

The adolescent girl and the scrubby looking drifter made a strange pair, people who knew them recalled later. Lucas, then about 40, was 5-foot-9 and weighed about 150 pounds. He was described as a man with matted, dark brown hair, a scum-covered glass eye, greasy grimy clothing.

Conversely, Frieda was described as "a sweet girl, well cared for by (her older woman relative), a girl who didn't run the streets."

It was in 1979 that the first of the women Lucas claimed to have slain were killed, officers said.

During a robbery at a motel on Kings Road on November 27th, Elizabeth Diane Knotts, 31, was shot to death. Two weeks later, Debra Lynn O'Quinn, 18, was stabbed to death in her home, but her skeletal remains were not discovered in a wooded area near Mount Pleasant Road until Dec. 10, 1979.

In 1980, five more women fell victims to the self-described "moonlight killer," Terry said. The first killing that year happened on January 5th. Jamie L. Collins, 76, was beaten, stabbed to death and sexually assaulted in her San Juan Avenue home. A similar killing took place on March 27th.

This time the victim of a beating and stabbing was Jo Scheffer, 45. Her nude body was found in a day care center. Not quite four months later, Regina Azell Campbell, 24, was strangled to death. Her body was found underneath a car on July 12, 1980—next door to the home of her grandfather, who was Police Chief Howard Basil of Neptune Beach.

Another woman was strangled to death eight days later. The body of Tammy Keel Conners, 19, was found in a ravine in Hanna Park.

Three days before Christmas, 1980, Brenda Elaine Harden, 28, the mother of two children, was found stabbed to death in her home on Miss Muffet Lane. She was found lying on the floor by her husband.

The eighth Jacksonville slaying allegedly admitted by Lucas in a videotaped statement given to Detective Terry was that of Shirley E. Ogden, 58, a transient. She lived just a few blocks away from the boarding house where Lucas, Toole and Becky then were staying. Her body was found in an alley on April 14, 1981.

Meanwhile, Becky Powell's older woman relative who had

29

cared for her and who had been the dominating influence in the circle of Lucas, Toole and the girl, died as a result of a heart ailment in June, 1981. Becky was placed in a state foster home at Auburndale, Florida. Six months after the girl was placed in the state home, Lucas and Toole went there and helped her to escape, investigators said.

They brought the girl back to Jacksonville to live with them.

Late in 1981, Lucas left Florida, taking Becky with him. From then until Lucas' arrest at Montague, Texas in June, 1983, the strangely-matched couple drifted from state to state, sometimes traveling in junk cars Lucas bought and abandoned along the road, but mostly hitchhiking. Lucas earned some money by doing odd jobs as a repairman and shade tree mechanic.

Detective Terry said that Lucas told of killing other women in Jacksonville, but officers could not find any bodies. Lucas related that he had killed an elderly woman and dumped her and her car in a pond along Interstate 95.

"We found an old car, but no old woman," Terry said of the police search that was made in the spot designated by Lucas. "We did find some alligators."

Terry was bothered by the knowledge that Lucas got away with an unknown number of killings for so long a time, even after spending time in prison and mental hospitals for murdering his own mother and trying to kidnap two teen-age girls.

Lucas even claimed that he had killed four women on the day that he was released from prison in Michigan.

Detective Terry said, "What bothers me is that he went to so many places and kept such a low profile that he never was caught. He never did anything to get caught. He says, 'I killed so many, I get my dates and times and places mixed up sometimes.' "

Strangely enough, Terry said, Lucas recognized him as a Jacksonville police officer when Terry came to Montague County jail to talk with the suspect for the first time. The detective said that Lucas reminded him that they had met on a street in Jacksonville when Terry was working on the robbery detail. The officer wondered if Lucas was thinking to himself then, "If only you knew what I've been doing."

But, the suspect couldn't have been too concerned, unless it was about the prospect of being caught, the detective noted.

"When he saw a woman by herself, something hit him," Terry said. "Henry has no feelings of remorse. He says there's no need to feel sorry about them, because they're dead."

Lucas's detailed knowledge of the eight Jacksonville woman killings brought an announcement from Jacksonville Sheriff Dale Carson that the sheriff's department was closing the books on the homicides about which Lucas had given statements.

The Duval County medical examiner, Dr. Peter Lipkovic, told newsmen at a news conference in Jacksonville on Sept. 22, 1983, "As far as I'm concerned, the mystery is over. I don't think he is going to take credit for something he did not do."

The biggest factor in clearing the books of the eight slayings was Lucas's furnishing intimate details that only the killer could know, the medical examiner said.

Lipkovic said that in the case of 76-year-old Jamie L. Collins, Lucas described in his taped confession how he bludgeoned her in bed, dragged the woman into the living room, cut her throat, raped her and poured feathers from a ripped pillow over the body.

At the time of the murder, investigators did not make public that the body had been dragged from one room to another or that pillow feathers were found at the crime scene.

"That's more than a coincidence," said the M.E. "You can think of an active imagination, but this is a little too much." Lipkovic said Lucas described the scene in details that were known only to the killer and the medical examiner.

However, Sheriff Carson said that the evidence in the series of slayings would be turned over to the State Attorney's Office to determine if indictments should be returned by a Duval County grand jury. At this writing, formal indictments had not been returned.

But Florida officers said they didn't expect to get custody of Lucas for a long time anyway. They based their belief on the charges pending against Lucas in Texas — some capital murder charges that, if Lucas were convicted, could bring him a death penalty. The punishment for capital murder in Texas is either life imprisonment or death. The death penalty can be given if a jury finds that the defendant is a continuing threat to society.

"We don't have any hopes whatsoever of getting him back in Jacksonville," said Lt. Jim Suber of the Jacksonville Sheriff's Department homicide division.

State Attorney Ed Austin said Florida would be hesitant about trying Lucas in the Jacksonville slayings because of sentences meted out in Texas.

"We'd have to look carefully about using taxpayers' money to bring him back here to do the very same thing," the state prosecutor told reporters. "It can be wasteful to duplicate a good solid conviction from somewhere else that would bring about the same ends."

In mid-October, 1983, the Ouachita Parish homicide task force at Monroe, Los Angeles sponsored a conference attended by 80 officers from 20 states to compare information and outstanding murder cases with the cross country slayings admitted by Lucas and Toole. At the end of the three-day meeting, Lt. Joe Cummings of the Monroe Police Department told reporters that either Lucas or Toole, or both, had been linked to 28 killings in 10 states. He also said officers were looking at the pair in at least 69 other murders.

In the ensuing weeks more charges were expected to be filed against both suspects, the homicide investigators announced.

But the homicide men said the full extent of the pair's killing spree may never be confirmed.

Detective Terry of Jacksonville, who had grilled both Lucas and Toole at length, told reporters, "Toole told me they have killed someone in every state in the Union except Alaska and Hawaii."

32

Police in Hollywood, Florida announced another sensational development in the coast-to-coast murder probe on Oct. 21, 1983. Ottis Toole, who already was serving a 20-year prison term in Florida for two arson convictions, had confessed to the slaying of 6-year-old Adam Walsh of Hollywood.

Assistant Police Chief Leroy Hessler of Hollywood disclosed to reporters that "Toole killed Adam Walsh by himself. We feel quite confident that Toole is the individual who killed Adam Walsh."

The little boy vanished from a department store in Hollywood in July 27, 1981. His head was found floating in a canal near Vero Beach 15 days after his disappearance. Medical examiners were unable to determine the cause of death.

The youngster's disappearance set off a statewide but futile search. Adam's parents launched a personal crusade for passage of a national law that would enable local police agencies to ask for help from the FBI in missing children cases and permit the FBI to put the names and descriptions of missing children into the National Crime Information Center computer.

The parents lobbied Congress to enact such a law. When it was passed, they were present at the White House when President Reagan signed the Missing Children's Act in October, 1982.

The abduction of Adam and the heroic efforts that ended with the new law later was told in a television drama titled "Adam."

Ironically, the TV movie aired the week before Toole gave what Hollywood police said was a signed confessed admitting the boy's kidnaping and slaying.

Toole led officers to a site where he claimed to have buried the boy's body, but investigators were unable to find anything, said Hollywood Police Chief Sam Martin.

But Chief Martin added, "Certain statements this man has given us have convinced us." He said Toole related to homicide detectives details that only the killer could know.

"We were satisfied with the answers we got," said the

33

chief. Martin related that Toole told of driving to the Fort Lauderdale area for the sole purpose of abducting someone. Martin said Toole told investigators that he spotted Adam on the sidewalk outside the store and lured him into his car with promises of candy and toys.

Authorities disclosed that it had been the work of Jacksonville Detective Terry that elicited the confession from Toole. Terry had been talking to Toole in the Duval County jail at Jacksonville for about a month as the result of a statement given by Henry Lucas implicating Toole in an arson homicide.

As a result of the information supplied by Lucas and subsequent investigation, Toole was indicted for first degree murder and arson in the death of 64-year-old Nicholas Sonneberg of Jacksonville. Sonneberg died on Jan. 4, 1982 from injuries he received in a fire at a wood-frame boarding house that had been torched, police said.

Toole was indicted for the fire death on Sept. 8, 1983, which resulted in his being brought from prison to the Duval County jail.

It was in early October that Toole started asking Jacksonville officers whether they had ever been to Fort Lauderdale, Detective Terry said. Terry was preparing to go to the three-day murder conference at Monroe, Los Angeles when Toole asked him the question about Fort Lauderdale.

When Terry asked the suspect why he was asking, Toole allegedly replied, "I have something to tell you, but we'll talk about it when you get back." Terry interviewed Toole after returning from Louisiana. Toole said he knew something about "the murder of a little boy in Fort Lauderdale," Terry said.

The Jacksonville detective immediately contacted the police in Hollywood, Fla. That night the Hollywood investigators flew to Jacksonville to quiz Toole.

During the police interrogations, Toole first blamed Lucas for the killing of Adam Walsh, Terry related. But Terry got busy and determined that Lucas had been in Wilmington, Delaware, in jail when the boy disappeared.

Confronting Toole, Terry told him, "I know Henry didn't

34

do it, because Henry was in jail at the time. Did you kill that little boy?"

Terry said that Toole broke into tears and exclaimed, "Yes, I did."

After Toole's alleged admission, detectives from Hollywood again grilled the suspect. They announced afterward that Toole had made a signed confession to the boy's slaying.

Investigators did not reveal details of the killing, except that Assistant Chief Hessler said, "It made Charles Manson sound like Tom Sawyer and Huckleberry Finn."

The police official told newsmen that of the homicides that Toole talked about, the killing of the Walsh boy seemed to be the only one that bothered him. "He was remorseful about hurting this young boy," said Hessler. "He broke down and cried when he talked about killing Adam."

But on Nov. 1, 1983, Toole recanted and claimed he had not confessed to killing Adam Walsh. His court-appointed attorney announced at a press conference that Toole "denies having made that confession and he denies killing Adam Walsh."

Hollywood, Fla. police information officer Tony Alderson said after Toole's denial, "we would be extremely surprised to have a homicide suspect not, somewhere down the line, deny his confession. That's just the way you play the game." At this writing, Toole had not been charged or indicted in the Walsh boy's death, although police reiterated that he had made a signed confession.

On Nov. 8, 1983, the trial of Henry Lucas for murder in the slaying of his 15-year-old common-law wife, Frieda "Becky" Powell, began in state district court at Denton in Denton County, Texas. A jury of seven men and five women was selected to hear the testimony.

The defense attorney said that he would try to show that Lucas was guilty of voluntary manslaughter, not murder, in the girl's killing.

The court-appointed attorney told reporters he thought the slaying was a crime of passion, not premeditated murder. District Attorney Jerry Cobb said Lucas should be found guilty of murder because the killing was a deliberate, intentional act. He said voluntary manslaughter was applicable in cases such as a barroom brawl that results in a death, but not in such a brutal killing as Miss Powell's.

The defense tried to block the admission of a 27-minute video-taped confession that Lucas made to Texas lawmen in Denton.

Claiming Lucas was under the influence of a mind-altering drug when he made the confession, the defense lawyer said, "At the time he gave the confession, he was not in control of his facilities to voluntarily give that confession."

But presiding Judge W.C. Boyd, after considering statements by medical authorities, ruled the confession was admissible. In the tape that was played for the jury—shown on two screens—Lucas described in a calm voice how he stabbed Frieda Powell to death on Aug. 24, 1982 and cut up her body in "teeny little pieces."

At the start of the tape, Lucas told an investigator, "I don't want a lawyer."

Lucas said in his statement:

"Frieda Powell was fifteen when she died. I met her through her uncle Ottis (Toole)." He said he and Frieda were living in Stoneburg, Texas when the girl decided to return to Jacksonville, Florida.

On the night of the murder, the two were hitchhiking when they stopped in a wooded area near Denton to spend the night. The tape of Lucas' continued:

"Me and Becky got in an argument about going back to Florida. I kept pleading and begging with her, and the more I begged, the more we argued. We argued for a while. I took all of my clothes off and Becky took off all of her clothes except for her panties and bra.

"We were arguing and cursing each other. I told her we were going back (to Stoneburg) the next morning, regardless. She hauled off and hit me upside the head. That was it. That's when I hit her with a knife. I picked it up off the blanket and brought it around and hit her in the chest. I doubt she ever knew what hit her."

Lucas said he then completely undressed the girl and had

sex with her body.

"After that I cut her up in little, teeny pieces, and I stuffed them in three pillowcases, all except her legs . . . And I drug them back out in the field." Lucas related that he took all of their belongings and threw them away.

Lucas' voice cracked as he described his feelings about killing the girl. "I came back to bury Becky. I wanted to bury the rest of her, but I just couldn't do it."

In the tape made to Denton police detective Larry Brearley, Lucas said also:

"I hope that you can find all of her. That's what I hope. Like I said, I didn't leave her in no pretty sight."

"You're not just telling me this to make me happy?" the detective asked.

"I am saying it because it is the truth," Lucas replied.

The defense called Lucas himself to the witness stand. After testifying he and the girl had argued about returning to Jacksonville, Lucas testified: "I tried to explain to her about going back to Florida. I knew if I went back I was going to be arrested for probation violation, and she was going to be arrested for running away from a girls' school." Lucas said he stabbed Becky in the chest with a knife before he realized what he was doing.

"During the argument, she swung her hand around and hit me upside the head—and at that moment, she was dead," Lucas testified, sobbing uncontrollably. "I just remember she hit me and she was dead."

The defendant said he stabbed the teenager with a knife that they carried for protection on their hitchhiking trips.

"I'm not going to cover up the fact that it happened by my hand," Lucas sobbed. "I saw her sitting there with a knife in her. There was nobody else out there in the field."

Lucas also testified that he recalled "talking" to his victim as he mutilated her body. He said he returned to the murder site "weeks later, months later."

"I couldn't stay away," he said. "I was in love with Becky."

Lucas denied having sex with Becky after she was dead. He said he told the authorities that because it was what they wanted to hear. He said Texas investigators knew that he had been accused in Michigan of having sex with his mother's corpse, and they asked him if he had done that with Miss Powell.

"Nobody would believe the truth," said Lucas. "They wanted things their way."

However, Texas Ranger Ryan testified that Lucas first mentioned having committed necrophilia with Miss Powell in a June 15th interview with the Ranger and that he made the statement voluntarily.

In final arguments before the jury, the defense attorney asked that Lucas be acquitted or found guilty of voluntary manslaughter because he had acted on impulse. "Becky Powell didn't mean anything to anybody except to Henry Lucas," the lawyer told the jury. "And Henry Lucas took her life, but didn't mean to do it."

District Attorney Cobb said in summation, "From his own testimony, he loved this lady, and I don't doubt that. I think what happened is, Becky Powell told him, 'I'm going to Florida and I don't care if you do.' He didn't want to live his life away from Becky Powell."

The jury deliberated about three hours before returning its verdict. They found Lucas guilty of murder.

Lucas, who sat quietly as the verdict was read, told newsmen as he emerged from the courtroom, "It's just what I expected."

Next, the jury considered the punishment to be assessed. After about three hours of deliberation, the jury on Nov. 10, 1983 returned a verdict of life imprisonment.

Lucas said when leaving the courtroom, "Death, that's what I asked for. I'm going to get it." He indicated he might enter guilty pleas in the capital murder indictments against him that could bring the death penalty.

Lucas shook hands with the prosecutor after signing his sentence judgement, telling the DA that he had "done a good job."

Lucas' defense attorney read a one-page letter that he said Lucas had written to the press. It said:

"I don't have any hard feelings toward any of the people involved in this case here in Denton. I have not tried to win. If I ever decide to win, I can do so. But because I was responsible for the taking of Becky's life, I do not wish to win. And I have set forth to see that no man can win for me, unless I want it done.

"I'm sorry that people have to be used to gain what I want to happen. Yes, I used you all to gain my own peace of mind."

The defense attorney also read a note that Lucas had written to him. It read:

"I'm going to get 75 years or life. But I don't care. I've already given myself to death. I know I will be with Becky in time to come."

District Attorney Cobb said that chances of Lucas being tried in all the cases in which he is charged diminished with the life sentence.

"You need to try him several times because you've got to have a backup to make sure a person like this goes to the penitentiary," he said. "But ultimately I believe he will not be tried in all other cases."

Texas Ranger Ryan, who talked to Henry Lucas so long and took his statements concerning perverse sex, mutilation and murder, will never forget the drifter with one eye.

"That first night, to sit there and listen to someone talk in detail about all those murders . . . In one night he goes through forty murders, what they (the victims) said, what he said, where he stabbed them, how he stabbed them. It can't help but affect you if you value human life at all," the Ranger said.

"I went from being enthusiastic to where I had to force myself to go in and talk to him. I'd rather have done manual labor than talk to Henry another day."

Both defendants were given life terms.

Hillside Strangler

by Chris Edwards

For more than a year he was the will o' the wisp murderer who seemed to be strewing girls' naked bodies all over the Los Angeles landscape, but frustrated detectives knew that sooner or later, he had to make one big mistake that would mark the end of the trail for the Hillside Strangler.

It all began with the strangulation murder of 18-year-old Yolanda Washington on the night of October 17, 1977 and ended — at least for Los Angeles — on February 17, 1978 with the death of Cindy Hudspeth, 20, whose body was found crammed in the trunk of her car that had been shoved off a mountain road.

In between the slaying of Washington and Hudspeth were eight other murdered young women — all like the first and last — the victims of rape and strangulation and, occasionally, sodomy.

It was the most vicious spate of murders to plague Southern California since the days of Charlie Manson and his Helter Skelter "family" of male and female executioners. The chronology of what came to be known as the Hillside Strangler case goes something like this:

Miss Washington, a 20-year-old waitress who had served jail time for prostitution, was lured into the car of her killer, raped, strangled and stripped and then discarded like a broken toy on a brushy hillside in Los Angeles' Griffith Park. It hardly rated a line of type in the newspapers. Such murders are not uncommon in big cities.

Less than two weeks later the body of Judith Miller, a 15-year-old school dropout and familiar figure along the sleazier parts of Hollywood Blvd., was raped, sodomized and strangled. Her body was found on October 31st in a bed of African daisies on Alta Terrace in La Crescenta, a foothill suburb of Los Angeles.

Elissa Kastin, 21, was last seen leaving the cafe at Hollywood and Vine where she worked as a waitress. Her body was found on November 6th in Glendale — and like others, had been raped, sodomized and strangled.

Because Kastin and Miller had been found in their jurisdiction, the Glendale police took more than a passing interest in the murders and speculated they both could have been the victims of the same killer. It was the first such assumption to be made in what became an incredibly tangled case.

On November 20th the ravished body of Sonja Johnson, 14, and her schoolmate, Dolores Cepeda, 12, were discovered in Elysian Park in the central section of Los Angeles. The young girls, who had been on a shopping tour when they vanished, were missing for several days before their bodies were found.

Also on November 20th, the body of Kristina Weckler, 20, was found in Highland Park. Three days later the nude body of Jean King, 28, turned up on a hillside overlooking the Golden State Freeway in Los Angeles.

And on November 28th, residents of a quiet street in Sepulveda saw two men escorting Lauren Wagner, 18, into what looked like a black and white police car. The following morning her body was discovered on a hillside road in the Mt. Washington area of the city. Like the other young women she, too, had been strangled and raped.

Kimberly Diane Martin, 17, a nude model, was found dead in the Silver Lake area 10 hours after she was lured to a vacant apartment on December 13th by a phone caller who had contracted for her services.

The next victim was Miss Hudspeth, the 20-year-old cocktail waitress.

Then the epidemic of killing stopped in Los Angeles just as suddenly as it had started. In its wake it left one hell of a lot of frustrated and puzzled cops.

Because the killings took place in widely scattered police jurisdictions, it was several weeks before crimes were matched and their similarities noted.

It was not until November 23rd that a coordinated effort was mounted by the Los Angeles Police Department and Sheriff's Department and the Glendale Police Department. They pooled their information, in what by now had been tagged the Hillside Strangler Task Force.

Teams of newspaper and TV reporters also moved in on the case by delving into the background of the victims, looking for similarities that could possibly lead to the killer—or killers.

The big question was, who and in what way were any of the victims connected? What, if anything, did they have in common? Why and how were they chosen for death?

This much was determined: Four of the victims, Miller, Martin, Washington and King, were known to have been part of the Hollywood street scene. But the others couldn't have been more different: Johnson and Cepeda, the two schoolgirls, had never been to Hollywood. Kastin was seeking a career as a dancer. Weckler was a student in a well known art center college.

By a strange coincidence, Weckler had once lived across the street from Hudspeth, the cocktail waitress, but so far as could be determined they had never met. Miss Wagner was a business college student who seldom went to Hollywood.

The work of the Strangler Task Force became a high priority matter as the weeks and months went by. Thousands of tips poured in and most were thoroughly investigated. Some were disposed of rapidly when it was apparent they were coming from cranks, or obvious nuts, compulsive confessers or disgruntled relatives and acquaintances with personal axes to grind. But for the most part, virtually every good lead was painstakingly checked—all without success.

During periods of peak operation 134 sworn officers and eight full time employees of the LAPD were operating within the task force.

This did not include numbers of specialized Metro Division officers who were called in on a part-time basis. By February, 1978, a total of 30,400 investigative man-hours plus another 15,815 hours in paid overtime had been logged by the LAPD.

The Sheriff's Department had 19 officers assigned to the task force with special bureaus standing by if needed. During one four month period alone, sheriff's deputies logged 60,800 man hours on the case and in one month overtime was nearing 12,000 hours.

For a case that started out with the routine killing of Yolanda Washington, it became the most extensively investigated case in Los Angeles history.

Lt. Ed Henderson, commander of the task force, found it necessary from time to time to order some of his men to go home and get some rest. Asst. Chief Daryl Gates said his men "won't lie down until they fall down."

Said Asst. Chief Daryl Gates of the Task Force detectives, "We have to send them home because they are apt to lose their perspective when exhaustion sets in. They are not as sharp as they should be."

In speaking to the press on the frustrating investigation, Glendale Police Chief Duane Baker commented, "This is like looking for a thread and trying to unravel it. If we were lucky we would have found the thread by now. But here the thread hasn't even presented itself yet."

Meanwhile, sections of the county involved in the investigation became armed camps. Gun shops did a land office business, karate classes were full, and demands for guard dogs increased as never before. Terror ruled neighborhoods that had always before been terror-free.

Several suspects were picked up during the course of the investigation, but generally it was clear from the start that any case against them was too leaky to hold any water.

Each day the complexity of the puzzle grew. Was the Hillside Strangler one man or two, as in the case of Miss Wagner?

43

Or were there several copycat killers?

Said Lt. Dan Cooke of the LAPD: "You think you have driven him underground because there are no more murders. Maybe he is in custody on another charge. Or has he left the community?"

There was no doubt about it. The Hillside Strangler—or stranglers—was a wily one—or two, or three. And a task force, an aggregation of the finest detectives in the country, were stumped—and admitted it.

That is the time in any bizarre murder case that the shrinks enter and dispense their expert analysis, solicited or not. The Strangler case was no exception. Here are a few of their offerings:

The Strangler is a man who doesn't live with a woman, which would include as suspects widowers, single men, and divorced men. Another psychiatrist concluded the killer was a white man in his late 20s or 30s. Another identified him as a Hispanic who had made a hobby of studying weird murders.

Others concluded the Strangler was unemployed, passive and cold. Still others tabbed him as a psycho who had been released from a mental hospital, the product of a broken family, a prolonged bed wetter, and as a man who is cruel to animals.

Another portrait described him as a cruel and oversexed man who could not have sex without violence. He might be a loner but then again he might have a lot of friends who may or may not know the guy is a kook.

He might to some degree pick on street women because they are easily available. But how does that explain the murders of the virtuous victims? Or he may have turned against all women because one of them gave him a venereal disease. He is not crazy in the true sense of the word, just sick. But then again, he is really crazy.

Still another doctor concluded that mass murderers are usually people who are psychiatrically ill. But another said sex murders are rarely committed by people with identifiable mental illness.

So where did all that expertise leave the Strangler Task Force?

Were they to look for a white man or an Hispanic? He doesn't live with a woman?

Is he a kook, but not a "crazy" kook? Had he been a persistent bed wetter? Or is he a loner who, on the other hand, could have a lot of friends?

The more the detectives examined the psychiatric speculation, the more the feeling closed in on them that they were back at Square One—exactly where they started when Yolanda Washington was murdered.

The time rolled by until Jan. 13, 1979 when a long distance phone call from the town of Bellingham, Washington was made to the Los Angeles Police Department.

Bellingham Police Chief Terence J. Mangan, a former priest who gave up the cloth for the badge, wanted to talk to someone in the Strangler Task Force.

There had been two murders in Bellingham. Karen Mandic, 22, and Diane Wilder, 27, had been strangled on the night of Jan. 11th and the bodies had been found the next day in the trunk of Miss Mandic's automobile.

Evidence at the murder scene and statements of witnesses pointed the finger of suspicion at Kenneth Bianchi, a handsome 27-year old security guard and half-baked private eye who had offered the two women a "surveillance" job—to house-sit a residence—the night they were murdered. He was taken into custody an hour after the bodies of the Western Washington University juniors were found.

In the suspect's home officers found a stolen power saw and five stolen telephones. He was charged with having stolen property in his possession. But witnesses had linked him to the two murdered girls and bail was upped to $150,000.

When Bianchi was arrested in Washington, Chief Mangan, on a hunch, had Capt. Dan Fitzgerald call the LAPD but the captain was unable to reach anyone on the Strangler Task Force. The next call he made was to the Sheriff's office in Los Angeles and he was put right through to a Task Force officer.

The officer in Los Angeles listened as Fitzgerald told him of the two strangulations and informed him that LA officers would be on their way to Bellingham that night to talk to

Bianchi. Dudley Varney of the LAPD and Sgt. Frank Salerno of the sheriff's office were dispatched at once. The officers in Bellingham learned that Bianchi had been in the Washington city for 10 months and had gone there from Los Angeles because his girl friend was pregnant and wanted to be near her parents when she gave birth to the child.

What intrigued the investigating officer was that Bianchi left Los Angeles immediately after the Hudspeth murder and never returned. Significantly, the Hillside Strangler killings in Los Angeles stopped, but now two young women were strangled in Bianchi's new nesting ground.

For six months in 1977 Bianchi had lived in the same Glendale apartment building as Kristina Weckler, LA police determined, and at one time he lived across the street from Cindy Hudspeth. He once lived in the Hollywood apartment building where Kimberly Martin was killed. And for a period of time he worked with the sister of Yolanda Washington at an insurance company. It looked like the Task Force was getting off Square One.

In the Bellingham jail, Bianchi was booked for grand theft and then for the murder of the two coeds. And eventually, he was booked on suspicion of committing the 10 Strangler murders in Los Angeles. But his case in Washington would have to be settled before he could be returned to California.

Asked if there was hard evidence to link Bianchi to the 10 slayings, Chief Gates said, "Yes," but then he ducked behind a "no comment" when asked to elaborate. The law enforcement officers also told the press that they were working on the assumption that at least one other man was involved in the killings, but they didn't say why.

Los Angeles County Sheriff Peter Pitchess and Deputy Police Chief Gates revealed that detectives had been searching the Glendale home of an Angelo Buono, 44-year-old cousin of Bianchi, with whom Bianchi had lived for a period of time in 1976.

And when it was disclosed in April, 1979 that officers had been searching the Glendale home of Buono, it was also revealed for the first that Bianchi's cousin was named as a "suspect." Although he was not taken into custody, cops kept a

24-hour surveillance on him.

All of which would indicate that the lawmen suspected that Buono was implicated in the murders with Bianchi but they lacked the hard evidence to justify a formal complaint from the office of the district attorney.

Eventually Bianchi was charged with the murders of the Washington coeds and ordered to stand trial. It appeared that it would be a long time before he would be brought to Los Angeles to face the murder charges in the Hillside Strangler cases. Washington was not about to release him to the California jurisdiction until they had picked him clean.

But at least for the first time in months the weary Strangler Task Force had two names to work with as strong possibilities. No longer were they groping in the dark for faceless, nameless suspects.

Moreover, while Washington had Bianchi safely in jail, the Los Angeles officers had bought themselves some time. But they kept an eye on Buono.

Bianchi was a native of Rochester, N.Y. who came to Glendale to live in 1975. He attended a community college where he majored in police science and tried several times — unsuccessfully — to get on with various police departments.

He tried his hand at being an ambulance driver, but police work was his first love. So he took on the next closest thing — a job as security guard, or what some cops call a door knob rattler, a rent-a-cop. At least that job gave him a uniform, a badge, a gun and some aura of authority.

Task force officers in Los Angeles have speculated for some time that their quarry had used his badge and his uniform to lure some of his victims to their deaths. For months the feeling that the killer was either a security officer — or even — God forbid! — a legitimate police officer — was high on their list of possibilities.

Friends and associates in California described Bianchi as strange and said he carried an attache case that contained a bogus police badge, a California Highway Patrol identification card, and some photographs of nude women.

One of his stories was that he did undercover work for police agencies. He was a braggart, telling friends that he was a psychologist from Columbia University. When anyone doubted it, he would produce an obviously phony degree purchased from a mail order house.

All this meant nothing or little to the police. But what did interest them was that a year before his capture in Washington, Bianchi had been identified to Los Angeles police by at least two persons as a possible suspect in the Strangler case.

But nothing ever came of those tips—they were just two among the thousands upon thousands that poured into the office of the task force during the months they sought The Strangler. They were just not convincing enough to warrant special follow-up investigations.

One of the tips for example, came from an individual who said Bianchi once asked him, "What would you think if I told you I was the Hillside Strangler?"

Had Bianchi been checked out thoroughly by the police they would have learned earlier in the game of his coincidental relationships with some of the victims.

Bellingham Police Chief Mangan was convinced that Bianchi was planning a new string of strangulations at the time of his arrest for the murders of the coeds.

Mangan said Bianchi had planned another killing the next night in the same house where the coeds had been raped and murdered. In Bianchi's possession police found a list of names of girls who had agreed to pose in the nude for him.

Said Chief Mangan, "I can't prove it, but I am certain in my own mind that he was going to set up those women for killing."

Bianchi had obtained the names from a list at the University of Western Washington of women who registered to be nude models in art classes conducted there.

"He was such a good con man," said the chief, "one of the women couldn't believe he was anything but a nice, sincere guy. We couldn't convince her she could have been number three up here."

Evidence that linked Bianchi to the murders of the coeds included fiber from the rug in the house where the murders were committed. The FBI matched the fiber to those found on the clothing of the women and to Bianchi's clothing.

Police in Los Angeles sought without success for evidence to link Buono to the Los Angeles killings. Detectives had gone over his small yellow frame house on Colorado Street in Glendale, and his upholstery shop adjacent to it, convinced but unable to prove that some of the Hillside killings took place there.

Eventually, they had to admit that although their gut feelings indicated he may have been Bianchi's partner in at least some of the crimes, they could not supply enough evidence to convince District Attorney John Van de Kamp to file murder charges—or any other kind of charges—against him.

After his arrest, Bianchi had pleaded not guilty to the murder of the Washington coeds, but during a court appearance on March 31, 1979 he changed that plea to one of not guilty by reason of insanity, meaning, in effect, that he was admitting the killings but was not responsible for them.

A panel of six experts was appointed to examine him. One doctor called Bianchi the classic example of a split personality with the hidden personality not normally seen.

Psychologist John Watkins of Montana called Bianchi a "very pure psychopath" whose hidden personality seized control of the normally mild-manner Bianchi.

But, Watkins insisted, "Bianchi's underlying personality would threaten me a good deal. He would get up and stride around. I was never quite sure that he would not attack me."

The psychologist said Bianchi was not aware of his second personality until he was told about it by experts. Watkins said the dual personality stemmed from Bianchi's unhappy childhood.

While the wheels of justice were grinding away in Washington, law enforcement officers were working up their case against Bianchi in Los Angeles. On May 9, 1979 they charged him with five of the 10 Hillside stranglings, along with 16 other felonies, including conspiracy to commit murder, kidnapping, rape and sodomy in a complaint filed in Municipal Court before Judge Gabriel Gutierrez.

An unidentified "John Doe" was named as an accomplice in 11 of the 16 "overt acts" committed in connection with the five murders.

There was little doubt that the "John Doe" named in the complaint was Angelo Buono. The police and assistant district attorneys never backed away from calling him a suspect, even when he threatened to file suit against them for defamation of character.

On one occasion, Buono told the press, "The only thing I have to say is that I haven't did nothing.

"They (the investigators) can do anything they want but they won't find nothing because I ain't did nothing."

Buono, the father of six children from two marriages, charged that the police by calling him a suspect had disrupted the lives of his family and ruined the upholstery business he operated next door to his home.

Buono's residence had been searched several times by deputies armed with search warrants. At one time during April, 1979, Buono's house had been sealed for five days while extensive laboratory tests were conducted.

A sheriff's spokesman said the house was being examined in connection with the death of Judith Lynn Miller, the third victim of the strangler. Here again the press could only speculate that officials were suspecting that Miss Miller had been slain in that house.

Chief Gates continued to state, "I would have to say we are looking at Buono and I am sure you would classify him as a suspect." But never did Gates spell out the accusation more clearly, other than to say, "He's had a relationship with Mr. Bianchi and from other things we have learned, I think he is a suspect."

Speaking of the police interest in him, Buono told the press, "Hell, I don't know what else they can do to me. They've done everything else. They got guys following me around. They even got some of my friends talkin' about me. They can't do much more to me than they have already done."

Buono said he had received threatening phone calls and letters since the allegations made against him by the police.

Buono continued, "I'm in jeopardy and my kids are in jeopardy. They've even been hassled at school. There is some kook out there some place who wants to kill me."

Commenting on Bianchi, Buono said, "All I ever did was

do my aunt a favor by letting him stay here for a while. I didn't see much of him after he moved out. I told him to leave because he wouldn't get out and get a job. Because we didn't have nothing in common.

"He used to come over and watch television once in a while or we would go out to dinner or something. Everything has turned to shit since he stayed here."

Asked if he had any idea who Bianchi's accomplice could have been, Buono replied, "I don't have any way to know. All I know is if he did them things (the slayings) they (police) ought to get his ass!"

Returning to his trouble with the police, Buono said, "I didn't do nothing and I don't think they should bad-mouth anyone until they know they did something. They told me they were spraying stuff on the walls of my house to see if there was any fingerprints. They later told me they didn't find none."

That was pretty much the way things stood on the Hillside Strangler murders until Friday, October 19, 1979 — the day the roof fell in on Buono.

In court in Washington for a hearing on charges that he killed the two coeds, Bianchi suddenly broke out in tears and pleaded guilty to killing the coeds. Moments later he admitted guilt in five of California's Hillside murders.

Bianchi told the judge in the Bellingham courtroom, "Your Honor, I can't find the words to express the sorrow I feel."

Minutes later and hundreds of miles away in Glendale, Calif., Angelo Anthony Buono was arrested at gunpoint in his upholstery shop and charged with 10 counts of murder. He surrendered without a struggle.

The fast-moving and coordinated action by authorities in Washington and California climaxed the two-year investigation of the Hillside Strangler Murders.

Bianchi had appeared in the Bellingham courtroom for what was to have been a hearing to determine whether he was mentally competent to stand trial for the murder of the coeds.

Instead, the defendant, wearing a bullet-proof vest under his neat three-piece suit, changed his plea from innocent by reason of insanity to guilty to the coed murders, in exchange

51

for a promise that Washington authorities would not seek the death penalty against him.

Then it was disclosed that Bianchi had also agreed to plead guilty to five counts of murder in Los Angeles, along with one count of sodomy, and one of conspiracy to commit a felony in connection with the Hillside Stranglings.

It was then learned that California authorities had agreed not to seek the death penalty for Bianchi in the Hillside murders if the confessed killer agreed to blow the whistle on Buono and become a material witness against him. And before Buono knew what was happening, he was slapped into jail and charged with taking part in the 10 Hillside murders.

He was scheduled to be arraigned in Los Angeles Municipal Court the following Monday—the same day Bianchi was to be brought to Los Angeles to face up to the murders he had admitted.

Chief Gates declined to specify what evidence might connect Buono and Bianchi to the killings, other than Bianchi's statement. However, in California statements of accomplices cannot stand on their own weight and must be supported by corroborating evidence. But Gates did not appear to be concerned. He did say, however, "We believe we have other witnesses that will be very helpful in the trial."

Bianchi turned on Buono in the Bellingham court after he had entered his guilty plea and, in tears, told the court, "There is no way I can take away the pain that I have caused others and no way I can ask forgiveness of anyone." Then he added, "Before I can begin to live with myself I must face up to what I have done and I must do everything I can to get Angelo and to give my life (to psychiatric study) so that hopefully someone won't follow in my footsteps."

Whatcom County Prosecutor David McEachren asked for consecutive life sentences for Bianchi for the Washington murders, saying, "The murders could not have been more carefully planned on a calculated basis by a really cunning man." He said the only reason he did not seek the death penalty was because "there is an accomplice in Los Angeles and that person can only be prosecuted with Mr. Bianchi's assistance."

It was agreed that Bianchi would be confined to a maximum security institution for the criminally insane in California because such a facility is not available in Washington.

Veteran prosecutors said Bianchi's confinement in California might range between 20 and 25 years, and then he would face another 26 years in Washington.

Said Prosecutor McEachren: "There is no question in my mind that he will never be set free."

The complaints filed in Los Angeles on Oct. 19th alleged a total of 25 felony counts with Buono and Bianchi being jointly named in 22 of the counts.

Both men were charged with conspiracy, pimping and pandering, extortion, kidnapping, rape and murder. Buono was charged with two counts of sodomy and Bianchi with one count.

If found guilty, Buono could get the death penalty. Because of the plea bargain, Bianchi could get a maximum of life in prison.

There is no doubt that Bianchi's fear of the death penalty in Washington is what led to breaking the Hillside Strangler case wide open.

Buono had been playing it cool, and with good reason. Repeated searches of his home found nothing to link him to the murders. The district attorney's office was unable to lay a glove on him. He insisted he was going to sue the police for defaming him. The Washington prosecutor admitted that without Bianchi's testimony it would be difficult to convict Buono.

Buono, like Bianchi, was a native of Rochester, N.Y., being born there in 1934. The two men were not blood cousins but related by adoption. Buono worked as an upholsterer in various parts of the Los Angeles area until he settled down to his own business in Glendale.

A fellow worker who had known Buono for 11 years described him as a "hell raiser" and a ladies man. Friends said he would approach women on the street whom he didn't even know and make a sex pitch to them. Sometimes he could get his face slapped, they said, and sometimes he would score. He was also described as a soft touch for women.

Buono's former boss said, "He had more women running after him than he could handle."

The district attorney's office declined to reveal details of the crimes charged against Buono and Bianchi. However, a lengthy criminal complaint on file does establish a pattern of sex and violence in the murders. Motion picture films depicting sado-masochism were found in one of the Glendale apartments where Bianchi formerly lived.

According to the complaint, Buono and Bianchi met in Buono's home in Glendale on Oct. 17, 1977 and plotted the first of their grisly crimes. They allegedly talked "about having sex with a girl and then killing her." The unlucky first victim, allegedly, was Yolanda Washington.

According to the complaint, Miss Washington was picked up off the street voluntarily and handcuffed and then raped.

She is believed to have been strangled in the car and her body dumped on a hillside near Griffith Park. Between the dates Oct. 17, 1977 and Feb. 17, 1978, nine more young women would die in a similar manner.

The two handsomely rugged men allegedly left Buono's little house on the night of Oct. 23, 1977 seeking another victim; Buono assertedly picked up Judy Miller, 15, on Sunset Blvd. and took her to Buono's house. There she was raped, sodomized and strangled. Her body was discarded in La Crescenta.

According to the complaint, five of the victims were kidnaped; the others entered the Buono house willingly or were deluded by subterfuge.

According to the complaint, all the young women, with the exception of Miss Washington, had been killed in Buono's house. But apparently numerous searches by police failed to find any physical evidence of this.

The complaint says Miss Kastin was kidnapped in Hollywood, Jean King was "persuaded" to get into the car with the two men; the two young schoolgirls were kidnapped off a street corner.

Miss Wecker was persuaded by Bianchi, who lived in the same apartment house, to accompany him to a party.

Lauren Rae Wagner was abducted off the street near her

home. Kimberly Martin was kidnapped from an empty apartment where Bianchi had once lived and at which he arranged to meet her for a nude modeling session.

According to the complaint, Cindy Hudspeth accompanied the two suspects to the upholstery shop and then to the adjacent house in which she was murdered.

The complaint charges that each of the murders was carefully planned in advance; earlier in 1977 the two men allegedly discussed the possibilities of opening a house of prostitution and recruiting girls in Phoenix to work in California, but it never worked out.

Kenneth Bianchi went back into court, in Los Angeles, on Oct. 23rd, pleaded guilty to five counts of murder and was sentenced to six life prison terms. The sixth term was imposed on a conspiracy-to-commit-murder count, and an additional five year sentence was added for a count of sodomy.

Said Superior Court Judge William B. Keene, "I wish I had the power to have the sentences run consecutively but in this state they must be merged as a matter of law." Two additional life sentences for murder were imposed on Bianchi in Washington.

Commented Los Angeles Prosecutor Roger Kelly, "It is extremely unlikely, bordering on the impossible, that Bianchi will ever be released."

There is little doubt that prosecutors in Los Angeles will make every effort to bring down the death penalty on Buono if they can convict him. But whether or not he dies in San Quentin's apple green gas chamber or spends the rest of his life in a cage there will depend on a jury and the California courts.

But what of the Hillside Strangler Task Force that tirelessly pursued the killers of the 10 girls for more than 20 months only to have the case solved by a squealing accomplice?

Twenty of those hard bitten Homicide detectives "celebrated" the successful conclusion of that case—no matter how it was solved—in the back room of a downtown Los Angeles restaurant with generous portions of booze.

Said Det. Bob Grogan, "We toasted the girl. Each man toasted 'my girl,' the one whose murder he had investigated. It won't make it better, but at least we know who did it."

Said Grogan, "I may forget the case someday, but I'll never forget the girls."

Added Grogan, "You can't believe the wild goose chases. We were never sure whether we were wasting our time or not."

Sgt. Dudley Varney said, "I spent more time at the coroner's office than I did at home. I ended going there on the way to work fearing there would be more girls." Sgt. Bill Williams said, "I couldn't sleep at night knowing there would be more deaths."

Commenting on the fact that the puzzling case was solved miles from the scene of the killings in Bellingham, Wash., Varney said simply, "I'm just glad it was solved."

Sgt. Williams added, "We were so close." And Grogan didn't hide his envy of the Washington copsy by saying, "I'm disappointed. I wish it had been us."

As we go to press, further legal actions in the case of Angelo Buono are pending. It should be remembered, however, that until or unless Buono is found guilty of the charges against him by a jury of his peers after due process, he is entitled to the Constitutional presumption of innocence.

Snuffing Lives Was
His Fiendish Passion!

by Bill G. Cox

The differences between the small cities of Odessa and Midland in Texas are as sharply defined as night is from day.

Both cities saw their economies skyrocket during the oil-boom days of the Permian Basin in West Texas. Odessa was the blue-collar city of oilfield workers and oilfield-related service companies. It eventually had some skyscraper office buildings, but in the beginning it was a rough-and-tumble oilpatch town of quickly-thrown-together buildings and residences and bars and honkytonks—a brawling town of old frontier style.

Midland, 20 miles to the east on Interstate 20, was a little Dallas from the start. Almost overnight, as new oil wells were sunk and developed, skyscraper office buildings sprang up, their towers tightly cluttered in the downtown area and visible for miles to anyone approaching the city. Here were located the offices of the independent and major oil firms and their executive staffs. It was a white-collar town, with a fancy petroleum club instead of honky-tonks and bars.

Over the years, Odessa changed its face, too, becoming not only a large petrol chemical center, but also a stable and church-filled town, with burgeoning new suburban shopping centers and an increasing population that upped its census figure to around 90,000. It has modern schools and a branch of the University of Texas.

In the early 1980's, both Odessa and Midland saw a nosedive in their economies as the bottom dropped out of the oil market.

It was in this locale of two strangely different but closely related cities that the bizarre tale of a tall, lanky, odd-looking businessman began to unfold in a packed district courtroom. He went on trial in January 1988 to legally determine if he was a cold-blooded and calculating prisoner of at least three people—two women and a man—or an innocent victim of coincidence and circumstance.

Certainly the descriptions of the 34-year-old defendant's character, as portrayed by law enforcement officials on the one hand and his family and friends on the other, were as blatantly different as the two cities of Odessa and Midland.

He had often represented himself in conversation with friends as a U.S. secret agent, part of an assassination team that traveled around the world killing assigned victims with a .22-caliber pistol equipped with a silencer. He represented himself as a counselor and therapist for friends with personal problems, but his therapeutic methods were bizarre and deadly, if the courtroom evidence were to be believed.

The hard-hitting district attorney described the accused man as someone who controlled his friends through shared paranoia and later killed them when he tired of them.

"He likes to be the power that snuffs out life," declared the prosecutor. "He likes that supreme power. He was fascinated with death. He was completely coldblooded."

Conversely, this strange-appearing man was seen by his attorney, friends and relatives as perhaps eccentric, but really just an ordinary guy—perhaps a Walter Mitty personality in his fantasies of intrigue and death; a loving father and husband, even though he may have played around a bit; an active church man and youth worker; an individual who would go without things himself to help someone and who "wouldn't hurt a fly."

Above all, his backers said, he was an innocent victim of coincidence in the bizarre deaths of the three people who were his friends and business associates, and maybe—in the case of the two women—his lovers.

The first of the strange and mysterious deaths was re-

58

ported in Odessa on the hot summer day of August 16, 1983. It began with a phone call from a fellow employee of 26-year-old Lisa Blythe Krieg to Lisa's father. The caller was David A. Dowler, a sales representative for the same oil-field firm where Miss Krieg worked as a secretary.

Dowler told her father he was concerned that Lisa had not shown up for work at the Midland office. Alarmed by the call, the father drove to the Odessa address where his daughter lived. His worst fears were realized when he entered the apartment.

The shocked parent found Lisa Krieg's partially clothed body in bed. She was dead.

Lisa's health had been of deep concern to her father and other relatives and friends for some time. It was known that she had suffered from an eating disorder known as anorexia nervosa, a disorder in which victims sometimes starve to death. A justice of the peace called to the scene as acting coroner — a legal requirement in all unattended deaths — ordered an autopsy. There was nothing in the apartment to indicate anything other than death from natural causes — no signs of forced entry or violence, no physical injuries immediately apparent on the body.

And when the autopsy was performed, the pathologist's finding was that Lisa Krieg had died from the ravages of anorexia nervosa as suspected. Yet, stories were going around that made her friends wonder if that was the cause of death.

The weird story was related to Lisa's ex-husband and a young woman friend of hers. Telling the story was Dowler, the co-worker who had notified Lisa's father of her absence and expressed concern that something might be wrong.

Dowler called the ex-husband on the same day that the body was found and told him that Lisa had killed herself with cyanide that Dowler had provided. According to Dowler, he had gone to the Odessa apartment himself when Lisa failed to show up for work. He said he had found her dead in bed and completely nude. Dowler related he had partially dressed the body after cleaning the woman, in order to make her death look natural.

The ex-husband didn't know what to believe. He knew

Dowler as the teller of some weird stories, all of which sounded pretty unbelievable.

Dowler had told him that Lisa had been involved with him in a U.S. sponsored secret mission. Moreover, said Dowler, he had saved Lisa's life twice when assassins tried to kill her because of her participation in the secret mission. Dowler boasted he had killed the two men who made the attempts on Lisa's life.

The ex-husband decided not to call police about Dowler's story because he was afraid police would think he was crazy.

A few days after Lisa Krieg's burial, Dowler told a similar story to one of Lisa's friends, adding that he'd tried to convince Lisa not to use the cyanide to kill herself.

Dowler added an especially juicy bit of information in his tale to Lisa's friend. He said Lisa had left a note saying, "I love you, Dave." The friend was bewildered by the story, too. She didn't think of going to the police about it. All of Dowler's acquaintances knew him as a spinner of stories that taxed the imagination, to say the least.

But for the time being, Dowler's claims of Lisa Krieg's self-inflicted death didn't reach the ears of law enforcement officers. The natural-death ruling eliminated the need of any police interest.

But Lisa's friend continued to be haunted by the chilling words of Dowler when she had asked him how much cyanide Lisa had taken. The somber Dowler, whose height and extreme leanness of features gave him the appearance of Ichabod Crane, had replied: "Bless her heart, she took enough to kill six people."

Unfortunately, those words wouldn't reach police ears until about five years later, when events would once again bring into question the death of Lisa Krieg.

But in 1983, her death went on the records as a "natural" death.

On February 12, 1986, another Odessa resident was found dead under mysterious circumstances. The dead man's name was Juan Antonio "Tony" Casillas, 29. His fully-clothed body was discovered sprawled on the kitchen floor in his apartment.

Police officers and a justice of the peace acting as coroner went to the scene, following up the "body found" report as is routine procedure in sudden deaths. There was nothing in the apartment to indicate foul play. No forced entry, no tossing of the place as in a burglary or robbery, no signs of violence on the body.

Casillas, it turned out, was a partner in a one-hour photo service in nearby Midland. His partner was David Dowler. No one made any special connection at the time that he was the same David Dowler who had reported another death three years earlier—that of his fellow worker, Lisa Krieg.

Again, it was Dowler who had set off concern about Casillas' welfare.

Dowler phoned Leza Kay Chandler to ask if she would check on Casillas, who had not reported to work at the Midland photo shop that morning. Dowler was wondering if something might be wrong. As those who knew him were aware, Dowler always seemed to be having premonitions about his friends.

He called Leza Chandler at her Odessa apartment because she was Casillas' ex-wife. The woman, in turn, got on the phone to her present husband, and asked him to find out if Casillas was all right.

Dowler also alerted another friend, a man who ran a photo shop in Odessa. Within a short time, both men went to Casillas' residence in response to the phone calls.

When they entered after ringing the bell and receiving no answer, they found Casillas dead on the kitchen floor.

When police and the acting coroner arrived at the scene, their investigation indicated that the death probably had been a natural one. But relatives and friends were not aware that Casillas suffered from any disease or condition that might suddenly have claimed his life, such as high blood pressure or a heart ailment.

The acting coroner ordered an autopsy. When the autopsy was conducted by an Odessa pathologist, standard toxic tests were run that showed that the death might be drug-related. The pathologist told investigators that he could not identify the drug or chemical that might be responsible for the death.

With the investigation continuing, the death was tentatively listed as natural, pending identification of the substance found in the body.

The family of the sudden-death victim felt that there might be more to Casillas' death than the initial facts revealed. He had not shown any suicidal tendencies, nor did they know of any big problems he might have been facing. No valuables were missing from the apartment, as far as could be determined, except for personal and business papers in a leather case.

Casillas habitually carried the leather case with him, according to friends and relatives. As far as they knew, there would have been no reason for anyone taking these papers.

Casillas and Krieg were acquainted through their mutual associations in their work with Dowler, but there seemed to be no other link in the unexplained deaths. At that time, no one really paid much attention to the fact that both deceased persons were involved with the suspicious David Dowler.

Eight months later, another young Odessa resident died unexpectedly. This time, the death occurred in full view of several witnesses, including relatives of the victim, Dorothy Jane Nesbitt, 29. She dropped dead at an arts and crafts show in the Ector County Coliseum on November 29, 1986.

Dorothy and two women relatives had been browsing through the exhibits at the show. As one of the women later related to investigators, "We were sitting up in the seats. We saw Dorothy looking from booth to booth, and she looked up and waved at us." The booths were set up on the coliseum floor, at a lower level than the spectator seats that ringed the area.

A few minutes later, Dorothy, who had bought a hot dog and soft drink, joined her relatives in the seating section.

"We were chatting," said the relative. "She never said a word about not feeling well . . . She never said anything. She had her Coke on the floor, and I thought she had leaned over to get it."

Instead, the young woman's head hit the seat in front of her, then she slumped to the concrete floor. When medical help was summoned, it was found that Dorothy Nesbitt had died on the spot where she collapsed.

The family and friends were stunned by her death.

The young woman, who had graduated some 10 years earlier from an Odessa high school, was employed as a secretary for a health organization in Midland. She'd had a mostly ordinary life. At the time of her death, she had been separated from her husband.

As far as had been known, Dorothy hadn't suffered from any serious diseases or conditions. In fact, relatives could offer no possible reason why she had suddenly keeled over dead at the arts and crafts show.

An autopsy was ordered. The report later released to the family was that Dorothy had died as the result of a malfunctioning heart valve.

On the afternoon of June 28, 1987, Leza Kay Chandler, 30, an elementary school teacher and former wife of Tony Casillas, was discovered dead on the bed of her Odessa apartment. Once again, it was David Dowler whose "premonition" that something was wrong led to the finding of the school teacher's lifeless body . . .

Dowler telephoned another woman friend of his, Martha Donnelly, to tell her about his strange feelings. He had awakened from a deep sleep the previous night, he said, with a strong feeling that something had happened to Leza Chandler. He asked Martha, who also was a friend of Leza's, to please go to her residence and find out if she was okay.

When the woman asked Dowler to accompany her, he said he had not dressed yet.

Martha made a phone call to the Chandler residence.

After a few rings, the phone was answered by a young child, whom the caller recognized as Leza's 2-year-old daughter. "I can't wake mommy up," the little girl said.

Now fearful that something really was wrong, Martha called back Dowler and again asked him to go with her to the Chandler home. Dowler was adamant about not going, adding that "it might look bad" if he was present. Unable to persuade him to accompany her, Martha Donnelly went to the address on East 53rd alone.

When she entered, she spotted the child playing quietly

beside her mother on the bed. The youngster was completely nude and covered with red fingernail polish, which she apparently had picked up and opened. Leza Chandler's body was cold; it was apparent that she was dead.

Police officers who responded to the death call found no evidence that foul play was involved in the young woman's demise, though there was no immediately apparent reason why she had died. A cursory examination revealed no marks of physical violence on her body.

The house was in order; there was nothing visible to indicate that entry had been forced by anyone, or that a burglar had prowled through the residence. In fact, the investigators could find nothing that might answer the question of how the school teacher had died. Answers, if any, would have to await the results of the autopsy ordered by the acting coroner. But the detectives were thoroughly suspicious.

If for no other reason, there was the one bit of information related by Martha Donnelly that set off a loud alarm bell within their investigative instincts. It was that the mysterious David Dowler had again been involved in voicing concern about one of his "premonitions" that all might not be well with a friend, and that premonition had led to the finding of another body.

To the detectives who had investigated the earlier deaths of Lisa Krieg, Tony Cassillas, and Dorothy Nesbit—all of whom had been friends, business associates or acquaintances of Dowler, and who were acquainted with each other—Dowler was having "premonitions" about too many people who ended up dead of some unknown cause.

With Leza Kay Chandler being number four in that fatal category, Odessa police detectives decided to launch an intensive probe into all of the sudden and unexplained deaths.

The first step would be additional comprehensive tests on the body tissues of the four people who, on the surface at least, had died "natural" deaths. The pathologist who had performed the autopsy on Lisa Krieg still had possession of organ samples removed from her body. This was also true in the cases of Cassillas and Nesbitt, so the bodies would not have to be exhumed.

But now the body samples would be submitted to a higher degree of forensic testing by lab experts other than the local pathologist. Also, body samples from Leza Chandler would be sent to a forensic laboratory in Forth Worth.

The team of Odessa detectives involved in the baffling multi-death probe included Detective Sergeant Richard E. Hirst and Detectives Mickey Browne and Gregory Travland. The sleuths gathered together all of the reports on the four strange deaths.

They worked closely with the local pathologist who had autopsied the bodies, and whose findings would be studied by other lab experts as the toxic search for what might have caused the deaths was expanded.

The detectives also put together an in depth "backgrounder" on David Dowler. During this phase of the probe, their investigation would take them to Albuquerque, New Mexico, where Dowler had grown up and lived until moving to Odessa in 1981. The investigators would also follow leads on this unusual character to Dallas and Austin, among other places.

As the officers put together the dossier and profile on Dowler, he shaped up as something out of the pages of intrigue fiction. They learned he was the son of a U.S. Air Force colonel and his Japanese wife. In his teenage years, Dowler had been an above-average "B" student at an Albuquerque high school. He'd been a member of the wrestling team. Other interests had included electronics and ham radio activity.

He'd attended the University of New Mexico for three years but had not been graduated.

He took courses in electrical engineering, physics, chemistry, and mathematics. He also was interested in karate, to the point that he held a black belt in the deadly art of oriental combat.

People were attracted to the tall, extremely skinny, dark-haired man with the strange eyes. His brows were dark and thick. He had a large nose, a straight-line mouth, eyes that were described both as hypnotic, and cold and calculating.

As the detectives talked with numerous witnesses, David

Dowler emerged as a man who easily integrated himself with people, especially individuals on the higher intellectual level: people in the arts, those in education, those actively involved in religious faith, and work. He seemed to get along well with children. Kids liked him, as did most people who were drawn by his nonstop conversation, not to mention the weird stories he told.

But his friends and acquaintances were never sure whether they should believe all his tales. They did stretch the imagination just a tad. While presenting himself as a friend to turn to in need or when having emotional problems, he at the same time claimed to have been a secret agent, a part of an assassination team that went around the world executing assigned victims.

He frequently talked of death and all its aspects. It was almost as if death were a hobby with this tall, slat-like man. He seemed fascinated with it. A video entitled "The Faces of Death" was one that he viewed often. It showed humans and animals dying or dead.

Later, Detective Browne would described Dowler as similar in his character, his talk and his influence on his circle of friends and associates, to Pennsylvania killer William Bradfield, who was convicted of the bizarre 1979 murder of a school teacher and her two young children. Bradfield, a high school English teacher, with a gift of gab that included boasts of "secret agent" assassinations and some sexual preoccupations out of an X-rated movie, was the subject of a best-selling book by police writer Joseph Wambaugh titled, *Echoes in the Darkness*.

"David Dowler has a personality very much like that of William Bradfield," Browne remarked.

But it was a side of Dowler that his relatives and friends couldn't believe. For instance, one relative described him as "the greatest uncle in the world."

"David is one who goofs around, jokes a lot, but he will do without to help someone else," said one family member. "You'd be surprised at people who borrowed money from him and never paid back . . . David would even let his own work slide to help someone else."

Said another kinsman, "Anybody who's been sick or ill—he's always tried to come out and visit. Or at least make a phone call. He's always taken somebody under his wing."

As their investigation deepened, the detectives would have to agree with that statement, at least to some degree.

When the report was received on the results of the autopsy on Leza Kay Chandler and the additional tests by the Fort Worth forensic lab, the detectives had at least one important fact for certain—they knew *how* the school teacher had died.

The pathologist said that death was attributed to acute chloroform poisoning.

The pathologist explained that chloroform is a "clear, colorless, volatile liquid with a strong ethereal smell and a sweetish, burning taste." It can be used to induce general anesthesia by inhalation of the vapor. Chloroform can cause death when the person inhaling the vapor does not get enough oxygen.

Though no longer used as an anesthetic, chloroform is often used in organic chemistry work and for synthesis and extractions in chemical manufacturing. "It's a very widely used compound," the medical expert noted. "For instance, I've got a jug of it sitting here in my office. You can find it in virtually any college laboratory."

The compound is inexpensive and can be bought from chemical supply companies by anyone who presents a photo identification, the detectives learned.

One possibility that the investigators now needed to check out was whether Leza Chandler might have committed suicide by administering chloroform to herself. No evidence that the compound was used had been found in her bedroom. Officers rechecked the residence to make sure, but no chloroform was found anywhere in the home.

From friends, the police investigators learned that Leza Chandler had been concerned about personal problems. Among the problems were domestic difficulties with her husband, from whom she was separated. There was talk, too, that David Dowler had offered to help her through that emotional storm. There were even stories that Dowler had talked of using chloroform to induce a hypnotic state that would

67

allow the woman to use her subconscious mind to find answers to questions that troubled her.

As detectives continued to sort out Dowler's role in the lives and deaths of his circle of friends, an unexpected development occurred. Martha Donnelly, the woman who had found Leza Chandler dead after receiving the call of "concern" from Dowler, contacted detectives. She was deeply concerned about things she was hearing from Dowler, in relation to the string of sudden deaths of people both she and Dowler had known as friends.

"Something's not right about all the things that have happened," the anxious young woman told Detective Browne. "I want to tell you what I know."

She wasn't sure whether to believe the strange stories that Dowler related. But, in her opinion, especially in light of Dowler's call and subsequent refusal to accompany her to Leza's home, there was something definitely wrong in the activities of this man so totally engrossed in death. After talking to the investigators about her relationship with Dowler in recent days, she agreed to a plan to get Dowler's conversations on record.

Martha Donnelly agreed to carry a hidden transmitter so that police could tape her conversations with Dowler. A policewoman did the job of wiring the witness for sound. The witness also gave permission for a secret microphone to be installed in her apartment. The mike was installed by Intelligence Agent Ronnie Watson of the Texas Department of Public Safety, who was working with the local detectives on the investigation.

In all, the tape recordings in July 1987 of conversations between Dowler and Martha Donnelly ran nine and a half hours in length. It was a bizarre and chilling story that unfolded in the recorded conversations that took place at a shopping mall and in the witness' apartment.

Dowler again talked about his "premonition" that caused him to alert Martha that something might be wrong at the Chandler residence. Martha pursued the question that had bothered her from the start, telling Dowler, "I don't understand why you wouldn't go with me. You sent me over there by myself, knowing what I would find there."

Dowler's voice replied; "I didn't know for sure what you would find. I don't know why I didn't go. I just didn't." Then he explained again that "it would have looked bad" and reiterated that he hadn't been dressed at the time she called. Dowler maintained that he "often" got these feelings when his friends were in danger.

In the taped conversations, Dowler extolled the use of chloroform for therapeutic hypnosis, saying that the drug was safe for this purpose, unless too much was inhaled by the user. "It can't kill you unless you drink a gallon of it," he told Martha Donnelly.

He carefully explained that chloroform put people into a "twilight state" that permitted them to delve into their subconsciousness in matters that were of personal problems. Kay Chandler had expressed interest in this technique of self-analysis, but had never gone through with the idea.

Dowler advanced a reason for the woman's death. He told Martha that he believed Kay Chandler's estranged husband had killed her because he was extremely jealous of Dowler's and others' relationships with Kay. Moreover, said Dowler, the estranged husband had a "hit list" of other people he intended to kill. Ominously, he added, both Dowler and Martha Donnelly were on that list.

Dowler had a plan. He told Martha that he could easily kill Kay Chandler's estranged husband without detection. He said he would wait for the man at his apartment and splash cyanide into his face when he showed up. Or, as an alternative, Dowler said he could throw the homemade and deadly poison on him as he jogged past Dowler in a parking lot.

The listening investigators also heard Dowler blame the deaths of Lisa Krieg and Tony Casillas on Kay Chandler's estranged spouse. Dowler again characterized the man as an insanely-jealous husband who feared that Kay Chandler would go back to her ex-husband, Casillas.

Dowler related that although the estranged mate was jealous of Dowler, too, Dowler had rejected Kay's sexual advances when she propositioned him twice. Dowler believed

Martha Donnelly would be the estranged husband's next victim. But he recommended "taking out" the would-be killer first.

"There's all kinds of ways of doing it," he said. He outlined a plan in which Martha could assist in the extermination of the estranged husband by acting as "lookout" while Dowler did the job.

Dowler built himself up as a killer, telling the witness on the tape-recording that he had been part of a 12-man government assassination team that travelled the world killing assigned victims with .22 pistols equipped with silencers. He claimed that during his work as a government agent he'd had to "take out six guys."

In addition to the tape-recording, the investigators also made a video record of the outside of Martha Donnelly's apartment and also the front of Dowler's photo shop in Midland, where they had also met.

In all, as the detectives later listened to the tape in its entirety, they were aware that they had a primary suspect who admittedly had a knowledge of chloroform and cyanide, claimed he could kill without being detected, and had had close relationships with the three victims. His fantasy about being a government assassin (which the sleuths quickly checked and eliminated as nothing but plain bull) aside, Dowler had said enough to tangle himself in a growing chain of evidence.

Following up Dowler's claims about Kay Chandler's estranged husband, the detectives grilled the man at length. The husband told the investigators that he believed his wife and Dowler were indeed having an affair. But he said he had never thought about harming her or Dowler. Asked about his whereabouts on the night that Kay Chandler was thought to have died, her husband said he had seen his wife that evening about 6:00 p.m. when he picked up some laundry. He had then left and talked to her on the phone at 9:00 p.m., when he asked her to go to church with him the next day.

During that conversation at nine o'clock, Kay Chandler had mentioned that David Dowler was with her at that time, the husband related. He told the detectives that he had visited at a friend's apartment from 9:00 p.m. to 11:00 p.m., then had been at his own apartment the rest of the night. He emphatically denied having anything to do with his wife's death.

As the detectives pressed the probe into the deaths of the three victims, they turned up another witness whose recollections were intriguing. On the day Lisa Krieg's body was found, this witness related, Dowler had told him that Lisa had killed herself with cyanide powder Dowler himself had provided. Further, Dowler had claimed to this witness that he'd gone to Lisa's residence and cleaned up the body to make her death appear natural. The witness said he hadn't told police about Dowler's statements at that time, because he figured they would think he was crazy.

Dowler had made all sorts of far-out statements, even about being a government agent, the witness told the investigators. The man had called the FBI to check out this particular claim of Dowler's; he hadn't heard anything back from the agency. "But whenever one of my friends dies, he seemed to know all about it," the witness said of Dowler.

Another witness told the officers that she had been informed by Dowler that Lisa Krieg killed herself because "if she couldn't have him, she didn't want anyone."

Still another witness had something to say about the death of Tony Casillas, in relation to Dowler's actions. About a week before the death of Casillas, said the witness, Dowler had phoned to have her read him a formula from a book he had loaned her. The book was titled, *A Poor Man's James Bond,* and the recipe Dowler had requested was for the deadly poison, cyanide. The witness said that Dowler had later denied having killed Casillas.

This conversation took place when they met at Casillas' funeral, according to the witness, who added Dowler explained that Casillas had died because he made a mistake in brewing a batch of homemade cyanide.

It was now August 20, 1987. The detective team working long hours on the probe had conferred with Ector County District Attorney Eric Augesen, who had been overseeing

71

their hunt for evidence in the bizarre case. The district attorney reviewed what they had, including the lengthy tape-recording with Martha Donnelly that revealed Dowler's personal knowledge of exotic poisons as well as the intimate lives of the victims.

It was decided to get a warrant for Dowler's arrest, and a search warrant for his home.

Among the information alleged by the detectives in the application for the arrest and search warrants, filed with Justice of the Peace R. G. Hungerford, were:

A witness had given a sworn statement that Dowler had planned to spend the night with Kay Chandler at her apartment, the night of her death that was later attributed to acute chloroform poisoning.

A witness had given police "lengthy and detailed information about Chandler, her death, and Dowler, all of which has been verified by independent sources through investigations conducted by Odessa police officers." The "information" referred to was the audio-video tape-recordings made of Dowler and Martha Donnelly.

A witness said that bottles containing chloroform were in Dowler's residence on a "continuing basis for a period of time, dating back to January 1986, and up to the present time." Furthermore, said another witness who made an affidavit, Kay Chandler told a friend that Dowler had offered to give her chloroform "reducing her to a hypnotic state."

According to the witness, Kay had told the friend a personal problem she was having with her family that she could not resolve. The witness related that Dowler planned to ask Kay questions while she was in a hypnotic state, "questions that she had previously written down for him to ask, allowing her to answer said questions."

"David Dowler further alleged that her answers would come from her subconscious mind as a result of the hypnotic state induced by the ingestion" of chloroform, the affidavit said.

Based on the information in the affidavit, the justice of the peace issued a warrant for David Dowler's arrest on the charge of murder, alleging that he killed Kay Chandler with acute chloroform poisoning on the night of June 27, 1987. A search warrant for the suspect's home was also issued.

Dowler was arrested as he drove away from a residence he had been visiting. Pulling him over to the curb and making the collar were Detectives Browne, Hirst, Travland, Don High, and DPS Agent Watson. He offered no resistance. At the same time, the officers found a .22-caliber Ruger automatic and two silencers for the gun inside Dowler's car. The silencers appeared to be home-made — one constructed from a racquet-ball canister and the other from a metal tube.

While Dowler was taken to the police station for questioning, other investigators searched his residence. Among the items found by detectives and taken as evidence were two bottles containing traces of chloroform. A copper heating stand and two rubber bottle-stoppers were also taken for laboratory testing.

After being informed fully of his legal rights, Dowler was confronted with the results of the several-months' investigation into the deaths of his friends. Dowler gave a voluntary statement admitting that he had been with Leza Chandler on the night she apparently died but denied that he killed the woman.

Dowler related in the statement that he brought a film container filled with chloroform to Leza's apartment after she had asked him to perform a hypnotic experiment that might help solve her accumulating personal problems. She asked Dowler to put her under a chloroform-induced trance in hopes of delving into her subconsciousness. Dowler said that after talking about five minutes, he and Leza went into a bedroom. After lying down on the bed, she placed a chloroform-soaked cloth over her mouth. After a few minutes, her speech became slurred, said Dowler, and she told him she was too tired to continue with the hypnosis. She fell asleep and Dowler left with the chloroform and the rag saturated with the chemical, going out the back door.

Considering the witness statements they had gathered, detectives felt that they had good reason to doubt the version of Leza Chandler's chloroform episode as related by Dowler. He was taken before a justice of the peace, who set bond of

$500,000 on the charge of murder filed in Leza's death. He was also charged with two counts of carrying a prohibited weapon as a result of the pistol and two silencers found in his possession at the time of arrest.

He was remanded to the Ector County Jail to await presentation of the case to a grand jury. On August 31st, the suspect's attorney sought to reduce Dowler's bond, and a hearing was held in state district court.

Detective Travland testified that video and audio tapes were made from a police surveillance van on two occasions— once when Dowler and Martha Donnelly talked together for over five hours in a Midland shopping mall, and again when the two conversed in Martha's Odessa apartment for several hours. One video film showed the two talking in the mall; the second one showed Dowler arriving and entering Martha's apartment.

The detective related that the recorded conversations included plans Dowler made to kill Leza Chandler's former husband: "In the tape, he describes how he would set him up and kill him," said Travland. "He wanted (Martha Donnelly) to be what you would call a lookout woman while he was in the apartment."

The detective also testified that Dowler said on the tape that he knew how to "make arsenic and cyanide to kill someone."

After calling several character witnesses, including a minister who testified about Dowler's church work, the defense was successful in getting the defendant's bond reduced from $500,000 to $100,000. He did not make the reduced bond, however.

On September 8, 1987, an Ector County grand jury returned an indictment charging Dowler with murder by chloroform poisoning in Leza Chandler's death.

Meanwhile, the Odessa detectives and the Ector County Sheriff's Department continued to investigate the other deaths—those of Krieg, Casillas, and Nesbitt. The main evidence needed was the cause of the deaths. That badly needed information came late in September when the final toxicology reports from the Fort Worth forensic lab were released.

The Odessa pathologist who made the initial tests released the report to police, and later the press. It showed that both Lisa Krieg and Tony Casillas had died from cyanide poisoning. The tests showed that Lisa's body contained 7.7 micrograms per milliliters of cyanide in her blood. The pathologist said the minimum lethal dose is at least 1.1 micrograms per milliliters.

The report also revealed that 9.7 micrograms per milliliters of cyanide were present in the blood of Casillas.

"They had what would be considered a lethal dose," said the pathologist. The medical experts said that cyanide is not too difficult to obtain. As a poison, it interferes with the metabolic process of the body at the cellular level. With the toxicological evidence in hand, the investigators now planned to fully brief the district attorney on their evidence in the two deaths and seek additional charges against Dowler.

Meanwhile, a relative of Tony Casillas speculated to reporters that the Casillas' killer might have hoped to fool authorities because of the timing of the death. At the time, newspapers across the nation were bannering stories about accidental cyanide poisonings from the consumptions by the victims of an over-the-counter pain-killer.

The sleuths also continued to check into the strange death of Dorothy Jane Nesbitt, who had dropped dead while attending the arts and crafts show, but additional tests failed to indicate any other cause of death other than a malfunctioning heart valve, as disclosed in the original autopsy. There was no evidence to link her death to those of the other three friends of Dowler, even though the woman had known Dowler and the victims. The circumstances had to be marked down as coincidental.

In December 1987, after the district attorney's office presented the evidence to the grand jury, two more murder indictments were returned against David Dowler, charging that he killed Krieg and Casillas with cyanide. The defendant was placed under additional bond of $200,000.

Dowler's trial was set to begin in January 1988 in Judge Bill McCoy's 358th State District Court in Odessa's modernistic-looking courthouse.

In a preliminary hearing, the defense attorney attempted to block the use of the video and audio tapes of Dowler's conversations on the grounds that his legal rights had been violated. The key witness, Martha Donnelly, took the stand to testify that she was not coached by police on what to say when she met with Dowler. A detective told the court that the purpose of filming and recording what happened between her and Dowler was to monitor the meetings for the safety of the witness. The judge ruled that the defendant's rights were not violated because he was not in custody at the time the tapes were made. The judge also ruled that the prosecution would have to prove a common link between the three deaths before the Krieg and Casillas cases would be mentioned in the trial of Dowler in Leza Chandler's death.

Dowler would be tried in Chandler's death first.

Testimony in the Chandler homicide started on January 19th before a six-man, six-woman jury. After opening statements, the state introduced the testimony of the local pathologist that Leza Chandler had died of acute chloroform poisoning.

The pathologist told the jury that Leza's body contained two to seven times the amount of chloroform required to be lethal. He related that the woman must have continued to inhale chloroform three or four minutes after the chemical rendered her unconscious for her body to have absorbed such a large amount of chloroform as revealed by the autopsy.

The testimony of the pathologist was a striking blow to Dowler's claim that he had left, taking the chloroform and chemical-soaked rag with him after Leza said she was too tired to continue the experiment.

The pathologist said Leza probably died within minutes after receiving the lethal dose.

When grilled on cross-examination as to whether he thought the chloroform was administered by someone other than the victim, the doctor answered that he thought it was unlikely that she had done it herself, because no chloroform containers were found in her residence.

The defense attorney asked if it were not possible the chloroform had been in some other container and evaporated before police arrived.

"But the container wouldn't have evaporated," replied the pathologist.

It was the audio-video tape recording of the conversations between Dowler and Martha Donnelly that gripped the attention of the jury and courtroom spectators. They appeared spellbound as the glib-tongued Dowler made his series of bizarre claims and theories about the deaths of three friends.

He talked of making undetectable poisons with which he could kill people and get away with it, of his ruthless activity as a government agent-assassin, of the plans of Leza Chandler's husband to kill other people including Dowler and Martha Donnelly and how they could beat him to the punch, of his ability to help friends with his chloroform hypnosis and therapy, how "you would have to drink a gallon of it" for chloroform to be fatal.

Leza Chandler's estranged husband, whom Dowler had said on the tape had a "hit list" including the defendant and Martha Donnelly, took the stand and denied all of the accusations levelled by Dowler. He related that he talked on the phone to his wife on the night that she met her death, at which time she told him Dowler was there. The husband said that he believed Dowler was having an affair with Leza, though Dowler said on the tape that he had turned down the woman's sexual advances twice.

The witness also testified that Dowler told him he was a government agent and member of an assassination task force, that he could build bombs, had many weapons, and "he didn't have a problem killing anyone."

Dowler lowered his eyes and shook his head during the husband's testimony, but his expression remained stoic, as it did throughout the trial.

The voluntary statement given by Dowler after his arrest, in which he had claimed he had left Leza sleeping but alive when he left her home with the chloroform, was introduced by the state, which called Detective Browne as a witness. Chloroform bottles, the copper heating unit, and other items found in the defendant's apartment were also admitted into evidence.

Out of the presence of the jury, District Attorney Augesen told the judge that he planned to show Dowler was guilty of three poisoning deaths—those of Krieg and Casillas in addition to Chandler. The defense attorney countered that the tape recording, in which the deaths of Krieg and Casillas were discussed by Dowler, showed no similarity to the crime for which he was being tried to the other two deaths. He asked for a mistrial for the tape having been shown to the jury.

But the district attorney persisted that he would have evidence to prove the three deaths connected, and that he would essentially be trying three murder cases instead of one.

The judge denied the defense request for a mistrial, ruling that the tape showed Dowler's "scheme and design." Similar crimes can be introduced when the prosecution is seeking to show a pattern within several offenses.

The D.A. lost no time in trying to prove his theory when the trial resumed before the jury.

Called as a witness was a Forth Worth toxicologist, who testified that traces of cyanide were found on two rubber bottle-stoppers and a copper heating stand that police had confiscated from Dowler's home.

The expert witness also testified that traces of chloroform were found in the two bottles also seized in the search.

Under cross-examination, the doctor said it would be virtually impossible to determine whether the cyanide found on the items in Dowler's home was the same that killed Krieg and Casillas. "Results show that cyanide caused their deaths," he said. "That's all I can testify to."

Both the forensic expert from Fort Worth and the Odessa pathologist told the jury that Krieg and Casillas had more than enough cyanide in their bodies to have caused the deaths, citing the amount of cyanide in their blood as revealed by the extensive tests.

Saying that Casillas had 9.7 micrograms of cyanide per milliliter of blood and Krieg had 7.7 micrograms, the Fort Worth lab expert said that in the cyanide cases he had seen in his career that "one to two micrograms have led to death."

The prosecution put on five witnesses who testified that Dowler had told them he had given cyanide to Krieg and was with her the night she died. One of the witnesses said the defendant told her that Lisa Krieg killed herself with cyanide he had given to her and that he had "cleaned her up" to make her death look natural.

Another witness testified that Dowler called her a week before the death of Tony Casillas and asked her to read him a formula for cyanide from a book he had lent her.

She added that Dowler later denied killing Casillas, saying the man had died because of a mistake he made in brewing a homemade batch of cyanide.

When asked repeatedly by the defense attorney whether police had any direct evidence that Dowler forced fatal amounts of poison on Chandler, Krieg, and Casillas, Detective Browne answered that Dowler had said in the secretly recorded conversations with Martha Donnelly that Krieg and Casillas died of cyanide poisoning. The conversations had been recorded long before the toxicological results showed that the two bodies contained amounts of the poison, Browne said.

"Only the killer would know this," the detective declared.

As the defense prepared to present its case, Dowler's attorney told the jury in opening remarks that he would prove Dowler was home with a friend most of the night before Leza Chandler's body was found the next morning. The lawyer said he also would show that chemicals police found in Dowler's home were used to make fireworks and that Leza was "scared to death" of her estranged husband, from whom she was in the process of getting a divorce.

"There is no evidence that David Dowler killed Leza Chandler," the defense attorney asserted.

The first witness called by the defense was the son of a prominent Odessa official, who said he was with Dowler most of the night before Chandler's body was found in her home.

The witness, who occasionally worked at Dowler's Midland photo store, said he was staying at Dowler's residence on the night of June 27, 1987. He said Dowler was there most of the night, except for a period from about 8:30 p.m. to 10:00 p.m. He related that he was a light sleeper and would have heard Dowler leave during the night, had he done so.

The witness also told the jury that Dowler had taught him how to inhale chloroform. He said he had used the chemical about four times to sleep or to relax tight muscles in his back. Testifying that he had seen several people use chloroform in Dowler's presence, he added he had never seen Dowler administer it to anyone.

The witness further testified that Leza Chandler had told him she was afraid of her husband.

But a psychiatrist who had counseled Leza's husband for about a month in 1987 said that his patient suffered from a "simple depression" because of stress resulting from his failing marriage, but was not abusive. "He appeared depressed and upset, but he was never psychotic," said the psychiatrist.

The defense had questioned Leza Chandler's husband on the stand in relation to Dowler's allegations made to Martha Donnelly on the tapes that the husband had a list of people he wanted to kill, because of his mental condition.

Responding to the defense questions, the husband said he made arrangements for his wife and himself to see a psychiatrist in an effort to save their marriage.

His former wife had gone to only two sessions, he recalled. The witness said he had been diagnosed as being depressed and that anti-depressants had been prescribed. He denied suggestions that he had been physically abusive to Leza Chandler.

He said he and his wife had separated in February 1986, and he had moved out of their home.

In final arguments before the jury in the guilt or innocence phase of the murder trial, the prosecution characterized David Dowler as a manipulative murderer who enjoyed controlling people and then watching them die. D.A. Augesen told the jury that Dowler was someone who controlled his friends through "shared paranoia" and later killed them when he grew tired of them.

"He likes to be the power that snuffs out life," said the D.A. "He likes that supreme power."

He argued that Dowler convicted himself in his comments in the nine and a half hours of taped conversations with Martha Donnelly. "They aren't only the ravings of someone who is strange and bizarre," he said. "They are confessions."

Dowler's attorney described him before the jury not as a killer, but as "one of the biggest B.S. artists he'd ever seen.

"You have a complicated, bizarre case, but that doesn't mean you have a crime." He said his client had no motive for any of the killings, nor had the state proved that Dowler administered the fatal dose of chloroform to Leza Chandler.

The defense lawyer pointed out that the unusual deaths of Dowler's three friends "are as consistent with suicide or accidental deaths as they are with homicide. Even more so."

He continued, "My client not only lies when telling the truth would be better, but he runs around on his wife. But the fact that a person lies or runs around on his wife doesn't mean he killed somebody."

Turning to the death of Leza Chandler, the defense attorney said that since the time of death had not been determined, nobody knew whether Dowler could have been with her at the time. The district attorney countered that though the exact time Leza Chandler had died wasn't known, Dowler would have killed her anyway.

Just as Dowler had had "feelings" that Krieg and Casillas were about to die, his "sixth sense" told him that Leza Chandler was next, the district attorney told the jury. "She was dying," said the prosecutor. "It was a total question of when."

Early on the morning of January 27, 1988 — six months to the day after Leza Chandler died from chloroform poisoning — the jury returned its verdict after deliberating for six hours.

The verdict was guilty of murder.

Later that day, the punishment phase of the trial began, with the same jury facing the job of determining what Dowler's punishment would be.

D.A. Augesen urged the jury to give Dowler the maximum sentence under the law — life in prison.

"The man is a vicious murderer," Augesen declared. "He doesn't need to walk the streets of our community again. Ninety-nine years to life is far too cheap for what he did, but that's all we can do with the facts and the circumstances."

The defense asked for a term of 10 to 20 years in the state penitentiary. The defense lawyer asked the jury to consider Dowler's family—his wife and two small children—when assessing his punishment. "The ultimate punishment will be given by somebody higher than in this courtroom," he said.

But after only 30 minutes' deliberation, the jury decided to go as far as the law provided. The jury set punishment at life imprisonment. Even with that sentence, Dowler could be paroled within 15 years, but he still faces trial on the other two murder indictments.

The D.A. later told newsmen that he would have preferred to seek the death penalty for Dowler. But he pointed out a 1984 change in the state's capital punishment law meant that the maximum sentence would have to be life in prison.

"But capital punishment is what the man really deserved," said the D.A. "If anyone deserved it, he did."

Augesen praised the astute work of the Odessa Police Department in bringing Dowler to justice in the complicated case: "It's time someone said something good about the police department's work on this case, because they are the cause of the verdict of guilty."

In turn, Detective Browne, who led the investigations in all three deaths, lauded the district attorney's office: "I think it had an extremely complicated case, but the jury came back with the right verdict. The evidence was overwhelming."

And as one of the jurors put it, "We felt we had to virtually ensure he wouldn't re-enter society. I thought life in prison would have an impact on David Dowler. He seemed to show no remorse throughout the trial and the sentencing phase."

Meanwhile, Dowler's attorney said the verdict would be appealed to a higher state court on grounds that some of the evidence admitted should not have been, especially the tape-recording.

Dowler is being held in the Texas Department of Corrections, pending outcome of his appeal and the two murder indictments yet to be brought to trial.

EDITOR'S NOTE:

The names Dorothy Jane Nesbitt and Martha Donnelly are not the real names of the persons so named in the foregoing story. Fictitious names have been used because there is no reason for public interest in the identities of these persons.

The Green River Killer!

by Gary C. King

On Thursday, July 15, 1982, two young boys were enter-taining themselves by bicycling along a path which runs along the banks of the Green River in an area just north of the Meeker Street Bridge in Kent, Washington, located in south King County near Seattle.

The summer of 1982 would be a summer they would never forget, no matter how hard they tried, because what started out as a day of brightness and high spirits for the two boys quickly turned into a haunting nightmare when they looked down the banks toward the river from the path above. What they saw was the dead body of a teenage girl partially submerged and snagged in pilings near the bank of the Green River.

When the King County authorities arrived at the crime scene, located near a popular lovers lane, they treated the obvious homicide routinely by following proper police pro-cedure, just as they would treat any other such case. What the cops didn't realize as they fished the young lady's body out of the river, and wouldn't realize for some time yet, was that the macabre discovery they were dealing with was only a sample of what was yet to come. It would ultimately tie in with the murders of at least 25 additional females whose bodies or remains would be found over the following two years in or near the vicinity of the Green River near the Seattle-Tacoma International Airport. The case at the time of this writing would become the biggest active murder investigation in the United States.

The young victim of July 15, 1982, the first victim of what was to be called the Green River Killer, was a cute, 5-foot-4-inch blue-eyed blonde, somewhat chunky at 140 pounds. Although her body was bruised and bloated, the cops guessed that the girl was a teenager and, because of several tattoos on her body, the investigators reasoned that positive identification would not be too difficult to attain.

They entered the victim's physical description into their notebooks and described the tattoo of a Harley-Davidson motorcycle emblem on her back, the tattoo of a cross entwined with vines on her left shoulder, two butterflies just above her left breast, a unicorn on the left side of her lower abdomen and a tattoo of a heart entangled with additional vines on her left forearm. Suspected cause of death was listed as strangulation, which was confirmed following a thorough autopsy by the King County coroner's office.

The victim of July 15, 1982 was soon identified as 16-year-old Wendy Lee Coffield, who had been reported missing from a foster care home seven days earlier. The identity was confirmed visually by a close relative, who also told the investigators that Wendy disappeared after she left the foster care home to spend the night with her grandfather.

Background investigation of the victim revealed that Wendy was a persistent, incessant runaway who dropped out of high school and took to the streets, eventually selling her body as a prostitute to help support a drug habit and to otherwise help sustain her troubled life. In addition to prostitution, Wendy managed to build a criminal record for herself by stealing lunch tickets at her high school prior to dropping out, and was sent to a juvenile detention facility for the theft. When she returned home in May, 1982, she stole $140 worth of food stamps from a neighbor and was convicted, resulting in her being returned to the juvenile detention facility. After a short period of incarceration, she was released to the custody of the foster care home and was subsequently murdered, leaving investigators with no solid leads to point them in the direction of a prime suspect.

Time slipped forward to August as detectives made little or no progress with the Wendy Coffield case. King County authorities also had several other unsolved murders involving young females linked to prostitution on their books, but were treating them as separate cases due to the lack of similarities regarding the killer's method of operation. It wasn't until August 12, 1982, when the body of 23-year-old Deborah Lynn Bonner of nearby Tacoma was found a half mile upstream from where Wendy Coffield's body had been found in the Green River, that the police were able to make a connection linking any of the cases together.

The sleuths still had a string of unsolved murders of young women, some of which were linked to prostitution and some of which were not, that they had to deal with as separate cases. But there were striking similarities regarding the murders of Wendy Coffield and Deborah Bonner, which prompted the detectives to theorize that their deaths were the work of the same man, thus allowing them to combine the two into one case.

After checking the latest victim's background, the detectives learned that Bonner had been involved in prostitution activities in Portland, Oregon, for which she had been arrested several times. They also learned that she had made numerous collect telephone calls from Portland to Seattle, which established a link to King County where her body was discovered.

As King County authorities worked around the clock attempting to make even a little headway with the Coffield-Bonner case, a Seattle-area self-described psychic volunteered to help by attempting to pick up psychic images of victim Wendy Coffield, ultimately achieving some startling, if not useful, results.

Laura Thompson, the psychic, and a friend went to the area of the Meeker Street Bridge in Kent on a pleasant weekend evening in August, the area where Wendy Coffield's body was found floating in the Green River, in hopeful anticipation of picking up psychic images. Shortly after parking in an area near the bridge, Thompson later reported that she began picking up the name Opal and, as a result thought she should be looking for a car by that name, but spelled O-p-e-l. However, no such car was spotted.

At approximately 2:00 a.m., Thompson and her friend heard a scream coming from the river that made their blood run cold. Wasting no time, they followed the stream and caught a brief look of a tall, slender man taking long, giant steps, but not quite running, across a clearing near the river. He got into a car, at which time Thompson was able to glimpse the man's profile. Thompson and her friend followed in their own car in hot pursuit, but were unable to catch up with the man because he was driving a car "that was all souped up. I was driving sixty miles an hour but he knew how to drive. He took the curves like an expert," she said. Although Thompson was unable to catch up with the car to get a license number, she was at least able to give detectives a sketchy description of the man driving the speeding vehicle.

"He's white," said Thompson, "has brown hair, thin legs and I'm not sure of his age, but he walks with a long stride with long, slow-swinging arms." Admittedly, it wasn't much to go on, but, according to one detective, police from agencies around the country have used psychics and have at times achieved positive, desired results The key, however, of being able to use psychic results effectively is dependent on the investigators' ability to find and gather hard evidence which will stand up in court.

Thompson, who fears for her own safety because of media attention surrounding this case and for which reason a fictitious name has been used here, says that a good deal of her psychic ability is related to rapes and murders of younger age girls and women and claims 90 percent accuracy. "In the beginning," she said of her psychic experiences, which began at age 17 (she's now in her forties), "I thought it was depressing, because I would see people I care about die and accidents happen to them." Now she uses the voice of her subconscious to help authorities whenever possible, but says that she is not able to recognize the "location, identity or meaning" of most of her psychic experiences.

One thing is certain, though: On the weekend night in August, 1982, when Thompson and her friend were parked by the Meeker Street Bridge trying to pick up psychic signals, they were indeed having a high degree of success for, on Sunday, August 15th, King County authorities discovered the nude and decomposed bodies of three young black women floating in the Green River near the area where Thompson was parked. The victims were later identified as Cynthia Jean Hinds, 17; Marcia Faye Chapman, 31, and Opal Charmaine Mills, 16.

"I was parked there (near the bridge) the night Opal Charmaine Mills was killed," said Thompson. "I had been picking up the name Opal."

The day after the three latest victims' bodies were found, August 16th, the King County authorities had no doubts that they had a serious problem on their hands—a problem that frighteningly resembled the area's numerous "Ted" killings, eight years earlier. In that reign of terror, several young women were brutally slain in serial-type killings attributed to suspect Ted Bundy, then an inmate on Florida's Death Row. As a result of the discovery of the three latest victims, a 25-member unit known as the King County Task Force (later to be called the Green River Task Force) was formed to investigate the homicides.

Background information revealed that one of the latest victims, Marcia Faye Chapman, had been arrested by King County authorities for prostitution along "the strip" near Seattle-Tacoma International Airport (Sea-Tac), a busy avenue where there are many cheap, sleazy motels frequented by prostitutes, pimps and their customers. Chapman lived near the airport, police said, which is not far from the Green River where the bodies were found. Police said that victims Cynthia Hinds and Opal Mills, however, had not been convicted of prostitution, but had been associated or linked to "the strip" area and that some of the victims knew each other.

Although it was revealed early in the investigation that Wendy Coffield had been strangled, police refused to reveal the causes of death of the other victims at this point. But, according to King County Police Major Richard Kraske, task force investigators were theorizing that the five victims, two whites and three blacks, were killed by the same person who disposed of their bodies by tossing them into the Green River on separate occasions. Police also said that because of this series of obviously connected murders, additional un-solved homicides would be looked at again and compared with the Green River killings.

One such killing that was looked at again by the investi-gators was of 15-year-old Patrisa Jo Crossman, whose blood-soaked body was found on June 13, 1982, lying in shrubs outside an apartment house near Sea-Tac Interna-tional Airport. According to King County Homicide Detec-tive Larry Peterson, the slender young girl had been raped and repeatedly stabbed. Peterson said that Crossman, linked to prostitution activities in Seattle and Portland, had been "a chronic runaway for over a year," and was well-known on several Portland street corners.

"It's very tragic," Peterson remarked. "They don't believe there are risks. They believe that it always happens to the other person, that they won't get into a car with a bad guy," he said, predicting that young prostitutes would continue to be murdered.

Another death looked at by investigators in the wake of the so-called Green River killings was that of Leann Vir-ginia Wilcox, 16, also known as Renee Virginia Ramirez, of Tacoma. Wilcox's body was found lying in a field in nearby Federal Way, Washington, on January 22, 1982, and autopsy results revealed that she had been strangled. She, too, had been linked to prostitution and, like Crossman and Bonner, Wilcox's activities had been traced to Portland. However, investigators linked Wilcox to a specific pimp and believed that she may have been killed to prevent her from testifying against the pimp in a Seattle prostitution trial.

Still other deaths were scrutinized again by King County

authorities to determine whether or not any links exist between those deaths and the Green River killings. Among those cases looked at again:

Angelita Bell Axelson, 25, whose decomposed body was found June 18, 1981—she had been strangled;

25-year-old Desiree Hawkins, a convicted prostitute who had been beaten to death with a crescent wrench in Kent, Washington, on July 4, 1981 (James Patrick Laherty, 33-year-old taxicab driver, was charged and convicted in Hawkins' death and was sentenced to 20-years in prison);

19-year old Virginia Kay Taylor, a nude dancer, whose corpse was found, strangled on January 29, 1982, in a vacant lot near South Seattle Community College;

16-year-old Joan Lucinda Reed Conner, who was found strangled the following month after leaving her home to sell Campfire Girl mints;

Theresa Kline, 27, who was found strangled after having been seen hitchhiking on Aurora Avenue in Seattle on April 27, 1982.

Of the 12 known victims being looked at here, six were found to have been linked to prostitution—Wendy Coffield, Deborah Bonner, Marcia Chapman, Patrisa Crossman, Leann Wilcox and Desiree Hawkins. Two of the known victims, Cynthia Hinds and Opal Mills, had no convictions for prostitution but had been linked to "the strip" area near Sea-Tac International Airport, which is frequented by pimps and prostitutes. Four of the known victims—Theresa Kline, Joan Conner, Virginia Taylor and Angelita Axelson—had no links to prostitution or to "the strip."

In order to avoid "copycat" killings and to provide detectives with a way in which to verify that they had the right man in the event an arrest were made, certain key elements of the case, such as causes of death, were kept secret, particularly after it had been established that several of the killings, namely the deaths of Coffield, Bonner, Chapman, Hinds and Mills, could be linked to a single killer. Before such a link had been established, though, it had been revealed that Coffield was strangled and, according to a source close to the investigation who did not want to be identified, several of the killings were carried out in precisely the same manner.

By August 19th, King County investigators had compiled association charts on the victims to determine if any common friends and acquaintances existed between them, and special attention was given to the five victims whose bodies were found in or near the Green River. As the 25-member task force worked around the clock to piece together bits of evidence they had gathered, King County police spokesman Pat Ferguson reiterated the importance behind the reason investigators remained tight-lipped as to how the women were killed.

"That is one of the few things we have in common with the killer right now," said Ferguson. "The killer knows how he or she killed them and so do we, so that will help when we focus in on a suspect." Ferguson would not disclose whether or not police believed that the killer was male or female, but said that the FBI was putting together a psychological profile of the killer for the task force. "We've got a lot of work to do. It's progressing, but slowly," he said.

By the end of August, 1982, prostitutes working the Tacoma-Seattle area became frightened because of the prostitute slayings there. As a result of their growing fear, several hookers fled to Portland because they felt it was safer to work there, among other reasons.

"I'm afraid to work up there (in Seattle)," said one prostitute who fled to Portland shortly after prostitutes began getting murdered in Seattle. "There are a lot of girls from Seattle here because of that. Besides, it's so hot in Seattle the police don't let the girls work."

By September, 1982, investigators reported that they had more than two dozen people under investigation and felt more optimistic about the case in spite of the fact that the 25-member task force had so far been unable to turn up enough evidence to point them towards one suspect. Also by this point in the investigation, police sources had been quoted as having said that all the Green River victims had been strangled. Some of them had been strangled with items of their own clothing.

Three weeks passed without any additional bodies turning up, and the special task force members worked energetically as they attempted to put the pieces of their horrible puzzle together. But in spite of their efforts to find the killer and their emphatic warnings to the numerous street-walkers in the area, the bodies continued to pile up, serving only to keep the investigators stymied despite the numerous profiles of possible suspects they looked at.

On Saturday, September 25, 1982, the discovery of the nude body of a young woman found tangled in heavy underbrush in a wooded area just south of a Sea-Tac International Airport runway was added to the growing list of slayings attributed to the Green River Killer, dead proof that he was still committing his hideous acts of violence in the Seattle area, even though he had dumped the latest victim's body six miles from the location where five of his victims had been dumped in or near the Green River.

"We feel there is a connection with the other (five) homicides (found in or near the Green River)," said police spokesman Frank Kinney.

The latest victim was identified as 17-year-old Gisele Lovvorn who, like some of the other victims, had worked as a prostitute along "the strip." However, unlike some of the others who chose the life of being a hooker, background information on Ms. Lovvorn revealed that she'd been a drifter looking for thrills and was known to mix her "work" with pleasure, an unsavory lifestyle that ultimately ended with her violent demise before she saw the age of 18.

By the end of September, 1982, investigators with the Green River Task Force felt reasonably certain they could narrow the scope of their investigation to include only those six victims found in the vicinity of the Green River between July 15, 1982, and September 28, 1982. Even though several of the Seattle slayings had gone unsolved, in which several of the victims were strangled, task force investigators cited notable differences between those slayings and the slayings they were now attributing exclusively to the Green River killer. They would not elaborate on just what those differences were out of fear of jeopardizing their case, but did say they believe all of the so-called Green River victims died at the hands of a single man whom the investigators theorized was likely a deranged customer.

Meanwhile, as speculations surrounding the Green River case began to circulate and grow, two teenagers from south King County were reported missing, last seen in late August. According to police spokesman Kinney, Terri Renne Milligan and Kase Ann Lee, both 16, "fit the general profile of the Green River homicide victims," a fact which prompted police to theorize that the two missing teenagers may be the crazed killer's latest victims.

"There is no evidence to indicate that they also are victims," said Kinney, "but the possibility cannot be discounted," particularly since the two girls fit the profile of the other six victims. An appeal was made to the public to help find the two girls, and their names were added to a list of possible victims.

In an unusual move on Monday, October 4th, a middle-aged Seattle ex-cab driver named Tom Davis contacted news media from the local area and announced that police considered him a prime suspect in the Green River killings because he came to them and offered to help in the investigation. Davis told reporters that he suggested to detectives that they check out two other cabbies in the area, but they instead focused their attention on him.

"I feel like I've got absolutely nothing to hide because I haven't done anything," said Davis, who admitted that he knew five of the six victims and said that he flunked a lie-detector test when he denied to detectives that he killed the women. The ex-cab driver, who had two convictions related to car thefts, said he flunked the tests because he had a nervous disorder which prevented him from passing such tests. He added that he got to know five of the victims because he associated with "street kids."

When asked abut Davis, King County police acknowl-

93

edged that they had questioned him extensively but denied that the investigation had been narrowed to the point where the task force was focusing on a single suspect. The task force, it was reported, had in fact looked at the profiles of more than 2400 possible suspects in a tedious process of elimination. "I'm sure this guy is under some suspicion . . . but somebody is reading a lot into something that is very questionable," said Sergeant Don Rutherford.

Meanwhile, an FBI profile of the Green River killer indicates that the perpetrator responsible for the strangling deaths of the six women found since mid-July had a deep hatred of women, might be a married man who probably came from a broken home and quite possibly hates his mother. The profile states, or suggests, that the killer is probably between 20 and 40 years old and white, a heavy smoker who likes to drink but is fairly intelligent and likes the outdoors, possibly a fisherman or a hunter. The killer may have a background of sexual crimes and/or assault.

The profile suggests that the killer likes to drive and craves publicity, with a strong compulsion to return to the scenes of his crimes. The killer probably has knowledge of where the bodies have so far been discovered, and has possibly posed as a police officer to gain his victim's trust. The profile suggests that the killer chooses prostitutes to prey upon because their lifestyles make them the most accessible or approachable, or he may pick prostitutes because he simply hates loose women.

Unlike mass murderers, who usually know at least some of their victims (as in the case of Seattle's Chinatown massacre, in which 13 victims were killed) and kill them all at the same time, the serial killer stalks strangers and kills them one by one over an extended period of time and quite often involves different locales where the killer travels from city to city or state to state. A Justice Department report suggests there are at least 35 serial killers operating in the United States, including the Green River Killer.

According to Robert D. Keppel, chief criminal investigator for the Washington attorney general's office and a consultant to the King County Police Green River Task Force, serial murder is one of the rarest forms of homicide in spite of the number of victims who die at the hands of a single killer and is probably one of the most, if not the most, frustrating types of homicides for an investigator to deal with. One of the reasons that serial murder is so frustrating and different to deal with is that the killing has usually gone on for quite some time before lawmen recognize the connections between the victims and can link them to one killer.

"Most of the time you're right in the middle of the serial by the time you recognize it," said Keppel, who has investigated or consulted on 10 serial murder cases ranging from the Ted Bundy killings to the Atlanta child murders and now the Green River case. "If you're right in the middle, and here we are with sixteen deaths, imagine how many he's done beforehand!" Keppel believes the Green River case began prior to the finding of the first bodies in or near the Green River in the summer of 1982, citing that the killer may be the most, or at least among the most, prolific serial killers in the history of the United States.

"The obvious difference (in this case) is that the volume of calls in the Green River case is a lot less," said Keppel, "to the extent of thousands of calls less than we received in the 'Ted' case," citing the fact they had witnesses who could describe the suspect in the "Ted" case. Witnesses could also describe his car, how he approached some of his victims, the way he walked and even certain mannerisms. Unfortunately, detectives are getting no such calls in the Green River case.

"You have to understand," said Keppel, "there is a difference in victims. In the "Ted" case, the type of girls that were missing were just what everybody fears: Someone like their own daughter is the victim. In the "Ted" case you had a little bathing beauty on a beach in front of 20,000 people. All of a sudden she'd disappear and be found dead a month and a half later. You had people who were taken from their basement bedroom and beaten to death in the middle of the night. You had people that were in a tavern and taken away.

You had people who were on a college campus and feeling depressed and just needing somebody to talk to and just happened to be talking to the potential killer."

According to task force investigators, public silence has greatly hampered the lawmens' efforts in the Green River probe. So far, investigators have been unable to determine the type of car the killer drives, and in most of the cases the cops have been unable to determine when a victim first disappeared. Even worse is their inability due to lack of witnesses to develop a description of the killer himself. According to Keppel, a good deal of the phone calls the task force receives are simply about "crazies" running loose, but Keppel points out that serial killers, particularly the Green River Killer, are more intelligent and clever than that.

"They appear to be bright people," said Keppel, "clearly literate . . . street-wise . . . What they do, other than kidnap and kill, they look like the normal public when they're doing it. They're not standing out in the middle of Pacific Highway South with a bloody knife in their mouth chasing prostitutes.

"Right now," said Keppel, "he's stuck mainly to prostitutes, but his M.O. could change," as did that of Hillside Strangler Kenneth Bianchi, who started out murdering prostitutes but later changed his M.O. to include other females. "You also have to remember that serial murderers generally are cruisers and travelers," said Keppel. "They put a lot of mileage on their cars. He (the killer) could very easily have gone to Portland or to Vancouver, British Columbia for some reason. It's a rather well-known fact that the natural path of prostitutes is from Portland to Tacoma to Seattle. If for some reason the killer felt the heat was on here (in Seattle), he may well look to other areas."

It is precisely for that reason that investigators studying the death of 17-year-old Trina Deanne Hunter, a North Portland black girl with a record for prostitution, are looking at the Green River killer as a possible suspect. Her body, nude from the waist down, was found in a swampy area near Battle Ground, Washington, on December 29,

1982, her head submerged in a shallow pond. An autopsy revealed that she drowned. A background check revealed that Miss Hunter, several months before she had been killed, told a judge that she was forced to work as a prostitute by a man she knew. Other than the fact that she was last heard from on December 7th, few other details were known.

The winter of 1982 passed gently into the spring of 1983 without the discovery of any new bodies that could be attributed to the Green River Killer. If there were additional bodies, they had not yet been found. However, the task force was aware of and looking into a couple of missing-person cases: Mary Bridgit Meehan, 19, of Seattle, was last seen on September 15, 1982. She had no history of prostitution arrests. Shawndra Lee Summers, 17, of Bellevue, was last seen on October 7, 1982. Still missing were Kase Ann Lee and Terri Rene Milligan, both 17.

Because the Green River killer seemingly took a break from his heinous activities beginning the fall of 1982, many people felt that perhaps he had stopped killing or had moved on to another area of the country that was not as "hot" for him. Captain Frank Adamson, who heads the Green River Task Force, did not share that view.

"Some people may have made the assumption in 1982 that the person was gone," said Adamson. "Clearly, he wasn't." The body of Carol Ann Christensen, a 21-year-old from Seattle, was discovered on May 8, 1983, in the vicinity of Maple Valley, Washington. Like several of the other victims she had been strangled, but she had no record of prostitution arrests.

"I still don't think he's gone. I don't think he's dead," said Adamson. "I think he'll be back. More bodies are going to be found—there's no doubt in my mind about that."

Meanwhile, additional missing persons were reported. Kimi Kai Pitsor, a 16-year-old from Seattle was last seen on April 28, 1983, and police suspect that she was abducted from a downtown Seattle street. If, in fact, she turned out to be a Green River victim, the scope of the investigation

97

would be widened to include the area of downtown Seattle. In addition to Pitsor, the task force learned that Yvonne S. Antosh, 19, from Vancouver, British Columbia, was last seen on May 30, 1983. However, it should be pointed out that at this juncture in the investigation there was no conclusive evidence that Pitsor and Antosh were in fact victims of the Green River Killer, merely cautious speculation.

In the meantime, it was learned that convicted killer John Norris Hanks of San Francisco was being looked at by King County authorities as a possible suspect in the Green River killings because of his presence in the Seattle area when several of the murders occurred and because, according to one investigator, "women start coming up dead" in locations where Hanks goes. Hanks served 5 1/2 years in prison for second-degree murder in the 1966 stabbing death of his sister-in-law, said police.

Furthermore, court records show that Hanks has been charged with twice assaulting his wife in Seattle in September, 1982, by choking her until she became unconscious and, according to police, he was arrested on March 3, 1977, in San Francisco and charged with the murder of Patricia Ann Crawford. However, those charges were dropped due to lack of evidence when his former wife refused to testify against him. More recently, though, Hanks has been charged with the June 21, 1980 strangling of 30-year-old Arnetta Oakes, an East Palo Alto, California woman whose body was found beside a creek bed in San Jose.

According to Lieutenant Robert Moir of the San Jose Police Department, Hanks was focused on as a suspect after a tedious investigation during which police learned that Hanks was a friend of Oakes. Charges were not filed until nearly three and a half years after Oakes' body was found.

"It was through scientific analysis of evidence, through criminalistics and crime lab analyses similar to that used in the Atlanta murders that we were able to focus on him . . . as a prime suspect (in the Oakes case)," said Moir, 14 months before Hanks was charged with the strangling.

According to police reports, Hanks allegedly told one of

his former wives that he felt powerful when he choked women, and the wife told investigators that Hanks assaulted her seven times, and during two of such assaults he allegedly choked her into unconsciousness. Furthermore, according to court documents, Hanks allegedly told a San Francisco police investigator in 1982 that if he were convicted in a San Francisco homicide case "he would confess to numerous other murders." At that time he was being viewed by police as a possible suspect in eight San Francisco homicides.

"We are looking at Hanks as a suspect because he'd been involved in similar types of assault in the past," said Sergeant David Maehren, King County Police Department. Aside from the Oakes case in San Francisco, however, Hanks had not been charged in any other homicides and Captain Adamson of the Green River Task Force said that Hanks had been ruled out of some "but not all" of the unsolved homicides being investigated in the Seattle area.

On Monday, June 13, 1983, the Green River Task Force had another body to consider as a possible victim in the growing chain of killings occurring in the northern Washington area. This time, however, the body was found some 50 miles southeast from the location where many of the other victims attributed to the Green River killer have been found. According to detective Walt Stout of the Pierce County Sheriff's Department, the nude body of a young woman was found floating in the Nisqually River near the entrance to Mount Rainier National Park at Ashford.

Stout described the victim as a white female in her mid-20s with red hair, approximately 5 feet 6 inches tall weighing 125 pounds. She had visible scars from old injuries on her right lower arm, and her left wrist and thumb. Stout said that the only items on her body were a pair of small pierced gold earrings with tiny green stones in their centers. Stout said an autopsy surgeon tentatively listed the cause of death as strangulation.

The victim was eventually identified as 27-year-old Kimberly Ann Reames of Vancouver, Washington, and, although Reames did not have any known involvement or activities relating to prostitution, there were some striking similarities with the earlier Green River victims.

For example, Reames was a young woman who had been strangled, and her nude body had been dumped into a river, though not the Green River. Although she had not been involved in prostitution, the subsequent follow-up investigation revealed that she had last been seen the evening of June 12th at a motel along "the strip" just south of Tacoma, where she had been staying with a female friend who, along with Reames, had planned to leave for the Midwest the next morning via Sea-Tac International Airport.

"There is, in all probability, no connection between the case of Kim Reames and the Green River murders," said Detective Stout. "My gut feeling is that it is not connected. You always look for common factors," he said in obvious reference to the striking similarities between the way Kim Reames died and the way the Green River victims were killed.

"Now," he continued, "I believe that what happened to Kim was the same type of thing that happened to a lot of those girls in King County. But there's just no way you can say they are all connected. I don't necessarily happen to think that the ones they're all calling 'Green River victims' are precisely that. There's no way to tell."

Although Kim Reames was not initially added to the list of victims officially attributed to the Green River Killer, task force investigators could not rule out the possibility that she was a victim, particularly if the killer had mistaken her for a prostitute on "the strip" on the night of June 12, 1983, where she had last been seen alive. For that reason, she was added to the list of possible victims which included Leann Virginia Wilcox and Trina Deanne Hunter.

The summer of 1983 brought forth still additional victims and more missing women police believed were possible victims, evidence that the killer was indeed still in the area or had returned from an absence at another location. The task force added the following women to their growing list of missing females, whom they feared to be victims whose remains would later be found or, worse yet, never located at all:

Constance Elizabeth Naon, 21, of nearby Burien, was last heard from on June 8, 1983. Background investigation revealed that she had a history of prostitution arrests. Others added to the list were: Denise Darcel Bush, 24; Shirley Marie Sherrill, 19, last seen alive in Portland; Sandra K. Gabbert, 17; Marie M. Malvar, 18, from Des Moines, Washington; Kell K. McGuinness, 18; Debbie May Abernathy, 26; Tina Lee Tomson, 26, and Tracy Winston, 20, also known as Tracy Gordon.

Among those victims whose remains were discovered and identified the summer and early part of fall 1983 were those of Shawndra Lee Summers, a 17-year-old who was last seen on October 7, 1982. The task force investigators revealed that her remains were identified on August 11, 1983, and also revealed that bone fragments found in a wooded area south of North Bend, which is east of Seattle near Issaquah, were identified on October 18, 1983, as those of Yvonne S. Antosh, 19, from Vancouver, British Columbia.

On October 27, 1983, bones identified as the remains of Constance Elizabeth Naon, 21, of Burien, were found about a block from "the strip," along with the bones of another woman who remains unidentified. Naon had last been heard from on June 8, 1983.

On Thursday, November 3, 1983, Leann Virginia Wilcox, whose body was found January 21, 1982, in a south King County parking lot, was taken off the task force's list of possible victims and added to the official list of Green River victims and, 10 days later, the remains of Mary Briget Meehan were discovered lying in a shallow grave less than a mile south of the airport, barely a block off "the strip" and just across the road from where Constance Naon's remains were found less than a month before. Because of the condition of her remains, the county medical examiner could only say that Meehan died "of homicidal violence of undetermined origin."

As the bodies continued to pile up and the list of possible victims grew it seemed, by the fall of 1983, that the Green River Task Force was not any closer to cracking the case than they had been from the very beginning. Naturally, everyone, police and the general public alike, wanted to know why.

"Usually, in a homicide, the suspect can be found somewhere in the victim's background," said King County Police Captain Michael Nault. "In this case that hasn't proven true. This crime is not personally oriented . . . but is someone who wants to kill prostitutes.

"We've been in contact with every major city in the United States and also with Interpol," Nault continued. "We've been able to determine certain suspects and to determine that there are no similar crimes anywhere in the country or anywhere in the free world.

"It is possible some victims may be the victims of a copycat killer," said Nault, "but the probability is that there is one killer."

At one point in the investigation, detectives considered the possibility that their elusive killer might have held a seasonal job in 1982, particularly since the killing seemed to stop from autumn, 1982 until April of 1983. If that were in fact the case, it seemed possible that the perpetrator of these heinous crimes may have been, and perhaps still is, employed in the tourist industry, an industry which provides an abundance of seasonal jobs in the Northwest each year from May through October.

Each year there are numerous jobs available in national parks, ferry operations, restaurants, hotels, motels and resorts as tour guides, cooks, waiters, waitresses, bartenders, desk clerks, maids and janitors. It was just such employment possibilities, as well as many others too numerous to mention here, that the task force investigators were, and still are, looking into, particularly since their killer seems to take a vacation from his dirty deeds from fall until spring. However, it should be pointed out that this is just one of many theories investigators are considering regarding the apparent seasonal slayings, and should not be construed as implying that it's the task force's only avenue of investigation and, more importantly, additional body discoveries could render that hypothesis obsolete.

As the investigation into the Green River killings continues, the task force occasionally receives helpful leads from unusual and unlikely sources. For example, recently the task force received a letter from a woman in Chicago who, after reading about the Green River killer in a Chicago newspaper, felt that task force investigators should be aware of an unpleasant and frightening experience she had at a motel on "the strip" in 1983.

According to Bob Keppel, task force consultant, the woman told investigators in her letter that she was apparently mistaken as a prostitute by a man who boldly confronted her and followed her for quite some distance until she managed to eventually shake him off and escape. She told the task force what she could about the man who assailed her, details investigators felt hopeful about involved one of the women on the task force's missing list, 26-year-old Tina Tomson, also known as Linda Lee Barkay. According to investigators the day Tomson disappeared, Halloween Day, a girlfriend had left her at a bus stop on Pacific Highway South at 11:00 a.m., and the girlfriend later told another friend that she hadn't seen Tomson since.

After the police had been alerted, detectives learned that Tomson had been arrested several times for prostitution and, as a result, her name was added to their list of potential victims, the first name placed on the list since June, 1983. Two of the missing women from that list were later confirmed as victims of the killer when their bodies or remains were eventually found, a fact which prompted detectives to consider the possibility that Tomson's disappearance might indicate that the killer was still at work on the last days of October, 1983 which would, of course, cast considerable doubt on the previous hypothesis that the killer stopped killing from fall until spring.

Knowing it was important to track Tina Tomson's last

103

known activities, which could, ultimately bring the cops closer to their elusive killer, detectives checked court records to learn her last known address. The court records indicated that she resided at a North Seattle apartment complex; when the cops arrived at the complex and talked with the manager, they learned that no one by the name Tomson or Barkey had been a tenant there. Knowing that prostitutes often provide false addresses when arrested, the cops felt that they'd hit another dead end. However, betting on a longshot, they showed the missing woman's mug shot to the manager, who told them she looked familiar.

Admittedly, it didn't seem like much help. But by backgrounding Tomson, the investigators learned some contrasting information which, if she turned out to be a victim, would show that the killer was still operating in the fall of the year, had picked a victim whose prostitution activities took place on Aurora Avenue North instead of the usual Sea-Tac airport strip in the south end of King County, and that the killer had chosen a victim who, at 5 feet 10 inches and 140 to 150 pounds, was larger than any of the others on the missing or the dead list. It was enough to make the cops wonder if their killer had changed his M.O. If he had, only time and the discovery of new bodies would tell.

During the course of this intensive, continuing investigation, the Green River Task Force had been expanded to 45 investigators due to the possibility of a large group of victims, some of which have not been involved in prostitution and may indicate for the first time in the investigation that the killer is selecting women other than prostitutes. As a result Kimberly Ann Reames, 27, whose nude body was found in the Nisqually River in June, 1983, and previously thought not to be connected to the Green River case, was added to the victim list because, perhaps, the killer's "signature" being left behind at many of the sites where his victim's bodies have been found. Police would not elaborate on the killer's "signature," and would only say that it links the known victims.

In spite of a $25,000 reward fund for information "resulting in the arrest and prosecution of the person or persons responsible for the Green River murders," not to mention the stepped-up efforts of the increased task force, bodies attributed to the killer continued to turn up in late 1983 and early 1984, and new names of missing women were added to the missing list of potential victims.

Laura Thompson, the self-described psychic who said she received images of victim Opal Mills in August, 1982, found part of a skull near an Auburn, Washington cemetery in December, 1983 after being led to the location by psychic images. The skull was later identified as Kimi-Kai Pitsor, 16, of Bellevue, who had last been seen in downtown Seattle in April, 1983.

In the spring of 1984, Thompson returned to the location where she found part of Pitsor's skull, located about 25 miles east of Seattle near Interstate 90 and state Highway 18. Thompson said she was led to the location by an intuitive "voice" or "vision" of Kimi-Kai Pitsor, to search for another body.

"Kimi's vision told me to go back, that I missed (the body in December), to check a little bit farther," said Thompson. As a result of the vision, Thompson walked approximately 70 feet from a service road into an alder grove where she found a skeleton lying on a clear sheet of plastic, covered by a dark sheet of plastic. When she uncovered the skeleton, she said, some of the bones adhered to the dark cover sheet. She said the skeleton had long, dark hair, but refused to reveal any additional details out of fear that a copycat killer might crop up or that the killer might change his M.O.

As the investigation continued, new names were added to the missing list. Among those were: Carrie Rois, 16; Patricia Lee Osborn, 19, last seen January 24, 1984; Martina T. Authorlee, 18, who was last seen in downtown Seattle on May 15, 1983; Mary Bellow, no age or details available; Debra Lorraine Estes, 16, also known as Debra Lorraine Jones, reported as a runaway in July, 1982, and was last seen on "the strip" on September 14, 1982, and had prior "contacts" with police for prostitution and theft; Becky Marrero, 20, also known as Rebecca Murrero, Vicky Johnson and Rebecca Fashaw, was last seen on December 2, 1982, when she left home after receiving a phone call, and was a friend of Debra Estes; Joanne Michelle Hovland, 16, also known as Joanne Michelle Harbard, reported missing on March 16,1983, and was last seen on May 8, 1983, when released from an Everett, Washington detention center, had prior "contacts" with police for prostitution; April Dawn Buttram, 17, also known as April Manuel, last seen leaving home on August 4, 1983, and Mary Exzetta West, 16, also known as Alisa Annette West, last seen on February 6, 1984.

Several victims whose bodies were found and added to the dead list appeared previously on original and updated missing lists. Among those were: Debbie May Abernathy, 26; Terri Rene Milligan, 16, and Sandra K. Gabbert, 17. Although the remains of Joanne Michelle Hovland were found in a wooded Snohomish County site she was not immediately added to the official task force list of 26 dead victims, some of which have not yet been identified. Among those remains found and identified and added to the list of 26 dead are: Cheryl Lee Wyms, 18, who police say did not fit the mold as do most of the other victims; Alma Ann Smith, 19; Colleen Renee Brockman 15; the remaining victims on the list of dead have been previously mentioned, with the exception of those remains that are still unidentified. It should be pointed out that investigators are also looking into the death of Amina Agisheff, 36, who was reported missing on July 7, 1982, and whose skeletal remains were found on April 20, 1984. Agisheff had no links to prostitution, and has not as yet been added to the official list of victims.

Has the killer struck in 1984? Captain Adamson, head of the task force, thinks not. Will he strike again?

"I'm not optimistic that there won't be any more (victims) if we don't catch him sometime soon," said Adamson, whose task force has expanded its investigation into three counties. "Bodies have been found north and south of the airport and in the Green River," he said. Bodies have also been found off of Interstate 90 east of North Bend, about 35 miles from Seattle, and the killer has a tendency to "cluster dump" his victims, as many as five bodies found in close proximity to each other.

"The proximity of the last two skeletons to both Interstate 90 and Highway 18 was just the final link I'd needed to connect the North Bend ones with Green River," sad Adamson. "But there are quite a few similarities in the various scenes, enough commonalities for us to investigate . . . from the very beginning."

The Green River Task Force has looked at similar deaths in various cities as part of its on-going investigation, including Portland, Oregon. Between March 23, 1983, and April 23, 1984, the bodies of four female victims between 16 and 24 years old were found dumped at North Portland locations. All of the women were black; three died as a result of strangulation and one was stabbed.

According to Portland Police Detective David Simpson, the nude body of Essie Jackson, 24, was found on an embankment near Overlook Park and had been strangled. Simpson said Jackson had been arrested for prostitution, and that all four Portland victims had "similar backgrounds."

Tonja Harry, 20, was found dead of asphyxiation in the Columbia River Slough on July 9, 1983. The strangled body of Angela Anderson, 16, was found December 22, 1983 inside a vacant house, and the body of 19-year-old Vickie L. Williams was found tangled in some bushes near Lloyd Center Mall on April 23, 1984. She had been stabbed to death.

"We're extremely interested in the circumstances surrounding those cases," said Bob Keppel, task force consultant, "as we would be in Vancouver, as we would be in almost any city that we find out those prostitutes migrate to." But so far no firm links have been established between the Portland cases and the Green River case, leaving the Portland cases unsolved at this point.

107

When they are not studying aerial photographs in preparation for extensive searches in the wooded areas of King, Pierce and Snohomish Counties, task force investigators are busy studying profiles on their list of suspects numbering 500-600, sometimes narrowing their focus down to two or three names, but never narrowing their ever-fluctuating list to focus on one single suspect. Although they sometimes narrow their view to focus more on a given suspect at a given time, new leads and developments direct their attention in many different directions.

For example, at one point the task force's attention was drawn to a man who had been jailed on statutory rape and indecent liberties charges stemming from the complaints of two 13-year-old girls who lived in the apartment complex the suspect managed. The man had also driven a taxi in the Sea-Tac International Airport area and had purportedly witnessed another taxi driver kidnap a young girl from "the strip," but so far nothing has developed on either of those lines and task force investigators said they did not have anything that would link the man to any of the victims.

On another occasion, more recently, an "associate" of victim Alma Anne Smith, whose body was found April 2, 1984, near Star Lake Road south of Seattle, told task force investigators that Smith was picked up at 9:00 p.m. on March 3, 1983, by a man on "the strip," and was never seen alive again. Later that same evening Smith's "associate" was approached for a "date" by the same man. However, she refused the offer.

Smith's associate described the man who picked up Smith as white, 6 feet tall, 27 to 30 years old, weighing 160 pounds, with greasy-brown shoulder-length hair and light blue eyes. The man was driving a mid-1970s Ford pickup, dark in color, possibly blue, with large mirrors on either side. According to Green River Task Force spokeswoman Fae Brooks, the man is not considered a suspect in the case, but police do want to question him to discuss the activities of the victim. A composite drawing was released by Green River Police.

A short time later, former cab driver Tom Davis, who was earlier considered a suspect in the case, came back into the picture by reporting to task force investigators that he saw the man pictured in the sketch at a south Seattle convenience store.

Although Davis said he didn't know the man's name he said, "I know where he drinks," and added that if he could get the man's license-plate number he would turn it over to the task force. "That's as close as I'll come," he said. "He could have a gun."

In another development, at one point in the investigation the task force seized a list of 5,000 names of customers during a raid on a Seattle escort service by Seattle police. King County prosecutors alleged that the escort service was used as a front, and served to provide introductions to prostitutes. Of use to task force investigators was the customer index files, which included customers' addresses, business and employment information, telephone numbers, credit card numbers, dates the service was used, amounts paid and personal background information including the customers' behavior. The task force checked the files in an attempt to identify customers who were considered potentially dangerous, but investigators did not say whether or not they obtained any significant leads from the information.

There are other efforts being made and other avenues of investigation being pursued by task force members in their never-ending attempt to generate new leads, among those efforts being the reconstruction of the unidentified victims' faces from their skulls. For this somewhat macabre job the task force commissioned Betty Gatliff, 53, of Norman, Oklahoma, who worked as a consultant during the filming of the motion picture "Gorky Park," in which a detective used reconstructed heads to identify the mutilated and defaced bodies discovered in the frozen depths of the Moscow park.

Gatliff reconstructed two of the oldest unidentified skeletons found in the latter part of 1983, which added to her vast experience of 87 prior reconstructions. Once the reconstructions were complete, pictures were made of the faces and released to the public with the hopes they would trigger recognition in someone who could aid investigators in identifying the victims. Although officials admit there is only a 50-50 chance the reconstructions would trigger someone's memory, they said if any new leads were generated as a result of the reconstructions they would commission Gatliff to reconstruct the faces of six additional unidentified victims.

With a 45-member task force actively working on the case and the recent approval to purchase a $200,000 computer system to help track down the killer, not to mention the help of outside consultants like Bob Keppel, Pierce Brooks and Betty Gatliff, many are wondering why the killer hasn't been caught yet. Some say he's too clever, always outsmarting the cops. Others, like the co-founder of a support group called Families and Friends of Missing Persons and Violent Crime Victims, say the killer hasn't been caught yet because the public's attitude has been too lax and apathetic, perhaps because most of the victims have been prostitutes and the general public is less sympathetic toward that group of human beings, which makes one wonder what the public's attitude would be if it were Mr. and Mrs. Joe America's daughters who were being killed instead of prostitutes. Would they still be apathetic? Probably not, and most of those associated with the investigation of the Green River killings agree that the public would be less apathetic and more willing to help if they simply took a few moments to remember that the prostitutes killed by the Green River killer have families, too, who must survive and re-live the horrible ordeal again and again.

Does the Green River Task Force presently have any good suspects and, if so, what are the chances of an arrest in the near future?

"We have a lot of interesting information we're working on," said Captain Adamson, "but that's different from saying any particular person is a good suspect.

"I wish I could say we're closer to an arrest, but I don't

110

think I can say that."

The Green River Task Force says that 49 bodies have turned up, all of them young women, all attributed to the mysterious slayer. The cost of the investigation so far is $15 million. There were four prime suspects, but all were cleared.

The Task Force called on botanists, anthropologists, psychologists and psychics. It has solved seven unrelated murders while working on the Green River mystery. The last known murder occurred five years ago.

The frustration is monumental, but the probe goes on.

The Green River Task Force asks that anyone with information which might prove useful and helpful to detectives to please call them at: (206) 433-2051.

EDITORS NOTE:

Laura Thompson, Tom Davis and Richard Jones are not the real names of the persons so named in the foregoing story. Fictitious names have been used because there is no reason for public interest in the identities of these persons.

Terror Spree of
the Rampaging Rambo!

by Barry Benedict

Steve Vestal, 38, was one of the nicest guys you would ever want to meet. A church-going country boy, he grew up in and around Laclede County in southwest Missouri, and was known by just about everyone.

George Brewer, 43, and his wife Carol, 36, had lived in the county less than three years. They kept to themselves and wanted to keep it that way.

Steve was outgoing and personal. George and Carol were loners. Everyone liked Steve. Hardly anyone knew George and Carol. Under normal circumstances, it is unlikely the trio would have ever met, or that their names would ever be mentioned in the same sentence.

But the circumstances of mid-September 1987 were hardly normal.

Wednesday, September 16, 1987, began as a typical day for the Laclede County Sheriff's office, with the usual number of suspicious activity and stolen chicken reports to check out, write up, and if possible, act on.

The call received at 9:25 p.m. was a bit out of the ordinary. It came from the wife of Steve Vestal, who wanted to report her husband as missing. She said Steve was supposed to join her at the church in Phillipsburg for choir practice, only he never showed.

She had tried their home in nearby Conway and made the usual calls to friends and the Mid-American Dairymen office, where Steve was employed as a representative. No one had seen him since 6:00 p.m. when he left on the five-mile drive to the church.

Deputies checked the accident log. Steve's name wasn't on it. Nor did the state police, who cruised the interstate, have anything.

Strange, deputies admitted. Mighty strange.

Deputies began a search. They retraced the route Steve would have taken to Conway and checked neighboring police agencies for accident reports.

An APB was placed on Steve's 1966 Chevrolet pickup, along with the license number and a description of the driver.

At 9:30, Thursday morning, a deputy radioed headquarters with information that he had found a vehicle abandoned off the interstate about five miles north of Conway.

Detectives drove to a gravel road north of Interstate 44 near Highway B where they found a white Chevy van abandoned off the road.

The doors were open and the inside was drenched in blood. "My God, it looks like a slaughterhouse in there," one deputy exclaimed, looking inside.

The deputy who discovered the van ran a check on the license plate. It was registered to George Ray Brewer, 42, of nearby Niangua. A call was put through to the home but no one answered. A deputy was dispatched to check out the house, which turned out to be a mobile home. The deputy reported back that the Brewers weren't home and apparently hadn't been there for at least a day.

Almost certain of foul play, deputies spread out along the roadside and began a search for the missing driver and his wife. Lab teams went over the van and surrounding area, looking for clues. The vehicle was towed to the station for additional forensic work.

Laclede Sheriff Lawrence Rifenburg was informed of the searches for the missing dairy representative and the Niangua couple. He hurried to the scene where the search for the Brewers was under way.

Deputies, standing 10 feet apart, had foot-searched the waist-high grassy flatland on both sides of the gravel road and were now busy searching the forests that grew along the banks of a fast-running creek.

"So far we haven't found a thing," one detective said.

"What about Steve Vestal?" the sheriff asked.

"Nothing yet," the detective replied. Relatives and friends of the missing dairy representative had been talked to, but none had heard of George and Carol Brewer.

The three apparently didn't know each other.

The search continued until 5:30, when a call from authorities sent sheriff's detectives speeding to Lebanon, about 10 miles away.

They roared into a nearly vacant parking lot of a retirement home next to Glasconade Park where a police officer stood next to a white Chevy pickup.

Steve Vestal was slumped on the passenger-side floor, shot twice in the head.

The body was discovered by a woman who noticed blood leaking out of the truck on the parking lot pavement. She said she looked inside, saw the body on the floor and called police.

Deputies began a canvass of small businesses and residences near the retirement home. Witnesses said they had seen the pickup in the parking lot before noon, but didn't report it to police because they didn't see the blood, or know a search was on for the driver.

No one police talked to saw anyone enter or leave the pickup, nor had anyone heard any shots, suggesting that the shooting took place at another location.

The tragic news was no sooner broken to the Vestal family, when another call sent detectives racing back to the abandoned white van near Highway B.

Searchers were going over a wooded area about one half mile north of the van when they spotted a boot sticking out from under thick ground brush. They removed the brush and found George Brewer staring back at them, shot twice in the head.

Sheriff Rifenburg ordered searchers to continue looking for Brewer's missing wife, Carol, and the weapon or weapons used in the killing.

The search continued until nightfall when it was called off until daybreak the next morning.

Rifenburg held a news conference Thursday evening to explain the day's bizarre turn of events. "I honestly don't know if the two deaths are related," he said. "There are several similarities to the cases that make them look related, but we can't put together any logical reason why they're connected."

He said they had no suspects and no motive.

Detectives scrambled for clues in a baffling case that defied explanation. "Two dead, another missing and no motive," is how one sleuth summed it up.

A search was conducted of the Brewer home, but it produced no evidence that the home had been robbed or that the Brewers might be in any activity that might possibly explain an abduction and murder.

Witnesses said the Brewers were last seen driving from their home toward Conway between 3:00 and 4:00 p.m., Wednesday. They didn't return to the mobile home that evening and the van was discovered the next morning.

A few leads came from the coroner's office. According to the coroner, Vestal and Brewer were both shot two times in the side of the head at point blank range and had died within a few hours of each other.

The slugs were turned over to ballistics, which made the determination that they were fired from a .22-caliber weapon with a short or cut-off barrel. An examination of the misshapen slugs showed enough similarities to indicate that the same weapon had been used for both killings.

The murders were also linked by a shoe print found inside the Brewer's van. The print, outlined in a blood pool behind the passenger seat, showed a distinctive diamond-sole design such as those found on military boots.

A bloody toe print was found on Vestal's jacket. An analyst, comparing the size and shape of the toe print said it was very likely it was made by the same shoe that made the print in the van.

The search for Carol Brewer resumed Friday morning. Sheriff Rifenburg was skeptical she would be found alive. Lab examiners said there were two blood pools in the van made from two different blood types.

A command post was set up at a church in Conway to coordinate the search being conducted by 50 volunteers in separate areas.

Meanwhile, detectives checked out tips that were phoned in to police headquarters. One caller said he had seen Vestal driving his pickup apparently on the way to church Wednesday afternoon, with a passenger inside.

He didn't get a good look, however, and was unable to give a good description.

About an hour later, another witness spotted a hitchhiker near the spot where the Brewer's white van was located. The caller said he had picked up hitchhikers but passed this one by because he was scruffy looking and appeared nervous.

The sheriff's office released a composite of the hitchhiker late Friday afternoon. It showed a Caucasian male in his mid to late twenties with brown hair parted in the middle, and a scruffy beard and moustache.

On Saturday, volunteers combed the open fields and woods surrounding the spots where George Brewer was discovered and searched side roads the killer might have taken to dump the body.

At 1:30 p.m. a searcher was driving his pickup truck along a country road a mile and a half from the creek where George Brewer's body was found when he spotted something in a ditch.

As he said later, "I just happened to see what looked like a piece of cloth and I hollered out I had found something."

He got out of the truck and with two other searchers walked back to the ditch. Six feet below the road surface, he saw the body of Carol Brewer.

She was fully clothed and lay on top of heavy brush. Like the two other victims, she was shot twice in the side of the

116

head. The slugs were later determined to have been fired from the same weapon that had killed the others.

With the third victim found, police devoted all their efforts to finding the killer.

With the information that had been gathered, detectives theorized that the Brewers had been murdered between three and four o'clock Wednesday afternoon, followed by Steve Vestal, who had left his house for choir practice a little later.

The motive remained a mystery. The wallets of the two men and Carol's purse were missing, but Sheriff Rifenburg wasn't convinced robbery itself explained the killings.

"They didn't carry a lot of money," the sheriff said. "I am just not a hundred percent convinced robbery was the only motive."

On Sunday morning, more than 2000 mourners arrived early at the Conway Cemetery to pay last respects to their friend Steve Vestal. A gospel quartet performed, while he was eulogized as a dedicated family man and a deeply religious community leader. Flowers surrounded the casket as town people, many who had known Steve their whole lives, crowded close together, some sobbing openly.

In contrast, only a handful of people attended the Monday graveside services for George and Carol Brewer. As a newspaper reported, "they were, in death, as private as they had been in life."

Fewer than 70 persons attended graveside services at the cemetery in the small town of Niangua, where the Brewers had lived the past three years.

The minister who delivered words of comfort had never met the Brewers. Then again, neither had most of the mourners.

"I didn't know them, but I came out of respect for the dead," said one mourner. "I know how I would feel if something happened to someone in my family and no one showed up."

Left behind was a single spray of flowers signed "From Someone Who Cares."

117

Sheriff Rifenburg and his men worked straight through the week to develop leads on the killer or killers. They checked out sightings of the grizzled-faced hitchhiker and questioned a man who had been picked up for vagrancy the day after Steve Vestal disappeared. Nothing panned out.

Sunday evening, detectives received a report over the telex that two escapees from the Nevada State Penitentiary in Carson City might be headed their way.

The escapees were Daniel Adamik, 31, and Roger Hayward, 46. They had escaped August 28th by hiding in boxes being hauled from the prison in a garbage truck.

Adamik was serving a 20-year sentence for robbery and assault and Hayward a life sentence for sexual assault. They had been in prison since 1982.

Mugshot photos accompanied the Be-On-the-Lookout alert.

The detective who was trimming the telex wire let out a whistle and took the bulletin into the sheriff's office. "Look at this," he said.

The mugshot of Adamik bore a good resemblance to the hitchhiker seen near the Brewers' van Wednesday.

They did appear similar. But why would two cons on the lam kill three people for no reason then leave behind their getaway cars.

Sheriff Rifenburg couldn't answer the questions. "I got a feeling it ain't them," he told a detective.

His instinct proved right.

The search for the escaped cons chewed up time and manpower. Because of the number of calls, officers had to set up a command post at the First Baptist Church in Conway. Police followed up on dozens of sightings with none turning up the cons.

On Tuesday evening, a tired Sheriff Rifenburg slumped in his favorite chair in his living room and turned on the evening news.

There were the usual reports of fighting in far-off countries and latest public relations ploys by the Soviets, none of which had much direct bearing on Laclede county and the

118

search for killers and escaped convicts.

He listened with half interest when a news flash dated out of a small Texas town caught his attention. A man dressed up like Rambo had run amok and killed three people before turning the gun on himself.

Texas authorities were describing the murders as senseless.

"Just like ours," the sheriff thought.

The next morning Sheriff Rifenburg was on the phone to J.S. Ryzman, the police chief of Corsicana, Texas. That afternoon, Rifenburg and his detectives were headed to the small town, located about an hour's drive south of Dallas.

Corsicana is a slumbering community of 30,000. Few had ever heard of it, until a hail of gunfire and violence put it squarely on the map.

Tuesday afternoon Corsicana received a report of a shooting at Hulcher Services Incorporated. Investigators rushed to the small business where they found the company supervisor, Dennis James Wade, sprawled on the floor, his body riddled with bullets.

An eyewitness, shaking from shock but nonetheless alive, had called police. He gave the following report . . .

At 1:30 p.m., Howard Franklin Stewart, a 37-year-old former employee who had been fired six months earlier, walked into the business wearing camouflage fatigues and combat boots and brandishing a .22-caliber semi-automatic pistol in the one hand and a .38-caliber revolver in the other.

"I stood there for a few minutes and he just looked at me," the witness said. "Then he shot Dennis. He didn't say anything. He just did it."

After pumping 10 slugs into his unarmed former boss, Stewart holstered his weapons and clanked out of the office as if nothing had happened.

"Where is he now?" one of the detectives said.

"I don't know," the man replied. "He just shot Dennis and left."

An answer came over the radio. Investigators raced to a

119

steak house on Seventh Avenue near the downtown.

The popular eatery was about half full and a 34-year-old assistant manager was on duty when Stewart burst into the restaurant yelling for his wife, Brenda, who worked there.

Before anyone could say anything, he pumped off three shots into the ceiling and repeated his demand to see his wife.

The assistant manager bravely approached Stewart and told him that Brenda didn't come in until three.

"Okay, I'm going," he said and stalked out of the restaurant.

The assistant manager told police that she went to the phone to notify Brenda that her estranged husband was acting crazy and coming her way, guns in hand.

"I was afraid he might shoot her," she said.

She said Brenda thanked her for the call but said she was not going to leave the trailer.

Sheriff's deputies and police officers sped to the trailer park on Park Row Road. They got there in seconds, but it was already too late to help Brenda.

The pretty, chubby-cheeked waitress lay dead in the bathroom of the mobile home, her body riddled with bullets and the walls sprayed with her blood. Her current boyfriend, Edward Persons, was also dead. His body was found in the master bedroom, riddled with .22-caliber slugs.

Stewart was on the front porch. Still dressed in Rambo fatigues, he was crumpled in front of the door, half his head blown away.

"Christ, Almighty," one of the detectives growled. The bodies were covered with sheets until measurements and photographs were taken and detectives could figure out what happened. They were then taken to the medical examiner's office in Dallas for the autopsies.

Officers went to a camping ground on Lake Halbert, where Stewart had been living the past few weeks out of his van. Opening the side door, they found two pit bulldogs, belonging to Stewart, lying in the back of the van shot to death. One of the dead dogs was the mother to six puppies who were suckling the dead mother's breast.

The dogs had been dead a short time and apparently murdered before Stewart went on his rampage. Lying next to the dogs were several more weapons and two Claymore mines, which scared detectives silly until it was discovered they were not armed.

The motive for the rampage was rage, pure and simple. Stewart had been dismissed from his job, and had recently been separated from his wife.

A witness who talked to Stewart days earlier quoted him as saying that he couldn't stand the thought of another man making love to his wife and, "If I can't have her, no one will."

The explosion of violence sent Corsicanians reeling. Dennis Wade had been a devoted family man who loved to fish and hunt. Just about everyone liked the affable Kentucky native.

The same went for Edward Parsons. "I met Ed through Brenda and I can tell you there was no finer man alive," said a pal.

Brenda, because of her job at the Seventh Avenue steak house, was perhaps the best known of the three. Voted one of the best waitresses in Corsicana in an October 1986 newspaper poll, she was described as "a gal who always had a smile and a happy hello and made customers feel special."

Brenda, just 36 and mother of two, had a pretty face, an hourglass figure and a perky personality. Everyone who met her liked her.

People wondered what she ever saw in Howard Stewart, who, some said, had a sullen disposition, rarely smiled and had a tendency to fly off the handle. In recent months, Stewart got the nickname Rambo after he shaved his head, took to wearing combat boots and camouflage clothing, and carried a .22-automatic machine gun with a 50-bullet clip strapped to his leg.

His few expressions of love were mostly saved for his two pet pit bulldogs which he trained daily. "Frankly, the only thing that really surprised me about what happened was his killing the dogs," a former friend of the Stewart couple said.

Rifenburg arrived in Corsicana and questioned detectives investigating the town's most sensational murder case. He later viewed the crime scenes, and talked to the medical examiner and lab technicians.

By the time he left, the sheriff was convinced Stewart was the right man.

The investigation continued in Laclede County with detectives questioning a couple who lived outside Lebanon, Missouri, bus station ticket sellers, and several other witnesses, including a deputy sheriff.

At a press conference Thursday, Sheriff Rifenburg said that bullets and bloody shoe prints had linked Stewart to the murders in Missouri and Texas.

"We are glad it's over," the sheriff said, showing relief. "It's a relief that we're not still looking for someone who might still be out there."

The sheriff said ballistics showed that bullets used to gun down the three persons in Missouri had been fired from the gun that killed the three persons in Texas and was worn by Stewart when he committed suicide. The combat boots he was wearing at the time of his death had also been linked to the Missouri crime scenes.

The sheriff said Stewart was a native of Macoupin, Illinois, who had lived in the Lebanon area for about five years before moving to Texas in 1985.

Bus ticket stubs and witness interviews created the following scenario: On September 9th, Brenda Stewart took her husband to the Corsicana bus station and put him on a bus bound for Missouri.

Stewart had been telling people that he needed to get away and might hurt somebody.

He arrived in Lebanon sometime on September 10th or 11th and went to the summer home of a relative. He spent the next few days building a car port onto the house and taking target practice with his .22-caliber full automatic which he kept strapped to his leg at all times.

On the morning of September 16th, he left the house

dressed in camouflage fatigues and carrying a backpack and his beloved full automatic. He said before leaving that he was going to hitchhike back to Texas.

Sometime between 3:00 and 4:00 p.m., George and Carol Brewer left their home in Niangua. The route they took would have taken them right by the interstate where Stewart was trying to get a lift home. Shortly afterward, both were shot to death.

Police believe that after killing the Brewers, Stewart continued hitchhiking and caught a ride with Steve Vestal, who had left home and was headed to choir practice in Phillipsburg.

"It was something Steve would do," a witness said. "He would always try to help out a hitchhiker or someone in need."

After killing Vestal and abandoning his pickup in the parking lot next to Glasconade Park, Stewart returned to his relative's home around midnight.

The relative said when Stewart arrived, "He looked tense and depressed."

He left Lebanon by bus on Friday morning September 18th.

After returning to Corsicana on Saturday, Stewart spent a day or two with friends shooting guns and camping out in his van at a campsite by Lake Halbert.

On Tuesday morning, dressed in Rambo fatigues and armed with two guns, he killed the two dogs in his van, then he drove across town where he shot to death his former boss Dennis Wade.

Then, after shooting up the steak house in search of his wife, Stewart raced to the mobile home park where he found Brenda and boyfriend Edward Persons.

Police believe Stewart shot Persons first, then went after Brenda, who had locked herself in the bathroom. After spraying the door with bullets, he kicked the door open and killed Brenda who cringed in a corner, unable to get away.

Police believed Stewart had planned to escape after killing his wife, because he left his truck motor running. He likely

123

changed his plan to suicide after hearing the police cruiser which arrived at the mobile home park just seconds after Stewart put a bullet to his head.

Witnesses told police that Stewart had threatened to kill his family, but no one really believed him.

Stewart also told several people over the weekend before the Texas shootings that he had killed three people in Missouri.

Again, no one thought he was serious.

Rifenburg said investigators had been unable to determine what Stewart's motive was for shooting the Brewers and Vestal.

He said he was looking into reports that Stewart had had a quarrel several years ago with one of Vestal's fellow employees, but added there was no evidence the killer knew Vestal or the Brewers.

Perhaps there wasn't a motive. "This thing had been building for a long time," said one law enforcement officer. "It looks like he just exploded and these unfortunate people happened to be in the way."

Satan-Loving Night Stalker!

by Turk Ryder

Six hundred people jammed the tiny City Council chambers on July 11, 1985. Their anguished faces were tilted toward the man who stood before them at the podium. They had come to hear good news.

But John D. Elder, police chief of Monterey Park, a suburban community of 100,000, 20 miles east of Los Angeles had nothing good to report.

Instead, the ramrod straight, silver haired chief asked for their help.

"We have a multi-agency task force at work," he said. "Two hundred detectives are working the case this very minute. But they can't do it alone. It will take a combination of police and citizen efforts to break the case. Help us. Be our eyes and ears out there. Tell us what is happening. Do not hesitate to call. We cannot do it alone."

No one had to be reminded to call police. Since the killings began, switchboards were swamped at every police station and sheriff's substation in the West San Gabriel Valley.

The man they were afraid of was the most sought after killer in memory. The small army of detectives was larger than the one assembled to solve the Hillside Slayings, the Freeway Killings, and other celebrated cases.

His face was on every front page and at the top of every newscast. In some parts of Southern California his scrawny pock-marked face was better known than those of television celebrities.

Physically he wasn't much—25 to 30 years old, six feet tall, with brown curly hair, and gapped front teeth that were stained and badly decayed.

He went by various names—Valley Invader, the Valley Intruder and the Walk-In Murderer, but the name most police and news agencies settled on was "The Night Stalker."

It didn't matter which one you chose, because people knew who you meant, and it sent shivers up the spine.

The Stalker had been linked to 14 killings and 15 rapes, kidnapings and beatings in the San Gabriel and San Fernando valleys.

Worried residents feared they would be next. Police knew he wouldn't stop.

"They can't stop killing," explained a Los Angeles sheriff's detective. "They are rabid dogs who have gone insane and won't stop biting and biting until they are dead."

Until August, however, there was no multi-agency task force, no panic in the streets and talk of a rabid dog killer on the loose was confined to a handful of Los Angeles Sheriff's detectives.

One was Detective Gil Carrillo, a gravel-voiced veteran investigator with the Los Angeles Sheriff's homicide detail who had been working a murder case out of Rosemead east of downtown Los Angeles.

On Sunday morning, March 17th, Carillo was called to a condominium on the city's eastside, where he found the body of Dayle Okazaki, 34, sprawled in a pool of blood on the kitchen floor.

She had been shot point blank in the forehead with a .25-caliber pistol and died instantly. Her roommate had also been shot, but had survived and was recovering at a West San Gabriel Valley hospital.

The gunman had entered through the garage and forced the rear door that led into the kitchen. He then burglarized the condominium, shot the two roommates and fled.

The investigation revealed the killer likely had experience as a burglar. He left no fingerprints in the condominium

126

and was careful about selecting jewelry and other valuables he took.

Condo residents said they did not hear the shots or see anyone suspicious near the complex Saturday night or Sunday morning.

The detectives distributed drawings of jewelry taken from the condo to pawn shops in the area, and ordered police notified immediately if someone tried to pawn the items.

One piece of evidence surfaced during a search of the parking garage, when detectives discovered a baseball cap bearing the logo of the rock band AC/DC.

Carrillo knew little about the band except it was a "heavy metal" group popular with the teenagers.

The hat had no identifying tags or markings and was sold at hundreds of retail outlets, making it virtually untraceable.

The detective saw no connection between the group and the murder suspect. He was still working the case on a part time base in July when a police computer programmer dropped a four page computer readout on his desk.

"Look at this," the clerk said.

Carrillo had requested a computer check of violent crimes in the San Gabriel Valley which showed similarities to the Okazaki murder. Carrillo scanned the single spaced readout and cursed between clenched teeth.

Sergeant Frank Salerno walked by, holding a cup of steaming coffee and asked him what was up.

"Look at this," Carrillo said tersely.

Since the Okazaki investigation, there had been eight other murders under investigation.

Salerno read through the computer printout and let out a low whistle. A trim six footer, 46-year-old Salerno was something of a living legend at the Hall of Justice building. He had tracked down the flimsiest of clues in cases almost nobody remembers and, a few years back, played a key role in an investigation few can forget—the notorious Hillside Strangler case, the sex slayings of 10 young women and girls in 1977 and 1978.

Since then, Salerno had become an authority on serial killers—killers who murder for psychological reasons and continue to kill until they are caught.

On March 17th, the same evening as the Okazaki murder, Tsal-lian Yu, a 30-year-old Monterey Park woman, was pulled from her car near her home and shot several times. She died the next day.

Ten days later, Vincent Zazzara, a 64-year-old retired investment counselor was beaten to death and his 44-year-old wife Maxine stabbed to death by an attacker who entered their ranch-style home in Whittier.

Two months later, William Doi, 65, was shot to death in his Monterey Park home and his wife raped.

On May 29th, an 84-year-old widow and her invalid 81-year-old sister were beaten to bloody pulps in their Monrovia home.

Salerno continued reading through the computer list. It was like a Who's Who of horrors.

On June 27th, Patty Elaine Higgins, 32, was slain in her Arcadia home. Her throat was slashed. Five days later, and less than two miles away, Mary Louis Cannon, 77, of Arcadia, who fought off two bouts of cancer, was beaten then murdered, her throat slashed ear to ear.

The list also included assaults and rapes that occurred in the neighborhoods of the murder victims or had similar MOs that linked them to the murders.

On February 25th, a 6-year-old Montebello girl was snatched from a bus stop, zippered into a sleeping bag, and taken to the Silver Lake district where she was raped repeatedly before being freed.

A month later, a 9-year-old boy was kidnapped from his Monterey Park home and sexually assaulted before he was left in Elysian Field, near Silver Lake.

On March 20th, an Eagle Rock girl was kidnapped and sexually molested by a man who broke into her family's home at night.

This was followed by the rape of a teenage babysitter who fell asleep in the home of a neighbor. The rapist entered through an open window.

Salerno put down the readout and went to his boss, homicide Captain Robert Grimm. He told him about the murders, rapes and beatings the computer had linked together.

"There are a lot of dissimilarities, too," Salerno said. "Some victims were shot, others beaten. My hunch is, it is the same guy."

Grimm went with the sergeant's hunch. "You and Carrillo are on the case full time," he said. "I will give you more men as you need them."

Salerno and Carrillo began their new assignment by going back to the computer to check on crimes for the San Fernando Valley, south central Los Angeles and Orange County.

The computer sped through the thousands of crime reports submitted by law enforcement agencies and came up with one.

During the early morning hours of June 5th, a gunman burst into the bedroom of a Sun Valley home, shot to death Chainarong Khovanath, 32, sexually assaulted his wife and beat senseless their 8-year-old child.

He then fled in a maroon colored Pontiac Grand Prix with a damaged right fender. The car had been reported stolen.

The sheriff's detectives were still gathering information in the case when they received a phone call from Monterey Park police Lt. Joe Santoro.

"He's struck again," Santoro said. He grew suspicious when earlier that morning he entered the Monterey Park home of Joyce Nelson, and found the 61-year-old grandmother and assembly line worker beaten to death.

Santoro had a gut feeling this was not an isolated incident, that the murder was connected to the others, and that a madman was out there killing and killing and killing.

That afternoon Monterey Park Police Chief Jon D. Elder and Los Angeles County Sheriff Sherman Block talked urgently by phone and agreed on the concept of a multiagency task force to investigate the string of murders.

Elder was particularly concerned because the killer had struck three times in his city.

"That son of a bitch has scared the hell out of this city," he said.

The fear soon spread.

On July 11th, Elder stood before 360 citizens in the Monterey Park City Council chambers and asked for help.

"He is out there, somewhere, and we need your help to catch him," he said. "Be our eyes and ears. Tell us what you see."

Fearful residents had already taken to arming themselves against the mad dog killer. One gunshop owner told the Associated Press that gun sales had picked up about 75 percent in the last month. "People are tired of all the violence," he said. "They want to protect themselves."

Hardware stores also reported a run on dead bolt locks, sliding door and window lock devices and security home alarm systems.

There was also a run on rifles and shotguns, and exotic weaponry like "stun guns and lazar guns" because there was no 15-day waiting requirement to take them home, like there was on handguns.

Police also noted an increase of self appointed neighborhood security patrols, who cruised the streets in the early morning hours jotting down license tags of strange cars and stopping pedestrians and drivers who looked suspicious.

One of the patrollers was Police Chief Elder, who worked behind the desk during the day and took to the street at night.

Police officers feared the armed homeowners might accidentally shoot an innocent bystander thinking he was the killer, and requested residents use caution and call the police, instead of taking matters into their own hands.

One side effect was a 30 percent reduction in reported burglaries for the month of July.

"People are armed and staying up late," one sheriff's detective noted. "Burglars want this guy caught like everyone else. He is making it bad for business."

The investigation was complicated because the killer did not follow patterns of the typical serial killer.

He prowled freeway corridors, and lurked in quiet, cozy suburban neighborhoods. He pulled victims out of cars and broke into their homes through open doors or jimmied doors.

The Stalker shot the men, then turned on the women. Some were handcuffed to beds or door handles, while others were tied up with extension cords. They were raped and sodomized and terrorized repeatedly.

Afterward, "he stuck the shiv in deeper" according to one investigator, and toyed with his victims, snacking on leftovers in the kitchens of some victims. He raped one woman and then ordered her to cook him a meal. He gouged out the eyes of another victim.

The terror decimated many of the victims who lived. Some became hysterical when questioned by detectives. Others could remember nothing of the assaults, erasing the horror from their minds.

Still, police artists had enough to create a composite sketch, which was released to the media in mid-August. It showed a narrow-faced man of Latin descent, with large almond shaped eyes, bushy eyebrows and curly dark brown hair worn in bangs.

An updated composite showed the stalker with a billed hat, such as the one found at the home of victim Dayle Okazaki.

The Stalker composite and the announcement of a $10,000 reward by the Los Angeles County Board of Supervisors lit up the Southland police switchboard. In one week alone, police recorded almost 1,000 tips from witnesses claiming to have seen the Stalker.

Ironically, most of the calls came when the Stalker was not anywhere near Los Angeles.

On August 17, an LA sheriff's task force investigator received a phone call from San Francisco police requesting details of the Stalker case.

"I think he struck here," said Detective Frank Falzon.

Falzon and his partner Detective Dave Klotz had been called that morning to investigate the murder of Peter Pan, a 66-year-old accountant shot to death at his Eucalyptus Avenue home in the Lake Merced area.

The killer entered at 2 a.m. through a window of the two level house, shot Pan while he lay in bed then turned the gun on his wife, who was wounded in the head but survived.

The killer ransacked the house and fled.

The San Francisco detective had followed Stalker bulletins on the police teletype and noticed similarities between the Southland murders and the Pan case.

One similarity was striking; before leaving, the killer had drawn a pentagram on the wall — a figure that denotes Satanism or black magic worship. The pentagram and references to black magic had shown up in homes of other Stalker victims.

Los Angeles detectives flew to San Francisco. No one on Eucalyptus Avenue had seen anyone matching the Stalker's description, or had heard or seen anything suspicious. But the murder was undoubtedly the Stalker's doing, a fact confirmed by ballistics which matched the slug to a gun that was used in other Stalker shootings.

As San Francisco police worked to solve the murder, the Stalker struck again, this time in Mission Viejo, a placid upper middle class community in Orange County, south of Los Angeles.

At 2:40 Sunday morning August 25th, the Orange County Sheriff's Department received a call on the 911 emergency line from a woman who said her boyfriend had been shot.

Patrol officers rushed to the home on Christina Drive, followed by a Medivac crew and sheriff's detectives.

They found the 29-year-old business executive lying on the bed, a bullet lodged in his skull. The girl friend had been awakened by a gunshot, and saw her boy friend had been shot by a man standing at the foot of the bed holding a smoking pistol.

She described him as 6 feet tall, 25 to 30 years old, with curly hair and stained, gapped teeth.

He grabbed her by the front of her night gown and pulled her from the bed. She was raped repeatedly.

Neighbors hearing of the assault were terrified. The other assaults had occurred north of Orange County.

"We didn't think it would happen here," one resident told the *Santa Ana Register.* "Everybody leaves their windows open in the summer here. Who would have thought this would happen?"

Until then the Night Stalker had been able to slip in and out of neighborhoods without detection.

This time, however, luck changed hands. A teenager was in his parents' garage working on a motorbike when he spotted an orange Toyota station wagon that he thought was suspicious. He called the police and gave them a partial license number.

The sighting occurred one mile away and ninety minutes before David Crew was shot to death.

The vehicle was listed as stolen from Los Angeles Saturday evening. The owner told police he was eating dinner in Chinatown when the car was pinched.

An all points bulletin was issued on the stolen car with instructions the driver was to be considered armed and extremely dangerous. Patrol officers were not to approach the vehicle if found abandoned but to keep it under observation and notify headquarters immediately.

Monday morning the owner of a health food store in the Westlake district west of downtown Los Angeles spotted a Toyota parked in the lot of his small shopping center.

The following day the car was still there and he notified police. Unaware it was the most sought after vehicle in California, he told police, "I keep an eye on who parks here and write down their license numbers. Otherwise, my customers got nowhere to park."

The police thanked him for his diligence.

Four plainclothesmen staked the Toyota out until the next

morning, hoping the Night Stalker would return.

Afterward, the vehicle was loaded onto a flatbed and taken to the Orange County Sheriff's Department, where the state of the art scientific methods were applied to lifting prints and other evidence from the vehicle.

The first method involved using Superglue fumes, which reacts to moisture in fingerprints, turning the prints white. With the other, a laser beam was used to enhance prints that were smudged or wiped clean.

It was the laser method that produced a partial print on the driver's side window.

The print was sent to the state Department of Justice, which had recently purchased a $10-million computer system, that could search through the millions of prints on file in a matter of hours.

Meanwhile, tips flooded law enforcement agencies, sending the 150 detectives involved in the search for the Night Stalker, in all directions.

A tipster told police that the Night Stalker was named Rick and that he frequented Skid Row hotels. Rick was tracked to a liquor store at Sixth and Main streets where the night clerk identified Rick from an artist sketch as a person who had bought candy bars and bottles of wine.

"The guy was a loner," the clerk said. "He might say hello but he never looked at you and he talked to himself. He had real bad teeth. I told him the candy bars weren't any good for him but he didn't listen."

Detectives combed downtown hotels. At the 600-bed Hotel Cecil a night clerk said Rick had spent a couple of days at the hotel. Detectives checked out the name on the registration and discovered it was fictitious. So was the rest of the information on the card.

Meanwhile, sheriff's investigators noted that several Stalker victims lived near construction sights and were busy combing employment lists to see if the suspect might have worked as a laborer.

In San Francisco, meanwhile, Detectives Falzon and Klotz traced a necklace believed stolen by the Stalker, to

Lompoc, California, 300 miles south of San Francisco. A woman said a man she knew slightly showed her the jewelry and said he would sell it to her cheap.

She paid him for the necklace; several days later she looked in the paper and saw a composite drawing of the Night Stalker, saw it resembled her friend, right down to the rotting teeth.

She called the local police who put her in contact with the San Francisco authorities.

The woman said she knew the man only as Rick and that they met while she was seeing friends in the Bay area.

Rick was friendly enough, she said, but was something of a loner. He seemed harmless, a dopey kid from Texas somewhere who had a sizeable cocaine habit and talked a lot about Satanism.

The woman in Lompoc provided the detectives with names of two friends in the Bay area who knew Rick.

One lived in San Francisco's Haight Ashbury. "Yeah, Richard," the friend said. "Richard Ramirez. From L.A. He was up here a few weeks ago."

But Los Angeles detectives were one step ahead of the Bay sleuths. As Falzon and Klotz searched rundown East Bay localities for Richard Ramirez, Los Angeles Police chief Daryl Gates met with Los Angeles Sheriff Sherman Block and Orange County Sheriff Brad Gates.

They knew the suspect was Richard Ramirez. It was his partially smudged print that was found in the abandoned getaway car.

The question was what to do next. If they released his photo and description to the news media it might spook him and give him the opportunity to escape or destroy evidence.

On the other hand, the composite sketch wasn't working out, and if Ramirez's face was plastered on the front pages and television news, it might lead to a quick arrest.

It was a gamble, but one the three top law enforcement officials decided to take.

On Saturday, Labor Day weekend, Californians got their first good look at the Night Stalker suspect.

"We are certain we have the right man," said police Chief Gates, at a press conference. "We believe he is armed and dangerous and advise anyone spotting him not to try to make an arrest but to notify us immediately."

Richard Ramirez, 25, was a pot smoking drifter from El Paso, Texas who had lived in the Southland for the past two years.

His name and fingerprints were entered into the state Department of Justice computer after he was arrested for a December 1984 car theft in Los Angeles.

It was a fluke that the computer had his fingerprints. The system was brand new and the only prints that had been fed into the new system were those of offenders born after a certain date.

News media descended upon a modest neighborhood on El Paso's east side and interviewed residents about their notorious neighbor.

Most were shocked that the scrawny kid with bad teeth they had grown up with was capable of hurting anyone, much less commit a string of atrocities that made him the target of a nationwide manhunt.

"We knew him as a burglar," said one neighbor. "We nicknamed him 'Fingers' because he was always stealing stuff."

A shop teacher at El Paso's Jefferson High School said Ramirez had been a quiet boy who they remembered primarily for his truancy.

"He had a few friends, but basically he was a loner," the teacher said. "No girl friends, I don't even remember him ever dating anyone. He was in and out. Nobody really missed him when he dropped out."

A neighbor who lived a few doors down from the simple single story home where Ramirez grew up told the reporter, "In about 8th grade he started sniffing glue. I know that. I guess that's how he got started on drugs. From that, he went to marijuana."

Another said the mugshot of Ramirez on TV looked nothing like the person they grew up with. "He had a completely different look on his face from the last time I saw

136

him. He's got a crazed look on his face that he didn't have when he was here. I would sure like to know what changed the guy."

Police sure wanted to know where he was. Despite hundreds of sightings phoned in over the Labor Day vacation, Ramirez remained on the lam.

It looked like the gamble had backfired and only driven the Night Stalker underground.

Then Sunday afternoon the clerk of an East Los Angeles grocery store looked up from his racing form and saw a customer pick up a copy of La Opinion, the Spanish newspaper.

Suddenly, he screamed and dashed from the store.

On the cover was Ramirez's mugshot and a story that mentioned him by name.

The clerk saw the man's face as he fled and recognized him immediately.

He dashed out into the street and yelled, "Stop him! Stop him! It's the Night Stalker!"

A block away on Hubbard Street a woman was headed for her car when a man ran from behind and grabbed her purse. She hung on and he punched her in the stomach.

She screamed but didn't let go. Her husband heard his wife and gave chase. Other neighbors followed. No one knew who the stranger was except he had punched a woman and they were going to run him down and kick his ass good.

The stranger jumped a fence, raced through a backyard, and out an alley that led back to Hubbard Street.

One of the pursuers caught him from behind and whacked him hard across the back of the head with a fence rod. The stranger slumped to the ground and covered his head.

The man continued beating him with the rod. A small crowd formed. Los Angeles sheriff's deputy Andres Ramirez was on routine patrol when he received the radio call to break up the brawl.

He arrived in his black and white cruiser and found four angry men beating and punching the man who was curled in a fetal position on the sidewalk.

"That bastard punched my wife," one of the men yelled.

"Yeah, I saw it," another said. "He tried to rip off her purse."

Andres Ramirez put handcuffs on the bloodied suspect and brought him to the cruiser.

"Thank goodness, you showed up," the man said. "They would have killed me for sure."

The deputy took a long look at the man in the back of the cruiser. The face bore striking similarity to Richard Ramirez, the Night Stalker suspect.

The deputy had the same last name and had taken a lot of ribbing at the station house, even though they were not related.

"You're Richard Ramirez, aren't you," the deputy said.

"Yeah," he replied.

A crowd of forty persons surrounded the cruiser. They pointed fingers at the man in the backseat and said, "That's him, that's the Night Stalker."

As word spread, dozens of residents poured out of homes to view the most infamous murder suspect in memory.

Police cruisers quickly descended upon the neighborhood to prevent what could have become a lynch mob. Ramirez was taken to the county jail where he was questioned by task force investigators before he was booked into county jail on suspicion of murder.

Police and public breathed a welcome sigh of relief. "There is still a great deal to do, but, yes, our search for the Night Stalker is over," said Los Angeles Chief Deputy District Attorney Gilbert I. Garcetti to members of the news media.

Ramirez, meanwhile, was kept on 24 hour suicide watch in a solitary wing of Los Angeles County Jail.

Attorneys came and went—some famous, like Melvin Belli, who declined to represent Ramirez, others not so famous.

Whoever the attorney, it will likely be years before Ramirez is ready to go to trial.

Since his arrest, the gangly Texas drifter has been charged with committing 14 murders and 21 assaults.

For much of Los Angeles, the horror story ended on Labor Day Sunday when angry citizens ran down a purse snatcher.

As a Monterey Park resident noted, "We can put away the guns and get back to normal."

On October 24, 1985, Richard Ramirez pleaded not guilty to the charges of killing 14 people over the last 13 months. The plea was entered in Los Angeles Municipal Court after Judge Alva R. Soper reluctantly allowed him to change attorneys again. Since his arrest on August 31, Ramirez has been represented by five attorneys.

Police say that the suspect is obsessed with satanic worship. In court he displayed a pentagram on his left palm. The symbol is a five-point figure that is sometimes used as representing the devil. When he was led from the courtroom, Ramirez shouted, "Hail Satan!"

It must be assumed, however, that Richard Ramirez is not guilty of the charges against him until he has been proved guilty under due process.

Illinois' Homosexual
Homicide Horror

by W.T. Brannon

The macabre tally is now 33 bodies of young men uncovered.

The case that was destined to become the most spectacular in the criminal history of the Chicago area, if not the most astonishing in the annals of illegality in the United States, began for the police of Des Plaines, Illinois a few hours after dinner time on Monday, December 11, 1978.

At that time a call was received at Des Plaines police headquarters from a woman who, in a somewhat shaky voice, said that her 15-year-old son, Robert Piest, had disappeared.

What were the circumstances? the officer asked.

The woman said she lived with her family on Craig Drive in Des Plaines. This was her 46th birthday and a party was planned for her. However, the son, Robert, could not be there because he had a part-time job as a clerk at a drug store on Touhy Avenue. He was scheduled to get off at nine o'clock.

His mother said she told him she would drive to the drug store to pick him up, and the family decided to wait until Robert got home to cut the cake. Mrs. Piest drove to the drug store, arriving about 8:50 p.m.

When it was time for him to quit work, Robert put on his

coat, joined his mother and the two started for the front door. Then Robert stopped.

"Wait a minute, Mom," he said. "I've got to see a man about a construction job that will pay me five dollars an hour. I'll be only a few minutes."

She nodded and stepped back away from the door and watched him leave. She knew that $5 an hour was about twice what he earned at the drug store. When he said he'd be back in a few minutes, she assumed he meant from 10 to 15 minutes.

She waited 15 minutes and Robert didn't return. She waited another five minutes and he still was not there. She decided this was long enough.

She went outside, looked both ways on the sidewalk. There was no sign of her son. She hurried to where her car was parked and drove home.

The family had seen nothing of Robert.

It was generally agreed by the family that Robert was not the sort who would keep his mother waiting. He was the kind of boy who would keep his word or let his mother know why he couldn't—unless something had happened to him.

The mother strode to the phone and called the police. That, she concluded her account, was all she could tell.

Did she have the phone number of the drug store?

She did and gave it to the officer. He had a missing persons report on the desk where he sat and she gave him answers to the questions on the official form.

Copies of the report were typed and one of each was sent to Chief Leroy Alfano and Captain Joseph Kozenczak. The report disturbed Kozenczak, who had a 15-year-old son of his own. He was up early the next morning, Tuesday, December 12th. He checked the night's reports which showed that all cruising squads had searched for the missing boy, but nothing at all new had been learned.

Captain Kozenczak had discussed the case at length with Chief Alfano and it was decided that an intensive, in-depth investigation would be made of the case.

Investigators were sent to the Piest home, where they

141

learned from the parents that Robert was an unusually well-mannered boy, an ambitious, hard-working youth who was very anxious to advance. He was characteristically dependable, reliable and trustworthy.

Because of these traits, Robert never had any trouble getting a summer job during school vacation or a part-time job when he was going to school. The parents assumed this was the reason the contractor had offered him five dollars an hour—an unusually high rate of pay for a 15-year-old.

Who was the contractor?

The parents didn't know his name or address, but they supposed his office was not far from the drug store, which was on Touhy Avenue. Otherwise, Robert would not have told his mother he would be back in a few minutes.

Before he left, Captain Kozenczak obtained the names and addresses of Robert's known friends. One of them was the captain's 15-year-old son, who attended the Maine Township West High School, the same school Robert attended.

Because they would be in school, Kozenczak would not be able to question the boys on his list. However, there was a slim possibility, hardly worth considering, that Robert had spent the night with a friend and that he had gone to school as usual. So the captain went to the school.

The principal sent his secretary to Robert's home room. She returned within a few minutes with the news that Robert had not come to school that morning and nobody had called up to give a reason, such as sickness, for his absence. This was very unusual—in fact, it never had happened before.

Robert's records showed that he was an honor student, that he always was given a top grade in deportment and that he was active in athletics, that he was a letter-man, having won it for excellence in various sports. He was "straight as an arrow," the police officials were told. He was regarded by his teachers and his fellow students as an all-American boy. He was considered remarkable in that he found the time and energy to participate in school athletics, work at a part-time job, do his homework and maintain a high average in

142

school.

The high school principal promised to contact the police at once if he learned anything at all about what had happened to Robert.

The boy's friends were in school and Captain Kozenczak knew he would have to wait until mid-afternoon, the time most of them came home. Meanwhile, he went to the drug store where Robert worked part-time.

The night pharmacist who usually was on duty at the same time Robert was, said the last he had seen of the boy was the night before when he got off at nine o'clock. He recalled that Robert's mother had come to pick him up and remembered that she waited inside the store while her son went on an errand. She waited only a few minutes, then left. He assumed she had joined Robert just outside the front door.

Captain Kozenczak had noticed that the drug store was unusually clean and parts of it appeared to have been renovated. He asked the pharmacist if any work had been done on the interior.

Yes, the pharmacist replied. He said the interior had been remodeled and the work had been completed only a short time before.

Was there anything unusual about the work?

There was just one thing, the pharmacist said. Practically all the workers were teenage boys or young men. The contractor had been in the drug store several times while his boys were at work. On several occasions he had been seen talking to Robert Piest. The druggist said the contractor's name was John Wayne Gacy, Jr.

Did the pharmacist hear what they were talking about?

Apparently the contractor was trying to lure Robert away from his drug store job. The druggist said he believed that the contractor had offered the boy much more than he was being paid for his work at the drug store.

Was Robert especially skilled in repair work? The druggist didn't know, but he assumed that was the case. Otherwise, why should the contractor offer a larger salary? Unless . . . Unless . . . Captain Kozenczak shuddered at the alter-

143

native. He continued questioning the druggist and learned that Gacy's office was in his home on Summerdale Avenue. This address is in an unincorporated section of Cook County, in Norwood Park Township, near suburban Rosemont and east of O'Hare International Airport, the world's busiest airport.

Although Gacy's home was not in the jurisdiction of the Des Plaines police, the drug store which he recently remodeled was. Captain Kozenczak found Gacy and asked him to come to the Des Plaines police headquarters for questioning. He promised to come early the next morning.

The Rosemont police were notified and promised to stand by in the event they could help in the investigation.

Although Captain Kozenczak was convinced that Gacy was probably the only one who could tell the police what had happened to Robert, he and Chief Alfano were not taking this for granted. They sent investigators out to question the boys whose names had been given to them as friends of Robert.

The news that Robert was missing had leaked out at school and the boys were not surprised to see the officers. None of them could furnish any information that might help to locate the missing youth.

However, several of Robert's friends knew about his impending employment by Gacy. He had told them about the possible job offer. He was to see the owner of "PDM" one more time before he accepted the job and quit his job at the drug store. Presumably, he had gone to see about the job on the night he disappeared.

Meanwhile, Cook County Sheriff Richard Elrod had been notified. The sheriff had passed the word on to his chief of police, Edmund Dobbs, and his assistant, Lieutenant Michael Clarn, and Sergeant Harold Anderson, commander of the sheriff's Niles station and Investigator Irv Kraut, also of the Niles station.

Some of Robert's friends who knew of the job offer told the investigators that PDM stood for Painting, Decorating and Maintenance. Most of the firm's work was remodeling and most of the workers were teenage boys.

The questioning of Robert's friends turned up nothing else.

The following morning, Wednesday, December 13th, John Wayne Gacy, 36, a chubby, well dressed man with dark hair and a mustache, about five feet eight inches tall and with a jaunty step, appeared at Des Plaines police headquarters.

Although he was questioned at length, he denied knowing what had happened to Robert Piest. He finally agreed to meet the officers at his home at four o'clock that afternoon. He was waiting when the police arrived.

The police looked around the two-bedroom yellow brick ranch style house, but the only thing of special interest they found was a receipt for a roll of film to be developed. The officers kept the receipt with Gacy's permission.

From Gacy's house the Des Plaines police drove to the Piest home in Des Plaines. Shown the receipt, they said that the name on it was a girl that Robert knew. He had volunteered to take the film to a place to have it developed and had received the receipt. He planned to pick up the developed film and give the pictures to the girl.

How did it get in the Gacy house? Police speculated that Robert had been lured to the Gacy house while he had the receipt in his pocket. Had Robert resisted a sexual assault and, in the struggle did the receipt drop out of the boy's pocket?

This was speculation, and not nearly enough evidence to get a warrant. But the officials were convinced there was probable cause, and they set out to obtain more evidence.

Deputy sheriffs along with Des Plaines investigators were assigned to the case and kept Gacy under surveillance around the clock.

Meanwhile, the Chicago police were asked for help and began checking the records. Missing person reports for the past several months were checked, especially those involving boys in their middle and late teens. More than half of the teens reported missing had returned home. Many others had been found by various law enforcement agencies, and the fate of the balance — about one-fourth of those missing —

still was a mystery.

The inquiries instituted by the Chicago police, aided by State Attorney Bernard Carey and his staff, Sheriff Elrod and many of his investigators, soon turned up information about Gacy. He was born in Edgewater Hospital in Chicago, on March 17, 1942. He grew up on the north side of Chicago, attending public schools. After his graduation from high school, he enrolled in a business college.

When he had completed the business course, he moved to Springfield, the state capital, and took a job in a shoe store. In 1963 he met a young woman whom he courted and who became his wife the following year.

Police located the mother of his two children and she agreed to talk to them if they would withhold her name. Gacy and his wife had two children and his wife said he was a good father. She also said he was "a likable salesman who could charm it right out of you."

But, she added, he was "always trying to build himself up," and "occasionally did crazy things." She cited one instance when he was driving to work and joined the mourners in a funeral procession. A policeman saw him cut into the procession and ticketed him for a traffic violation.

In 1966, Gacy's father-in-law hired him as manager of the fried chicken restaurants for which he held the franchises. They were in Waterloo, Iowa, and Gacy moved his family to that northeast Iowa city.

When the police contacted people in Waterloo who had been acquainted with Gacy, they were told that he was extremely well liked. He liked to attend parties and to be the center of attention. But he worked long hours taking care of his father-in-law's fried chicken places.

One businessman, who said he was one of Gacy's closest friends, said Gacy was always working on something, such as the local chapter of the Jaycees.

"He was always working on some project," said the businessman, Jack Dale. "The Jaycees were his whole life." Dale said that Gacy also was the chaplain of the Jaycees chapter and that in 1966 he had been voted the second best chaplain of the Jaycees in Iowa.

In 1967, the Blackhawk County Attorney's office in Waterloo began receiving reports and rumors that Gacy was not the jolly good fellow he appeared to be. One rumor was that teenagers were employed at the fried chicken places and that these boys often were invited to parties given by Gacy, who served them whiskey and encouraged them to engage in sexual activities.

"It wasn't just one incident," said Assistant County Attorney David Dutton who was assigned to the case. "It was going on for a few months before it came to our attention."

Prosecutor Dutton carried on a discreet investigation that disclosed Gacy as a classic example of the Jekyl-and-Hyde character. Cook County authorities found an attorney who was familiar with the grand jury testimony. He told of the testimony of one teenager.

The boy told the grand jury that Gacy gave him whiskey, then proposed a pool game where the loser would perform a sex act. The teenager refused, he testified, and Gacy forced him into a bedroom at knifepoint, chained his arms and legs and began choking him. When the boy went limp, Gacy stopped and unchained him.

After other testimony, Gacy was indicted on a charge of sodomy involving another boy. In 1968 he was convicted of sodomy and sentenced to serve 10 years in the Iowa State Reformatory at Anamosa.

His friends and many people in the county were stunned. At the time he was indicted he was a candidate for the 1968 presidency of the Jaycees.

He did all sorts of charitable acts—sending buckets of fried chicken to the boys' club, doing Christmas shopping for underprivileged children and always was ready to do a favor for a friend.

"People couldn't handle it," said a Des Moines businessman, formerly of Waterloo.

Gacy told people he was being framed and many of them believed him. He said the reason was to keep him from being elected president of the Jaycees.

"It was all so hard for us to believe," said Dale. "He was such a good doggone Jaycee."

A Jaycee chapter was being organized in the reformatory and Gacy worked very hard to expand it. He was assigned to cook and make salads in the prison kitchen. Prison officials said he was good natured and worked very hard in the kitchen.

He continued to be a good Jaycee in prison, taking over the chapter then being formed, working hard in any spare time he had to line up prospective members.

"He was a model prisoner, a good worker, but you had to watch him—he wanted to be the boss," said the man who was Gacy's supervisor. He said Gacy staged banquets for the Jaycees which were so popular that inmates competed with each other for the opportunity to work on them.

"He was quite a businessman," said another official. "He seemed like a regular guy, not weird at all."

"All he really wanted was for everybody to like him," said Jack Dale.

In 1969, Gacy's wife divorced him.

Eighteen months after he entered the reformatory, he was released on parole and the parole board stipulated that he could spend the parole time in Chicago.

In Chicago, he was arrested on February 12, 1971 for picking up a teenager at the bus station, taking the boy to his apartment and trying to force him to engage in a sex act. A date for trial was set but the case was dismissed when the boy failed to show up.

He bought the two-bedroom yellow brick house in Norwood Park Township. It was sparsely furnished. Shortly afterward, in 1972, his parole term was completed and he was released. Not long after that he met an attractive young woman and courted her with the zeal for which he was known.

"He swept me off my feet," she said later. She had been married before and was the mother of two girls. She and Gacy were married and she and her girls moved into Gacy's home. She also moved her furniture.

One day she found some wallets, apparently belonging to teenagers who had disappeared. When she asked about them, she said he exploded with fury.

148

She said Gacy told her that he had troubles in school and had been taken out of high school several times in a straitjacket.

In 1975, Gacy started his own business, the PDM Contractors, about the time his second marriage broke up. The couple was divorced on May 2, 1976. Gacy continued to operate out of his yellow brick ranch-style house.

The contracting business prospered and Gacy hired dozens of teenagers and young men. Police found one man of 28 who told of going to Gacy's house to see about a job. He said Gacy made a sexual advance and when he tried to break loose, Gacy became very angry and said he had a gun and it would be easy enough to kill him and dispose of the body.

"As a matter of fact," he quoted Gacy, "I have already killed some people." The young man said he didn't believe Gacy at the time.

But a 46-year-old friend and business associate of Gacy's said he had no trouble believing Gacy who, he said, told him a couple of weeks before that the police had him under surveillance. "They're trying to pin a murder on me," he was quoted.

This man said he asked Gacy if he had killed anybody and he replied that he hadn't.

Meanwhile, the Chicago police had dug up missing person reports and separated the teenage boys, of which there were many. There were very few adult young men. Some parents or loved ones who had filed the missing person reports agreed to provide pictures if they might be helpful.

From December 14th to 18th, Gacy was kept under constant surveillance. Known acquaintances and business associates were questioned. This yielded nothing.

On December 19th, lawyers for Gacy filed a civil rights suit for $750,000 against the City of Des Plaines and its police department, charging illegal searches and seizures and that they were harassing him and destroying his reputation.

The same day, Des Plaines investigators, using the receipt for the film and information received from acquaintances, obtained a search warrant for Gacy's house and the property surrounding it. Accompanied by Cook County sheriff's investigators, the officers went to Gacy's home and he admitted them.

Gacy was accused of holding Robert Piest against his will. The police threatened to tear up the floor if Gacy didn't tell them where they could find the boy. Gacy denied that the boy was anywhere in or near the house.

The questioning continued, and finally Gacy admitted he once had been forced to kill a man, but he insisted it was in self defense.

He said he buried the body under the concrete floor of the garage. Then he led the investigators to the garage located at the end of the house to the right of where the driveway ended.

Using a can of spray paint, Gacy marked the spot on the floor under which he said the body was buried. The police didn't believe him. There was an easier way than digging up the concrete to find out if he was telling the truth.

The officers went back to the house, and looking through closets they found a trap door that led to a crawl space under the floor. Crawling inside they found the cadavers of three teenage boys and various parts of other bodies!

One of the officers said they'd better notify the medical examiner, who is in charge where deaths are concerned. He said he had the medical examiner's home phone number, where he almost certainly would be at this hour—almost 10 p.m.

The officer was assigned to find a phone and tell the medical examiner what they had found.

Dr. Robert J. Stein, Cook County Medical Examiner, was about to get ready for bed when the phone rang. He is an early riser who gets to his office on weekdays about 5:30 to six a.m. That means he needs to retire early.

When Dr. Stein answered the phone, the caller identified himself as a policeman for the sheriff.

"There's a body or something in the crawl space of a ranch house near Norridge," the policeman said. Then he gave the address. Dr. Stein telephoned his office and asked an assistant to bring coveralls and meet him at the Gacy

150

house.

Then Dr. Stein left his home in Highland Park, a plush community of about 35,000 population, about 30 miles north of Chicago on Lake Michigan. The drive to the Gacy home, only a few miles southwest of Highland Park, required only a few minutes.

His assistant arrived with coveralls while the sheriff's men were telling him of their suspicions of Gacy. Dr. Stein pulled on the coveralls. He was shown the closet leading to the crawl space. "I opened the door and, my God, there was the odor of death," he said later.

Letting himself down through a trap door, he then dropped onto the wet, sodden dirt of the crawl space. Dr. Stein turned on a flashlight and immediately saw what his practiced eye recognized as human bones. First were the skeletal remains of two human arms.

Dr. Stein came back up into the house and ordered the whole place sealed and roped off. Guards were posted all around the house and other buildings on the property. Then Stein drove home.

But he was back the next morning with fresh coveralls. He ordered the removal of the floor of the house — and then they began finding the bodies. The medical examiner located three bodies and ordered them taken to the Cook County morgue where autopsies would be performed.

"They were six feet down in some cases," Dr. Stein said.

"What kind of man would do such a thing?" he was asked.

"A schizophrenic, of course," Dr. Stein replied. "More than that, who can say?"

Bodies and bones were not the only things found in that crawl space. There were various kinds of jewelry, items of clothing and loops of rope around the necks of the three bodies removed that day. All of these might be of some use in determining the cause of death, in identifying the victims, and possibly helping to lead to the killer.

The medical examiner had several dental specialists at his disposal and he hoped that dental charts filed with missing person reports would identify the victims. At the time he

151

didn't know how many there would be.

That day, December 22nd, Gacy was questioned at considerable length. The finding of four bodies and parts of other bodies the night before made Gacy realize that he couldn't deny complicity in those murders. He began to talk.

From the time he had become an adult, he had sought to gain the status of a big shot in the business world, but his queer sexual urges had punched holes in that ambition.

After the police had learned of his conviction for sodomy in Iowa and the later murders in the Chicago area of teenage boys who resisted his sexual advances, he was asked if he was a homosexual. He admitted he was, despite his two marriages and his fathering of two children.

Current developments had wiped out any chance of his becoming a VIP in the respectable world, but there was no limit to the heights he might attain in gay circles. It has been theorized that he began to talk in a way that would make headlines. He knew there were several ways he might beat the rap: he could plead insanity and temporary insanity. A good lawyer could think up other good reasons why he should plead not guilty, so he might as well shoot the works.

Under questioning by the police, Gacy assertedly said that during the past three years, he had killed 32 teenagers and young men after forcing them to have abnormal sexual relations with him against their wills. Of these, 27 had been buried on this property — one under the concrete floor of his garage — and five others, including Robert Piest, were disposed of in other ways he told police.

Asked what he had done with Robert's body, he said he had tossed it into the Des Plaines River a short distance south of Joliet in Will County. He was asked also about the body found in the river in November, but denied any knowledge of that one.

All right, where are the others? Chief Dobbs asked.

Gacy said he would draw them a picture. He drew a neat diagram of each of the 27 he had buried. Most of them were in the crawl space, four feet under the house. The depth became six feet or more where the bodies had been buried.

He gave the names of six of his victims and he was shown two pictures from the missing person files. He said he didn't know their names, although they were victims, also. He said they were not among the six he had named.

The following day, December 23rd, the police began an intensive search of Gacy's property. Papers, wallets and other personal property of missing Chicago-area boys were found, some in the house, some in the crawl space, other items in the storage shed.

Meanwhile, Dr. Stein and assistant medical examiners began performing autopsies on the four bodies recovered so far, starting first with efforts to identify the victims.

Dr. Stein has an unusually well equipped laboratory and all the instruments needed for the autopsies. One of the best known and most efficient pathologists in the world, he is acquainted with Dr. Lester Mooto of Guyama, who is in charge of the investigation into the Jonestown massacre. When the numerous bodies were discovered there and the case was headlined world-wide, Dr. Mooto had called Dr. Stein and they discussed the problems facing Dr. Mooto. Dr. Stein offered Dr. Mooto the use of his facilities if it became necessary.

Dr. Stein took his medical degree at the University of Innsbrook in Austria, and did his post graduate working in pathology. This accounts for his being on friendly terms with pathologists on an international basis.

Dr. Stein's father was an engineer and he attended public schools in Brooklyn. In his senior year in high school, the school had a visit from Dr. Charles Norris, who was the first New York medical examiner. Young Stein was so impressed with Dr. Norris' talk about legal medicine that he was led to become a pathologist.

In their investigation of the Gacy victims, Dr. Stein and his assistants used dental charts and X-ray and other instruments in trying to identify and establish the cause of death of the victims.

The investigation stopped for the Christmas holidays on December 24th and 25th, but, police, pathologists and others were back at work early on December 26th. Among the others were divers who began dragging the Des Plaines River at a point a short distance north of where the body was found in November to a few miles south of Joliet where Gacy said he threw the body of Robert Piest, according to police.

Some of the investigators searching the house found several of Gacy's papers, as well as a batch of business cards. In addition to the name of his construction company, there was a line in the left lower corner identifying Gacy as a Democratic precinct captain.

However, after the charges against Gacy had become public, a Democratic commiteeman denied that Gacy was a Democratic precinct captain. He said he'd seen one of the cards but hadn't made an issue of it because Gacy appeared to be well liked and could be an asset.

Many people in the Norwood Park and Norridge neighborhoods agreed that Gacy was well liked; one reason was that he liked to entertain children. He had two clown outfits that he had designed himself. He wore them to children's parties and benefits. Most people who had become acquainted with him since he had moved into the neighborhood liked him. He appeared to be very fond of children.

Four more bodies were found in the crawl space. Like the first three, underwear and wash cloths were stuffed in their mouths. This was to become a sort of trademark of Gacy victims. In November, before Gacy had become a suspect in a murder case, a teenager was found in the Des Plaines River, with Gacy's trademark, the boy's underwear, stuffed in his mouth.

Sheriff's investigators who were trying to identify the boy thrown in the river had obtained a dental chart from his parents at the time he was reported missing. After the body was pulled from the river, the chart was compared with his teeth and he was identified. It was not until after Gacy was arrested for the murder of Robert Piest that he admitted the murder of the boy pulled out of the river. This brought the body count to ten.

On Wednesday, December 27th, using the diagram on

which Gacy had marked off the places where he said he had buried 27 of his victims, the investigators searched each spot. One place that promised to be productive was the crawl space under the northeast section of the house where Gacy had indicated that he had buried a body.

"We have no doubt we will find twenty-seven bodies in the places he has shown us on the diagram," said one investigator. He added that so far the diagram had been accurate.

What appeared to be trenches had been dug in the crawl spaces, as if they had been prepared in advance. This turned out to be true when a teenage boy came to Chief Dobbs and told him that Gacy had hired him to dig trenches two feet deep in the crawl spaces.

Most of the bodies had been covered with lime to make them deteriorate more rapidly. Some were no more than skeletal remains, others were bones that had come apart from the skeletons. Most of the skulls were intact. Dr. Stein and his associates used their knowledge and skill to rebuild the skeletons from the bones.

By the end of the day, eight more bodies had been found under the crawl space in Gacy's house, boosting the body count to 18.

Meanwhile, the medical examiner and his associates had completed some of the autopsies and had found that the cause of death of most victims had been strangulation, some manual, some by choking with ropes tied very tightly around their necks.

One of these investigators said: "Most of the skulls are intact and only one of them had good teeth. The others all needed a lot of dental work, thank goodness."

His reasoning in this was that boys who needed much work on their teeth would have distinctive dental charts that would help to identify them.

The investigator said it appeared that the first victims were buried in concrete—one in the garage floor and two covered in cement in the crawl space. For some reason Gacy apparently gave up cement and decided to have trenches dug in the crawl spaces. The trenches were only a few feet down.

"When he ran out of trenches in the crawl space," said the investigator, "he really got reckless and began dumping bodies in the river, despite the fact that someone could have seen him."

Police said Gacy had told them he had dumped five of his victims into the Des Plaines River in Will County south of Joliet from the Interstate Highway 55 bridge. These included Robert Piest, whose disappearance led to the beginning of the spectacular investigation.

On Thursday, December 28th, four more bodies were found in the crawl space and under the direction of Dr. Stein were removed to the county. This brought the body count to 22.

Officials were still trying to identify the body dumped in the river in November, before any of the missing boys had been linked to John Gacy. The sheriff's missing persons bureau listed a teenage boy who, on July 31, 1975 was reported missing. A dental chart was obtained and it was compared with the teeth of the boy taken from the river.

The comparison definitely showed that the youngster pulled from the river a month before was John Butkovich, who disappeared on July 31, 1975. John had been working for a man named John Wayne Gacy, but quit about a month before he disappeared. Gacy didn't pay what was due him and on that last day of July he told his parents he was going to see Gacy to try to collect his back pay. They never saw him alive again.

He was reported missing to the police. The parents suspected Gacy for two reasons. The father was the owner of several rental buildings and he asked for bids from contracts. Gacy made a bid but didn't get the job. Then John went to work for him in his contracting business.

The parents never knew why John quit his job. Nor did they ever find out if he collected his back pay. The father called the police and an unidentified officer suggested that John was a runaway. The police were told about Gacy, but the parents heard nothing. The father called Gacy.

"I asked if police had talked to him. He always said no,

and told me he wished he could be of some help to me."

The mother sat on the living room couch crying.

"Everybody should know about their sons," she said. "Everyone who thinks it may be their son there should know for sure."

The "there" she referred to was the Gacy house. Ever since the investigation started, they had been expecting bad news.

"It is better to know," the father said.

The body count of 22 was the largest number ever linked to one individual, according to police records. Before that, there was a man named Herman W. Mudgett who preferred to use the name H.H. Holmes. He had a medical degree in Michigan, a home in Gilmanton, New Hampshire where one of at least four wives waited for him, but preferred to live in Chicago. On the city's South Side, he had erected a strange three-story building that came to be known as Holmes Castle.

During the Columbian Exposition of 1893, he advertised for young women to act as housekeepers and laboratory assistants. Several were hired and they were never seen again. In his laboratory on the third floor was a table where bodies were dissected. The bones were sent to the basement by a slide that emptied into an acid vat where they were decomposed.

The man calling himself Dr. Holmes got in trouble by collecting insurance on a man he killed. A Pinkerton detective trailed Dr. Holmes, the wife and three children and his three wives (each in ignorance of the existence of the others) to large cities in the United States and Canada.

The detective finally caught up with Dr. Holmes and he was tried for murder in Philadelphia. He was convicted and hanged in Moyaminsing Prison in Philadelphia in 1896. Various estimates were made of the number he slaughtered. Officials considered the most authoritative fixed the number at between 15 and 29. To people unaccustomed to super crime, this was colossal, and Dr. Holmes was promptly dubbed the Arch Fiend of the Century.

But the Twentieth Century was just around the corner

and in addition to a growth in population, there was an expansion in crime, especially murder emboldened by the abandon with which Prohibition mobs mowed down people with their sawed-off shotguns.

In 1973, 17-year-old Elmer Hensley led Houston police to three Texas gravesites where 27 men and boys were buried. Hensley told police he had killed Dean Corll, 33, in self-defense. He was acquitted but was charged with the 27 murders after he had accused Corll of masterminding the mass murders. He was convicted and sentenced to 594 years in prison. This beat the record of H.H. Holmes and those of other mass killers.

Hensley took an appeal and on December 20, 1978, the conviction was overturned by the high court, which ordered a new trial—one day before the first body linked to Gacy was found.

The search of the crawl space at the Gacy house continued on Friday, December 29th. Newsmen surrounded the house, picking up bits here and there, but mainly waiting for news from the medical examiner.

"Gentlemen," Dr. Stein addressed the reporters when he came out that night, "I have horrible news. Six more bodies have been exhumed."

The medical examiner added that there was still more evidence of bodies buried under the Gacy house. Sheriff Elrod and Captain Dobbs made plans for deputies to resume digging in the crawl space on Saturday.

Dr. Stein said there was "some evidence of other remains in the trenches along the south wall." This was an area that had not yet been searched. One quarter of the crawl space still had to be checked.

The medical examiner said that among the six bodies found that day, two were in the same trench, one upon the other, indicating that both had been buried there at the same time. Dr. Stein told the newsmen that the deputies had found a similar case earlier, two in the same grave, one on top of the other. This suggested that Gacy, the accused killer, had been afraid that he would run out of space.

The body count of 28 set a new record for the number of

corpses linked to one man. It exceeded the previous record by one, with a strong possibility that the number would grow.

While the digging was going on, Gacy's lawyer was being told by Circuit Judge John White of the criminal division that "Mr. Gacy will not appear in this courtroom because of fears for his safety."

Gacy's lawyer seemed stunned by Judge White's ruling and stated that he would protest to the chief circuit judge of the criminal division. However, Chief Criminal Circuit Judge Richard J. Fitzgerald had already made the decision. He instructed sheriff's deputies not to move Gacy from the Cook jail to Des Plaines. Although the distance was only 20 miles, he said the security precautions required would be enormous.

The five motions, including a plea for a psychiatric examination of Gacy, could be carried on without the suspect being in the courtroom.

Judge Fitzgerald said Gacy would remain in the county jail which adjoins the Criminal Courts Building at 26th Street and California Avenue in Chicago. Usually, when a prisoner is to appear in a courtroom, he is taken by deputies through an underground tunnel from the jail to the criminal courts building.

"It is a tragedy that a man cannot come to court to face the charges against him," said Gacy's lawyer.

Judge White granted two of the motions—to have Gacy examined by a private psychiatrist as well as by one at the Cook County Psychiatric Institute.

Another motion was for dismissal of the charge against Gacy accusing him of the murder of Robert Piest. The lawyers' ground for the motion to dismiss the charge of murdering Robert Piest was that the boy's body had not yet been found. Judge White said he would rule on the motion at the next hearing, which was set for January 18, 1979.

Bail was requested for Gacy because he was charged with only one crime and the evidence in that was scant. Judge White said he would rule on that also on January 18th.

The attorney asked that Judge White issue an order forbidding police officers, public officials, investigators or witnesses to make statements which would interfere with Gacy's right to a fair trial. White granted this motion.

Meanwhile, Dr. Lawrence Freedman, professor of psychiatry at the University of Chicago, said there was a tendency to stereotype mass killers, but that this was a mistake.

"We wrongly cling to stereotypes such as the assumption that a person who commits heinous crimes must go around looking monstrous," said Dr. Freedman, whose specialty is the study of violence.

Referring to Gacy, described by neighbors as a friendly, hardworking businessman who was popular for entertaining children while dressed in a clown outfit, "Someone who commits violent crimes is not always someone who looks dangerous, who looks like a killer," Dr. Freedman said.

"Aside from tending to be mentally imbalanced," Freedman added, "persons who commit mass murders often wish to be liked and admired. It is not inconsistent with their personalities."

Dr. Freedman noted the similarity between the Hensley murders in Houston and those attributed to Gacy. He said these were "rare incidents."

The Gacy case "is a horrible incident, but it must be seen as an isolated case, not as cause for greater fear of violence in our culture," Dr. Freedman said.

Meanwhile, in Texas, mass killer Hensley had been tried again and found guilty of the murders of 27 teenage boys and young men. However, as this was written, the judge had not set a date for sentencing Hensley, nor had he indicated what the sentence might be.

Inasmuch as Gacy reportedly had told the sheriff's police that he had killed 33 young boys and men, Sheriff Elrod and Chief Dobbs conferred with State's Attorney Bernard Carey and it was decided that search for other bodies would continue until 33 were found or it appeared that the others could not be found.

The search went on, but it was not until Friday, March 16th that the 29th body was found. It was unearthed in the crawl space under the Gacy house that still was standing.

Several times it had been ordered demolished by one judge only to have another judge stay the order. This went on until April 3rd, when the house was reduced to little more than a shell. Then on Tuesday, April 10th, final demolition began. Within a few days the entire house was gone.

On Friday, March 16th, only the driveway was left. This was not overlooked and the digging went on. That day, body number 30 was dug up. There was more digging and two more bodies were uncovered, bringing the total to 32.

More digging in the Gacy driveway and other parts of the property turned up nothing. The search would continued until one more body — number 33 — was found.

The digging yielded nothing more, but the men who were dragging the Des Plaines River worked on doggedly. They came to the intersection of the Illinois River near Morris.

Here they found body number 33. Using pictures, X-ray and dental charts, the body was identified as that of Robert Piest, the boy whose disappearance on Dec. 11th was destined to start the greatest search for bodies ever carried on in the Chicago area. It was to link 33 boys and men to one accused killer, the largest number in Chicago criminal history.

On Saturday, April 14th, the family of Robert Piest announced that a foundation would be established in Robert's memory. Present when the announcement was made were the boy's parents, members of the family, the family attorney and members of the Des Plaines Police Department.

A statement handed out by the family read: "The purpose of the foundation is to recognize the support those individuals and organizations or activities committed to helping reduce crime against children."

The father said the family felt they were not qualified to select those who would get annual grants and a board would be established. Its members would be from the areas of psychology, religion, journalism, medicine, law enforcement, child welfare, and members would be named by the Piest family. The Robert J. Piest foundation will be administered by the First National Bank of Des Plaines.

Several area residents and firms already have promised donations. "There's always more room for people to help out in this field of crimes against children," Mr. Piest said.

Assistant State's Attorney William Kunkle, who is in charge of the team that will prosecute Gacy, told Circuit Judge Louis B. Garippo that he plans to try Gacy first for the murder of Robert Piest. Judge Garippo was an outstanding assistant state's attorney for several years before he ascended the bench. During that first trial, prosecutor Kunkle said, the staff of assistant state's attorneys would try to introduce evidence from the 32 other sex murders for which Gacy was indicted.

One of Gacy's attorneys objected to this. "The State wants to have its cake and eat it, too," he told the judge. "They want to try one case and if they fail, be able to do it 32 more times."

John Wayne Gacy Jr., who'd been in the Cermack Memorial Hospital adjoining the jail after he complained of chest pains, was moved to the security ward of the Cook County Jail on Sunday July 1, 1979. He is now awaiting execution by lethal injection.

EDITORS NOTE:

Jack Dale is not the real name of the person so named in the foregoing story. A fictitious name has been used because there is no reason for public interest in the identity of this person.

Flooded The Valley
Of The Moon With Gore!

by Walt Hecox

He was the Jackal of San Francisco.

Boyes Hot Springs is a pleasant, slightly decaying relic of a time when the century was young and California's Valley of the Moon was a full day's journey, plus a ferryboat ride, from San Francisco. The village was almost sound asleep at three o'clock on the morning of April 14, 1989. But some people were awake, including the night clerk at the Sonoma Mission Inn, a splendid monument to the days when the entire town was a fashionable resort.

Also awake and abroad was the man with distinctly Latin features wearing rough work clothes who walked into the hotel lobby at 3:00 a.m. and wanted to check in. Shaking his head, the night clerk sent him away. Sometimes he wondered about people. Didn't the man know the cheapest single room in the place was priced at $95? That was the bare-bones bottom.

At seven o'clock in the morning, perhaps a dozen miles away, in middle-class, suburban Cotati, a man living on Lakewood Avenue thought he heard people screaming. Then the sound stopped and he pushed it from his mind.

A half-hour later, a man who lived directly across the street from Bob and Marion Richards' home on Lakewood Avenue noticed that the Richards' dog was outside. That

163

was unusual, he thought. The animal was never outside alone. He noticed that Bob Richards' car was gone. It was possible the dog had darted outside, unnoticed, when Bob left for work at the crack of dawn.

The man knocked on the Richards' door. Marion would want to know her dog was outside unattended. His knock was not answered. That, too, he thought, was strange. Ordinarily Marion Richards answered anyone's knock promptly. The neighbor waited a few more moments, knocked again and, when there was no answer, left, bewildered and just a trifle alarmed.

At 8:18 a.m. a sheriff's department dispatcher in nearby Santa Rosa, the Sonoma County seat, received a telephone call from the Kunde Ranch near Kenwood. "There has been a shooting," the dispatcher was informed. "A man has been wounded."

On the surface, the call, which sent Lieutenant Erne Ballinger and Detective Sergeant Mike Brown of the Sonoma County Sheriff's Department out of Santa Rosa, was somewhat alarming.

The incident appeared to be serious, disastrous. A man had been shot in the shoulder and the officers knew he was not critically hurt. Of more concern to Detective Brown and Lieutenant Ballinger was that the man with the gun had left the crime scene and was at large. He might use the weapon again.

Shortly after 8:35 a.m., Sergeant Brown and Lieutenant Ballinger, approaching the scene of the shooting, turned left onto a long, paved lane that rose gently up the slope under an arbor of magnolia trees. The drive curved left again as the hill steepened and rose to the crest of a gentle hill where they parked between the pillared porch of a spotless, shuttered, two-story farmhouse and a gazebo with a round, pointed roof, both of which overlooked the valley.

Ken Butti, the foreman at the Grand Cru Winery, waited for them, a blood-stained bandage on his shoulder, his pale-faced, shaken wife at his side. The winemaker was puzzled, angered and alarmed by what had happened.

164

Butti told the officers that one of the Grand Cru employees had driven to the Butti ranch house a short time ago, parked his car in about the same spot where the sheriff's department men had left theirs, and approached the porch where Butti was sitting. Ken recognized the car. He stood up and started down the steps.

The man, who had climbed out of an aging Ford LTD sedan that had seen better days, was not there for conversation. He leveled a .22 revolver at Butti, mumbled something the foreman never quite heard, and fired twice at almost point-blank range. The winemaker staggered back, wounded in the right shoulder. He heard his wife scream, then saw the man point his gun at her.

"I saw him pull the trigger and heard the hammer click, but there was no explosion," the wounded man told the detectives.

Mrs. Butti had been saved from death or serious injury by a misfire, the detectives decided later, probably because the gun was empty.

The injured man was hard-pressed to find a motive for the shooting. He told the detectives that the winery employee whom he identified as Ramon Salcido, a 28-year-old Mexican national who had migrated to the United States in the early 80's and was now a legal resident of his adopted country, was normally a good worker.

Lately, the foreman said, Ramon had been troubled by a marriage he thought might be falling apart. He was also in some kind of financial jam. The combination had affected his work, Butti explained. He had been forced to talk to the young man about his performance on the job.

He added that the conversation was friendly. Nothing had been said that indicated to Salcido that his job was in danger or might prompt the young man to retaliate.

Of course, the foreman reflected, Salcido might not, obviously did not, share his opinion. He had used his gun once. He might use it again. Based on the fact that he had been shot, Butti believed that if Salcido struck again it would be at the winery.

Sergeant Brown and Lieutenant Ballinger made arrangements for the wounded man to be hospitalized. They also helped Mrs. Butti make plans to leave home and stay with friends. She had witnessed the shooting and Salcido knew it. He had tried to kill her once. There was reason to believe that he might try again.

Then the detectives drove southwest, along tree-lined California Highway 12, toward the Grand Cru Estate Chardonnay vineyards and winery. They had obtained Salcido's Boyes Hot Springs home address from Ken Butti. Grand Cru was on the way. The officers wanted to stop at the winery and warn the workers there of the danger they might face.

Butti told the officers that Ramon Salcido was married to a truly gorgeous woman and was insanely jealous of her. The wounded foreman indicated that Salcido suspected the assistant winemaker at Grand Cru of making improper advances to his wife and he assured the officers that Salcido's suspicions were unfounded. But innocence, he added, might not protect the assistant winemaker.

A couple of miles south of the Kunde Ranch, where Ken Butti was wounded, Dunbar Road, a graveled byway, slashes right diagonally off Highway 12, forming a large, V-shaped piece of property. The Dunbar School is located there. A lofty chainlink fence marks the school-grounds' southern boundary, separating it from the Grand Cru vineyards.

A gate which more often than not is unlocked marks the end of Dunbar Road and the entrance to Grand Cru. Several hundred feet farther down the graveled road the winery and its inevitable tasting room are visible. The remote location of the winery is a standing joke among its employees and owners. Visitors who reach its tasting room are given a special badge. It reads, "I found Grand Cru."

Lieutenant Ballinger and Sergeant Brown found trouble on Dunbar Road before they reached Grand Cru that morning. Young grapevines, so tender and vulnerable that their baby roots were still protected by milk cartons, had been planted just inside the Grand Cru gate. Parked beside them, just off the access road, was an ancient automobile, a sports car of sorts. It was the dark and dusty Volkswagen Karmann Ghia that Tracy Toovey, 35-year-old assistant winemaker at Grand Cru, had been driving since he was a teenager.

Extended from the open door of the little car was the body of Tracy Toovey, half in and half out, his face shattered by almost a half-dozen bullets.

Sergeant Brown and Lieutenant Ballinger called for a physician, but they knew the youth was dead.

It was a Friday. Some children were visible on the baseball field and play-grounds of Dunbar School. There would be more in the classrooms. The officers knew that with a killer on the loose something would have to be done quickly.

The employees of Grand Cru were going about their tasks, oblivious to the fact that their foreman had been shot, that their popular assistant winemaker had been murdered and that possibly they were in extreme danger. Something would have to be done about that, too.

Half a dozen miles farther down Highway 12, past Glen Ellen and a couple of other rustic villages, was Boyes Hot Springs, where Ramon Salcido lived on Baines Street with his beautiful wife and three young daughters. Certainly the lives of Angela Salcido and her three daughters were in danger.

Sergeant Brown and Lieutenant Ballinger intended to do something about that personally.

The officers contacted their dispatcher in Santa Rosa and requested as much help as possible. They spoke to young, energetic Sheriff Dick Michaelsen and explained the problem. Dunbar School might have to be closed or at best the children there confined to their classrooms. The same was true for the employees of Grand Cru.

Salcido's friends and relatives should be contacted immediately. Any one of them might be in danger. Also, they might know where to find the person who the officers believed had killed one man, wounded another and attempted

167

to shoot a woman.

Considering the distances involved, help arrived quickly. Patrol deputies, more detectives and crime scene investigators arrived at Dunbar Road. Plans were made to close the Dunbar School and the staff there began calling the youngsters' parents. No child would venture out of the school without an adult escort that morning.

Sergeant Brown and Lieutenant Ballinger arrived at Baines Street at about 10 o'clock.

Among the area homes, the duplex occupied by the Salcido family is unusual, partly because it sits well back from the street and partly because it is obviously younger than its neighbors. But its white paint with blue trim is also fading and the large, dirt front yard is unkempt and dusty.

Blocking the officers' way to the front door were two tricycles and a little bike with training wheels, the type used by tiny tots. They stepped over the toys and noticed spatters of blood on the white paint.

Looking through a window, the detectives saw more bloodstains in the front room of the tiny apartment. They entered and almost stumbled over the body of a young woman. She was slender, her figure graceful, but the beauty the officers had been told about was hidden beneath bruises inflicted during the brutal beating and crusted blood that had seeped from bullet holes. She was dead and appeared to have been killed within the last few hours. Rigor Mortis was just beginning to stiffen her body.

The officers rushed through the house, fully alert. The killer might still be there. They were also looking for the children who owned the toys which blocked the front door. The officers followed a trail of blood and overturned furniture through the dwelling. Apparently Angela Salcido had tried to escape her killer, fleeing from room to room, until he caught and dispatched her.

Except for the body of Angela Salcido, the house was empty. When they concluded their search, the officers moved outside and spoke with a woman who lived nearby. They asked about the children who lived in the house and were told that they were very young. One was just under two years old, the neighbor said, another three, and the other four.

At the direction of Lieutenant Ballinger and Sergeant Brown, an all-points bulletin describing Ramon Salcido had been broadcast immediately after the shooting of Ken Butti. The suspect was described as 5 feet 9 inches tall, weighing 180 pounds, round-faced with good-looking, Latin features. He would probably be driving a 1979 brown Ford LTD that was somewhat the worse for wear.

The lieutenant called headquarters and added to that description the possibility that Salcido might have with him three daughters—Sofia, 4; Carmina, 3; and Teresa, about 22 months. He also asked that any of the wanted men's friends be contacted if possible and that the Cotati police be instructed to inform Angela Salcido's family of Ramon's apparent rampage. Ken Butti had indicated that Salcido did not like his in-laws. They could be in extreme danger.

At 10:30 a.m., Lieutenant Robert Stewart of the Cotati Police Department, accompanied by Officer Steve Conner and Reserve Officer Alice Caldwell, approached the Richards home on Lakewood Avenue in Cotati. Their knock was unanswered. Eventually they tried the front door, discovered it was unlocked, and entered the house. Later one of them described what they found inside as "a butcher shop."

Lieutenant Stewart and Officer Conner moved into the living room, just beyond the front door, while Reserve Officer Caldwell stood watch at the entrance. There was carnage in the living room, blood on the walls of the previously spotless home. There were bodies on the floor which the policemen had to step over as they moved from room to room, carefully, in case the murderer was still there.

If Ramon Salcido had committed the murders on Lakewood Avenue, he had decided against using his gun. Nor had he made it necessary for the officers to need a medical opinion to know that the people on the floor were dead. Twelve-year-old Ruth Richards' throat had been savagely slashed. Eight-year-old Maria Richards was lying nearby.

169

Her throat had also been cut from ear to ear.

Nearby was the body of 48-year-old Marion Richards, whose life had ended when the knife that killed Maria and Ruth also cut her throat. There was ample evidence in the room that the kindly, somewhat stern and straight-backed, deeply religious woman had fought savagely to protect her daughters. She had obviously been no match for the killer who entered her home that morning.

Away at work was Bob Richards, husband of Marion Richards and father of the two girls.

Moving through the house, searching it, room by room, the officers were sickened by what they saw. The killings made no sense. Certainly they were related to the murders on Dunbar Road and Baines Avenue in the Valley of the Moon, as well as the shooting of the Grand Cru foreman. It was impossible for the Cotati officers to even guess at the common motive.

A winemaker, a young and beautiful woman, a winery foreman, and now two children and their middle-aged mother . . . Their common bond was Ramon Salcido.

Lieutenant Stewart took in the scene. A veteran police officer, he had been hardened to brutal murders, but in this instance, detachment was impossible. He thought about the children. It was always the hardest when children were the victims.

Reserve Officer Alice Caldwell, standing by the door and watching the macabre search, was a veteran of several years as a regular officer on the nearby Novato Police Department. She shifted herself into a detached world as she stood by, looking on as though she were standing on another planet. She would stay detached, remote and aloof as long as she was on duty.

Back in Santa Rosa, Sheriff Michaelsen began to add up the score. Dead, so far, were Tracy Toovey, the Grand Cru winemaker, and Angela Salcido, the beautiful wife of Ramon Salcido. Three people had just been added to the list. They were, his detectives had learned from neighbors, Marion Louise Richards, a 48-year-old housewife, and her two

170

daughters, Ruth and Marie Ann.

The sheriff had every reason to believe the killer was Ramon Salcido, Angela's husband and the man identified by a sixth victim, Ken Butti, as the person who had shot him in the shoulder early that morning.

Beyond all that was the haunting thought that Lieutenant Ballinger and Sergeant Brown had reported that Salcido's three small daughters — little Sofia, Carmina and tiny Teresa — were missing. They had not been seen since the evening before their mother's body was found in the tiny duplex on Baines Avenue in Boyes Hot Springs.

The sheriff, like everyone else in Sonoma County, wondered if the little girls were still alive. Traveling with an alleged killer, they might not live long.

His primary task, the sheriff knew, was to put men in the field who could find the man who had just killed five people, but the thought of the little girls was uppermost in everyone's mind. Everyone in Sonoma County, it seemed, was praying they would be found before they joined the list of murder victims.

Meanwhile, detectives traced Ramon Salcido's history. Through the United States Immigration and Naturalization Service, they learned he had been raised in Los Mochis in the province of Sinaloa, Mexico. Los Mochis is located on Mexican national highway 15, which leads eventually to the fabled resort city of Mazatlan. But Ramon, raised by an upper-middle-class family in Las Mochis, was not interested in the Pacific coast city of Mazatlan.

His eyes, when he was a teenager, were turned north, toward the United States, where he had heard that a man could get rich and then return to Mexico to live out his life in luxury and wealth.

In 1980, Ramon Salcido had slipped across the border somewhere near Calexico, traveled to California's Central Valley, and found work in the vineyards near Fresno, where he met and married a woman who lived there. Through that marriage he obtained a "green card" and became a legal resident of the United States.

171

The Fresno union did not last. Salcido wandered north to the prime Napa, Sonoma, Mendocino Counties wine country, where he met and eventually married Angela.

Angela had been living in Santa Rosa with her parents when she met the young, handsome, worldly Mexican who could not, at the time, speak English. Angela was 19 years old and had never dated before meeting Salcido. She was a product of a cloistered world. Her parents, devout Catholics, disapproved of the fast-moving life of the '80s.

For the most part, Marion Richards kept her daughters at home and served as their schoolteacher herself. They were not allowed to play or associate with other children. An excellent seamstress, Marion made her daughters' and her own clothes and many of her husband's shirts. Until the day Angela met Ramon, the Richards family nevertheless seemed happy and content.

Then Angela began slipping out of her bedroom window at night to keep trysts with her Mexican lover. She did not know a word of Spanish and he knew few in English, but apparently they overcame the language barrier. They made love in the back seat of Ramon's ancient LTD. Before long it became obvious that she was pregnant. Angrily, Mrs. Richards had announced that her daughter would marry. But Ramon Salcido was hardly received with open arms by Angela's family. He was a disliked intruder and he knew it. He returned the dislike with a smouldering hatred.

Trouble loomed some 250 miles to the south, in California's central valley, for Salcido. He had neglected to divorce his Fresno wife, whom he had married in Reno, Nevada. Sergeant Brown and Lieutenant Ballinger, questioning as many friends and relatives of the Salcido family as possible, learned that Angela—who had been told by Ramon when they married that she was his first wife—had learned of the Fresno marriage.

By then, she had mothered three lovely daughters for Ramon and had been introduced to a world she had never known as a cloistered child in Santa Rosa and Cotati. More important, others had discovered her rare beauty.

To augment the scanty income Ramon's $8-an-hour salary from the winery, she had used her skills as a seamstress, learned from her mother, to build up a small dressmaking business. While making dresses she had been contacted by one of Santa Rosa's two modeling agencies. Executives there could see a future in television commercials for her. She began attending modeling school. Ramon, intensely jealous of his beautiful wife, had "hit the ceiling," in the words of a neighbor.

Salcido was apparently correct if he felt his marriage was falling apart. Friends and neighbors of Angela told the police that if she had known where to go or how to hide from her hot-tempered husband, she would have done so long before April 14, 1989. She was sick of his rages, his jealousy, his possessive attitude.

Violent quarrels broke out in the Salcido half of the duplex on Baines Street. The neighbors were aware of a lot of yelling and screaming. But they didn't think much about it.

Sergeant Brown learned that on March 11, 1989, Salcido's troubles in Fresno and his turbulent home life began to close in on him. A Fresno County judge ordered the winery worker to pay $511 a month in child support to his wife there. The same court ordered him to repay $5,807 to the Social Services Department there, representing payments made to his wife by the Fresno County welfare department.

From neighbors and friends, the detective also learned that Angela had been in contact with Salcido's Fresno wife. After consulting with her predecessor, the young woman had contacted Reno authorities and learned that Ramon had been married there. She also discovered there was no record of a divorce in either Nevada or California.

Another friend told the investigator that Angela had been ready to seek her freedom through an annulment. Only her fear of Ramon had kept her from making the move earlier. But the young woman's courage was growing. Several times in the past she had cancelled appointments to make television commercials because of Ramon's opposition, threats and temperamental outbursts. But another appointment

173

was scheduled for mid-April. A friend said she had asked Angela what Ramon had said about the date. "Oh, he hit the ceiling," Angela had replied. "But I'm not going to let him stop me. I can handle him."

Almost everybody under 90 years old was, according to Angela's friends, suspected by Ramon of making improper advances on his wife. One of his prime suspects was Tracy Toovey, the affable, charismatic assistant winemaker at Grand Cru. The people who provided that information also told the detectives that an affair between Angela and Toovey was totally impossible. Toovey, they said, was completely devoted to his wife and two small children.

Workers at Grand Cru told the detectives that Salcido's troubles were beginning to affect his work. Often he was late and at other times he would take a company truck and drive off to Boyes Hot Springs where he would cruise Baines Street to check on his wife's activities.

Until that time he had been a valued employee and the detectives were told that Grand Cru foreman Ken Butti had been counseling him, hoping to salvage a man who had been an excellent worker.

If the tales told by some acquaintances of Salcido's were true, Grand Cru and Butti might not have placed quite such a high value on Ramon as an employee or on correcting his deteriorating behavior.

The investigators looked at the list of names and believed, from what they had learned, that they knew how and why Salcido had selected his victims. What they could not explain was exactly what had ignited the fuse that touched off his rampage early Friday morning.

Salcido, Sergeant Brown learned, was a fairly heavy drinker and was at best a steady, recreational user of crack cocaine. People who drank with him at his favorite taverns liked him. They remembered him as a pleasant companion who sometimes brought his beautiful wife to both places.

Tracing Salcido's movements on Tuesday evening, April 13th, Sergeant Brown and Lieutenant Ballinger learned that he had been on a prolonged drinking binge that night.

People at both bars indicated that he seemed to be financing the booze bout with bottles of Grand Cru champagne, which he was selling for $5 each.

Neighbors of Salcido's indicated that it was not rare for the forklift operator to have a large quantity of the winery's champagne. They did not know how he got it, but they had their suspicions.

As probers followed Salcido's movement, trying to find some hint of where he might be hiding, they uncovered one reassuring piece of information. A schoolbus driver in Boyes Hot Springs reported having seen Ramon driving his LTD at 8:30 on Friday morning. The bus driver said three little girls were with him.

A report by the night clerk at the Sonoma Mission Inn had puzzled the investigators. He remembered a man in workclothes with Latin features attempting to check into the hotel at three o'clock in the morning. It might have been Salcido. The clerk had examined a photograph of Salcido and thought he was the man.

Radio and television reports describing the multiple murders were by then bringing a host of telephone calls to sheriff's headquarters. Salcido, it seemed, had been seen all over the western United States. Every lead had to be followed and all the leads, to that point, were false. Sheriff Michaelsen had every available person in his department working on the manhunt.

Of primary importance in everyone's mind were the little girls. Detectives wondered if Salcido simply meant to take them with him while he fled, probably to his native Mexico.

The men searching for him and the children were haunted by the possibility that he might use the knife or the gun he had used to kill his other five victims on them.

As the manhunt spread and the day waxed into afternoon, some solid clues began reaching the Sonoma County investigators. A routine check of the automated teller machine by employees at the Wells Fargo Bank in San Rafael, 30 miles south of Santa Rosa in Marin County, revealed that Salcido had attempted to withdraw money there using his credit card. His request had been denied; He was over-drawn.

Sheriff's officers immediately contacted Wells Fargo. They arranged for Salcido to have unlimited credit until he was caught. A trail of creditcard purchases and withdrawal would give law enforcement officials a trail to follow that might lead to his capture. The lives of three little girls were at stake. Wells Fargo executives agreed to cooperate.

A second report revealed that Salcido had purchased a set of workclothes, khaki shirt and trousers, in a San Rafael store with his credit card. Later that afternoon a third report reached Sonoma County investigators from San Rafael. The news was simultaneously encouraging and ominous.

Ramon Salcido's 1967 Ford LTD had been found parked on a San Rafael street not far from a Golden Gate transit terminal. The interior of the car was soaked with blood. A .22-caliber pistol was found on the front seat.

There was a note, handwritten in Spanish, on the seat. When translated the detective learned it said, "Forgive me, God, but this law made me do it. We could live better, me and my children but what can I do . . ."

Sonoma County officers told each other that the blood in the car might be Salcido's. There had been evidence at the Richards' home in Cotati that while Marion fought val-iantly to defend her children she might have stabbed her murderer.

But the same investigators were inclined to wonder how Ramon would board public transit with three little girls without drawing attention to himself. There was a chance he might intend to return to the LTD and continue his flight after dark.

Four detectives set up a stakeout near the car. They waited for hours, but Salcido did not return. Convinced that the fugitive had used public transit to cross the Golden Gate bridge where he might hide with drug-dealing friends in San Francisco, the probers cancelled the stakeout and had the ancient Ford towed to Santa Rosa.

From Wells Fargo executives, the sheriff's department in Santa Rosa had learned that early Friday afternoon that Salcido had attempted to withdraw funds from an automated teller at a bank in San Francisco.

From the Mexican consulate in Sacramento, the detectives received a report that a man had appeared there on Friday afternoon and asked for papers which would make it possible for him to travel to Mexico. The report was never verified. The clerk who had supposedly spoken to Salcido could not be found.

Between one and two o'clock on Saturday afternoon, while the futile search for Ramon Salcido and his daughters continued, a young man wandered along the edge of a quarry on State Gulch Road, which twists and winds through the lonely hills that separate Santa Rosa from Petaluma, its largest southern neighbor some 16 miles to the south.

The quarry bordered a county dump and the young man hoped to find a makeshift tool there which would help him lift a used camper-shell onto the bed of his pickup truck. He stopped when he saw what looked like two broken dolls lying on the grassy earth at the bottom of the embankment. A moment or so passed before the young man realized that he was looking at the bodies of two little girls. He ran to the quarry office and found the superintendent.

After calling for help, the two men returned to the quarry's edge. They stared at the two mute faces of a pair of little girls who appeared to be quite dead. Then they saw the third, a dark-haired little beauty clad in a filthy, blood-encrusted nightgown. She was sitting down, staring off into space, not making a sound.

The young man who had been looking for a tool ran back to the telephone to make sure an ambulance was on its way to the quarry. The superintendent scrambled down the bank and asked the little girl what was the matter.

She could not speak. The quarry superintendent could see why immediately. The little girl was Carmina Salcido, just a week short of three years old. Her throat had been cut from ear to ear. She was made mute then and has not said a word since, although surgeons assured her relatives that the operation was successful and that some day she would speak again.

The two doll-like bodies were those of Teresa Salcido, not quite two years old, and Sofia, who was almost four. Both of them were beyond help.

Ramon Salcido's death toll had increased from five dead and one wounded to seven dead, with two injured. The search for the little girls, at least, had ended. Tragic little Carmina was the one spot of relief in an otherwise miserable day.

By that time, the dragnet set up to capture Ramon Salcido had spread throughout the western United States and, secretly, into Mexico. Some local law enforcement authorities believed that Salcido was lying low, staying with friends in a drug-oriented underworld until he felt it was safe to travel to Mexico.

In Fresno, believing that Ramon Salcido might believe he had unfinished business with his wife and daughter there, law enforcement authorities moved the woman and her child to a new address. They planned to keep them under cover until after his capture. Around-the-clock guards were provided for the thoroughly frightened young woman and her little girl.

Some law enforcement authorities figured that Ramon would have difficulty finding a place to hide even with underworld friends. In their interview, few people on either side of the law have anything but contempt for a man who deliberately murdered little girls.

But for Sonoma County investigators, still working around the clock, a nightmare persisted. Salcido might make it to Mexico and fight extradition. Although an extradition treaty exists with Mexico, it had never been enforced when a Mexican citizen was involved. It was possible that Salcido might be tried in Mexico for his crimes, but Mexico has no death penalty. In Sonoma County, the men following Salcido's bloody trail felt that his was a capital case if ever there was one.

On the plus side, a series of trust funds had been established for the victims of Ramon Salcido. In addition to that, rewards totalling $40,000, topped by $25,000 donated by the Sonoma County Board of Supervisors, were offered for information leading to the arrest of Salcido.

In Fresno, despite the lack of confirmation in Sacramento, security measures around Salcido's wife there tightened. Clues indicated that the suspect was back in the central valley and would probably head south. Law enforcement officers in Fresno wondered if Ramon would head directly for Mexico or pause in the central California city for one more act of violence.

On the theory that Salcido would certainly cross state lines in an unlawful flight to avoid prosecution, the Federal Bureau of Investigation joined the search.

Sheriff's deputies in Sonoma County were hanging their hopes on another arm of the federal government — if Salcido reached Mexico. They knew that, scattered across Mexico's many states, working hand in glove with Mexican lawmen, was a thin, active line of Drug Enforcement Agency operatives. Some of those agents were located in Mazatlan, about 100 miles south of Los Mochis, Salcido's home town.

Mexican authorities were contacted and they promised to cooperate with the search. South of the border, Ramon was already known as "The Jackal of San Francisco."

Sheriff's detectives knew Ramon was heading south. A thin trail of ATM receipts marked his progress through the central valley. Always they materialized hours too late.

A telephone call from Los Mochis reached sheriff's detectives. A man who claimed he was Salcido's brother-in-law said Ramon was hiding out in his mother's house in the Mexican city. He reported that his sister thought he was a danger to everyone in his family and didn't want him there.

The Sonoma County officers contacted the DEA officers in Mexico City and told them what was happening. Agents there and the Mexican Judicial Police agreed to cooperate. But Mexico City is a long way from Los Mochis. The clos-

179

est DEA agents to Salcido were stationed in Mazatlan on the Mexican coast, where the Sea of Cortes opens into the Pacific Ocean, 100 miles south of Los Mochis.

On Monday morning, DEA agents from Mazatlan, with the Mexican Judicial Police, headed for Los Mochis. As they traveled north, a hitch developed in their plans. From Los Angeles, an enterprising reporter from the *Times* had traveled to Salcido's hometown and was asking questions in that city. Apparently hearing about the reporter, Salcido fled. He headed south to his grandmother's house in Orbabamoa. There had been room in his mother's house in Los Mochis. She was employed as a nurse and his stepfather was a civil servant. With both adult members of the family employed, they were considered well off and lived fairly comfortably. But in Orbabamoa, Salcido's grandmother's house was a crumbling shanty.

Salcido's move frightened his sister. Already alarmed and angry, she told the family that her brother should not be moving from home to home. After a short conference the family decided Ramon should travel farther south to Guadalajara, an inland metropolis between Mexico City and Puerto Vallerta.

Salcido's sister had no intention of allowing him to reach Guadalajara. She contacted the DEA and told them her brother would be taking a train south from Bamoa, site of the railroad station about two miles outside the village.

He headed for the railroad station late that night, getting out of his grandmother's house just in time to avoid several truckloads of Mexican Judicial Police. When the police raided and searched Salcido's grandmother's home and the house across the street, their quarry was gone.

Other Mexican police had traveled with DEA agents to the depot in Bamoa. There they found Ramon Salcido, waiting for his train. He surrendered without incident. The manhunt which had sprawled over 1500 miles and spread through two countries was over.

Back in California's Sonoma County, sheriff's investigators wondered what would happen next. District Attorney

Gene Tunney, son of the heavyweight boxing champion, promised to start early proceedings if that was necessary. He hoped there would be other alternatives. Mexico's record for allowing its own citizens to be extradited to another country was zero. People in the know in the United States were predicting that Salcido would be tried in Mexico, where there is no death penalty.

The people who knew did not count on the feelings of the people of Mexico or their president, Carlos Salinas De Gortari. Neither the people nor their president wanted any part of the man they called "The Jackal of San Francisco." Any reason to get rid of him was good enough.

Salcido himself had given the Mexican president all the reason he thought he needed. Ramon had told Mexican officials he was a citizen of the United States. The president of Mexico thought that over, decided that the fugitive had entered the country illegally and personally ordered him deported.

Back in Sonoma County, sheriff's department personnel decided they had better move fast before anyone south of the border had a change of heart. Deputy Craig Schulz, son of the famed originator of the comic strip, "Peanuts," who lives in Santa Rosa, was notified.

A short time later, Craig Schulz was piloting his father's private jet, with five deputy sheriffs as passengers, to Los Mochis.

Everyone on the plane knew there was no legal way they could transport Salcido back to the United States without his permission. The man was manacled, but technically he was returning to the USA of his own free will. Handcuffs or not, he never changed his mind.

He also did a lot of talking. Interviewed by a Mexican television reporter, he confessed all of his crimes on the air. To a San Francisco television reporter, he responded, "Not really!" when asked if he had any regrets.

Salcido admitted that on the night of April 13th, upset about the judgements in Fresno and his deteriorating marriage, he visited his favorite bar, drank until he ran out of money, and then continued his binge, financing it with the sale of bottles of Grand Cru champagne. To the booze he drank, he added a few liberal snorts of cocaine.

Arriving home when the bars closed, he found his three daughters there asleep and alone. Angela was gone. Still drinking booze and champagne, he cruised through town looking for her. When he didn't find her, he returned to Baines Street, loaded his three daughters into the LTD and headed toward the quarry. Standing at the edge of the big pit he cut their throats one after the other and dumped them down the embankment. Then he headed toward the Richards home.

Only chance, almost a miracle, saved little Carmina's life. She had landed on her head, lost consciousness and stayed in that position. The weight on her head had effectively closed her wound so the blood coagulated before she regained consciousness. Her sisters, who landed on their backs, bled to death. From there Salcido headed for the home of his in-laws in Cotati.

After the slaughter on Lakewood Street — Salcido left a dead body in three different rooms — he returned home, chased his wife through the house from room to room, and eventually killed her. Tracy Toovey was his next victim and Ken Butti, rather than the first, was the last.

The detectives listened to that blood-curdling story holding their collective breath, hoping Salcido would not demand his freedom before the plane reached the United States. Craig Schulz was forced to land in Hermosillo for fuel and the detectives waited impatiently. Anytime he wanted, Salcido could have demanded to be freed and could have walked away.

Not until the plane landed and cleared customs in San Diego, did the officers breathe freely. At last they were in the United States. The arrest warrants for seven murders were then served by the deputies traveling with Salcido.

The following Friday, Ramon Salcido appeared in a Santa Rosa Municipal Court to be arraigned on seven charges of murder and three of attempted murder.

Television cameras focused in on him while his old friends in his favorite Boyes Hot Springs saloon watched.

It was a strange scene. The television set, perched precariously above the bar, was suddenly tuned to the courtroom with Salcido occupying the center of the screen. Conversation in the bar stopped. Everything stopped. Glasses paused, midway to lips. People entered and halted in midstride. A man on his way to the bathroom froze for a moment, turned around, and stood still.

No one moved until the short arraignment was over. The faces of Ramon's old friends could have been carved in granite. They didn't move a muscle, blink an eye, twitch a lip.

When it was over, ice could be heard moving in glasses. Somebody sighed. Someone else coughed. But no one spoke. Not for a long, long time.

Salcido is in the Sonoma County Jail now, awaiting trial for the crimes of which he is accused. Detectives say that a mass of physical evidence, in addition to his confession, ties him to the crime and verifies his account of the murders and their sequence.

Of course, in accordance with due process as provided for by the Constitution, he must be presumed innocent of all charges until and unless proven otherwise in a court of law.

We've Captured The Most Dangerous Serial Killers!

by Jack G. Heise

U.S.A.
JULY 28, 1984

The man clad in blue jeans and a yellow T-shirt with a can of beer in his hand lounged on the bleachers overlooking the basketball courts in the playfield. An attractive young woman rested her head on his shoulder.

To the casual observer on the warm Friday afternoon of July 20, 1984, in Evanston, Illinois, they appeared to be a couple who had gone out for a stroll and stopped to rest.

But not to the keen eyes of Detective Susan Triquorea. Dressed in plain clothes and driving an unmarked car, she looked the couple over as she sowly cruised by the playfield.

Triquorea drove her car around the block and came back for another look. Driving past the playfield, she parked her car where she could still see the bleachers.

With difficulty to contain her excitement, Triquorea opened the mike in her car to give her name and location to the radio dispatcher at headquarters.

"I've spotted Coleman and Brown," she said.

"You're sure?" the dispatcher asked.

"Coleman has cut his hair short, but I'm positive it is the Brown girl," Triquorea responded.

"Don't try to take them!" the dispatcher warned. "Just keep an eye on them and I'll get backup units there right away. In the meantime, sit tight."

The report from detective Triquorea created a flurry of excitement and action. Police cars in the area raced toward the playfield while more officers sped to the spot from headquarters.

The couple Triquorea had sighted were Alton Coleman and Debra Denise Brown, labelled by the FBI at the time as the most dangerous serial killers in the nation.

Coleman had the dubious distinction of being only the 10th man in the 34 years the FBI had issued its "10 Most Wanted Fugitives" to have his name added as number 11.

For two months police agencies and federal officers had followed a bloody trail of kidnappings, rapes, robberies and murders that Coleman and Brown had left in six states.

It began on May 29, 1984, in Kenosha, Wisconsin, when nine-year-old Vernita Wheat coaxed her mother into letting her go with some acquaintances to Waukegan, Illinois, where they were to pick up a stereo.

The girl's mother had met the young couple and they seemed to be nice people. She became worried, however, when Vernita did not return home in the evening. In the morning, she called the police. Unfortunately, she knew the couple only by the names Paul and Diana Fisher. She did not know where they lived, as she had met them only at the times they came to her home.

The Kenosha police contacted the police in Waukegan with the information and requested assistance in locating the girl if she had been taken there.

While the search for Vernita was going on, 70 miles south of Kenosha in Gary, Indiana, seven-year-old Tamika Turks and her nine-year-old relative were walking home from a playfield when a couple in a car stopped them to ask directions.

With a promise of a dollar if the girls would get into the car and show them the way, the youngsters climbed into the vehicle.

Under the threat of being cut with a knife by the man, the girls were driven to a rural area where Tamika was raped. Her relative managed to escape and outrun the man who pursued her. The man gave up the chase, when the girl ran screaming toward a house.

Lawmen found the lifeless body of Tamika with numerous, fatal stab wounds in her body.

Tamika's relative gave police a description of the couple who had abducted them and killed Tamika. The description resembled the couple who had supposedly taken Vernita Wheat to Waukegan.

The information and descriptions were forwarded to the Waukegan police.

Chief Kenneth Rychman in Waukegan was almost certain he knew who the couple might be. He and his homicide detectives had been attempting to build a case against them for the murder of 15-year-old Gina Frasier.

Rychman pulled the rap sheet on Alton Coleman, a 28-year-old native of Waukegan, although he had most of the information in his head. Rychman had encountered Coleman while he had been chief of the Juvenile Division.

The rap sheet, as long as a man's arm, listed charges covering almost every type of crime from malicious mischief for breaking school windows, to auto theft, burglaries, robberies, rapes and suspicion of murder.

Born in the black ghetto of Waukegan Coleman had been raised by his elderly grandmother.

As a youngster he had a difficult time because of a vulgar nickname that had been pinned on him as the result of being a perennial bed-wetter. As Coleman grew older, however, he assumed a position of leader among the gangs along McAlister Avenue.

Shrewd and a smooth talker, Coleman was recognized by his shiny red pullover shirts and his Afro-style hair covered with a hair net and black cap. Coleman bragged that he had never held a steady job. He earned his living on the streets from gambling, thievery and conning elderly people by his beguiling manner.

His first sex offense, according to police records, was against a pre-teenage relative. The charges were dropped when the relative refused to testify against him.

Coleman spent his 21st birthday in jail on a charge of having raped a 17-year-old girl. Again, charges were withdrawn when she refused to testify, as did a number of other victims.

186

The investigators suspected, but could not prove, that the reluctance of the witnesses to testify was the result of threats of what he would do to them if he was convicted and then let out on parole.

The only hard time Coleman served was for a robbery conviction. While in the Joliet Correction Center, he was accused of having molested other male prisoners.

At this time, he underwent a psychiatric examination. The report stated that Coleman was considered to be a "pansexual, willing to have intercourse with any object, women, men, children, whatever."

It described Coleman as having "a grandiose personality, so self-centered that he could never realize anything could be wrong with him and unable to relate or care for others."

The young woman who had been living and traveling with Coleman for the past several years was 21-year-old Debra Denise Brown, another resident of Waukegan's ghetto.

The fifth child in a family of 11 children, and a high school dropout, Debra had been engaged to be married when she met Coleman in a bar and became "his woman."

Relatives saw little of Debra after she left to go with Coleman. The few times they did see her they claimed that she acted like a robot, doing the biddings of Coleman.

The day following the disappearance of Vernita Wheat from Kenosha, Coleman was due to appear in the Lake County Illinois Circuit Court for a pre-trial hearing on a charge of having raped a 14-year-old Chicago girl. He did not make an appearance.

And the day following the rape and murder of Tamika Turks in Gary, the police received a missing persons report for 25-year-old Donna M. Williams. Witnesses stated that she was last seen talking to a couple who resembled the descriptions given by the girl who had escaped from them at the time Tamika had been murdered.

Chief Rychman sent photos of Coleman and Brown to the police in Kenosha and Gary.

A relative of missing Vernita Wheat tentatively identified them as the couple she knew as Paul and Diana Fisher with whom Vernita had asked permission to go to Waukegan.

The young relative of Tamika Turks also allegedly identified Coleman and Brown as the couple who had abducted them and killed Tamika.

At the time the identifications were being made, the decomposing corpse of Vernita Wheat was found in a ditch outside of Waukegan. A postmortem revealed she had been stabbbed numerous times.

With tentative identification of Coleman and Brown as the abductors, Waukegan law enforcement authorities placed charges of kidnapping and first-degree murder against the pair of fugitives.

In addition, Chicago authorities requested federal assistance on a charge that Coleman was a fugitive from justice for failing to appear in court on the rape charge.

While the search for the fugitives continued, a young woman reported to the police in Detroit that a couple had entered her car while she was stopped for a traffic light and forced her, at knifepoint, to drive toward Ohio.

When the car ran low on gasoline, she drove into a service station and managed to escape. The couple took off in her car. She tentatively identified Coleman and Brown as the couple who had abducted her and stole her car.

Late the following afternoon, a couple in Dearborn Heights, Michigan, reported to the police that a man and woman had entered their home and robbed them. The couple said that when they were unable to convince the pair that they did not have additional money hidden in their home, they had been severely beaten.

They tentatively identified Coleman and Brown as the persons who had robbed and beaten them.

Coleman and Brown were reported to have been in Detroit two days later. A couple picked up two hitchhikers, a man and a woman. The male hitchhiker threatened them with a knife and robbed them. The victims were dumped out of the car on a rural road. They allegedly identified photos of Coleman and Brown as the hitchhikers who had robbed them and stole their car.

Later the same day another couple in Detroit reported that a man and woman had broken into their home, had beaten and robbed them and had taken their car. They tentatively identified Coleman and Brown as the persons who had attacked them.

As the search for the fugitives was concentrated in the Detroit area, the police in Toledo, Ohio, received a report from a couple that a man and woman had invaded their home, robbed them of $190 and stole their car. They allegedly identified Coleman and Brown as the assailants.

As the police in Toledo were searching for the car that had been taken after the robbery, a man and woman came to the home of Virginia Temple.

They said they had been hitchhiking and ran out of money and asked if they could spend the night at her home.

Despite the fact that the 30-year-old Mrs. Temple had five children and lived on welfare in a small house, she invited them in, fixed them a meal and let them spend the night.

In the morning the couple were gone and so was Mrs. Temple and her eldest nine-year-old daughter Rachelle. The younger children, ranging in age from one to six, went to the home of a neighbor. They said they didn't know why their mother and Rachelle would leave them without fixing their breakfasts.

Neighbors called the police. The youngsters told the officers about the couple who had come to their home and spent the night. Checking out the house, the officers noted what appeared to be signs of a struggle and bloodstains in the bedroom where Rachelle had been sleeping.

After the youngsters described the strangers who had been in the house, they were shown photos of Coleman and Brown. The children said they looked like the people who spent the night at their home.

Mrs. Temple did not own a car and the couple who came to the house had been on foot. The question was what had happened and where could they have gone.

A short time later, sleuths had part of the answer. Police Captain James Weigand and Detective Tom Cameron found the bodies of Mrs. Temple and her daughter stuffed into a crawlspace beneath the house. Both had been viciously stabbed to death.

The physical evidence indicated that Coleman had most likely attempted to rape the nine-year-old girl during the night and her mother had come to try to protect her.

With the latest murders credited to Alton Coleman and Debra Brown, police officers investigating the various cases met in Chicago to form a task force with a plan to capture the fugitives.

H. Ernest Woodby, agent-in-charge of the Milwaukee office of the FBI, conducted the meeting. He informed the group that the FBI was starting a new division that would be devoted solely to develop information concerning serial killers.

He said that the United States, which accounts for only five percent of the world population, produces three times as many serial killers as the rest of the human race and that there have been 120 serial killers reported in the United States over the past 20 years as compared to only 40 in the rest of the world.

Coleman and Brown fit the pattern of many of the serial killers in that they moved quickly from one place to another, making it difficult for investigators to catch up with them.

They varied from the norm only in that they were not selective of their victims. Most often, a serial killer will select one type of victim and go from place to place searching out only that type.

Christopher Wilder went from Florida to the West Coast and back across the country to New Hampshire abducting and killing young women he enticed by offering them jobs as fashion models. The Green River Strangler in Seattle, Washington, who had been credited with killing 25 young women, selected the victims he thought were prostitutes.

Albert De Salvo who confessed to being "The Boston Strangler" killed only elderly women. Elmer Wayne Henley, the Texas mass murderer, and John Wayne Gacy of Chicago killed only boys and young men. Ted Bundy, then awaiting execution in Florida, killed only young women.

Chief Rychman, who possibly knew Alton Coleman the best, reported that Coleman sometimes dressed as a woman to escape identification when he knew the police were looking for him. He said it was also a characteristic of Coleman to use a bicycle rather than a car while he was in a city.

"It's a clever ploy," Rychman said. "Who is going to suspect that a vicious criminal would be riding around on a bike?"

Agent Woodby reported that he had received word from Assistant FBI Director Oliver Revell that the bureau was adding Coleman's name to the list of the "10 Most Wanted Fugitivies" and that photographs and information concerning Coleman and Brown would be distributed to every police agency in the nation.

The immediate concern of the group was to get to the fugitives as quickly as possible before there were more murders.

Woodby suggested one course of action. He said he would issue a statement that the investigators believed Debra Brown was an unwilling accomplice of Coleman.

"I know most of you don't think this is true," Woodby said, "but she is probably pretty frightened by now and aware of the consequences, and it may be enough to entice her to voluntarily surrender."

The others agreed to go along with the FBI statement concerning Brown. The statement was issued, along with a warning for persons in the Great Lakes area to be wary of strangers and to keep an eye on their children.

On the same evening that the police officers were meeting in Chicago, a college professor from Williamsburg, Kentucky, was abducted from a motel room in Lexington while on a visit there.

A man and a woman entered his motel room and robbed him at knifepoint. Next, they forced him into the trunk of his car. It wasn't known that he was missing until the car was found in Dayton, Ohio. The professor was unhurt.

"All they wanted was my money and my car," he said. "I can be thankful for that."

The professor identified Coleman and Brown as the couple who had abducted him.

A 79-year old minister and his wife in Dayton weren't so fortunate, however. A man and woman broke into their home. After robbing them of the cash they had, the elderly reverend and his wife were severely beaten. They identified Coleman and Brown as the couple who had assaulted them.

While Dayton Police Chief Tyree Broomfield and his offi-

191

cers were searching for Coleman and Brown, a couple on bicycles rode up to a house where a 71-year-old man and his wife were holding a yard sale.

The couple on the bicycles expressed interest in a pickup truck with a camper that was being offered for sale. The couples went inside the house to discuss the purchase of the vehicle. Once inside, the man and his wife were bound and gagged.

After robbing the victims, the couple abandoned their bicycles and took off in the victim's car. The couple who were robbed identified Coleman and Brown.

Road blockades were set up around Dayton with the hope that the stolen automobile might be spotted before the fugitives abandoned it. However, if Coleman followed his usual routine, he would likely abandon the car within a short time.

The stolen car was located the next day alongside a car wash in Indianapolis. When the police arrived on the scene, they discovered that the 77-year-old owner of the car wash, Eugene Scott, was missing, as was his 1970 Chevrolet Biscayne.

A few hours later Scott's body was found in a ditch near Zionsville, Indiana. He had been repeatedly stabbed and shot four times in the head. Even more tragic was that the victim, Scott, had been murdered on his birthday.

A new alert went out for Coleman and Brown with the license and description of the stolen car.

The bloody exploits of the fugitives had become national news. Pictures of the wanted pair appeared in newspapers and on television.

"I don't know how much longer they will stay in this area," Agent Woodby informed the news media. "They know they are wanted for murder and have nothing to lose by committing more murders. We suspect that they may flee to some other part of the country."

On the Friday afternoon of July 20th, police in Evanston, Illinois received a tip from a caller who identified himself as having been a boyhood friend of Coleman.

"He was with that woman Debra Brown," the caller said. "I didn't talk to him because I was afraid he would recognize me, and he might have killed me."

He named the area where he had seen Coleman and Brown. When the police discovered the abandoned car of the elderly man who had been slain in Indianapolis, they knew that the tipster had been right about having spotted Coleman.

The big question was how long the fugitives would stay in Evanston. If they followed their normal pattern, it probably would be only a few hours before they abducted someone else and fled in a stolen vehicle.

Off-duty police officers were called back to duty to join the other officers combing the city for the fugitives.

Detective Triquorea spotted the wanted pair at the playfield about a quarter-mile from where the car had been abandoned.

Following instructions, she kept a watch on Coleman and Brown as the backup units sped to the area.

"It looks like the Brown woman is leaving," Triquorea reported. "Coleman is still in the bleachers."

"Let the woman go," she was told. "Just keep an eye on Coleman."

Sergeant George Scharm was the first officer to arrive after the alert had been given by Triquorea. Using his radio, he told Triquorea, "Wait until I take Coleman before you go after the woman."

Sergeant Kathryn Hynds joined Triquorea. They watched as Brown strolled across the playfield. Scharm entered the playfield and went up to where Coleman was sprawled on the bleacher seat.

Belying the tenseness he felt, Scharm gave no outward appearance of noticing Coleman until he was within a few feet of him.

Scharm whipped out his weapon, pointed it at Coleman's head and shouted, "Put your hands on your head!"

Coleman complied. "What's this all about officer?" he questioned.

"You know what this is all about," Scharm informed him. "You are Alton Coleman and you are under arrest on a charge of suspicion of murder."

Coleman laughed and appeared completely at ease as he gave Scharm another name and said that Scharm was mistaken in thinking that he was Coleman.

Triquorea and Hynds had already left their cars when they saw Scharm draw his gun on Coleman. They went up to Brown as she crossed the playfield, and both drew their guns and informed her that she was under arrest.

Brown did not deny her identity. She surrendered a purse she was carrying. Inside was a .38-caliber pistol.

More officers from the backup units arrived. Coleman was handcuffed. A search of his person produced a blood-stained knife in his boot. Another blood-stained knife was found strapped to his waist.

Taken to police headquarters, Brown admitted his identity and said he knew from reading the newspapers that he and Brown were wanted on numerous crime charges, including murder.

Advised of their legal rights, both Brown and Coleman chose to remain silent and be represented by an attorney.

They were taken before United States Magistrate Carl B. Sussman on the federal charges of being fugitives from justice.

United States Attorney Jeremy Margolis asked the court to set bond for each of the defendants at $50 million. When attorneys appointed to represent the defendants protested that it was excessively high, Margolis said, "No persons in this nation are a greater flight risk."

Magistrate Sussman set bond at $20 million for Brown and $25 million for Coleman, stating that the unusually high bond had been set "because this nation, this community, has been under a siege — a reign of terror, not knowing who the next victim might be."

Coleman and Brown were tried separately for the murders of Marlene Walters and Tonnie Storey in Cincinnati. Both were convicted and sentenced to death. Coleman was convicted and sentenced to death in Indiana for the murder of Tamika Turks. He was sentenced to die in Illinois for the kidnap and murder of Vernita Wheat.

The Yorkshire Ripper!

by Richard Walton

From court records, detailed reports of the murders of
13 women.

Waxwork pale and insignificant, a man who would vanish
in a crowd the moment he stepped into it, 35-year-old Bradford truck driver Peter Sutcliffe, who goes down in history
as "The Yorkshire Ripper" and Britain's worst mass-mur-
derer, gave police the runaround of the century as he butchered 13 women and tried to kill seven others.

He has left the police on his killing ground with very unpleasant egg on their face and there are already top-level
demands by Members of Parliament for an independent
public inquiry into their conduct of the five-year $8,000,000
investigation, apart from the internal one already announced by West Yorkshire's Chief Constable Ronald Gregory.

The much-vaunted and publicized 200-strong Ripper
Squad fell down badly on the job, for under a mountain of
paperwork and computer printouts, growing each day with
alarming proportion like the Quatermass Experiment of fiction, they already had all the facts needed to catch the killer
and had interviewed him nine times.

And when in a blaze of publicity, top detectives from all
over Britain were formed into a super-squad to help them,

Peter Sutcliffe hid a smile behind bloodstained hands when he killed again, for they were powerless to stop him.

So was an ill-assorted batch of crystal-gazers, soothsayers and mediums who offered help, most of it contradictory or confusing.

Praise there must be for some policemen, low down in the picking order, like the two uniformed patrolmen who came on Sutcliffe by chance one night sitting in his car beside another potential victim, a hammer and knife with him.

And praise also for stubborn young Yorkshire Detective Andy Laptew who put in a report that Sutcliffe should be seen again because he was probably their man, a report which was marked "File" for no immediate action.

Beset by red-tape bureaucracy and a lack of inter-force liaison where the crimes crossed police jurisdictional boundaries, the paper monster waxed fat on the flimsies thrust into its maw as the Ripper killed again and again.

The biggest blunder of all was an insistent belief that he came from England's North East Coast, which has a distinctive "Geordie" accent unlike any other British dialect. Sutcliffe was Yorkshire-born, an accent as disparate as New York to Mississippi Delta.

A tape cassette to be described later by Attorney General Sir Michael Havers as "a cruel hoax" had been posted to West Yorkshire's Assistant Chief Constable George Oldfield from Sunderland, in the heart of "Geordie" land, on March 22, 1979. The voice on the tape, taunting Oldfield with his team's apparent lack of success, purported to be the killer. And a letter with it was similar to others the police had received with uncannily accurate details of the killings.

That tape prompted the police to inform all other forces in the inquiry to eliminate from then on any man who did not have a "Geordie" accent, putting Sutcliffe, conveniently in the clear.

Sutcliffe's car had been logged by observers 46 times in vice areas where the Ripper preyed. On one of his nine interviews he was still wearing the boots which had left a print at the scene of one murder and he was questioned twice about a new 5-pound note from his pay envelope, found in the handbag of another victim.

Yet Sutcliffe was never, according to police, a suspect worthy of close surveillance. Chief Constable Gregory was to reveal later that there had been between 40 and 80 better suspects than the truck driver, some under 24-hour watch.

In all but two of the killings and attacks, Sutcliffe first struck his victims with savage hammer blows to the head, then repeatedly stabbed them in the stomach and elsewhere with knife or screwdriver.

Most of the victims had no chance, stalked from behind or, in the case of some of the vice girls, struck as they stopped on invitation to enter one of his many cars, which he changed before they became too well known.

Sexual intercourse occurred only once and there was a cold-blooded reason for it, but in six of the murders he lifted the women's bras to expose their breasts and, in his own words, "show them up for what they were."

The story began in 1969 when Sutcliffe was fined 25 pounds in Bradford for possessing "a housebreaking implement" at night. It turned out to be a heavy industrial hammer and that conviction went automatically on to criminal records and into the police computer. He was to tell them after arrest that he intended committing murder with it that night after being bilked out of 10 pounds by a prostitute.

Then in 1971, while prowling the vice area of Manningham Lane in Bradford with an innocent friend, Trevor Birdsall, he slipped away from their parked car for a few moments, but returned in panic crying out: "Drive off quickly!"

He was carrying a heavy stone in a sock and as he threw the missile out the window he told the surprised Birdsall that he had hit a woman with it. He was questioned by the police about that attack but the woman did not press charges. Again, Sutcliffe was to admit later that he meant to kill.

Birdsall was his companion again on August 15, 1975

197

and in no way involved in what followed when Sutcliffe left the car to follow 46-year-old Halifax housewife Olive Smelt as she walked home, never suspecting her danger.

Sutcliffe picked up something as he left the car which Birdsall did not see. He returned a few moments later saying he had tried without success to "chat the woman up."

In reality, he had approached her head-on and spoke to her about the weather. Then as Smelt hurried on past, anxious to ignore him, he struck her from behind with a hammer.

She remembered nothing else until waking up in the hospital with severe skull fractures and hacksaw cuts across her buttocks. Her life was saved by a passing motorist whose headlights had picked out Sutcliffe crouching over her. He fled back to his friend's car before he had time to finish her off.

Smelt was to insist to the police: "I know he was a Yorkshireman because he spoke to me."

Birdsall was to say nothing of his suspicions about his friend for years, but in November, 1980, he finally sent an anonymous letter to the police advising them to check up more closely on Sutcliffe's behavior, and then he made a written statement. Both vital documents went into the paper monster and were not regurgitated until after Sutcliffe's arrest.

Birdsall apparently had been content until the eleventh hour to believe what the police were saying—that the Ripper had to be "Geordie" and not his drinking and traveling companion.

Leeds, home of first murder victim Wilma McCann, a 28-year-old strawberry blonde divorcee, hides its red-light district in the rundown streets of Chapeltown where she lived. A fiery-tempered Scot from Inverness, she put her four children to bed on the night of October 30, 1975, changed into a pink blouse to match her hair and slipped out by the back door so neighbors would not see her head downtown.

Wilma called first in city center pubs where she was well-known. When they closed at 10:30 p.m., it was cold and foggy on the dismal streets and children were already begging pennies to buy firecrackers for the coming week's November 5th Guy Fawkes bonfire. Wilma smiled as she passed them and tossed over a few coins. She had one more call to make before going home, the Room at the Top nightclub, which she left about 1 a.m., carrying a plastic carton of curry and chips.

A trucker heading for the M62 motorway to Lancaster pulled up when she flagged him down, but when he realized she was a hooker — and a drunken one at that — he drove on. A West Indian in a flashy sports car picked her up but returned her a few minutes later to the motorway near Prince Philip playing fields. In thick fog nearby the Ripper sat patiently waiting . . .

At 7:20 a.m. the next day, milkman Alan Routledge saw what he took to be a discarded Guy Fawkes dummy on the playing fields bank and walked towards it through the swirling mist, but his younger brother, ten-year-old Paul, got there first and recoiled in horror.

Wilma's head had been bashed in with an engineer's ball peen hammer, the strawberry blonde head was caked with dried blood, and the face was a shapeless mass of bruises and lacerations. Breasts and stomach had been ripped open and she had been stabbed 15 times through the abdomen.

Most of her clothes had been ripped off and scattered, but a white plastic purse on which eldest daughter Sonia had scribbled the misspelled word "Mumy" was never found.

The police swung into action immediately, questioning motorway drivers and car-crawlers visiting the vice district, but the Ripper had been too thorough. There were no clues. Not even the curry and chips container remained.

Sutcliffe recalled later: "I had gone to the red light district and saw her on the road, stopping on impulse to give her a lift. I realized soon afterwards she was a prostitute, as she asked if I wanted business. I decided to take her into a field and started to hit her with a hammer when she became abusive."

Police began to think again then about the attack on Mrs. Smelt earlier in 1975 and an attack in nearby Keighley on 36-year-old Anna Rogulskj that July. Anna had been left for dead in an alley — again the Ripper had been disturbed by another motorist — and her injuries were so severe she was given the last rites of the Catholic Church. She recovered, but the terrible wounds turned new hair growing from her shaven head from auburn to gray.

Christmas arrived uneasily that year for vice girls all over the North of England. Some began to work in pairs for protection, but others told the police who advised them to stay off the streets: "We are terrified but have to go on working to keep our kids."

The second murder came on January 21, 1976, when prostitute Emily Jackson, 42, was found dumped behind a derelict school in Leeds.

High on the windswept Pennine moors just outside the city lies the village of Morley, infamous since as the birthplace of Black Panther killer Donald Nielson. Sydney Jackson and his wife Emily ran a shingle repair business and Emily often drove the van for him.

What villagers did not know was that when the fun-loving couple drove into the city at night, they split up. Sydney did a little quiet drinking in a pub while Emily toured the redlight district picking up customers in their van for a little sly hooking.

The Jacksons had met in 1963, the year of Queen Elizabeth's Coronation and the year when John Reginald Halliday Christie, Yorkshire's sex-killer, went to the gallows for murdering eight women in London.

Sutcliffe was later to sit on the same chair in the Old Bailey's main courtroom. So had Crippen and sex-pervert Neville Heath.

On the night of Jan. 20th, Emily Jackson settled their children in front of the TV, changed into a sweater, for the night was cold, and joined Sydney in the van.

They sat together for a time in the city's Gaiety pub, but

soon after six Emily finished her drink and left, driving the van down to Chapeltown to talk to the street-walkers.

When the pub closed at 10:30 p.m., Sydney was mildly surprised to find no sign of Emily and the van in the car park. He shrugged and took a taxi home.

When dawn filtered through the city smoke haze, a workman picked his way through an alley near where Wilma McCann had died. As he stepped carefully over the trash he saw a huddled shape in a cul-de-sac to his left. Curious, he approached it, thinking it might be an old tramp or overnight drunk. But when he bent down he spun around quickly, quelling the vomit rising to his throat as he ran for the telephone.

Emily's hooking days were over. She lay sprawled on her face, a bloodstained coat tossed over her, skirt and panties still on but the sweater pulled off and tossed aside with shoes and bag.

There was the same crushing hammer-wound to the head, establishing the Ripper modus operandi, and bloody drag marks on the ground showed where she had been struck down initially some yards away. After that, the Ripper had gone to work with his knives and 50 wounds were hacked or slashed into the body.

Meantime, the missing van had turned up, cheekily parked back at the Gaiety and used calculatingly by the Ripper to help his quick getaway in his own vehicle.

Police at a press conference on Jan. 23rd told crime reporters: "While this man, who shows every sign of being a psychopath, is at large no prostitute is safe."

Biggest surprise in the Jackson killing came for the villagers of Morley who had no idea Emily had been a "lady of the evening" on the sly.

They had only had one in the village before, recalled in Peter Kinsley and Frank Smyth's Pan book on the Ripper, "I'm Jack."

Her name was Ann Houghty, a sad little woman who supplemented vice earnings in wartime 1940 by selling doorstep scouring stones she stole off the railway line. She died violently, too — struck by an express train one night as she collected her loot.

Nearly a year passed before the Ripper struck again, but although the murder took place in a Leeds park used by prostitutes, the victim was no hooker but simply a woman down on her luck.

Her name was Irene Richardson, 28-year-old mother of two children, and she was in Chapeltown on the night of February 5, 1977 because she had booked a cheap room in Cowper Street.

She was last seen alive at 11:15 p.m., dressing in the best of her pitifully few clothes to visit a local club because she was lonely. It was a pathetic last-ditch attempt to meet someone who might give her a few moments of happiness. Instead, the Ripper brought her horror and death.

Sunday morning was bright and sunny with birds singing in the trees as John Bolton, a 46-year-old accountant, jogged through Roundhays Park, a famous place with mansions of rich merchants and TV and showbiz personalities on one side and colorful immigrant homes on the other. At night, however, the park is the haunt of hookers and curb-crawl motorists.

Trotting along in grass sparkling with fresh dew, Bolton spied Irene Richardson's body huddled on its side in the shadow of the sports pavilion. He veered across to speak to what he, too, thought would be a vagrant with a cheery, "Hello? What's the matter?"

When he had a closer peek, he was glad he had not taken an early breakfast. Richardson's face, when he cautiously brushed the long hair aside, caused him to stagger back in shock. The throat had been slashed and the eyes, glazed in death, were staring almost accusingly at him.

One leg had been removed from panties and tights and both calf-length boots had been stripped off. Bolton carried on his jogging — at three times the speed — for the nearest phone booth.

Over 11,000 people were interviewed in yet another abortive manhunt, but one important clue had appeared this time: a footprint found near the body was from a size seven industrial boot, so the killer was probably of medium height and working in the engineering or motoring business. And he had a phobia about hookers, because although Irene Richardson was not one, he had made it appear that she had stripped in readiness for sex.

Sutcliffe, incidentally, was still wearing those incriminating size seven boots on one of his many interviews with the police but not one seems to have made the connection.

On April 23rd he struck again, battering to death Mrs. Tina Atkinson, 33, in her Bradford flat, the first and only time he struck down a victim indoors.

Unlike his hookers to date, Mrs. Atkinson was a highly successful and relatively attractive one and released photographs do not do her justice. And she had many rich clients in the city, another famous woollen center which once had more millionaires than Texas. Its famous citizens included Britain's three top hangmen, Jim Berry and Harry and Albert Pierrepoint.

Atkinson, a divorcee and mother of three children, had a flat right in the heart of the immigrant colony where shops sell everything from spices to oriental sex potions and virility cream.

The night she died, the 5-foot, 7-inch beauty combed out her dark shoulder-length hair and left home wearing tight blue denim jeans, a blue denim shirt open to her navel and a short black leather jacket. It was pay night for the immigrants and money flowed like wine in the bars and clubs.

Mrs. Atkinson was a little careless that night and got drunk. She was refused a drink in one pub at 10:15 because of it but was still working the streets at 11:15, looking occasionally at her watch, for she had one inflexible rule. Tina never, but never, hooked on a Sunday . . .

All through the drowsy Sabbath day flies buzzed incessantly in the tiny room of her flat and for good reason. There was a surfeit of blood to attract them, including a gory handprint on one wall. Tina stared at the flies as they circled her ruined face but the eyes had been sightless for many hours.

Just before the pubs opened that night at 7 p.m., a friend, Bob Henderson, called at the flat. Pushing open the bedroom door when no one answered the bell, he stepped into chaos and when he took a closer look at the huddled form under the rumpled bedding, he paled and backed slowly from the room.

There was no way to recognize Tina from her features. They were a pulp of bloody bone chips and gore, but Henderson knew who owned the blood-soaked jeans and leather jacket.

Tina Atkinson died shortly before or after midnight. She had not been raped but had been the victim of a frenzied attack on the lower part of her body, especially the sex organs.

By the sultry summer of that year, professional hookers and enthusiastic amateurs were arming themselves, against the advice and warnings of the police. One girl bought a small fireman's axe to hide in her handbag, another a small cooking cleaver, a third dug out grannie's foot-long hatpin from the attic. Ice picks, long nail files and steel combs with the handle filed to a point became fashionable, wedged in among contraceptives in their handbags. Some hookers were openly asking police to let them carry Mace-style aerosols or tear-gas pencils, without success.

But when the Ripper struck again, the victim was a 16-year-old Leeds shopgirl who made the fatal error of taking a short cut after a date through a playground near the red light district on the night of June 25th that same year.

She was Jayne MacDonald who, ironically, lived only six doors away from the dead Wilma McCann in Chapeltown.

She had visited a bierkeller in the city center with boyfriend Mark James that night. Her father, Wilf MacDonald, who died of a broken heart two years after the murder, kissed her goodnight before she left home. As he looked, stricken dumb with grief at her mutilated corpse later, he recalled how she had last looked, clean and sweet, her fine silky hair perfumed like a spring flower. In the

204

morgue it was stiff and clogged with gore.

Singing the rowdy German drinking songs with other youngsters made Jayne and Mark hungry. They dined afterward on fish and chips and, because Jayne missed her last bus, Mark took her to his own house, hoping to borrow his sister's car to drive his date home, but the car was not there. They walked together toward Jayne's home and Mark left her a short distance from it.

She was seen walking toward home about 1:45 a.m., but unwittingly strayed near the notorious Roundhay Park. She was hurrying through the darkness—street lights had gone out at 11:30 p.m.—when the Ripper pounced on her from the shadows and struck her down with one of his hammers before dragging her behind a high wooden fence towards the childrens swings and some trees. Then he bent over the inert body for more of his grisly work.

A woman living nearby remembered hearing a man shouting obscenities from the playground about 2:00 a.m., but did nothing about it. It was the old story. What was so unusual about bad language on a vice beat?

Children visiting the playground next morning found the battered and mutilated corpse at 8:00 a.m. even as churchbells rallied the religious to prayer nearby.

When it was realized an innocent girl was the latest victim, all Leeds clamoured for justice and an immediate return of the death penalty. Sad that no one seemed to really care whether the hookers lived or died, but that is nothing new in vice murders, as the original Victorian Ripper murders in London's Whitechapel well showed.

The Ripper in Yorkshire, however, at last became national news, and George Oldfield, Assistant Chief Constable of West Yorkshire, was put in charge of a special Ripper Squad.

Oldfield was among the first to examine the body. Jayne's suntop with bare midriff and a checked skirt were untouched and her tights were undisturbed. There was neither clue nor weapon, but the characteristic injuries were there.

Inquiries took in a ten-year-old schoolboy's collection of

car numbers and the diary of a housewife who had jotted down car numbers after being pestered by curb-crawlers.

Oldfield was to become in the next few years the best known detective in Britain, with criminologists all over Europe and America watching his persistent, stubborn but fruitless efforts to run down the elusive killer.

By October of the year, the scene shifted across the Pennine Mountain chain into Lancashire when 20-year-old Jean Royle was found in Manchester.

On the eastern side of the huge city beyond the vice-beam slums of Hume and Chorlton lies that perfect haven of rest for some called Southern Cemetery, acre on acre of green lawns with serried ranks of tombstones, long-gone victims in the battle of life.

If you are not making the one-way trip, you visit the place for any of three purposes: to see a relative's grave, grow fruit and vegetables on surrounding allotments which flourish well in that enriched soil, or you sneak out there at night for a little vice on or behind a convenient tombstone, for as one hooker cynically puts it: "Southern Cemetery is an ideal spot. It's dead quiet and the residents do not complain."

"Scotch Jean" Royle fulfilled two of those conditions in time. She had sex with clients there and remained dead but unburied after the Ripper struck on the night of October 1, 1977.

Her body was found only a mile from the M63 which joins the trans-Pennine highway to Leeds and Bradford, and the Manchester police joined the hunt.

Detectives had suddenly realized that the motorways of Northern England were providing the killer with a quick and simple getaway route and the slum-clearance areas, razed by high-rise flat developers, were providing ideal killing grounds. The point is underlined even more forcibly in Michale Nicholson's book, "The Yorkshire Ripper," written, like "I'm Jack," before Sutcliffe was caught.

Unlike most Manchester hookers on the cheaper end of the vice beat, Jean Royle dressed modestly. On the night of her death she left her flat in Linbeck Crescent, Hume, at 9:00 p.m. to visit local pubs frequented by drug peddlers, hookers and pimps. The area is a warren of derelict property, old warehouses and vacant lots, infested with rats, cockroaches, skid-row characters, and . . . hookers—ideal territory for the Ripper to work in.

Early on the morning of Oct. 10th, an allotment holder at the necropolis phoned the local police making strange noises as if puking down the handset.

"I've found a naked woman in the grass near the cemetery fence," he gasped between retching noises. "It's awful! Oh, my God! Awful!"

Police soon found out the hard way why the caller had felt sick. The body had the most terrible injuries to date and the clothing had been hacked and torn to bloody ribbons.

It took some time to identify Jean Royle. It was a revolting mutilation in which the belly was ripped open, putrefaction had set in and rats had been at work too, gnawing and ripping at the ghastly remains.

She was positively identified by another hooker, who worked the same beat, Anna Holt, and by her husband, Alan Royle, who called on police when he read the tentative description issued to press and radio. He thought his wife had made one of her spontaneous visits to Scotland.

Police told Mr. Royle it would not be pleasant to see what was left of his slim little wife on the morgue slab. He gave them instead a glass she had drank from before leaving home. It was, fortunately, still unwashed and the fingerprints matched.

Police found a blank wall of hostility and silence in the vice community—public relations have never been at their best there—but they knew one thing. There was no way the body could have remained where it was found for nine days without being seen.

The report by pathologist Reuben Woodcock told a chilling story. Jean Royle had been killed about 40 minutes after leaving home on October 1st on waste ground near the cemetery, so the Ripper must have been her only "client" that night.

He had smashed in her skull with 11 powerful hammer blows, leaving the whole head and face one gigantic black bruise. Eighteen stab wounds to abdomen and chest followed and six to the right side, but then he ran off after dragging the body into a hedgerow. Yet again, car headlights had frightened him away.

Eight days later in the dead of night he returned, dragged the putrefying body into the open, ripped off and scattered the clothes and then bent over the body with a sharp knife to further mutilate it.

One slash ran from left shoulder to right knee and another tore open the abdomen, spilling out the already putrefying entrails.

Top Manchester detectives immediately raced to Yorkshire to talk to Oldfield and his team but yet again, nothing came of it. Senior Yorkshire cops were annoyed that the Manchester coroner and police had revealed the scope of Jean Royle's injuries while they had been reluctant to disclose details of their own murders, particularly to the press.

Perhaps they should have been less finicky, because rumors in Yorkshire ran wild that the Ripper rammed beer bottles or cans into his victims' vaginas, cut off their nipples and pulled out their entrails!

Had they but known it, police already had the Ripper within their grasp. In Jean Royle's handbag found near the body was a new five-pound note, serial number AW 51121565, soon traced to a batch issued to workers in the Bradford area four days before the murder. That note could not by normal banking or trade procedure have reached Manchester in that time. It had to have come from Jean Royle's one and only encounter that night, the Ripper.

Police issued an appeal to wives and mothers to examine their husbands' and sons' wage envelopes and they called at T & W. H. Clark Holdings, Sutcliffe's employers and one of the firms to whom those new notes had been issued by a Shipley bank.

For the first time, as police began interviewing the workmen one by one, they faced Sutcliffe in an interview and he survived it with almost detached calm.

He knew about that incriminating note only too well. That was why he risked returning over the Pennines to Manchester eight days after the murder to try and find the handbag, but in the darkness he could not find it. He tried to cut off the head with a hacksaw to carry away the hammering evidence of his trade mark, but that failed too, and he fled once more into the darkness to his parked car.

His alibi for the night of that return trip was very convincing. There had been guests at a house-warming party he and his wife Sonia had given in their new home and Sutcliffe drove them home afterward. But he also made a fast trip across the mountains to try and find that fiver afterward.

In order of death but not discovery, Yvonne Pearson was the next to meet destiny on a dark night.

The 22-year-old blonde Leeds girl with the page-boy hair style of Joanna Lumley from the TV Avengers spy series worked the red light district of Lumb Lane in Bradford and was the most professional of the Ripper's vice victims.

Dressing carefully with frequent visits to hairdressing salon and beauty parlor, she had worked as a call girl in Bristol, Birmingham, Glasgow and London, competing with the best in the business—if that be the qualification—in Shepherd Market, Mayfair, and around the luxury hotels of Park Lane and Bayswater. She had also broken successfully into the rather lucrative Arab customer market.

She knew full well the dangers of her trade. In November, 1977 a friend, Janie McIntosh, had been stabbed to death by an unknown killer in a London hotel.

Janie, originally a Bradford girl, had been a top-class call girl and the first in Britain to be prosecuted for selling her body Amsterdam and Hamburg-style in her own lounge window while living in the port of Southampton.

Yvonne Pearson also knew and had drunk with Tina Atkinson, so she knew the Ripper menace at first hand.

Because of that, she no longer took men home to her flat,

209

preferring to work the car trade on the street and she always carried a pair of long-bladed scissors to protect herself.

She told friends: "If you are going to get it, then that's it and it will be just my bad luck to get knocked on the head."

Twice she had been fined heavily for soliciting and was due to appear before Bradford Court on January 26th. That worried her more than the threat of the Ripper, because while in jail her two young children might be neglected.

On Saturday, January 21st, stars were twinkling like chips of ice in the blue-black sky when she gently closed her front door behind her for the last time.

When she did not reappear and was reported missing, police assumed she had jumped bail to avoid the court case and fled to another vice beat elsewhere in Britain until the heat cooled off.

Nothing more was heard of her until March 26, 1978, when a man walking across a patch of wasteland in Bradford saw an arm stretched out behind an up-turned old divan. At first he thought it was a tailor's dummy but when he moved forward, the sweet stench of death intruded on his Sunday morning solitude and he ran for the law.

The half-naked corpse lay under the divan and a carpet of dead leaves and rubble. Although badly decomposed, it bore the hallmarks of a Ripper kill but no mutilation. Again, Sutcliffe had returned to expose the body and make sure of its discovery.

Some clothing was sticking to the putrefying remains but the face and head had been smashed to pulp, although there were still some teeth in the jaw and the fingers gave up prints. A ring on one of them confirmed identity.

Woman Constable Lena Markovich aged 21, and only on the force ten months, dressed in the dead girl's clothing and a blonde wig to walk her last-known route, but no one recalled seeing Yvonne Pearson. She became just another statistic on the Ripper file.

When Sutcliffe eventually confessed he told police he shattered her head on the waste ground with a four-pound lump hammer and was about to finish her off when a car parked suddenly alongside his own a few feet away and he panicked. He hid behind the old divan with his victim, stuffing horse hair into her throat and mouth to stop her moaning. They crouched together, the killer and his dying victim, until the car drove off. Then he killed Yvonne by kneeling on her and kicking her in the chest until the sternum ruptured her liver.

In the same month, on January 31st, a beautiful half-caste hooker, 18-year-old Helen Rytka, was found in a timber-yard in the town of Huddersfield. Although not famed for its prostitutes, the town has a history of vice going back to Roman times. The word fornication comes from the Roman fornix — viaduct arches — under which ladies of leisure plied their voluptuous wares to the Roman legionnaires when they were not watching out for barbarians coming over the wall.

Hookers in Huddersfield have kept the tradition alive, using the railway arches of Great Northern Street.

Helen and her twin sister Rita were inseparable. Rita had had some success as an artist and Helen had turned to vice to finance herself into a dancing-singing career in showbiz. Rita helped her by acting as a "shadow" at night and the twins met at regular intervals on the streets.

Late on Tuesday, January 31st, Helen slipped into her work clothes of black lace undies, black jeans and sweater and an imitation fur jacket and they walked to their pre-arranged rendezvous in Great Northern Street outside a public convenience normally frequented by male homosexuals.

At 9:10 p.m., Helen went off in a car. The plan was to meet Rita again at the rendezvous in 20 minutes, but Helen never kept the appointment. Rita waited a while in the biting cold, then returned home, deciding that Helen must have broken the rule, perhaps, for a special customer but she never saw her twin alive again.

On the morning of February 1st, a trucker in the timber yard which lies just off Great Northern Street picked up a pair of black lace panties and showed them to foreman Melville Clelland. They both laughed. Someone, they assumed, had had a rare old time in the yard the night before, so they hung the frillies on a nail for other workmen to leer at.

But, when Rita reported her sister's absence to the Police and told them of the rendezvous plan, that yard was searched and Helen's body was found, naked, in the snow under a pile of timber.

Again, there was the battered head and slash and stab wounds common to a Ripper kill and the rear wall of the foreman's shed was spattered with blood, consistent with skull injuries splashing blood everywhere.

In his confession, Sutcliffe told how he had picked Helen up outside the public convenience and driven her to the deserted yard. When she began to undress in the car and he saw the dim outlines of her cafe au lait body he became sexually aroused in spite of himself, and for the first time.

Telling her he wanted to urinate, he climbed out of the car and persuaded her to get in the back seat, his usual technique of luring a victim within striking distance of his hammers. As she did so he hit her on the back of the head and she fell moaning to the ground.

Then he suddenly realised that two taxi drivers were turning in his direction about 40 yards away. Willing aside momentary panic, he pushed Helen flat, laid on top of her and had sex, as the only way he could think of to keep her quiet and explain why she lay moaning on the ground beneath him. Then when the taximen turned away, he hit the girl again on the head, stabbed her and threw timber over the corpse.

After the confession, the taximen were traced and confirmed Sutcliffe's callous account.

Be it fatalism or fanaticism of Yorkshire's hookers, the day after Helen Rytka vacated her beat outside the conveniences another girl took her place.

Helen had predicted her forthcoming death in a sad little poem written in 1975 and published in The Yorkshire Post:

"Loneliness is to live in a world where people do not care,
"Loneliness is to go outside to find no one is there,
"You fall down in despair on your knees in prayer,
"Asking God to rescue you from this cruel snare . . .
"I know I shall die as my years drag by.
"Oh, why was it me, Lord. Why?"

After this killing, the West Yorkshire Police Authority and then the press offered rewards for Ripper information and a local clergyman set up a collection-box appeal. The obvious result was even more paperwork for the police.

On May 16th the same year, a tired, disillusioned, sick and weary 40-year-old prostitute called Vera Millward became the next victim, again in Manchester's Chorlton district. A mother of seven, she was clubbed viciously to death and stabbed in the stomach before being propped up like a rag doll in the flower beds of the city's Royal Infirmary Hospital car park.

Vera, with only one lung and stomach pains only drugs could deaden, had told friends she did not have long to live. The Ripper shortened the odds. He found her when a regular client failed to turn up.

A male witness later told of hearing spine-chilling screams for help from the car park, cut off abruptly with a blood-curdling gurgle, but he thought it was a hospital patient having a nightmare.

In any event, a scream in the night is not uncommon in Chorlton and Hume.

The risks the Ripper took were enormous. The whole area was floodlit with 800 patients and staff in surrounding buildings and the park was in constant use by the night staff, visitors, shift-workers, prostitutes and their clients.

A 19-year-old innocent girl, Josephine Whitaker, was next to die on April 4, 1979, her body found 200 yards from her Halifax home in a good class residential district. The butcher had strayed from his usual path in more ways than one.

213

Miss Whitaker, a clerk, was found the following morning by early workers waiting at a bus stop opposite Savile Park. She lay, face down like a bundle of old rags, on the grass. The night before she had visited her grandparents to show them her new watch. They suggested she stay the night but she decided to walk home instead. There was nothing to fear in Halifax, she had said. But the Ripper was lurking in her path to strike her down from behind with his hammer, drag her into the park and mutilate her chest and stomach with his knife.

Her parents thought she had returned home and gone quietly to bed, and so did her young brother David, until he saw police in the park on his early morning paper-round and recognised one of his sister's discarded shoes lying in the grass.

Another vital clue had fallen into the police lap. Wounds on Josephine's body bore traces of a mineral oil used only in engineering shops and garages, and there was to be another. A bite on her left breast had been made by someone with a gap in his two upper front teeth. Sutcliffe had such a gap and it clearly showed in his frequent smiles.

On September 2, 1979, the Ripper kept his cold-blooded tape-recorded promise to the police that he would strike again when he murdered a 20-year-old Bradford University student, Barbara Leach. Her mutilated body was found a day later, bundled into a trash can under a piece of carpet only a few hundred yards from the city's new police station.

"Babs" died because she liked to take a walk before going to bed in her nearby flat. On that last night she told University friends as they all left a nearby pub:

"Who's for a walk, then?"

Tired, they all shook their heads but arranged to meet her the next day. Barbara shrugged and walked on alone to her death.

She was wearing trendy blue jeans with a badge on one back pocket reading "Best Rump," a long-sleeve cheesecloth blouse and red high-heeled boots.

By now, with yet another respectable girl butchered and

battered to death, police were warning that no woman was safe. Sutcliffe's own sister, Maureen, was carrying a knife in her handbag to protect herself from attack!

Asked why they had not called in Scotland Yard, Oldfield told critics with blunt accuracy:

"And why should I? They never found their own Ripper!"

Two more murders were to follow before chance, or fate, brought the Ripper to book. The first was the almost unpublicized killing of 40-year-old Marguerite Walls, whom he strangled after striking her down in Farsley, between Bradford and Leeds on the night of August 20, 1980, a marked departure from his usual tactic of mutilation, and the murder on the night of November 17th of a 20-year-old Leeds University student, Jacqueline Hill.

She was found next morning at the rear of a shopping centre not far from the University Hall of Residence where she shared a flat with four other girls, and this 13th kill was the most brutal of all, injuries shocking even the most hardened detectives in the five-year hunt.

She had been clubbed from behind like the others, then dragged on to waste ground for the mutilation. Her stab and slash wounds included a gouge into one eye that had pierced the brain. Tragically, Jackie had only recently moved out of a flat on the outskirts into the Hall of Residence because of the Ripper scare.

A woman later told police she had seen a couple standing in a well-lit street near where the body was found. In fact, what she had seen was Sutcliffe propping up his dying victim before dragging her away for his knife work.

Two young policemen were criticized for failing to find her body after a bloodstained handbag was found that night near the murder spot and handed to them. They searched the area for a few minutes but not thoroughly enough to find the body, which was not discovered until ten hours later by an early morning shopper, 30 yards from where the bag had been.

One of the civilians who found the bag, former Hong Kong policeman Tony Gosden, claimed that the policemen initially refused to search at all. Had they done so more thoroughly, he said at the time, the body could have been found and the Ripper trapped in the area.

After this sickening crime, Oldfield, who had had a heart attack through the stress of the hunt, was replaced by his second-in-command, James Hobson, temporarily promoted to Assistant Chief Constable, and in a move unprecedented in police history, five of Britain's top detectives from Regional Crime Squads were appointed to his team as advisers.

"Six Men Against the Ripper" were the headlines blazing across the British Press and Oldfield handed them the reins after five years of frustration and what he believed to be taunts on tape and a letter from the elusive killer.

Hobson knew the difficulties facing him only too well but was sure his super sleuths would get their man in time. In five years police had conducted 250,000 interviews, taken 32,000 written statements and logged five million cars in red light areas of the affected cities.

While there was spirited response to appeals for public help on one hand, even suspicious wives, mothers and girlfriends were telling police confidentially about their mens' behavior, some people were assessing police chances as pretty slim, like the crowd at a Leeds football match chanting in score-fashion: "Ripper 13 . . . Police Nil!"

Even the FBI offered help, including two agents from the Quantico Training Academy who visited the Bramshill Police Training College in Britain and prepared a profile on the Ripper, based on techniques 90 percent successful in the States.

But other criminologists were saying it needed luck to catch him, the kind that trapped Black Panther Donald Nielson, picked up for a minor offense by alert ordinary policemen. And that is precisely what happened, to the chagrin of high-ranking, highly-qualified detectives, although they were obviously glad to see him caught.

On the night of Friday, January 2nd that chance came the way of Sergeant Robert Ring and Constable Robert

Hydes, two uniformed officers on routine car patrol in the city of Sheffield, until then ignored by the Ripper.

As they passed a large disused building used by hookers, they spotted a Rover car parked alongside without lights. They strolled across to it. Sutcliffe was in the driver's seat with a well-known prostitute, Olivia Reivers, beside him. Sutcliffe claimed at first she was his girlfriend but the officers, disbelieving him anyway, made a quick double-check by radio on the Rover's registration plate. It turned out to be false.

They promptly arrested Sutcliffe and did a little detection work of their own. Searching bushes near the car, a hammer and knife were found. But for the intervention, Reivers might well have become Victim No. 14.

After police visited Sutcliffe's home in Bradford to talk to his wife about his movements—most of his killing trips had been made on nights when she was away doing part-time nursing—he asked to see her, and as she stood in front of him in the cell, he told her:

"I killed all them women, love."

Sonia Sutcliffe began to cry softly and then they sat down together to discuss whether or not to sell their $35,000 detached home in Garden Lane.

When Sutcliffe made his initial brief appearance at Dewsbury Court charged only with the murder of Jacqueline Hill, police fought to hold back jeering crowds trying to grab him with cries of "Hang him!"

Only then was it discovered how ironic had been the long hunt, for, in a way, Sutcliffe had been openly advertising himself. His photograph had appeared on a leaflet issued by his employers to potential customers. He had been the only driver available in the office when the photographer called.

His ultimate appearance at London's Old Bailey was to have been brief indeed, with agreement between prosecution and defense to accept his original plea of guilty to manslaughter on all 13 killings on the grounds of diminished responsibility but not guilty of murder.

Psychiatrists were unanimous in the opinion that he was

mad, a paranoid schizophrenic unlikely ever to be freed again, and it was also felt that it would be better in the public interest and to protect the feelings of relatives not to make details of the mutilations public through a trial.

But the trial judge, Mr. Justice Boreham, was having none of that plea bargaining in his court and he ordered a trial to proceed, with the jury, and jury only, deciding whether Sutcliffe was a madman not responsible for his actions or a cold-blooded murderer who knew what he had done.

Crowds were in near-riot proportion when the trial opened in the famous Number One court, some spectators for the public gallery having queued all night.

Elegantly-dressed wives of VIPs and City of London Aldermen contrasted vividly with sad-faced victims who survived, relatives of those who didn't, and even Sutcliffe's own wife, who appeared in court to sit behind the dock against his express wishes.

Sutcliffe, pale and drawn, seemed dwarfed by the awesome enormity of the court, but in front of him below the dock lay the tools of his trace on an exhibit table: hammers, a hacksaw, and an assortment of knives and screwdrivers.

He was to claim that the voice of God ordered him to kill prostitutes while he was digging a hole while employed as a gravedigger before he became a trucker, but Attorney General Havers warned the jury that Sutcliffe had been overheard twice in his remand cell saying that he hoped to fool everyone by saying he'd heard "voices," and was hoping to get off with a relatively short term in a mental hospital which he had referred to jocularly as "the loony bin."

The jury discounted the diagnoses of the eminent psychiatrists, and by a majority of ten to two found him to be a murderer, not a madman, guilty of 13 murders and seven attempted murders.

After the Attorney General had then told the judge and jury that Peter Sutcliffe should be locked up for the rest of his life, Mr. Justice Boreham passed concurrent sentences on the Ripper of 30 years for each of his 20 crimes.

He told Sutcliffe: "I am not going to seek words to describe the brutality and gravity of these offenses. The catalogue of crime speaks for itself."

Sutcliffe said not a word and went quickly to the cells below surrounded by five prison guards.

Now 25 children are orphaned through his crimes, his own family has suffered, and so have the relatives of the dead and those he tried to kill. Olive Smelt and Ann Rogulskj. And the other five: Maureen Long, 42, attacked on July 10, 1977, in Bradford; Marcella Claxton, 20, attacked in Leeds on Mary 9, 1976; Dr. Upadhya Bandara, 34, attacked September 24, 1980, in Leeds; Marilyn Moore, 52, attacked December 14, 1977, in Leeds; and Teresa Sykes, 16, attacked November 5, 1980, in Huddersfield.

Now the inquest on the Ripper investigation itself follows and a ripple of unease is running through the medical profession, too. Some psychiatrists are angry that their four colleagues who diagnosed Sutcliffe as a paranoid schizophrenic appeared to be on trial at the Old Bailey and not the killer. They fear the trial may become a precedent, with doctors having to explain their opinions in court, even when both sides agree.

But Professor Robert Bluglass, professor of Forensic Science at Birmingham University, defended the judge's decision to put the issue before a jury. He told a Sunday Telegraph reporter:

"The psychiatrists who gave their evidence were well aware they would be subject to cross-examination. Opinion is not immutable or immune from criticism."

The big question is: Would Sutcliffe have still been killing but for those alert officers in Sheffield? It's an open question.

Peter Sutcliffe himself says it was a miracle he was not caught earlier, because the police had all the facts. He pointed that out from the witness box.

And miracles are said to come only from Heaven.

Peter Sutcliffe is now serving a life sentence at Parkhurst Prison on the Isle of Wight off England's southern coast.

How He Butchered the New York Beauties

by Steve Govoni

Newspaper editors throughout New York State were hard pressed to remember a case so bizarre. For several incredibly grueling months, State Police investigators working out of Troop G headquarters in Loudonville, an Albany suburb and several scattered sub-stations had little time to draw any comparisons.

This much was certain: There had been no more sensational, or frightening, murder probe in decades. Granted, sex criminals and sadistic murderers are by no means rare in the headlines these days, but the search for and prosecution of, this particular elusive suspect had sustained the avid interest of all ages for more than 15 months. The reason was simple: Everyone who read the chilling reports soon realized that if they had the misfortune to cross paths with this killer, their names might also have been listed among his victims.

What began as a report of a "missing couple" in the Adirondack Mountains developed into a full-scale probe into four murders. The probe was climaxed by investigation of the two lawyers who defended the man eventually charged with the crimes.

The terrifying carnage that summer of 1973 became an indelible blot on the memory of thousands of vacationers, campers, sportsmen and area residents in Adirondack Park, a vast tract of relatively unspoiled state and privately owned land in upstate New York. Stretching from just north of the New York State Thruway almost to the Canadian border, scenic mountains, plus hundreds of lakes and well-stocked streams, make the park larger than its neighboring state of Vermont.

It was the height of the tourist season, in fact, and the unusually dry, sunny weather had attracted a greater than average influx of young campers. Three of them became the object of a pervert's fantasized hunting season.

On Friday, July 20th, the body of Daniel D. Porter of Concord, Massachusetts, was found murdered in an Adirondack gully in the town of Johnsburg, near Wevertown in Warren County. He had been knifed four times. Bureau of Criminal Investigation (BCI) officers learned he was a Harvard graduate, and founder of and partner in the research company that conducted Senator George McGovern's political polls the previous year.

Investigators also learned that Porter had had a traveling companion, Susan Petz, 20, of Skokie, Illinois, a Boston University student. Some of the girl's belongings had been found in Porter's car, but a search the next few days turned up no sign of the attractive coed.

While troopers acknowledged that Porter was Miss Petz's boyfriend, after several days' continued search they said they had no reason to believe that she was anywhere near the area. A helicopter and bloodhounds were used early in the search but they were later withdrawn as about 50 troopers, forest rangers and volunteers concentrated on a ground search.

The area being scoured included neighboring Hamilton County, where thick underbrush, rocks, cliffs and dense forest made it virtually impossible to see anything from the air or to move on the ground with any success. The focus of the search was a vast mountain wilderness. Hamilton County is the least populous in New York State, with 4,714 people, according to the 1970 census yet the third largest with an area of 1,735 square miles.

An autopsy report estimated Porter was stabbed to death on July 17th, three days before his body was found. Troopers felt that heavy rain since then had helped to wash away some possible clues.

A description of Susan Petz was teletyped to all State Police barracks as the search in central Hamilton County continued. On July 29th, a man armed with a shotgun and knife invaded a campsite near Speculator, tied four young campers to separate trees and stabbed one to death.

The body of Philip Domblewski, 18, of Schenectady, was found tied to a tree about half a mile from the campsite in the densely wooded forest preserve. Only the month before, Domblewski had graduated with honors from a Schenectady high school.

By the time his friends, one a young woman, had freed themselves, they knew Domblewski was already dead. Piecing together the ghastly details, police learned that a husky bald headed man broke into the group's tent carrying a shotgun and led them off and tied them to trees, out of sight of each other.

As one State Police official described it later, the intruder told the young people: "I'm not going to hurt you. I just want your car." Nearby was his car, an orange Volkswagen.

According to police, the man had one youth tie the other three to different trees. The female survivor recalled "he seemed especially hostile to Phil." Indeed — the intruder plunged a long knife between Domblewski's ribs.

The survivors also told police the killer had swaggered about and boasted that he had killed before and would kill again. The man said he was already wanted by the FBI and state police.

Sparing the other three campers, the intruder forced one of the youths into the youth's car and fled, leaving his own car and the others behind. In the meantime, the two remaining survivors freed themselves — one hitchhiked to nearby Wells, the other to Speculator. Sheriff's deputies and state police soon cordoned off the scene, where they ran a quick check on the license of the abandoned Volkswagen and learned that the car was owned by one Robert F. Garrow of Syracuse.

While mug shots of Garrow were being sent to state police, the knife-wielding killer freed his captive, left the youth and his car, then fled on foot into the woods. A few hours later, the camper positively identified pictures of Garrow as the man who had knifed Philip Domblewski to death.

One of the largest, and what would become one of the most difficult manhunts in the history of the state, began to take form. Some 200 state troopers, sheriff's deputies, conservation workers, and forest rangers closed in on the spot where the killer fled into the woods. Bloodhounds soon picked up a scent, but very shortly became stymied by the dense underbrush which forced the hunters to take several detours in an effort to pick up the trail again.

Of little comfort was some background information on Garrow sent by Syracuse authorities with the suspect's mug shot. Garrow was a skilled woodsman, Syracuse police reported; thus it appeared likely Garrow could subsist in the woods without shooting game, the gunfire from which might betray him. The suspect could certainly take advantage of the area's many sources of food. He could always raid campsites for canned goods while campers were absent, and there were berries and vegetables like skunk cabbage and mushrooms, plus lakes with plenty of bass, pike and trout.

Meanwhile, speculation mounted as to whether Garrow might have been involved in another homicide. As searchers fanned out from that woodland slaughter scene, probers re-examined clues in the July 16th slaying of Mrs. Michael Slovak, 60, the wife of a Schenectady surgeon who was fatally knifed six times in a $45 robbery on her doorstep in Schenectady's Stockade area.

Although Schenectady police sought to question Garrow only in connection with the Slovak slaying, BCI investigators declared Garrow was a suspect in the slaying and disappearance of Daniel Porter and Susan Petz.

Garrow, the prime suspect in the weekend killing of Domblewski, was described as white, 5 feet 11 inches tall, weighing 210 to 220 pounds, baldish with brown hair, blue eyes and a tattoo on his left forearm consisting of the words "Mom and Dad" and a heart. Officials said he wore sunglasses and a hat most of the time.

Records showed Garrow was born March 4, 1936 in Dannemora, New York, had been imprisoned in Auburn, New York, and was paroled on August 12, 1968 to the Syracuse area. In 1961, Garrow had been sentenced to 10-20 years in prison after he pleaded guilty to first-degree rape.

According to a State Department of Correctional Services spokesman, Garrow was apparently "doing well" under the terms of his parole which would last until 1981, the maximum for the expiration of his prison term. Garrow had been working as a bakery mechanic in the Syracuse area.

On July 31st, two days after the Domblewski killing, Garrow's wife and son appealed to him to surrender in taped messages broadcast from a helicopter into the search area.

In the meantime, forest rangers helped state police investigate the confession of an area man—proved false—that he had killed the Petz girl and buried her body in a beaver flow. Rangers checked several such areas flooded by beaver dams and uncovered some poaching activities.

Nervewracking tension began to grip the corps of searchers after several days of stalking the elusive suspect. Troopers, armed with shotguns, semi-automatic carbines and bolt action rifles, converged on a 10-square-mile triangle near the Sacandaga River. Despite the help of two helicopters added to the search, the suspect ran a roadblock near Fly Creek then fled into the woods again.

Troopers began a methodical search of the more than 40 camps in the area for possible signs of the desperate killer.

Garrow was not swayed by the messages of his wife and son repeatedly broadcast to him by the helicopters that hovered over the tops of the spruce and hardwood trees that concealed him.

Officers at roadblocks throughout Hamilton County checked car trunks of outbound traffic. As the dragnet wore on, many tourists, frightened by the growing tension and police activity, packed up and went home. Sightseers were not allowed in search areas. Meanwhile, weary search parties took time out for mayonnaise sandwiches prepared by some volunteer with a strange palate.

Local residents dug out all available firearms in case they saw Garrow. Rumors that the wanted man had been sighted began to spread.

On August 1st, a red shirt believed to be Garrow's was found at Owl Pond, 9 miles east of Wevertown. The next day searchers discovered a lean-to believed to have been constructed by Garrow above a roadside rest area near Wevertown. Hours later, motorists reported seeing Garrow on a bridge 7 miles south of Hamilton County.

On August 3rd, the hunt concentrated on the Speculator area after police found water still warm atop a stove in a camp broken into four miles east of Routes 8 and 20. The following day, after sifting fact from fiction among the increasing number of reported sightings, police sealed off five miles of Route 8 following a reliable report that Garrow was in the area. Bloodhounds again picked up the suspect's scent, only to lose it again as darkness and thick underbrush thwarted searchers.

Temperatures dropped to 40 degrees on August 5th and frost appeared likely. However, rangers and troopers began to discern a pattern in Garrow's movement based on two positive sightings and the locations of several brush wickiups.

Total radio silence was maintained, except at every four-hour interval when search teams were expected to report and vital information was transmitted. State Police issued repeated warnings that Garrow was extremely dangerous but urged that he be brought in alive. Further police advisories said the BCI would do the shooting if Garrow should be cornered and did not surrender willingly.

Garrow was reported seen at a Speculator gas station on August 6th, but probers turned up no sign of the suspect.

Several days earlier, Garrow's sister told reporters, "He'll either kill himself or they'll have to kill him."

By August 7th, troopers led by Major Francis Stainkamp believed they had begun to close in on Garrow when it was reported that the fugitive had visited the home of his sister in Witherbee, Essex County, for 30 minutes. The house assertedly had been under police observation.

While BCI crime lab technicians examined hair found in the car abandoned by Garrow the first night of the search to determine if it might belong to Suzan Petz, troopers located another car believed to have been operated by Garrow in the Witherbee area.

The hunters were closing the ring on their quarry.

Increased undercover surveillance on Garrow's relative's Witherbee home paid off August 9th when Garrow's nephew inadvertently led police to the suspect who had been hiding in a thicket a half mile away.

At long last, Robert Garrow was flushed into the open by bloodhounds in a densely wooded area near Silver Hill Road. When he burst into sight he was carrying a rifle, later found to be a .30-30 Winchester, and running in a crouch on an erratic course, apparently trying to make himself a more difficult target.

Officers in the party which had found him shouted repeated commands to the fugitive to halt, but Garrow, who had successfully eluded capture in one of the most massive manhunts in the history of the Northeast, apparently thought he could outrun his pursuers. Ignoring the commands to halt, he scampered through the brush like a rabbit, changing his course with every few strides. Unless he was stopped, he would reach an even denser stand of timber where there was a good chance he might make good his escape.

That much was all too keenly realized by all the men chasing him, but it was Hillary LeBlanc, a conservation officer from Ballston Spa, who got the running man in his sights. When Garrow again ignored LeBlanc's one last shouted command to halt, LeBlanc squeezed off a shotgun blast that sent the running man tumbling.

Garrow, the father of two, was taken to a Plattsburgh hospital and listed in "guarded condition" after suffering a fractured left arm and wounds in the foot and back from the shotgun blast.

The nephew, David Mandy, 16, was charged with first degree hindering prosecution, a felony, then arraigned before an Elizabethtown justice and remanded to the Essex County jail.

Officials at Champlain Valley Physicians Hospital reported treating Garrow for two superficial chest wounds, a bullet wound of the left foot with no fracture, a shattered upper left arm and a bullet wound in that arm. Garrow underwent surgery to set his arm.

Hospital reports prior to X-rays described Garrow's condition as near critical, but State Police Major Donald Ambler, hopeful of the suspect's recovery, described Garrow as "one tough son of a bitch."

According to Ambler, Garrow was semi-conscious, couldn't say anything, and wouldn't respond to any conversation as he was lifted onto a stretcher. As for the capture, Ambler said officers had tried to "keep activity in the area, keep him off balance, keep him nervous," knowing only too well that Garrow could gain much strength if he stayed in the woods for a few days.

Troopers immediately apprehended Mandy when they spotted him moving in a northwesterly direction from his home toward Mount Tom. Ambler said the youth soon cooperated with officers, and the dogs picked up the scent, with the searchers close behind.

While doctors attended to Garrow, BCI detectives examined several similarities between the Domblewski and Porter homicides. Noting that Porter had been stabbed four times, probers discovered the fatal wound had been made by a blade that went into the body parallel to the lines of his ribs. Domblewski's wound was identical. Porter's hands were tied behind his back, officials announced to newsmen.

Detectives found nylon cord near the sites of both murders and later said they were of the same type.

According to Senior Investigator Richard C. Beckwith, Garrow began to be absent from his job "around the middle of July." A month earlier, Garrow was arrested near Syracuse and charged with first-degree sodomy involving two children. When he failed to appear in court, Onondaga County Judge Ormand N. Gale issued arrest warrants additionally charging Garrow with sexual abuse, attempted rape, unlawful imprisonment, possession of a dangerous weapon, criminal impersonation, and endangering the welfare of a child.

As news of Garrow's arrest spread throughout the state, acquaintances and neighbors recalled what little they knew of the suspected murderer. One Schenectady woman remembered Garrow at one time saying, "I'll never go behind bars again. It's too tough. The years of loneliness are just too much for you."

One of Garrow's Syracuse neighbors called him "a very odd neighbor" and said Garrow had insisted on constructing a six-foot-high redwood fence around his property shortly after moving into his two-story three-bedroom frame house in 1972.

But another resident said Garrow ". . . seemed awful nice."

In late 1972, a Syracuse police court judge dismissed charges of second-degree unlawful imprisonment and sixth-degree criminal possession of a dangerous drug against Garrow.

According to Garrow's lawyer, Frank R. Armani, the dismissed charge stemmed from a November, 1972 incident involving two student hitchhikers who, the lawyer said had planted marijuana in Garrow's car then called police and filed unlawful imprisonment charges against him.

Upon Garrow's arrest, Mr. Armani said "there was no hint of anything wrong until this." Describing Garrow as a model parolee, bitter after the alleged frame-up incident, the lawyer added that Garrow would have benefited from better psychiatric care in prison.

Adirondack Park residents, meanwhile, breathed more easily, with Garrow in custody. Some veteran investigators and long-time residents were reminded of another manhunt 20 years earlier. The fugitive then was James A. Call, 29, an AWOL Air Force major who killed a police officer and wounded two others in a shootout near Lake Placid.

Call led up to 550 state troopers on a 103-day chase through the Adirondacks from August to October, 1954. A Korean War veteran, Call made maximum use of his Air

Force survival training and broke into several campsites each week, stealing clean clothes as well as food and throwing bloodhounds off his scent.

Call was never apprehended in the forest. He managed to escape the wilderness area as autumn nights began to give way to fierce winter temperatures. Weeks later, he was arrested in Reno, Nevada on a burglary charge. A newspaper clipping in his pocket, about the Upstate New York shootings, gave him away. Call eventually pleaded guilty to second-degree murder.

Garrow was later taken to the Hamilton County Court House in Lake Pleasant, where he appeared in a wheelchair and pleaded not guilty. Throughout his convalescence from the gunshot wounds, Garrow remained silent about the murders of Porter and Domblewski and the disappearance of Susan Petz. Nevertheless, Hamilton County District Attorney William Intemann, Jr. had a strong enough case to secure murder and kidnapping indictments stemming from the Domblewski murder and the abduction of Domblewski's companion.

In the meantime, the search for Susan Petz continued, but with no success. Court-ordered psychiatric tests determined Garrow was fit to stand trial, in that, as New York law dictates, the suspect understood the charges against him.

As defense counsel and prosecutors prepared their arguments for pre-trial motions, State Police expanded their investigation when on December 1st, youngsters discovered a human foot protruding from the entrance to an abandoned mine shaft in Mineville, less than a mile from Garrow's childhood home. The body, dead nearly six months, was identified as that of Susan Petz.

The site was also one mile from where Garrow was shot and apprehended, and 50 miles from where Miss Petz's boyfriend, Daniel Porter was found stabbed to death. An autopsy revealed she had been stabbed once on the left side of the chest.

The murders of Porter, Domblewski, and Susan Petz occurred in three separate jurisdictions; Warren, Hamilton, and Essex Counties, respectively. Until investigators turned up more information, however, the actual location of the Petz homicide remained in question. Garrow continued his silence, and it remained speculative whether Miss Petz was abducted after the Porter slaying, then killed in Essex County, the state's second largest.

In the ensuing months, a massive investigation pieced together bits and pieces of information in connection with the Petz and Porter homicides, but Essex County District Attorney John McDonald and Warren County District Attorney R. Case Prime still did not have as solid a murder case as Hamilton County authorities.

Whether they did or not, there were enough charges already pending against Garrow for one to be reasonably certain that the accused eventually would have enough time in prison to write a perverted, sado-masochistic version of "Paul Bunyan" if he so desired.

After months of continuances, pre-trial motions and jury selections, Hamilton County D.A. Intemann began presenting his case on June 10, 1974 after the screening of almost the entire adult population of this Adirondack county finally produced a 12-member jury and four alternates. The trial took place in the county seat, Lake Pleasant, population—364.

In his opening statement, the prosecutor told the jury that Maribeth Collins, one of Philip Domblewski's companions, actually saw and heard what allegedly happened between Garrow and the victim.

The prosecution reconstructed the events of July 29, 1973 with the following chronology:

Around 8 a.m., Garrow threw open the flap of a tent in which the Collins girl and Michael Simmons, another camping companion of Domblewski, were sleeping.

Domblewski and Robert Elder had gone fishing earlier that morning.

The pair in the tent were ordered out "before your friends come back," the prosecutor told the court. It seemed the defendant had prior knowledge of the other people in the camp.

230

But Domblewski and Elder returned to the camp before the couple could follow Garrow's command. Garrow took the four into custody at rifle-point, ejecting a shell from the chamber to remind them it was loaded. The desperate man then walked the four up and down a back road as if he were looking for something.

Elder was ordered to tie Domblewski to a tree, and then Simmons. The defendant tied Elder to a separate tree, then lashed the Collins girl to a tree, and told her, "I'm going to take you with me, and I might let you go," according to Prosecutor Intemann.

Miss Collins heard voices getting progressively louder, the D.A. said. She also heard "vomiting and gagging" sounds and received no answer when she called to Domblewski.

Simmons was later able to untie his hands and run away through the woods, where he found his car and drove to nearby Wells for help.

Elder also freed himself and went to the aid of Miss Collins, but Garrow, who was crouched next to the tree where Domblewski was tied, recaptured the three at rifle-point.

When a search failed to find Simmons, said the prosecutor, Garrow told Elder, "You better find him or you're in real trouble."

Garrow and Freeman searched the country roads for Simmons for almost two hours, first in Collins' car, then in Garrow's Volkswagen. At one point, Garrow told Elder to park the girl's car back in front of the tent to make it look as if it had not been moved. Meanwhile, Garrow waited in the bushes for Simmons' return.

When other people from Wells finally arrived at the camp, Elder bolted toward safety and shouted. "He's got a rifle and he'll shoot!" Intemann said.

However, no shots were fired at the time. Garrow escaped through the woods, but was spotted later in his car on a nearby road.

Spectators in the packed-courtroom re-positioned themselves in the uncomfortable wood chairs in anticipation of the prosecution's first witnesses, Philip Domblewski's camping companions.

"All the directions were with his rifle," Elder told the court. Elder's testimony substantially agreed with the earlier recollections of Miss Collins and the Simmons youth.

Elder recalled that while he was held captive he did not see a hunting knife in the sheath of the assailant's belt. Elder also identified several items of clothing as similar to those worn by his assailant; he then identified a rifle produced as evidence by the prosecution as the same gun wielded by the man.

The three young witnesses said that they had tried to be sympathetic to their captor. They testified they offered Garrow such things as their car keys and told him they too had been in trouble.

A relatively brief cross-examination did not shake any of the major points of the camping companions' stories, and courtroom observers began to sense the makings of a plea of insanity in the case.

One of Garrow's defense lawyers, Francis Belgc, asked each of them if they thought the man who held them captive, and whom they identified as Garrow, was "a nut."

Miss Collins testified that Garrow had been so calm that at first she thought he was a forest ranger. Simmons agreed and said the man had shown no anger during the incident.

At the opening of the trial, the prosecutor moved to bar defense counsel's use of any psychiatric testimony because the defendant allegedly had not cooperated in psychiatric tests.

In fact, Garrow had been examined by four psychiatrists. Intemann introduced all four psychiatric reports confident that the jury would believe the subsequent testimony of one doctor to whom Garrow fully narrated the events leading to Philip Domblewski's death.

The prosecutor acknowledged that Garrow had claimed amnesia in the other three psychiatric tests, but he argued that this was just another way of Garrow saying he would not cooperate with the tests. Intemann based his contention on a recent Court of Appeals ruling which held that a defendant must cooperate with mental examinations to be allowed the use of psychiatric testimony.

County Court Judge George W. Marthen reserved decision on the motion.

Several State Police witnesses gave their versions of the 12-day manhunt for Garrow. One of them, Trooper Michael J. Kelleher, who was manning a roadblock near the Domblewski murder scene the night of June 29th, said he saw a Volkswagen speed out of the area about 1 a.m. on July 30th. Kelleher testified he chased the car but lost it on the winding mountain roads, and later found the car abandoned on a side road off old Route 30.

Following the testimony of troopers and Domblewski's friends, Intemann began to depict the sequence of events surrounding the crime by telling a series of witnesses. Of the key witnesses, four added particularly vivid fragments of what happened July 29th to the mosaic being recreated for the jury.

— An Amsterdam woman said she saw an orange Volkswagen with old New York license plates on old Route 30 about 11 a.m. July 29th. The driver looked out his window and smiled at her, the woman said.

— The woman operator of a restaurant in Wells who said she phoned State Police in Fonda that morning described Simmons as "nervous and highstrung" after fleeing the murder scene.

— Two Wells men who followed Simmons back to the old Route 30 death scene recalled how Simmons had almost fallen at their feet when he came running out of the woods. "He's gonna kill me, he's gonna kill us all!" one of the men quoted Simmons.

The same witness, a licensed guide, testified he saw a man—in dress similar to the camper's description of the man they identified as Garrow—rustling through the brush away from the area. After Elder described roughly the .30-30 rifle carried by Garrow, said the witness, the two men attempted to seal off the area because of the ". . . pretty heavy gun."

— BCI Investigator Gerald B. Luck said he found an unused .30-30 caliber bullet in front of the campers' tent the

233

day after the homicide.

On June 13th, the pathologist who performed the Domblewski autopsy detailed what the prosecution alleged was a "methodical" stabbing. Dr. Jack P.M. Davies, who said he had conducted more than 30,000 autopsies, testified the victim's five wounds were "so evenly and parallel spaced" that there was no real indication of a "fight or frenzy."

According to Dr. Davies, a professor of pathology at Albany Medical College, Domblewski died of a five-inch wound which penetrated his heart and left lung.

"He died very suddenly but not, I think, immediately," Davies testified.

Later that day, Judge Marthen granted the district attorney's motion requesting the judge to consider advising the jury at the trial's conclusion of the possibility that Garrow had not cooperated with three state-hired psychiatrists.

The judge explained that if there was no doubt that Garrow had not cooperated with the court-appointed doctors, such a determination could preclude any plea of insanity.

After Dr. Davies testified there was vomitous material around the victim's face, Garrow's two defense attorneys, began cross-examination, with the trial's first overt indication that Garrow would be depicted as insane at the time of the Domblewski killing. After several questions by Belge, the doctor stated that brain damage need not be evident in persons certified as insane.

Another preview of the defense's strategy came when Frank Armani, the other defense counsel, asked one witness whether wiretaps were possibly used in the hunt for Garrow. Successful objections by the district attorney thwarted this line of questioning, but the jury was told of a note, made by one investigator, which read: "Fly to Ticonderoga with applications for wires."

Counselor Armani vowed to "rigorously pursue the wiretapping issue if it involves subpoenaing the president of AT&T to the local switchboard operator in Lake Pleasant. When I suspect my office phone has been tapped, I will use any and all legal means to expose it."

In his questioning, Defense Attorney Belge noted that the

police had questioned the defendant's sister and brother-in-law without knowledge of Garrow's visit. The brother-in-law testified police came to his house the morning after he had phoned the defendant's wife about Garrow's visit.

According to the brother-in-law, news of what car Garrow was using was broadcast after Garrow's visit to his home.

The prosecution concluded its case, a five-day presentation, with the testimony of its 32nd witness, Ralph Marcucio, a State Police senior lab technician. Marcucio said the vomit of Domblewski matched a yellow substance found on a shirt which witnesses previously stated was worn by Garrow on June 29th.

Referring to the substance found on the shirt allegedly worn by Garrow, Prosecutor Intemann asked. "Was this identical to the particles found in the decedent's stomach?"

"Yes, sir," Marcucio answered.

In earlier testimony, a Syracuse optician identified a pair of prescription sunglasses taken as evidence near the Domblewski murder scene as having been sold to Garrow in 1971.

The prosecution's case, to this point, consisted of strong circumstantial evidence. Although a routine defense motion for acquittal on the grounds of insufficient evidence was quickly turned down. The district attorney had not produced an actual eyewitness to the killing. Two witnesses indicated they had heard the sounds of death; another had said she saw "motion."

The jury pondered the chain of evidence and testimony laid out by the prosecution. With the widespread publicity surrounding the case ever since the initial search for Garrow, many upstate New Yorkers undoubtedly had the defendant already convicted in their minds, but everyone waited curiously for the convicted rapist's defense argument.

Little was known of what witnesses Defense Attorneys Belge and Armani would call in efforts to instill "a reasonable doubt" in the minds of the jury although one psychiatrist was expected to support an argument that Garrow was innocent by reason of insanity.

Excitement mounted during the weekend as many observers speculated over what methods the defense would utilize to demonstrate Garrow's insanity at the time of the murder. For such an argument to be convincing, veteran court-watchers agreed, Garrow would have to take the stand and come close to appearing like a lunatic. Yet the question remained: If the defendant did indeed testify on his own behalf, would his lawyers elicit *every* mystery and idiosyncrasy in Garrow's past, or would the prosecution ultimately use the defendant's testimony to its own advantage?

The courtroom buzzed with such wonderings that Monday morning, until a gravel-like voice suddenly interrupted, "All rise . . ." Judge Marthen took his seat behind the bench and pounded the gavel for the proceedings to reconvene.

"The defense calls Robert F. Garrow Sr.," the lawyer announced.

A puzzled, amazed, and avidly expectant gallery focused instantly on the gaunt, bespectacled defendant. Attendants helped Garrow from his wheelchair toward the witness stand.

Within minutes, Garrow had admitted his responsibility for *four murders and several sexual assaults over the years!*

The electrified chamber heard the bakery mechanic implicate himself in not only the Domblewski homicide, but also in the murders of Susan Petz, Daniel Porter, and 16-year-old Alicia Hauck of Syracuse.

Miss Hauck's decomposed body was discovered December 9, 1973 in a heavily wooded area of Oakwood Cemetery near Syracuse University when a university student stumbled across the girl's remains. Syracuse officials determined that the girl had been murdered, and positive identification of the body was made by her dentist and her parents, who identified a ring found near the body.

The girl was attending a Corcoran High School summer session when she was last seen on July 11th.

Garrow said he picked up Miss Hauck hitch-hiking and drove to an apartment complex area near his home. The girl had intercourse and other sexual relations with him without resistance, Garrow claimed in his testimony.

236

Theodore Bundy during his trial for the murders of two Chi
Omega sorority sisters on January 15, 1978

Angelo Buono, implicated by his cousin, Kenneth Bianchi, as an accomplice in the Hillside stranglings

Kenneth Bianchi, the confessed Hillside Strangler, as he testifies against his cousin, Angelo Buono

Albert De Salvo, the Boston Strangler, in custody after his escape from the Bridgewater, Massachusetts State Hospital for the Criminally Insane

David Berkowitz, the "Son Of Sam" killer

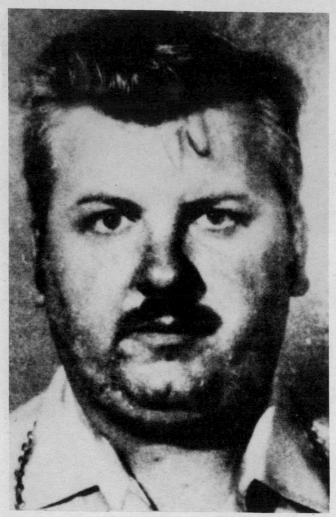

John Wayne Gacy, Jr.

Seventeen-year-old Elmer Henly leads an officer to grave sites at High Island, Texas.

Henry Lee Lucas (left), sentenced to death in Texas, leads law enforcement officers to the site of a double homicide in San Luis Obispo County, California.

An argument ensued, Garrow said. "Then she grabbed the knife and everything went berserk after that."

After walking home, Garrow said, he could not recall where he had been when asked by his wife. "But I was as happy as could be," the defendant added.

According to Garrow's testimony, the trip that led to Philip Domblewski's senseless death resulted from ". . . the pressure" following the bakery mechanic's indictment for rape and sodomy involving two 10-year-old girls in Geddes, a Syracuse suburb.

Persistent headaches and "lost periods" clouded his memory at that time, the defendant indicated. Shortly after he bought coffee and doughnuts at a Speculator diner, Garrow related, he approached the four campers' tent asking for gas. Soon Domblewski and Elder pulled up in a second car.

"That's what happened and I went berserk because of the pressure," Garrow said.

During the next two and a half days, Garrow's answers varied from vague to specific in his confession to four murders within a month.

"Embarrassed," tearful, at times ashamed, Garrow testified he took Susan Petz captive after fighting with her boyfriend, and then lived with her for three days.

Although Garrow rarely mentioned the names of his victims, the identification from his testimony was clear. He said he knew the man (Porter) had died but that he did not recall stabbing him.

Remembering Susan Petz as "Carol," Garrow's testimony revealed that Miss Petz's death stemmed from an argument about her removing her blouse. The young woman had picked up a knife and cut his hand before she died, according to Garrow.

After depicting himself as a wanderer who sometimes would leave his home and not remember where he had been or what he had done, Garrow began to tell the court his life story, however abbreviated. Under questioning by his defense counsel, Garrow recalled his days as a youth when his parents made him work on a farm. He admitted he had been in trouble at an early age.

"What kind of trouble?" asked the lawyer.

"The same kind I've been in all my life," Garrow replied.

The confessed killer told the court he had had sexual intercourse with animals on the farm because he didn't have any friends.

After 40 minutes of testimony, Garrow broke down in tears. It appeared that his love life was a particularly heavy psychological burden. He said he was 17 when he first kissed a woman, and 22 when he first had sexual intercourse with a woman. While in the Air Force, Garrow said, he had been disciplined for selling "dirty pictures." Later, the defendant testified, he had been sexually involved with a male Albany attorney.

When asked about a past arrest in Albany on rape charges, Garrow testified he remembered the incident although he "didn't know it happened" at the time.

Garrow served eight years in prison in connection with that arrest. His homosexual relations continued in prison, according to testimony.

His voice noticeably dry and strained, Garrow said he had taken many educational courses while in prison. The courses ranged from mathematics to typing to theology, the defendant stated.

The convicted rapist and confessed murderer then said he believed in God and knew the ten Commandments, including the fifth commandment, "Thou shalt not kill."

Within minutes, Garrow broke down again, and there was a short recess. The defense had wasted no time in its bid to persuade the jury that Garrow was innocent by reason of insanity. For such a verdict that panel would have to concur unanimously that the defendant was suffering from a mental disease or defect at the time of the crime that made him unable to realize the consequences of his actions or to know right from wrong.

Under questioning by Norman Mordue, special assistant for the prosecution, Garrow bewildered many court observers when he said he had no advance notice he would be called to testify.

"If my attorneys think it is best for me, that's it," Garrow

238

stated. Although acknowledging he had been advised several times of his right against self incrimination, a resigned Garrow told the prosecutor, "I'm living on borrowed time, anyway."

His two lawyers soon found themselves the focus of another controversy. In a drama-packed news conference, they disclosed that they did not reveal for six months that they had seen the bodies of Alicia Hauck and Susan Petz, because they were bound by the confidentiality of a lawyer-client relationship.

The attorneys said Garrow told them where to find the bodies. They photographed the bodies, but did not report the discoveries to police or to the father of one of the missing victims.

"I spent many, many sleepless nights over my inability to reveal the information, especially after Mr. Petz came in from Chicago and talked to me," Mr. Belge said.

Mr. Belge said he and Mr. Armani wanted to advise both sets of parents where the bodies were located, but could not reveal such confidential information because ". . . it was a privileged communication" between lawyer and client.

The conflict, which, as of this writing has yet to be resolved, is between legal ethics and confidentiality. Lawyers are generally committed to keep a client's confessions of an actual crime in confidence. But at the same time, the lawyers cannot hide such physical evidence as a weapon, or a body.

According to many legal authorities, the problem of a lawyer's duty when his client informs him about a criminal action is "a gray area." On the other hand he is privileged and bound to keep in confidence a client's confession of a completed crime. On the other hand, he is not permitted to conceal physical evidence from the prosecution.

In response to the lawyers' disclosure, a somewhat perturbed William Kirwan, State Police Superintendent, said he wondered whether such confidentiality was against the public good. "It just doesn't set right," he said.

Although both lawyers also acknowledged that they had destroyed photographs, negatives, maps and taped statements because of the lawyer-client privilege, many lawyers agreed they were within legal boundaries. Others found the act unconscionable and called for official censure.

The dispute soon shed light on another aspect of the Garrow case when the Hamilton County district attorney said he had been "outraged" by a plea bargaining attempt at a meeting in Syracuse September 7, 1973. According to Intemann, Attorney Belge offered to locate the two bodies "in return for our accepting a plea of manslaughter in the second degree."

Intermann said he refused the offer. Belge then tried to cop his client to a first-degree manslaughter plea, the prosecutor indicated.

On June 21st, a defense psychiatrist spent most of the day on the witness stand. Dr. Franklin G. Reed stated he had examined Garrow five times and found him suffering from a "combination of what is termed an anti-social personality and latent schizophrenia."

Regarding the defendant's awareness of the Domblewski murder, Dr. Reed said, "I think he had a substantial impairment in his capacity to appreciate what the act entailed and that it was wrong."

According to Reed's testimony, "a new project came to his (Garrow's) mind and that was to steal the woman" when the defendant first approached the campsite and saw two of the campers.

"The moment he saw him (Domblewski), Mr. Garrow hated him," the doctor said ". . . at that moment, probably he knew he was going to kill him."

Whether or not Domblewski said something that provoked Garrow to stab him, the psychiatrist indicated, "he (Garrow) saw red, he heard whispers that were like space sounds, and he stabbed him."

Dr. Reed added that he didn't think Garrow really appreciated ". . . what it is to be a human being."

The next day, Saturday, the defense rested its case following testimony from a psychiatrist, who stated that just recounting his initial encounter with Garrow "gives me cold hands."

In the meantime, the prosecution continued its cross-examination of Garrow, who testified in his second day on the stand that "everything went haywire" in his life a few weeks before the four murders.

But Garrow's composure cracked again under vigorous questioning by the assistant prosecutor. The defendant's second day of testimony came to an abrupt end after he frequently protested he was "confused" and "mixed up" about the events of July, 1973.

"Everything's a mumbo-jumbo in my mind," Garrow said as he broke down, crying and trembling. "Just leave me alone for a while, please."

When the trial resumed the next day, Garrow concluded his testimony, although he still insisted he didn't remember the crimes at the time they were committed. Garrow asserted his recollections were derived from what he heard in court testimony and during earlier questioning by police and others.

Later, his two sisters testified about the defendant's unhappy home life. They indicated Garrow received harsh discipline from his parents.

Subsequent testimony revealed that the telephone in Garrow's Syracuse home had been wiretapped after the granting of a court order during the manhunt for him.

"It was a terrifying experience," Dr. Jerry Morrow said.

Dr. Morrow told the court how he had the defendant fantasize killing him in order to make him reconstruct the Domblewski murder.

"He put his head down, a few seconds transpired, and when he looked up, the pupils in his eyes were twice the size they were when he looked down," the psychiatrist said. "He was shaking. He had a look in his eyes that gives me cold hands just recalling it — absolutely terrifying."

It appeared, from the doctor's testimony, that Garrow's rage was vented with the killing of Domblewski.

Why were the three other campers spared? Dr. Morrow quoted Garrow:

"I don't know. I felt more relaxed. The pressure was off, something like that . . . maybe I should have done it. I always like to slaughter hogs. I would drink the blood, and I would take it back and my mother would make blood pudding . . ."

As a rebuttal witness, Assistant Prosecutor Mordue called a third psychiatrist, who testified that Garrow suffered from an anti-social personality disorder.

Dr. Francis Durgin stated he could not determine any other mental or emotional illness. When questioned about the defendant's spotty memory of the details of the four homicides, Dr. Durgin said he could find no medical reason for his inability to recall these events.

On June 27, 1974, the seven-week trial culminated when the jury of seven men and five women, after about two hours' deliberation, found Garrow guilty of murdering Philip Domblewski.

On July 1st, Judge Marthen sentenced Garrow to 25 years to life in prison. After hearing the sentence, Garrow said from his wheelchair, "All I can do is say I'm sorry."

A motion to appeal the conviction was filed. Shortly thereafter, Onondaga County District Attorney Jon Holcombe, in Syracuse, said "we anticipate further prosecutions regarding the Alicia Hauck killing."

A few days after his conviction, Garrow told an Albany newspaper reporter he felt his testifying prejudiced his whole case. "I think it was going better for me before," Garrow said.

On July 2nd, Garrow began serving his maximum sentence for murder at the Clinton Correctional Facility in Dannemora, New York.

"I don't look forward to his being much of a problem child," the prison superintendent said. "We've got a lot like him here."

EDITOR'S NOTE
Maribeth Collins, Michael Simmons and Robert Elder are not the real names of the persons so named in the foregoing story. Fictitious names have been used because there is no reason for public interest in the identities of these persons.

Texas Homosexual
Torture-Murder Horrors!

by Redmond Travers

It was not, at the outset, anything unusual for a police blotter, not even that of Pasadena, Texas, a thriving petrochemical center nudging Houston's southeast flank. Violence is neither commonplace nor rare in Pasadena; with over 100,000 persons congregated within a given area, a certain amount of murder and mayhem is to be expected.

So there was nothing extra-portentous in the call received by the Pasadena police dispatcher at 8:20 a.m. the morning of August 8, 1973: a fatal shooting at 2020 Lamar, reporting party awaiting arrival of police.

No, the radio patrol officers and detectives who responded had no inkling of the Pandora's box of horrors that awaited opening, no idea that the one incident would mushroom into a *cause celebre* that would send a collective shudder of revulsion rippling around the world and boggle the minds of millions.

The house at 2020 Lamar was a white frame cottage on a tree-shaded street of similar middle-class residences. The officers were met at the door by three obviously nervous and frightened youths, two boys and a girl. They identified themselves as Elmer Wayne Henley, 17, Timothy Cordell Kerley, 20, and Rhonda Louise Williams, 15, all of Houston.

Henley, a slight youth with a wispy mustache and a sparse goatee, said the home was that of Dean Allen Corll, 33, an electrician employed by the Houston Lighting and Power Company.

243

"I killed Dean!" Henley said in a shaking voice. He surrendered a .22 caliber pistol.

Dean Corll lay in the hallway of the small house. He had been shot four times in the chest and head. He was a trim, dark-haired man with finely-etched features. Even in death he appeared handsome.

Corll's violent death quickly began to shape up as a case of self defense, based on Henley's account. He said that Corll, a friend for "a couple of years," had invited the three of them to a party at the house the night before; during the course of the evening all four had taken to sniffing paint fumes, and Henley, Kerley and the girl had rendered themselves unconscious. Henley said that when he awakened, he found Corll in the process of handcuffing him.

Henley said that Kerley and the girl, naked, were spread-eagled on a six-foot board with holes, a pillow affixed to the top, shackled to the slab of plywood with manacles. Their mouths were taped, Henley added.

"Dean said he was going to kill us all, but first he was going to have his fun," Henley went on. The "fun," said Henley, would be forcing the boys to submit to unnatural sex acts. The youth said Corll was armed with a knife in addition to a pistol.

Henley said Corll abruptly dragged him into the kitchen, threatening him with the weapons.

"I started sweet-talking him," Henley told the officers. "I told him I would kill them for him if he let me go. I promised I'd torture and kill them if he'd unhandcuff me, so he did. He told me to rape the girl and said he'd take the boy."

Henley said he talked to Corll for a few minutes, then went to the bathroom. When he returned, he said, Corll had placed the pistol on the table and was near the two intended victims.

"I picked up the gun from the table," Henley stated. "I told him to back off and stop what he was doing. I told him I would kill him if he came at me. He said something and came at me and I killed him."

Henley said he was stunned and terrified at the demonic side of Corll's nature, a side he'd never encountered before.

He turned to Detectives David Mullican and Sidney Smith. "While he was threatening us, he said he'd killed others and had buried them, near Hiram Clarke Road," Henley blurted.

Kerley and Rhonda Williams told the Pasadena officers virtually the same story, although neither could recall Corll clearly stating he'd killed and buried victims previous to themselves.

An inspection of the house turned up the "torture" board — a type the officers recognized as one commonly used in sado-masochistic sexual orgies; a keenly-honed bayonet; and a quantity of pornographic material, most of it relating to homosexual activities. A gas mask lay on the unmade bed.

The three young people were taken to the Pasadena police station to make written affidavits while other officers completed a detailed search of Corll's home. But although every nook and cranny was examined, every scrap and slip of paper examined, every inch of wall and floorboard scrutinized, there was nothing to indicate that anyone other than Dean Allen Corll had met death in the house.

Corll, the neighbors said, had lived in the house only a few months. He was a bachelor, and once mentioned that his father had given him the home. If uncommunicative, and somewhat of an enigma, Corll had been a pleasant neighbor.

"He was a quiet, polite guy who took care of the place and tinkered with cars in the yard. He used to have a Corvette he liked to work on a lot," said one man who lived adjacent to Corll.

According to his neighbors, Corll was always neat and well groomed himself, but most of the young men who came and went were "almost hippie types," with long hair, and often wearing dirty clothes.

"And they came and went at pretty odd hours," said the one man.

A woman said she had noticed a pattern with Corll. "He always drove away in that white van on Saturdays and came back on Sundays," she said.

Yet another neighbor gave some background on Corll. The man said he had known Corll's father since 1951. The man said the father had divorced his first wife, and Dean had

245

been reared by the ex-wife, but kept in close touch and on good terms with the father, an electrician at Baylor College of Medicine. The second wife had died of leukemia, said the neighbor.

The informant hadn't been "close" to Dean Corll, but he had never learned anything or heard anything that would discredit the slain man in his eyes. It was a view shared by all the slain man's neighbors. No one had ever heard a disturbance at the Corll cottage until this morning. Everyone in the neighborhood was shocked at the accusations leveled by Henley.

An inspection of the white van disclosed some heavy plastic, similar to a roll of heavy plastic found in the house. The van also had hooks on the side panels that did not appear functional as lash holdings, but otherwise the interior was devoid of suspicion.

Henley, meantime, had calmed somewhat and was waxing voluble. He said he'd met Corll through a mutual friend, David Brooks, who lived near him in the Heights at one time, and had since seen Corll often, frequently drinking beer with the electrician. He said Corll recently had talked of quitting his job and traveling, and he, Henley, had contemplated going along, taking Rhonda Williams with him.

"Once he said we'd go to Dallas, and another time he said to Reno," Henley stated. "He was supposed to be in some kind of organization that he could get money from. He talked of thousands and thousands of dollars.

"I didn't really believe this, because Dean lived poor. He just had a TV, no stereo and just a transistor radio. He'd be broke once a month when the bills came in."

Henley was uncertain of the exact location where Corll had allegedly buried the victims he spoke of, but recalled that Corll had once pointed out a boat shed he rented, and recalled it was somewhere off Hiram Clarke Road, in Houston's southwest sector. Henley offered to assist officers in locating the boat stall for inspection.

Since Hiram Clarke Road lay inside Houston, the Pasadena officers contacted Houston homicide officials, and a team of Houston detectives, Karl Siebeneicher and D. R. James, joined Mullican and Smith and the witness, Henley.

After a few hours of cruising the Hiram Clarke Road area, criss-crossing the sparsely-populated here, thickly-populated there, neighborhood, Henley pointed to a row of off-water boat storage sheds.

"There, Dean rented one of those stalls. No. 11, I think," Henley said. The row of sheds was owned by a woman who lived nearby, and she confirmed that No. 11 was rented to Dean Allen Corll, and had been since November 17, 1970.

When the detectives entered the shed, they found a sleek new automobile parked inside. Henley denied ever seeing the car. A check of license registrations showed the car to be stolen, taken some days past, from a Houston parking lot.

The officers inspected the earthen floor of the shed, 15 feet wide and 35 feet deep. In places, the soil did appear to have been disturbed recently, especially against the north wall. The detectives contacted the inspector in charge of the Houston jail division and trusties armed with shovels and other digging paraphernalia were sped to the scene. Newsmen at the police station noted the activity, and a horde of television and newspaper reporters and photographers descended on the scene.

The story that ensued was to make gruesome headlines around the world and even generate Papal comment at the Vatican in Rome. The address 4500 Silver Bell (that of the boat stall) would become a universal designation as familiar as 10 Downing Street.

The squad of jail trusties had been at work only a few minutes that afternoon of August 8th when the shovel wielded by one prisoner uncovered a portion of plastic. Carefully, the dirt was removed until a six-foot plastic sheath, enclosing what was patently the body of a human, was bared. The wrapped body was lifted from the shallow grave.

"There's another one beneath it," commented an officer.

There was. Like the first corpse, this one, too, was wrapped in heavy plastic and coated with lime. The lime had contributed to advanced decomposition of both bodies, and it was impossible to tell if the bodies were those of boys or girls, or how long they'd been in the ground.

Henley, whose information to police had led to the discovery, said they were boys. He seemed mesmerized by the grave-probing activity, which, in the next hour, yielded two more bodies, or rather, the skeletal remains of two bodies. These, too, were wrapped in plastic and the flesh had been consumed by lime.

A newsman asked the youth if he knew any of the victims. With tears trickling down his face, Henley nodded. "I knew Marty, and Marty's there. And David, I grew up with him and he lived next door, and I went to school with Charles."

He fell silent then, and slumped on the ground beside a squad car, weeping.

A fifth body was unearthed. And a sixth. Then a seventh. When the eighth body was found, at midnight, the detectives called a halt. The digging would resume next morning. A heavy police guard was placed around the boat shed, and Henley was taken to the police station for food and rest. Fully warned of his constitutional rights, he waived them, and said he'd discuss the case freely the next day after he'd had some sleep and was refreshed. He seemed relieved as he was placed in a solitary cell with a cot.

The detectives conferred with the shift commander, Lieutenant Breck Porter, while others pulled missing persons reports on juvenile or young adult males turned in over the past three years.

Henley had identified Marty as Marty Jones, David as David Hilligiest and Charles as Charles Cobble. The missing person reports reflected a David Hilligiest, 13, who had lived next door to Henley on West 27th, had been reported missing on the night of May 29, 1971, when he left his parents' home to go swimming and never returned. Cobble, 17, who also lived on 27th Street, and Jones, 17, of nearby Arlington Street, had been reported missing only two weeks past. The reports disclosed, however, that the boys had called home a few days later and had said they were sharing a rented room and making their own way.

On July 27, 1973, both boys had contacted their fathers, saying they were "in trouble and needed $1,000 each." No word had been had from either since. Relatives said they had feared the boys were involved with narcotics pushers and needed the money to go elsewhere in the state or nation.

"I think all three of them are among the bodies we recovered," observed Detective Siebeneicher.

Lieutenant Porter agreed. "I don't think Henley's told us all he knows," added the wiry officer. "I have a strong feeling that more than one person is involved in this sadistic, perverted work.

"No one person could have done it. In thirty-two years of police work, I have never seen anyone capable of doing such a thing alone."

A search was initiated for David Brooks, named by Henley as a close intimate of Corll's, and the next morning excavation at the boat shed was resumed. While the trusties wielded shovels, police quizzed Kerley, Miss Williams and Henley.

The girl and Kerley steadfastly denied knowing any more than they'd already related to police. Henley was talkative, but evasive. He said he'd known that the Cobble, Hilligiest and Jones youths' bodies were in the shed because Corll had told him he'd killed the boys after sexually violating them. But Henley said he didn't really know whether Corll was telling the truth or not. And, he added, he was afraid to go to police because he was fearful of Corll.

The discoveries in the boat shed of Thursday, August 9, 1973, were enough to make headlines around the world and to bring newsmen to Houston from all over the globe. At mid-morning, Detective James emerged from the shed, obviously shaken.

"It's wall-to-wall bodies in there," he said tersely.

It was not an exaggerated statement. By noon, another nine corpses had been unearthed. Some were skeletons only. The others were badly decomposed. Only one body was in a recognizable state. That of a young boy, it appeared to have been placed in the shallow grave only a few days past. All the bodies were dispatched to the Harris County Morgue, where teams of pathologists, headed by famed medical examiner Dr. Joseph Jachimczyk, labored around the clock to effect identification.

The same day, the case, in a shocking magnitude that strained the sensibilities of the average citizen, was put into sharper focus when David Brooks, 18, was taken into custody. Almost immediately, on confrontation by officers, Brooks allegedly blurted out a spine-chilling tale of cold-blooded murder, homosexual sex parties and sadistic orgies that staggered the imagination.

Brooks said Corll was the sado-masochistic mastermind of a sex-and-murder triumvirate in which he and Henley were tools, Henley as a participant and he, most often, as a procurer and observer.

He said that he and Henley, for two to three years, had acted as agents for Corll in procuring teenage or young adult males for Corll, who, after taking the victims captive at gunpoint or knifepoint and satisfying his homosexual lusts, would kill the boys and then bury them, alone or with the aid of Henley and Brooks, one or the other, or both together.

Brooks accused Henley of killing several of the victims.

"But I never killed anybody," Brooks insisted.

He said the victims were runaways, young teenagers known to him or Brooks, hitchhikers or young vagrants. Many were friends of his or Henley's from childhood.

Brooks said he knew of "twenty-five to thirty" sex slayings, but he also said that Corll had talked of killing others in other cities and places where Corll had lived.

Brooks said he and Henley were sometimes paid up to $200 to procure victims for Corll's murderous passions. He said he'd met Corll three years ago while visiting Houston from Beaumont, and later became close friends with Corll, he said, and sometimes was paid $5 to $10 by Corll for engaging in homosexual activities with the electrician. He said that after knowing Corll for several months, he introduced Henley to Corll and Henley became a part of the gruesome operation.

Brooks said his first knowledge that Corll was raping and killing young boys was gained when he walked into an apartment on Yorktown, where Corll then lived, and saw two naked boys strapped to a board and Corll, also naked, sexually violating the two victims.

"What are you doing here?" Brooks quoted Corll as asking angrily. He said he placated Corll, who then offered Brooks a new car not to mention the incident. Brooks said he later received the car, and was driving it at the moment. He said he had since married.

He made a written affidavit, a horrifying statement of mass murder that was chilling in its aspects. This is the statement, in its entirety, given by David Brooks:

"My name is David Brooks. I am 18 years old and I live at 1445 Pech with my wife Bridget.

"The first killing that I remember happened when Dean was living at the Yorktown townhouse. There were two boys there and I left before they were killed. But Dean told me he had killed them afterwards. I don't know where they were buried or what their names were. The first few that Dean killed were supposed to have been sent off somewhere in California.

"The first killing that I remember being present at was on 6363 San Felipe (an apartment rented by Dean Corll). That boy was Ruben Haney. Dean and I were the only people involved in that one. But Dean did the killing, and I was just present when it happened.

"I also remember two boys who were killed at the Place One apartments on Mangum (another address of Corll). They were brothers and their father worked next door where they were building some more apartments. I was present when Dean killed them by strangling them but again I did not participate. I believe that I was present when they were buried, but I don't remember where they were buried. The youngest of the two boys is the youngest that was killed I think.

"I remember one boy who was killed on Columbia Street at Dean's house (a home previously owned by Corll in Houston). This was just before Wayne Henley came into the picture. Dean kept this boy around the house for about four days before he killed him. I don't remember his name but we picked him up on 11th and Rutland. I think I helped bury this boy also, but I don't remember where it was.

(Brooks said Corll used High Island, across the bay from Galveston, and a beachhouse tract of land near Rayburn Reservoir in East Texas as burial sites, in addition to the boat

251

shed.)

"This was about two years ago. It really upset Dean to have to kill this boy because he really liked him.

"A boy by the name of Glass was also killed at the Columbia address. I had taken him home one time, but he wouldn't get out because he wanted to go back to Dean's. I took him back and Dean ended up killing him. Now that I think about it, I'm not sure whether it was Glass I took home or another boy. But I believe that it was Glass.

"It was during the time that we were living on Columbia Street that Wayne Henley got involved. Wayne took part in getting the boys at first and then later he took an active part in the killings. Wayne seemed to enjoy causing pain and he was especially sadistic at the Schuler address (another of Corll's numerous Houston residences over a period of years).

"Most of the killings that occurred after Wayne came into the picture involved all three of us. I still did not take part in the actual killing but nearly always all three of us were there.

"I was present when Mark Scott was killed at the Schuler Street address. I had told yesterday this in my witness statement about Mark Scott being at the Schuler house but I did not say that I was present, which I was. Mark had a knife and he tried to get Dean. He swung at him with a knife and caught Dean's shirt and barely broke the skin. He still had one hand tied and Dean grabbed the hand with the knife. Wayne ran out of the room and got a pistol, and Mark just gave up. Wayne killed Mark Scott and I think that he strangled him. Mark was either buried at the beach (High Island) or at the boat house.

"There was another boy killed at the Schuler house, actually there were two at this time. A boy named Billy Balsch and a Johnny and I think that his last name was Malone. Wayne strangled Billy and he said 'Hey, Johnny,' and when Johnny looked up Wayne shot him in the forehead with a .25 automatic. The bullet came out his ear and he raised up and about three minutes later he said, 'Wayne, please don't!' Then Wayne strangled him, and

252

Dean helped.

"It was while we were living on Schuler that Wayne and Dean got me down and started to kill me. I begged Dean not to kill me and he finally let me go. I told about this in my witness statement and that part of my statement was absolutely true. (Brooks apparently gave a first statement full of falsehoods, although police will not comment due to a court order prohibiting further disclosures of what the defendants in the case have stated.) It was also at this address that they got Billy Ridinger and what I said in my witness statement about him was true. (Brooks apparently refers here to a statement he made to newsmen concerning a boy he said was visiting Corll and himself and Henley on one occasion. He said Corll handcuffed the boy on a pretext of showing the youth a trick, and thereafter Henley wanted to kill the boy, but was persuaded not to by Corll.) I took care of him while he was there and I believe the only reason he is alive now is because I begged them not to kill him.

"Wayne and Dean got one boy by themselves while we were on Schuler. It was a tall, skinny guy. I just happened to walk in the house and there he was. I left before they killed this one.

"In the first apartment we lived in at Westcott Towers (another Corll address) I think that there were two boys killed. These were both young boys from the Heights area but I don't know their names. Wayne accidentally shot one of them. This was about 7 A.M. I was in the other room asleep when this happened. Dean told me that Wayne had just come in waving a .22 and accidentally shot one of the boys in the jaw. The bullet just went in a little and then it was just under the skin. They didn't kill the boy right then. They killed these two boys later on that day.

"Dean moved to the Princessa Apartments on Wirt and I remember him getting one boy there by himself. He wanted me to help him but I wouldn't do it. I didn't want to mess with this one because I had someplace I wanted to go so I tried to get him mad (the victim) so he would leave but he wanted to stay.

253

"Dean grabbed the boy and within three minutes of when he grabbed him I was gone. At that time I was using Dean's car so I was in and out all the time. After the Princessa Apartments Dean moved to Pasadena. I know of two that were killed there. One was from Baton Rouge (Louisiana) and one was a small blond boy from South Houston. I saw the boy from South Houston for about 45 minutes. I took him a pizza and then I left and he wanted me to come back. I wasn't there when either of these two boys were killed. I did come in just after Dean had killed the boy from Baton Rouge, that one was a different day from the blond boy.

"In all, I guess there were between 25 and 30 boys killed and they were buried in three different places.

"I was present and helped bury many of them but not all of them. Most of them were buried at the boat stall. There were three or four buried at Sam Rayburn, I think, I am sure there are two up there. On the first one at Sam Rayburn I helped bury them. Then the next one we took to Sam Rayburn when we got there Dean and Wayne found the first one had come to the surface and either a foot or a hand was above the ground. When they buried this one a second time they put some type of sheet on tops of him to keep him down.

"The third place that they buried was on the beach at High Island. This was right off the Winnie (Texas) exit where the road goes to the beach. You turn east on the beach road and go till the pavement changes which is about a quarter or a half a mile and the bodies are on the right hand side of the highway about 15 or 20 yards off the road. I never actually buried one there but I always drove the car. I know that one of the graves had a large rock on top of it. I think there were five or more bodies buried at this location.

"The bodies on the beach are in a row down the beach for perhaps half a mile or so. I am willing to show officers where this location is and I will try to locate as many of the graves as possible.

"I regret that this happened and I'm sorry for the kids'

families."

David Brooks' own father witnessed his son's signature on the damning document.

Confronted with Brooks' accusations, Henley confessed that he'd been misleading police, and was himself deeply involved in the mass murder ring. He said he thought he'd killed nine of the victims himself, but wasn't sure of the exact number. Like Brooks, he said there were possibly "twenty-five to thirty" victims, but there might even be more, since Corll had hinted at a similar operation in Dallas, where Corll lived for a time. But he said he knew of no names and no burial sites other than those of which had firsthand knowledge.

He, too, offered to guide police to gravesites near Sam Rayburn lake and High Island, an offer that was promptly accepted.

A large posse of Houston, Pasadena and state officers converged on the Rayburn lake site, near a beach home owned by Corll's family. A large contingent of newsmen tagged along with the posse. After driving around for a while, Henley pointed out a narrow clay road leading to a sandy clearing near the lake.

"Down there," he said. He pointed out two seemingly undisturbed spots, but when workmen shoveled away the top soil, the bodies of two more victims were revealed. Like most of the others, the corpses were naked, decomposed, wrapped in plastic and covered with lime.

"Who's in the graves?" asked a reporter of Henley.

Henley sighed. "Just some boys I helped Dean get. He raped them, killed them and buried them. I helped him," Henley replied.

He paused. "Billy's buried out there."

"Who's Billy?"

"Billy Lawrence," said Henley and then fell silent.

In all, four bodies were unearthed at Rayburn, all, Brooks and Henley insisted, that had been buried there to their knowledge. A thorough search of the land around the site using backhoes and bulldozers, failed to turn up any more bodies. The searchers moved on to High Island, with Henley still making intermittent comments about his part in the slayings. He would not go into detail on any of the killings, but said his role in the beginning was that of being only a procurer for Corll.

"He offered to pay me $200 as a beginning price," Henley told newsmen.

"He paid me some of that."

He said his two-year relationship with Corll began to get to him in recent months. "He made me feel pretty grotesque," said Henley.

"Dean had a lust for blood. I was tired of him doing things like that."

At High Island, Brooks and Henley first pointed out a large rock. They said a body was beneath the rock, according to Corll. They said they weren't sure, since they had not helped bury anyone there.

"Dean pointed it out about six months ago, and said, 'This is where I buried one of those boys I told you about'," Brooks told Detective W. L. Young.

Workers removed the rock and commenced digging. Less than three feet down in the sand, they uncovered a skeleton wrapped in plastic. Shards of flesh were on the feet bones.

One hundred yards distant, Brooks and Henley pointed out a second site. Digging yielded another skeleton, this one unwrapped. Long black hair still clung to the skull.

Digging over the next three days resulted in the discovery of four more bodies, bringing the total recovered to 27 and making the Corll-Henley-Brooks operation the greatest mass murder case in the annals of the 20th Century, surpassing California's Feather River mass murder of 25 men in which Juan Corona was convicted this year.

While search operations were going on, pathologists and police were seeking to identify the various victims, a task, Dr. Jachimczyk pointed out, that might never be completed.

Unless the skull was intact and the victim had identifiable dental work or identifiable bone fractures, identification from a skeleton alone would be very difficult. And old, healed fractures would not necessarily be proof, said Dr. Jachimczyk. In some cases, perhaps, the victim would be known only as to age and sex, both of which could be determined from the bones.

It had already been established that all the victims were young boys or males verging on adulthood.

In ensuing days, however, police and pathologists, using dental records, other means of identification, and through correlation of Henley's and Brooks' accounts of victims known by name, and drawing on dates, times and places of contact recalled by the two, effected positive identification on 14 of the victims, including Jones and Cobble.

Others positively identified:

William Lawrence, 15, son of a Houston Post employee, missing since the first week of June, 1973. Identified by father.

Donald Edward Waldrop, 15, and his brother Jerry Lynn Waldrop, 13, who disappeared from their Heights home in January of 1971. They were identified by their clothing.

James S. Dreymala, 14, last seen August 3rd, 1973, when he rode his bike to a friend's home. He called his father that night and asked to spend the night with the friend, but was told to be home within 20 minutes. He never appeared. His body and the bike were found in the boat shed, and the youth was identified by fingerprints. He was the last victim of the three, police theorize, or so Henley and Brooks insist.

James Eugene Glass, 14, who vanished from a church meeting in December of 1970. Identified by dental records.

Danny Michael Yates, 15, who vanished in company with young Glass. Identified from dental records.

Ruben W. Watson (identified by Brooks as Ruben Haney), 17, who left home August 17, 1971, to attend a movie and never returned. Identified from dental charts.

Wally J. Simoneaux, 14, who left home October 2, 1972, to spend the night with Richard Hembree, 13. Both boys disappeared from Hembree's home that night. Simoneaux was identified from dental records.

Richard Hembree, identified from dental records.

Jeffrey Alan Konen, 18, a student at the University of Texas, who vanished September 25, 1970. Identified from dental records.

Raymond S. Blackborn, 20, of Baton Rouge, last seen in

June, 1973, when he left his trailer home in Houston to hitch-hike to Louisiana, where his wife and child resided. Identified from dental records.

Johnny Delone, 16, who ran away from his Heights home in May of 1972. Identified from dental charts (he was identified as Johnny Malone by Brooks and Henley).

Other victims among the 27, police feel certain, although positive proof is lacking, include:

David Hilligiest.

Gregory M. Winkle, 16, who vanished in company with Hilligiest.

Frank Aguirre, 19, who disappeared in March of 1972, after leaving his job. Aguirre at the time was dating the Williams girl.

Mark Scott, 19, who disappeared December 22, 1972. He was a friend to both Corll and Henley. Named as a victim by Brooks.

Homer Garcia, 15, who disappeared from his home July 17, 1973. Lived near Henley.

Willard Branch, Jr., 19, who disappeared in July of 1971.

Of the dozen instances where cause of death could be definitely established, Dr. Jachimczyk said all had been shot or strangled, or both. In some instances, pistol slugs suitable for ballistics comparisons were recovered and turned over to police. Detectives, however, have refused to make public results of the tests in relation to the gun that killed Corll and other handguns that may have been recovered.

What manner of men were Brooks, Henley and Corll?

Hundreds of police and newsmen joined in an attempt to provide an insight into the pasts and personalities of the three.

So far, each emerges as an unlikely fiend, despite the mind-boggling evidence of their depravity. Nothing in the backgrounds of the three, as so far known, indicates that any of the three displayed the symptoms of the psychopathic, deep-seated emotional disturbances usually exhibited by sado-masochistic sex killers.

David Brooks: Son of divorced parents, but officers say there was nothing in the dissolution of his parents' marriage that would tend to create a homicidal trauma. He lived with his father in Beaumont after the divorce, then moved to Houston with his father, a contractor, some three years ago. In Beaumont and in Houston, David Brooks was a C and B student before dropping out of high school to get married. He was never in trouble, and was liked by those who knew him. If he made the drug scene, his father had no knowledge of it. His involvement in the sex murder ring stunned both parents.

"But I love him," said the mother, who now lives in Louisiana. "That doesn't mean I condone anything he's done. It's a real shock."

Brook's father cannot pinpoint anything in his son's formative years to explain the terrible deeds the youth has admitted.

Elmer Wayne Henley: One of four sons of divorced parents, never in trouble and never on drugs, according to his mother, who talks freely about her son. She knew both Corll and Brooks. Henley met Brooks in the ninth grade, shortly before Henley dropped out of school. Henley's mother says Brooks and her son were not always good friends, for sometimes they would quarrel and not see each other for days or weeks. Brooks was not talkative, she says, and sometimes criticized her for what Brooks considered too rigid disciplining of her children.

"I like to know where my kids are," she stated. "David told me my kids could take care of themselves and to leave them alone."

Henley's mother cannot comprehend the enormity of Wayne's crimes, but said her son told her he was deeply involved and quoted Henley as saying, "Momma, be happy for me because now at last I can live." She said her son had told her he had confessed in detail, "everything, just everything," to police.

"I don't understand how he lived with it," she said. "He never told me a thing about it and he was always so considerate. He is a generous, kind-hearted boy. I just know he is."

She is equally astonished at the dark, unsuspected portrait of Corll that has been made public. "He was such a nice, polite man who loved to be around kids." She said she only saw Corll display irritation once, when she was kidding him about his age. "His eyes would flash when I joked about his age," she said.

"Dean treated Wayne like a son. And Wayne loved him like a father. I know Dean must have done something terrible to Wayne to make Wayne shoot him. Dean loved to be around kids and prattle with them about cars or fishing."

Henley's mother said Corll was a frequent visitor in her home. Corll ate Easter dinner with the Henleys. Corll worked on her car. She said Corll sometimes piled 10 to 12 neighborhood children into his van and took them joyriding. She said Wayne, Brooks and Corll were often together on weekends. She said they told her they were working on cars at a warehouse "near the Hiram Clarke Road power station where Corll worked (for the Housing Lighting & Power Company).

"About four months ago, Wayne began seeing a lot of Dean Corll," she continued. "He spent the night over at Dean's with David Brooks almost every Sunday."

Corll's mother, struggling to make a living for her three children, opened a candy store in Vidor, selling homemade pralines to local outlets. Corll himself frequently gathered pecans from the woods that were used in the sweet discs. He continued to help his mother in the candy business after graduation from high school.

At 21, he returned to Fort Wayne for two years to take care of his aged and widowed grandmother. He took a job in Indiana and faithfully sent money home to his mother. When he returned to Texas, his mother, brother and half-sister lived in Houston. Soon after, his mother, using the family kitchen as a factory, established the Corll Candy Company, with herself as president, Dean as vice-president and his brother as secretary-treasurer. Dean Corll was drafted into the Army at 24, on August 10, 1964, and trained at Fort Polk, Louisiana. He went through radio repair school at Fort Benning, Georgia, and was posted to Fort Hood, Texas, where he was discharged honorably on June 11, 1965, under the Army's hardship discharge system. His record as a soldier was spotless, and fellow

GIs recall him as a "good guy, quiet and helpful." No taint of homosexuality attached to Corll in the Army.

Back home, Corll immersed himself in the family candy operation. The firm grew and moved to larger quarters, across from an elementary school. Dean Corll took an apartment by himself a block from the candy factory. He was generous to the school children, and became known as the "Candy Man" of the Heights.

David Hilligiest knew him, says the boy's mother.

"David would come home, all excited, saying the man was giving away candy to the children," she said. "It was the talk of the neighborhood. I had a funny feeling about it. Then I heard that this man was inviting the children into a back room where he kept a pool table. I could understand the free candy, maybe, but this other sounded a little peculiar to me." She told David never to visit the candy man again, but doesn't know whether the child went back or not.

Corll maintained a close, pleasant relationship with his father, who settled in Houston in late 1954. In 1968, his mother dissolved the candy firm and moved with her daughter to Colorado. Dean Corll's brother took a job as a machine operator in Houston. Dean decided to become an electrician like his father, and apprenticed himself in a training program maintained by the Houston Lighting and Power Company.

If there was anything odd about his demeanor, it was his penchant for moving from apartment to apartment, house to house. Only one hint of the horrors Brooks and Henley say occurred behind the various doors has emerged. A former manager of an apartment complex where Corll once lived says a maintenance man found some bullet holes in the door of an apartment shared by Brooks and Corll in 1971. The door was replaced, and when Corll and Brooks moved a month later, a steel plate was found fastened to the inside of the new door.

Corll's mother has a tenacious faith that her son is innocent. She emphatically insists he was a tool of Brooks and Henley.

"He was used," she says firmly. In a copyrighted Chronicle interview, she told of a telephone conversation she had with her son, Dean Corll, on August 4, 1973, four days before his death.

Dean called her, she said, and she first asked him how he was doing.

She quotes him: "All right, but, Mother, I'm in trouble. I'm going to drop out of sight." A pause, then: "I could take an overdose."

His mother says she protested: "You're not on dope!"

Corll replied: "No, but it would be one way of getting out of this."

His mother continued: "Then he told me, 'I can't talk about it,' so I didn't ask him." But she told Dean, "Taking your life will not solve your problems. You'll have to carry your problems to the next life, so you might as well start now." She recalls Dean answered, "Mother, it might be easier to start over in another life."

She says she thinks now Corll called her "right after those last two murders. He found out what those boys were doing." She said she mailed her son a letter, some candy and an inspirational book. "Now, they can't find his books, his clothes, nothing," she says. "The Sunday before he was killed, I called him. There was no answer all day. That night, about seven o'clock, he answered the phone and said, 'I've been dodging somebody.'" She said Corll then talked of coming to Colorado and helping in a candy factory she'd established there.

Her son was a joy and a help to her all his life, his mother added. Dean Corll was an obedient son. Polite. Kind to animals, children and old people. He loved humanity.

He was no homosexual. He planned to get married to a girl he dated in Houston.

He was studious, interested in the classics, cars, music, all the normal things a normal young bachelor is interested in. He loved and was devoted to his family, father, mother, sister and brother.

"Does this sound like a man who would murder and do all those horrible things he is accused of?" asked the mother.

She released an "open letter" to the world. It is reproduced here:

"My heart is heavy with sorrow; not only for the loss of my

262

son, but also for the loss of all the boys and people whose lives they touched.

"To David and Wayne, you may have the best defense lawyers the world can offer but your best defense is God. You can lie, plan, and plant evidence to shift the blame to one who cannot defend himself, but you surely know that your days on this earth are numbered, whether it is behind bars or walking the streets. We are not concerned with your bodies, but we are concerned with your souls — 'And the truth will set you free.'

"If you knew where to find the bodies of these children, you also have a list of names. Please set the anxious parents' hearts at ease, and see how much better you feel.

"I am not trying to solve this mystery, as I know nothing about the case. I only know that Dean loved both of you. He did things for you that you could not do for yourself but you cut off the hand that fed you. Dean cannot help you now. He loaned you his truck to go on dates. He borrowed money from the bank for you, a Vet (Henley reportedly got a used Corvette from Corll).

"Would he have rented the boat shack to bury bodies in and still loan it to friends and the family to store furniture in and help them move in? Would he ever stoop so low as to have had those wild parties in a house belonging to his father whom he adored? He was not a sex maniac or a sadist. You might be able to convince the type of people who drag their children to see bodies dug up out of the earth that this is true, but the people who knew Dean, worked with him, raised him, will never believe these terrible accusations . . .

"The tear gas pencil and gas mask on the bed proves to me and the world that Dean was not going to shoot you. He only wanted to live and let live. The torture boards were also planted, and where are his clothes and the books I sent him on 'Help For Today' and 'This Thing Called You' by Ernest Holmes?

"Parents, pray for your children, and children, write your parents. What a wonderful world this could be if we all turned to God for guidance. The police department could solve all their problems if they too really and truly asked God for help.

God does not protect us from the law, He is the law. The law of love, life, happiness, prosperity and success.

"I cannot help but wonder if the digging would have stopped if the record had not been broken . . ."

The digging has not stopped. Police have explored yards and vacant lots wherever Corll had lived, dug up additional miles of beaches and lake shores that Corll was known to haunt.

They seek the answer to some of his mother's questions, and hundreds of their own.

Why were not shots or cries ever heard from any of the residences in which Corll and Brooks lived? Why did none of those reputed to have escaped his clutches contact police? Were some youngsters buried alive, as has been rumored in the Heights? Questions, questions, questions.

At this writing, a grand jury probe of the mass murder ring is underway. Billy Ridinger, Kerley, Miss Williams and many others have been heard in secret sessions.

Henley and Brooks are held without bond on indictments returned against each, accusing each of four counts of murder. A sanity hearing for both has been ordered by a judge, over the objections of their attorneys.

More than 100 lawmen are still working on the case, spurred by a burning question: Are there still more corpses to be unearthed, further footnotes to the horror story?

Perhaps, during the legal hearings scheduled for Henley and Brooks, some of the questions may be answered.

But in all likelihood, all connected with the case agree, the answers to most of the questions posed—and any reader can pose scores of his own—went to the grave with Dean Corll.

Including one concerning Corll himself.

Was he a dupe and a pawn, or a man to stand side by side with the arch-fiends of recorded history?

The Mistakes That Trapped "Son of Sam"

by George Carpozi, Jr.

July 29, 1976. A warm, moonlit night, a Thursday. The time was 1:10 a.m. A vivacious dark-haired girl, her tresses falling in a pleasant flow to her slender shoulders, sat easily in the parked car chatting animatedly with her pretty brunette companion who also wore her neatly-coiffed hair in a long sweeping style.

Eighteen-year-old Donna Lauria occupied the passenger side of the front seat nearest the sidewalk and 19-year-old Jody Valente was behind the steering wheel of her 1975 blue Oldsmobile that was double-parked outside the six-story yellow brick building on Buhre Avenue, a quiet, tree-lined street which looked more like a neighborhood in the suburbs than a residential section of New York City.

The locale was just three blocks from the southern perimeter of Pelham Bay Park, one of the few expanses of verdant land in the Bronx and less than two-thirds of a mile from the craggy shore of Eastchester Bay. The neighborhood itself hadn't yet been contaminated by the blight afflicting so many of the borough's other residential and business communities being transformed into burned-out, uninhabitable ghettos.

So caught up were Jody and Donna in their free-flowing, easy-paced, carefree banter that neither heard the call from the sidewalk.

"Hi, Donna . . . Hi, Jody," the voice greeted.

At that moment Donna had been telling Jody about a funny incident that had happened to her the day before at her job as an emergency medical technician for a private hospital ambulance service in Manhattan.

The girls had just returned from a night out. They had met a couple of hours earlier following a date Donna had with her 21-year-old fiance who worked as a paramedic with Donna for the Empire State Ambulance Service at New York Hospital.

At the sound of their names, the girls turned and looked toward the sidewalk.

"Hello, Mom," Donna called out. "Hi, Dad . . ."

Her parents were just returning themselves from an evening out when they spotted their daughter and her friend.

"Coming up soon?" her mother asked.

"Be up in a minute, Mom," Donna promised.

The parents went upstairs to their apartment on the fourth floor where their other two children, one 19 years old, the other 14, were asleep.

No sooner had they gotten inside than the parents were startled by a series of loud explosions from the street, followed immediately by the shrill outcry of a woman. They hurried to a window overlooking the street and were terrified by what they saw.

There was Jody Valente struggling out of the car and then limping in the middle of the roadway in what seemed like an aimless back and forth jaunt of the street.

"Help me! Help me!" she was screaming.

The Laurias didn't wait to see anymore. They shouted to their sons, who by now were out of bed, and they all rushed downstairs to the street.

Meanwhile, Jody's outcries awakened many residents in that predominantly Irish and Italian neighborhood and they gaped with inordinate curiosity and bewilderment from their open windows.

They were able to see now what the Laurias couldn't see from inside the stairwell that they were descending at this

266

very instant. Jody had finally returned from her inexplicable middle-of-the-street zigzagging and hobbled in a straight, direct path finally to the other side of the car where Donna had been sitting.

Crying out, "Donna! Donna!" Jody opened the car door and her girlfriend toppled limply out of the front seat. Her body fell like a weighted sack, head first out of the car and hit the pavement with a sickening thud.

As the onlookers from on high gasped in horror, Jody exploded anew with anguished screams.

Just then the Laurias burst out of the apartment building. The sight of their daughter's unmoving body sprawled on the street beside the car generated cacophonous, hysterical outbursts by the family.

Her parents and brothers knelt beside Donna in a desperate but futile attempt to minister first aid and comfort. Then they quickly sensed the utter uselessness of their efforts.

From the large flow of blood from the back of the head, it was obvious even to those nearest and dearest to her that there was nothing they could do for Donna. Even if Jody Valente was not broken up and weeping uncontrollably — and bleeding from the left thigh — she couldn't have been expected to apply any lesson she had been taught up to then as a nurse in training.

She couldn't have helped her friend.

There wasn't anything anyone could do for Donna Lauria now . . .

It was up to the ambulance doctor from Jacobi Hospital to make it official by pronouncing the victim D.O.A. — dead on arrival.

Jody, who'd been shot in the left thigh and was bleeding profusely, was given emergency first aid at the scene, then taken to the hospital. Her condition wasn't critical and doctors placed no prohibition against her being questioned by the police.

That task fell to Detective Ronald Marsenison who obtained the following account from the young woman who

267

described the events of the evening: Donna's date with her beau, the girls' get-together, and their drive to Donna's apartment where Jody was to drop off her friend and then go to her own home on nearby Hutchinson River Parkway.

Then Jody went into the significant details about those moments that led up to the shooting:

"Donna had left the car after her parents had gone upstairs. I was about to drive away but Donna came back to the car to say something she had forgotten to tell me before. It had something to do with our vacation plans that we were making for this summer.

"Then all of a sudden a man . . . he wasn't very tall . . . appeared on the sidewalk and came toward the car on the side where Donna was sitting. Without saying a word, he pointed a gun and fired two or three shots.

"I believe the first shot hit Donna in the head . . . She slumped back in the seat. I'm not sure when I was hit . . . with the second or third shot. But, as you can see, he got me in the thigh . . ."

What did the killer look like, Marsenison wanted to know?

He had a wide face with a nose whose tip seemed slightly pinched, eyes that "appear to stare at you," and hair that was brown and curly.

"How tall was he . . . how much would you say he weighed?" the detective asked.

"About 5 feet 8 . . . and I'd say around 175 pounds," responded the only eyewitness to the murder.

"Would you recognize him if you ever saw him again?" the sleuth asked.

Jody nodded vigorously.

"I'll never forget him," she said.

Other detectives interrogated Donna's parents as well as her brothers.

Anyone who might have reason—no matter how remote, how far-fetched, how unlikely—to harm Donna, they inquired?

There was instant and unanimous agreement that Donna

268

had no enemies.

What did the parents know about Donna's boyfriend?

Police investigations often hit on what many consider to be cruel and inhumane approaches in searches for clues and evidence that can conceivably help to solve a crime. No detective was suggesting that the young man Donna planned to marry was even remotely suspected of complicity in the crime. Yet asking questions about him and all others who knew and associated with Donna was part of the routine.

Checking out such innocent, uninvolved persons eliminates them from suspicion and clears the path which authorities had to travel on the way to the ultimate solution of that senseless outrage perpetrated in this quiet Bronx neighborhood.

After daybreak, detectives went on a door-to-door search for possible eyewitnesses or for information which could aid the investigation.

No one could add anything more to what the sleuths had already learned. But the neighbors were unanimous in their praises of Donna, who had lived all her life in Pelham Bay Park.

Detectives wished they could explain why a killer stalked out of the night's black shadows and took Donna Lauria's life. Because if they could explain that, then they'd know who the killer was—and they'd have him in custody.

Their investigation at the murder site was augmented by the detectives from the Crime Scene Unit which entailed photographing the street between its two nearest intersections. Mayflower and Pilgrim Avenues; shooting numerous interior and exterior photos of the car (and of the body before it was removed to the morgue for autopsy); dusting the car for fingerprints inside and out; finetooth-combing the street, its gutters, and sidewalks for any conceivable clue—a matchbook cover, a discarded pack of cigarettes, anything that looked as though the killer had dropped or tossed it away—which could help put police on his trail.

The most telling bit of evidence that the teams of detectives ultimately drew out of their investigation was the conclusion of the ballistics experts on the type of weapon used in the crime.

It was a most unusual gun and the two lead slugs found inside the car — one fired wildly and one that tore through Jody Valente's thigh, along with the one later removed by the medical examiner from the victim's head — gave conclusive proof that the survivor of the savage attack wasn't hallucinating when she reported the assassin had wielded what looked like a legendary six-shooter.

Indeed he had, for the three bullets were big .44-caliber slugs!

The killer had come armed with a gun right out of the sagebrush and cactus country of the Wild West. It was the same gun that Buffalo Bill and Jessie James and the Dalton Brothers and Bat Masterson once unlimbered from their holsters when they had reasons to shoot from the hip.

But the man who pulled the trigger of the .44-caliber revolver in the Bronx that early morning of July 29th didn't have the style that the good and badmen of the West had when they fired the six-iron — with one hand.

As Jody Valente explained it vividly and with total certainty to Detective Marsenison, this killer held the gun with two hands — one hand on the grip, the other underneath to steady the trigger finger. He also went into a semi-crouch — just as the cops on TV have been firing their guns at the bad guys.

The unusual caliber of the gun and the killer's peculiar stance and style of firing the weapon didn't make an immediate impact on the investigators. But in time this information and evidence would become increasingly more significant and, indeed, indispensable to the case as the search ultimately generated into a trackdown of a psychopathic killer that commanded greater numbers and more intense concentration by the posse of lawmen rounded up in that manhunt.

Actually the weapon's caliber would grow to be the one all-important link between the gunman who killed Donna Lauria and the largest police force in the United States that was engaged in the search for him.

But in the hours after Miss Lauria was slain and Miss Valente was wounded, the unexplained attack took its place as a more or less routine crime on an unusually busy mid-week night of criminal activity. The killing of Donna Lauria and the wounding of Jody Valente was but one of five separate shooting incidents that confronted detectives in three of New York City's five boroughs and left the statisticians at police headquarters shaking their heads in puzzlement at the freakish outbreak of gunfire that night.

By dawn's early light, the terror of the night translated into a startling statistic—the rampaging gunman had visited an unsuspecting city and left one dead, 9 wounded, and an 11th intended victim a lucky near-miss.

But among all the victims of that warm, moonlit night of July 29th, only two would matter in the realm of future investigations and searches for the man who took Miss Lauria's life and caused bodily injury to Jody Valente.

Yet at that time no one—not even the police who investigated Donna Lauria's baffling murder and Jody Valente's shooting—could envision then what time would bring:

The deep, abiding, vivid fear of a psychopathic assassin with an inexplicable penchant to kill and maim girls with long, brown hair.

The .44-caliber killer!

Four months had now gone by and it was a Friday night. The bone-chilling snap of another approaching winter was in the air everywhere. Certainly it was too late in the season to have hoped for continued warm weather, for this was November 26th.

Thanksgiving was a day gone already and a mere 24 shopping days remained till Christmas.

Friday night in the Floral Park section of Queens was never much different than in many other areas of the city where teenagers congregate. They gather on a favorite streetcorner, in a special hamburger hangout, or even at an out-of-the-neighborhood discotheque where they might sip a beer or two with a phony or forged I.D. card that adds a

271

critical few months for an underage person.

But on that Friday night, 18-year-old Joanne Lomino and 16-year-old Donna DeMasi had followed a more circuitous route to their preferred hamburger stand. They had first journeyed by bus and subway to Times Square and the Broadway scene for an evening at a rock movie.

The show let out shortly after 10:30 p.m. and Joanne and Donna were feeling the pangs of hunger. They could go for a nice, juicy hamburger with all the trimmings and a milk shake—but certainly not on the Gay White Way. Not the way it is these days—a deteriorated, seemingly endless tapestry of pornography and prostitution, with undesirables waiting at every corner and darkened doorway to solicit or dispense the illicit favors merchandised by those dregs of society.

Joanne and Donna plunked their half-dollar tokens into the turnstile slots and rode a graffiti-covered subway train to the IND line's Hillside Avenue station, the last stop. Then they caught the bus which ran further on along Hillside Avenue from Hollis to the city line for another 50-cent fare.

They got off at the corner of 257th Street in Floral Park, which was the site of a late-hours hamburger stand the kids of the neighborhood really dug.

After a satisfying snack and an exchange of pleasantries with some of the crowd—many of them neighborhood youngsters who attended nearby Martin Van Buren High School in Queens Village—Joanne and Donna left the corner burger shoppe and walked homeward in the quiet, virtually crime-free middle-class neighborhood of neat, detached one-family homes which abut the Nassau County line.

Joanne Lomino lived on 261st Street, which lies between 83rd and Hillside Avenues. Donna DiMasi's home was four blocks further, on 262nd Street, situated between 86th and 87th Avenues.

Since Joanne's home was more or less on the way to where Donna lived, the latter walked her friend to her house and sat with her on the front stoop to talk a while.

The time was 12:30 a.m.

It was somewhat overcast and the chill of approaching winter was very definitely in the autumn air, although it was still pleasant to be outdoors.

Their conversation ranged over a number of subjects and lasted for about 10 minutes. Then the two girls rose from the stoop they'd been sitting on. Joanne, who like Donna had long brown hair that reached down to her shoulders, descended the steps to the sidewalk. Donna reached into her purse for the key to unlock the front door of the two-story white-shingled house.

"Goodnight," she said, "see you tomorrow . . ."

Before Joanne could respond, there was an interruption caused by the sighting of an unfamiliar figure walking on the opposite sidewalk of 83rd Avenue.

The girls might not have given the stranger a second thought had it not been for the startling turn in direction he took after spotting them in front of Joanne's house. As he changed course abruptly, he also quickened his pace appreciably.

After crossing at the corner of 261st Street to the other side of the avenue, he headed straight toward Joanne and Donna, who stood their ground more in puzzlement than fright.

Yet concern was not completely absent from their thoughts as the man came into sight more clearly after passing under the street light.

He looked to be about 30 years old, perhaps 5 feet 10, or a little shorter, and about 150 pounds or a slight bit heavier. He was wearing an Army-type pea green, three-quarter-length coat for warmth against the early morning cold.

Still, neither girl felt any particular apprehension as the man moved closer, closer, even closer. To Joanne and Donna it seemed that he might be lost, that he was coming to them to seek directions.

And for a brief, fleeting moment their assumption appeared to be a correct one as the stranger blurted, "Say, can you tell me how to get to . . ."

273

Then an instant later Joanne Lomino and Donna DiMasi shrieked in horror.

The man had yanked a gun from his waistband and without a word began firing at the girls.

Donna cried in anguish as a slug tore through the fleshy part of her neck and shattered her collarbone. The impact came with such force that she toppled backward to the sidewalk, a fall later credited with probably having saved her from more serious injury or even death, had she remained on her feet and been struck by another of the four bullets the gunman had fired.

But not all the three other lead slugs went astray. One plowed into Joanne Lomino's back just as she had turned and was trying to unlock the door to summon her family's help.

Joanne collapsed on the concrete stoop with an agonizing scream.

By now, lights in the Lomino house and others in the block were flicked on as Joanne's family and neighbors heard the girls' startling screams of pain.

A next door neighbor pulled on his pants without even looking out the window. He was out of the house in a minute. As he would soon tell Detective Bernard Judge of the 105th Squad in Queens Village:

"I saw Donna lying on the stoop, screaming that she was dying. Her jacket was soaked through with blood. She was in terrible shape," he added grimly.

"I saw Joanne just sort of leaning against the house door, not saying anything much. She didn't seem to be hurt that badly, because she wasn't bleeding that much."

He said he didn't see the assailant.

But another neighbor did catch a glimpse of the fugitive.

"I just got a fleeting look," the detective was told by the eyewitness whose identity was not revealed by authorities because this person would be called upon to identify the gunman—if and when he was caught.

"What can you tell me about him?" Detective Judge asked the witness.

The man's height, weight, and clothing which the witness described dovetailed precisely with the portrait of the assassin that Donna had painted for authorities when she was questioned in the emergency room of Long Island Jewish-Hillside Medical Center in nearby New Hyde Park, before she was wheeled to surgery for repairs to her shattered collarbone.

Detectives were unable to question Joanne Lomino because her condition was critical. The bullet which struck her back had lodged in her spine. Her legs were paralyzed and, as she was taken to surgery, doctors gave her small chance of regaining the use of her lower extremities.

Back at the scene, the Crime Scene Unit and specialists from the police laboratory went through the rigorous routine of gathering whatever shreds of evidence the mysterious gunman might have left behind.

But there were rather few clues to recover. Aside from the bullet that doctors removed from Donna's collarbone and the other one from Joanne's spine—both so badly shattered that rifling marks couldn't be distinguished—the ballistics sleuths recovered the other two slugs that the gunman had fired.

Those were in far better condition than the bullets that had lodged in the girls' bodies. One of the stray slugs had struck the mailbox, the other was imbedded in the wooden front door.

These bullets would be analyzed later by ballistics experts and the riflings were to tell a revealing tale—that those bullets were fired from the very same .44-caliber "Wild West" revolver that had killed Donna Lauria and wounded Jody Valente four months earlier in the Northeast Bronx.

But did that finding strike an immediate recognition for the investigators of the Queens shooting?

Did the discovery prompt detectives in the Bronx to leap into action and make tracks to Queens to compare notes with the sleuths probing Joanne Lomino's and Donna Di-Masi's shootings?

No, the ballistics findings didn't precipitate such action

275

even though it was a mere 10 miles from the Baychester-Pelham Bay neighborhood where Miss Lauria died and her friend Jody Valente was wounded to the Floral Park neighborhood across the merging waters of the East River and Pelham Bay in Queens.

In fact, there were several direct express highway links between the two neighborhoods in the separate boroughs—roads that anyone, even a psychopathic gunman, would encounter little if any difficulty traversing from one juncture to the other in a matter of 15 minutes or so.

Of course the man who murdered and maimed in the Bronx may not have traveled between those two points on the same night that he wounded the two Queens teenagers.

The crimes had been committed four months apart.

In their investigation in Queens, detectives of the 105th Squad made no inroads in picking up the gunman's trail. The one solid witness, the one whose identity was kept under wraps, had also seen the assassin in flight—but only fleetingly.

"He ran quickly at first, the gun with its long barrel held in his left hand as he went," the witness told authorities. "Then when he reached the corner, I saw him slow down and begin walking. And that's when he disappeared from my view, when he turned the corner. Then he was gone . . ."

Did the witness hear a car start, or a car driven away?

"No, nothing at all," the witness responded. "Just the two girls crying and whimpering . . . that's all that broke the silence of the night, that's all I heard . . . except for the shots that woke me and brought me to my window . . ."

In time, when they were in condition to do so, Donna DiMasi and Joanne Lomino provided a police artist details of the gunman's face for a sketch. Their description, coupled with what the unidentified neighbor had contributed to the artist, resulted in a sketch of a man with a wide face and a nose whose tip seemed slightly pinched, eyes that had a "cold, steely look," and brown, curly hair.

Now, he was about to strike again . . .

The young man was behind the wheel of his sedan and the girl sat closely beside him in his embrace. They were supremely happy, for they were looking dreamily to the future, just two weeks hence — Valentine's Day — when they'd announce their engagement.

For 30-year-old John Diel and his 26-year-old sweetheart Christine Freund, the night was young, for it had been made for lovers. It was 12:30 a.m., just a half hour past midnight of that chill morning of January 30, 1977, a Sunday. Neither John nor Christine were in any rush to end their Saturday night date and return to their respective homes. They didn't have too many opportunities during the week to see each other because of their crowded schedules.

Their separate trans-Atlantic trails that ultimately led each to the borough of Queens and a meeting at a dance in Ridgewood Hall had their origins in neighboring European countries. Christine Freund emigrated with her family to America in 1957 and settled into a comfortable home on Linden Street in the Ridgewood section of Queens.

That was almost a month or so before Diel and his parents made the same move from Yugoslavia and eventually moved to Gates Avenue in that same community of Ridgewood.

Living as neighbors, the attractive Christine and the handsome John were fated to meet at that Saturday night dance in 1970 and become hooked on each other.

While they were soon to be betrothed and then married, dates for Christine and John had been rather infrequent in recent times. Her days were occupied as a secretary for a Wall Street brokerage firm. She worked in their midtown Manhattan offices on 42nd Street.

While his own days were free, John's nights were not because he was the bartender in a Ridgewood tavern. So except for a brief time together preceding summer at a mountain retreat where they'd vacationed, their only opportunity to be in each other's company was weekends.

On that particular Saturday night of January 29th, John and Christine had laid out in advance the entire itinerary

277

they planned to follow. They started the evening by going to the Continental Theater on Austin Street in Forest Hills, not too far from their Ridgewood neighborhood.

The movie was *Rocky,* a story not unlike the plot of their own love affair. After leaving the theater they walked to the nearby Wine Gallery where Christine and John had a late evening repast of cheese and crackers and wine.

It was now past midnight and the young lovers' schedule called for one more stop on their entertainment itinerary — the Masonic dance in Ridgewood Hall, the very place they met each other seven years ago.

Leaving the Wine Gallery, Christine and John walked slowly, arm in arm, along Forest Hills' quiet, crime-free streets to his car parked in Station Square, opposite the Forest Hills Inn and the Long Island Rail Road passenger station.

As they reached the car, John and Christine unclinched from their embrace and she walked to the door on the passenger side, alongside the sidewalk. He went to the driver's side and unlocked the door. He checked his watch as he got into the car. It was 12:30. Once seated behind the wheel, he reached over and unlatched the door so Christine could get in.

Meanwhile, he started the engine. It coughed and sputtered from the cold, but soon it was racing.

"Better warm it up a bit," he said to his girlfriend, reaching to pull Christine close to him.

She returned his embrace and they joined in a kiss for several long seconds. Finally John and Christine settled back in their seat for the short ride to Ridgewood Hall.

Diel was about to throw the shift into gear when a deafening roar and a terrifying crashing of glass made him jump back in fright. The first explosion was followed instantaneously by a second. Then a deafening silence ensued.

His mind for a moment was a blank. But then all at once he was fully and totally alerted to the reality of what had just happened. He realized it when he felt Christine's head sag onto his right shoulder. He called out her name, asking

278

if she was all right. There was no response. He crossed his left hand over to touch his sweetheart's face. He felt a warm wetness.

It was blood!

Gripped by the sudden terrifying events, Diel held stiffly to courage, not panic. He sensed that Christine had been shot. How badly he could not know. Yet the blood, flowing from a point over her right ear and her seemingly comatose state told him that her condition was serious if not critical — or even fatal.

With his left hand he shifted the latch and threw the door open. Then taking hold of Christine by the shoulders, he eased her as gently as he could upon the seat so that her head rested on the warm seat he had just moved from.

Then, slamming the door shut, he ran along the darkened, deserted street in search of someone, anyone, who might summon an ambulance or a doctor or any sort of help.

"Help! Help! I need help!" he yelled as he ran aimlessly, almost blindly in a direction he chose only because it was a way to go. But it proved to have been the right one, for when he reached the corner of Burns Street and 71st Avenue his cries, now at a hysterical level, were heard by a young couple passing by in a car.

They stopped. He told them what had happened. They told him to hop in. They drove him back to his car so he could stay with Christine. They then sped off and called police.

Within minutes, the familiar blue and white police cruisers, their dome lights ablaze, sirens screaming, roared to a stop beside Diel's car.

"Can't wait for an ambulance," one of the uniformed police officers wisely decided. "Let's take her in the car."

The policemen lifted Christine out of the front seat and carried her to one of the police cars. They laid her down on the back seat and her beau, squeezing in the floor area on his knees to comfort her, shouted, "We're ready . . . please go to the hospital right now!"

The police car sped at near 80 mph speeds to St. John's Hospital in nearby Elmhurst and pulled to a screeching stop at the emergency entrance.

A rolling stretcher was wheeled out and Christine was brought inside. Doctors, alerted ahead of time by police to expect a victim with a head wound, were standing by to receive the patient. A neurosurgeon had also been summoned after the hospital learned that the victim had suffered a head wound.

Besides the bleeding from over the right ear, Christine had also suffered a less critical wound on the right shoulder. The doctors agreed that both punctures had been caused by bullets—large caliber bullets!

And as police would soon learn after the slugs taken from the victim and a third one that ricocheted off the windshield were examined by ballistics—they were the same deadly .44-caliber bullets that had felled four victims earlier, one fatally.

Four earlier victims?

Yes. The police were about to make a startling discovery in the wake of Christine Freund's shooting—that still another victim had been struck by one of the .44-caliber bullets three months earlier in the Flushing section of Queens.

But that finding didn't occur until after ballistics experts established that the bullets fired at Christine Freund were the deadly .44-caliber variety.

Preparations were quickly made to perform surgery on her in the hope of removing the bullet which, as X-rays showed, had lodged in her brain. It was, of course, one of the most hopeless operations any surgeon could perform. For the plates, or negatives, showed that the bullet was imbedded in a portion of the brain that condemned Christine to a life of total paralysis—even if the neurosurgeon could have removed the bullet in surgery.

As it turned out, Christine Freund succumbed at 4:30 a.m. that Sunday before she could be taken to the operating room.

Now the police began to sense the outside possibility that

Christine's death could conceivably have had some link or relationship with the other seemingly senseless shootings of recent months—those of Donna Lauria and Jody Valente and of Joanne Lomino and Donna DiMasi.

Now enterprising newsmen for the city's newspapers began putting together stories that the senseless slaying of Christine Freund was conceivably the work of the same man who shot the two Floral Park girls and killed and wounded the two young women in the Bronx.

The stories soon spurred attention—and action—on the parts of Mayor Abraham Beame and Police Commissioner Michael J. Codd. They ordered greatly intensified investigations.

But not until still another young woman, a 20-year-old Columbia University student had been shot to death with a bullet from a .44-caliber revolver as she was walking home from the subway, less than six weeks after Christine Freund had been fatally wounded only blocks away from the latest depradation.

Before the narrative gets out of hand, let's backtrack to the autumn night of October 22, 1976. Carl Denaro, aged 20, is on a date with his girlfriend. She is driving his small sports car; he's in the seat beside her. They are in the parking lot of a tavern at 159th Street and 32nd Avenue in Flushing, still another Queens community not so far distant from Forest Hills where Christine Freund was destined to be fatally wounded some three months later.

Denaro and his date had an appointment with some friends at 2 o'clock in the morning following the Friday night outing with his girlfriend. It was at the tavern in whose parking lot his date drove the car.

Just as she pulled the car into one of the stalls, the girl and Denaro were startled by a series of explosions they thought were firecrackers.

As Denaro was to recall at a much later time, he felt a "ping" in his head and heard a crashing sound—actually a .44-caliber bullet tearing through the rear window of his car and slanting into his skull. Before he lapsed into unconsciousness, Denaro heard several other shots.

Terrified by the explosions and the sight of blood trickling from her boyfriend's head, his companion rushed into the tavern and screamed for help.

An ambulance took Denaro to Flushing Hospital and Medical Center where he remained for three weeks. A steel plate was implanted in his scalp during the surgery to repair the site where the bullet had entered. He also sustained permanent damage to the middle finger on his right hand.

"But I thank God I'm still alive to talk about it," Denaro told a detective who interviewed him after he had entered his period of convalescence at the hospital.

Why, everyone on the police investigation wanted to know, would anyone want to shoot Carl Denaro?

The answer that the cops came up with without much deliberation and delay was that Carl Denaro had dark brown, shoulder-length hair. Moreover, Denaro was sitting on the passenger side. Then consider, too, that the killer had approached from the rear.

He mistook Denaro for a girl!

Denaro, who recovered and had an opportunity to be interviewed, said he held no grudge toward the killer.

"I'm sure he's not in command of his senses," Denaro said. "I just hope the police catch him soon so they can treat him for his illness."

Carl Denaro's near-miss with death at the hands of a night stalker didn't generate any heightened suspicion that the attack could be linked with the one that had preceded it in July in the Bronx that claimed Donna Lauria's life and injured Donna Valente.

And a month after Denaro's harrowing experience when Joanne Lomino and Donna DiMasi were shot in Queens, there was no more thought given to the likelihood that a mad gunman was on the loose than when Christine Freund was blasted to death two months after that chilling episode.

Well, to say that no thought at all was given to the chance that a single assassin was on the loose would not be the truth. For there was at least one New York City cop, Detective Sergeant Richard Conlon, of the 15th Homicide Zone in Queens. While Conlon was quick to point out that the department was not leaning toward the one man theory, he himself was inclined to believe differently.

"If I had to guess, I'd say there is a nut running around with a gun," Conlon offered.

He made that statement on February 1st when more than 50 detectives were mobilized for the search of Christine Freund's slayer. But their search had been launched with no predisposition to link this murderous attack to any of the other savage forays. As in each of the other cases, this one received the same treatment, as though it were an individual case with no connection to any other.

But the time was not far off when the police were to suddenly face the stunning reality—that one madman lurking under the cover of night had felled six victims thus far and was about to claim his seventh on that blustery Wednesday night of March 9th . . .

It was just a few minutes past 8 p.m. when the front doorbell rang at the trim, one-family residence of Garabed Voskerichian on Exeter Street in the shadows of famed Forest Hills Stadium where the celebrated tennis championships are held.

The ringing was urgent and persistent. The door was opened by Mrs. Voskerichian who looked in astonishment at the woman standing on the stoop. She was a familiar figure in the neighborhood but Mrs. Voskerichian, who like her husband is an immigrant from Armenia and doesn't speak English very well, couldn't fathom the occasion of the woman's visit.

"Your daughter," the woman said breathlessly. "She fainted on the street and they are taking her to the hospital . . ."

Before the woman could voice a further explanation, Mrs. Voskerichian's 22-year-old son bolted out of the living room where the family had been watching television.

"What happened to Virginia . . . where is she?" he stammered, brushing past his mother and confronting the

283

woman at the door.

"Down by the entrances," the woman said, referring to the Forest Hills Gardens community, a private development of apartment houses and one-family homes such as the Voskerichians' dwelling.

"She is by the apartments at Dartmouth Street near Continental Avenue . . ."

Before she could say anything else, the youth took off in full sprint for that destination, two-and-a-half blocks away. But when he arrived, his heart almost stopped and his stomach was seized by a sickening feeling.

"Virginia . . . Virginia," he began sobbing.

Even her brother could see through his tears that Virginia was beyond aid. Her eyes were closed forever in her nineteenth year of life as she lay on the sidewalk in her Paris-styled winter jacket, a muffler wrapped around her neck, and peasant skirt with knee-high leather boots. Several books were on the sidewalk beside her body as was her pocketbook, which was unopened.

It was later established by Dr. Jacques Durosier, Queens County assistant medical examiner, that Virginia had been shot in the mouth with a single bullet fired at a range of no more than three feet!

The slug's impact shattered several of her teeth and tore through her mouth and head, lodging in the cranium near the spinal cord.

It would not be known for several hours by homicide detectives from Queens' 15th Zone that the bullet which killed Virginia Voskerichian was a .44-caliber—the same type of bullet that had taken the life of Christine Freund the previous January only a short block away!

That connection generated instant and concentrated searches for clues and the immediate assignment of 100 detectives in the trackdown for a killer that police now suspected was the man who not only killed these two Queens women but also shot and wounded the teenaged girls in the outlying Floral Park section of the borough.

But the Queens detectives were in for an even greater

surprise — after ballistics tests were conducted on the .44-caliber slug removed from Miss Voskerichian's head and was found to have the same riflings as the bullets which killed Miss Freund and wounded the Misses DiMasi and Lomino.

For the evidence didn't end there. With startling swiftness now, the boys at the lab took everything off the back burner, including the results of the tests on the .44-caliber bullets that killed Donna Lauria and wounded Jody Valente — as well as the slug that struck Carl Denaro in the head in that surprise October night attack in Flushing. That slug, incidentally, did not make its way into police hands until many days after the shooting. Denaro's girlfriend was cleaning his car while he was laid up in the hospital — and found the deadly lead pellet on the floor.

Detectives were as much at a loss to explain the seemingly motiveless attack on Virginia Voskerichian as they were in offering a reason to account for any of the other mysterious shootings.

To begin with, Ginny, a Columbia University coed who, unlike all the other victims, was alone, walking home from the Independent Subway Line's Continental Avenue station following classes at the college's Morningside Heights campus in upper Manhattan.

An elderly man came forward immediately after learning that Virginia had been slain on the street. He told detectives under the command of Captain Joseph Borelli, chief of Queens homicide, that he was walking home at about 7:30 to 7:40 p.m. when he heard a "pop" that he surmised might have been a firecracker.

A second or two later he said he saw a white youth, in his late teens, the man judged, running toward him. He was wearing a dark-colored stocking cap and a dark sweater. The witness described the youth as weighing about 160 pounds and being about 5 feet 9.

"As he came running toward me," the man told detectives, "I heard him saying, 'Oh, Jesus!' But I had no idea what he could have meant — until I learned that the young girl was murdered."

Virginia, who was a language major at Columbia's School of General Studies, apparently had seen her killer approaching, for gun powder residue was found on her books—indicating she may have raised them to her head to fend off the lethal bullet.

The force of the slug evidently catapulted her body face down into shrubbery alongside the apartment house on Dartmouth Street.

Another passerby, a youth of 19, unaware of either the shot that had been fired or of the presence of the stocking-masked young man fleeing the area, almost tripped over the girl's body as he rounded the corner from Continental Avenue enroute to his home on Exeter.

The young man quickly became a Good Samaritan. He kneeled, turned the girl over, and was going to try to revive her. But when he saw the blood coming from her mouth, he realized he could not help her. He ran to a police call box and reported what he had found.

The search for clues and evidence at the scene was an exercise in frustration, for other than the books that ultimately revealed the gunpowder residue there was nothing to tell police who might have committed the crime. Or why.

Virginia's brother, acting as interpreter for his parents and spokesman for the family, assured authorities that his sister had no enemies.

"It must be that crazy man who killed that other girl," he said, referring to Christine Freund's motiveless killing that had happened barely 300 yards from where Virginia was shot to death.

Captain Borelli and his men were thoroughly convinced that the same madman had fired the bullets that took Christine's and Virginia's lives. Especially so after Dr. Durosier removed the bullet from the victim's head during the autopsy and turned it over to police.

But, of course, that didn't establish positively that the bullet was fired by the same killer and the same gun that snuffed out Miss Freund's life. Yet that incontrovertible connection, the proof positive that police scientific probers always search for in their efforts to establish evidence that is admissible in court and which can help convict the accused, was not very far off now.

Police ballistics experts reached that crucial conclusion within hours after the slug from Miss Voskerichian's head was compared under the microscope with the bullet that killed Miss Freund.

The riflings were the same! But that wasn't all that came out of the laboratory sleuthing now. Now the analyzers made comparisons with the bullet recovered at the scene of Donna DiMassi's and Joanne Lomino's shooting, and those bullets also had the same riflings as the last two. Then the bullet that had wounded Carl Denaro was found to have those very same telltale grooves that are scored into a slug as it is fired through the barrel.

And then the terrifying truth, the total picture came into focus when the bullets that killed Donna Lauria and maimed Jody Valente were also found to have been triggered from that same .44-caliber revolver as all the other ones.

Now, without any question, a murderous assassin was on the loose. It certainly wasn't the first instance that a terrorist was running amuk in the city. Yet never was New York confronted with the awesome presence of an apparently psychopathic gunman such as this.

So far, all his victims were cut from an almost identical mold. They, all of them, had long, dark brown hair. Hair that fell shoulder length in every case — including Carl Denaro's. Most probably he was mistaken from behind as a girl, since his hair was long and he was sitting on the passenger side of the car.

Who was this maniacal gunman? Why was he killing and wounding by the numbers? How were police going to track him down before he struck again?

The questions were asked over and over but they repeatedly and unvaryingly defied any answers.

The last thing Mayor Abraham Beame wanted to do was

287

alarm the people of his city. There'd been enough woes brought on by a financial crisis which had received nation-wide notoriety. The constant, unrelenting threat of bankruptcy was a terrible burden for New York to bear. Yet now there was that ominous and awesome presence of an apparently deranged gunman.

Yet the Mayor and Police Commissioner Michael Codd had a duty and obligation to the 8,000,000 residents. The truth had to be known.

"We have a savage killer on the loose," Beame said at a press conference that he and Codd called in the Forest Hills police station. "He is singling out women with shoulder-length dark brown hair. We don't know why . . ."

Codd added that the approximate description of the twisted killer was that of a white male, 25 to 30 years old, medium build with a height of 5 feet 10 to 6 feet, well groomed, with dark hair combed straight back.

Beame urged the public to come forward with any information they may have on anyone they suspected could fit the mould of the killer.

"Don't use your judgment as to whether what you have is important or not," the Mayor implored. "Just come forward and tell police."

A special police number was established: 520-9200.

Young people in their teens and twenties were wearing their Sunday finery and looking out of place standing in the bright sunshine of the late April 20th morning outside St. Theresa's Church in the Baychester section of the Bronx. But it was a Wednesday, not a Sunday.

They were gathered there to pay their last respects to pretty, dark-haired Valentina Suriani whose life had ended much too soon. She was only 18, yet the madman who'd been terrorizing the city for nearly a year now, made no distinction when he struck Valentina down with a deadly cannon, the .44-caliber revolver.

It happened in a parked car once again, a car parked on the service road to the Hutchinson River Parkway about a block from Valentina's home on Hutchinson.

The time was 3 o'clock in the morning, Sunday, April 17th, for Valentina Suriani, an undergrad at Lehman College, and her beau, 20-year-old Alexander Esau, a handsome tow-car helper from Manhattan's Hell's Kitchen, this was a moment for smooching after a Saturday night date that ran into the wee hours.

Esau, who lived with his father in a fourth-floor walkup on West 46th Street, had stopped with his fiancee at a bachelor party in Miss Suriani's neighborhood. He had left Valentina in the car because Alex was merely paying a token visit at the party simply to convey his best wishes to the groom-to-be.

"Where's Valerie?" asked a friend and co-worker of Esau at the Luna Brothers Towing Company of West 46th Street in Manhattan.

"Out in the car," replied Esau, explaining that he just dropped in to wish the guest of honor well. "We're going to cruise around the neighborhood, Val and I."

Then Esau left and drove away with his sweetheart. They finally parked at the curb of the parkway's service road.

At about 3 a.m. a resident in a lower floor of an apartment house nearby heard four shots and called police.

Uniformed officers responded in radio cars and found what would soon be acknowledged as the .44-caliber killer's eighth and ninth victims. Miss Suriani, seated behind the wheel, had been shot in the head and she was dead. Esau was also wounded in the head—by three bullets. He was unconscious, his breathing was labored, his condition seemed critical.

He was taken by ambulance to Jacobi Hospital where he underwent immediate surgery. But some 18 hours later—at 9:38 p.m. Sunday—Alexander Esau became the .44-caliber killer's fifth fatality.

The scene of the murderous night marauder's latest foray was only five blocks from the scene of his first strike against Donna Lauria and Jody Valente nine months earlier.

Like all his other ambushings, he was careful to leave no evidence—no footprints, since concrete won't allow such

289

impressions, no fingerprints, since he touched nothing but his deadly Wild West artillery piece which he always carried away from each of his deadly onslaughts . . .

Hold on! No evidence?

At first it might have seemed that way. But the detectives finetooth-combing the area soon turned up a most startling documentation of the killer's existence.

It was a handwritten note in a uniquely-styled block letter format characterized by remarkably uniform slanting of the serifs at 45-degree angles. The lettering looked very much like a cartoonist's hand had drawn it.

The message was not divulged in its entirety but it was described as being general in nature and that the killer claimed he knew none of his victims . . .

A police spokesman described the page-and-a-half-long note as "mostly incoherent" and said it was "the product of a disturbed mind."

The note was taken to the police laboratory and analyzed for every conceivable clue it could yield about the writer. It was scrutinized by police handwriting experts and psychologists for an analysis of its writer; it was dusted before anything else for fingerprints. There were none.

The police were no closer to the .44-caliber killer now than they'd been before he struck Valentina Suriani and Alexander Esau.

But Police Commissioner Codd was no longer satisfied with searches for the mass murderer by the various detective commands that had jurisdiction over the killings and maimings committed in their precincts. Codd came to the conclusion that the investigation had to be conducted under the direction of a single supervisor in a unified command.

Chosen to head up that command was Deputy Inspector Timothy J. Dowd, who was moved out of Manhattan and put in charge of the case and the teams of detectives from the Bronx and Queens who'd been working on the various shootings—six in all—since the outbreak nine months earlier that had by now claimed five dead and four wounded.

In deciding to treat the Bronx and Queens as a common

290

hunting ground for the killer, Codd ended the treatment accorded the investigation from opposite ends of the bridges linking the Bronx and Queens. He placed 30 detectives from the two boroughs under the direct command of Inspector Dowd, who at the age of 62 had 37 years under his belt as a cop, and most of that period as a homicide sleuth.

"We're going to get this guy," Dowd said, frowning on the traditional use of "perpetrator" or "suspect." "We'll just spend as long as it takes. There's no way we can close the file on it. I can't wait till the end of this case. I just want to see what kind of human being this is who's been committing all these heartless killings and maimings."

The command post was set up in a bright, second-floor office in the modernistic Flushing Precinct, near by Shea Stadium where the Mets and Jets perform. This was Room 224 in the 109th Squad and the offices comprising this area were soon fully equipped for the task at hand.

Before the operation had settled too snugly into the staionhouse, psychological studies and profiles of the .44-Caliber Killer began surfacing. In those, he was viewed in part as possibly being under demonic possession or compulsion; that he was a paranoid schizophrenic; also that he was intelligent and reasonably well-educated, and conceivably religious to some extent.

Detectives John Beccone and Richard Ward even came forth with their theory that the killer had a car; that although no one had seen him arrive or drive away in a car, he was not a strictly foot soldier.

Thus Beccone and Ward, with Inspector Dowd's full blessing, went off to check State Department of Motor Vehicle records of all registrations by white males, aged 20 to 30, in the past two years in Queens and the Bronx. They wanted those records to make comparisons with the .44-caliber killer's note.

But as it turned out, they couldn't have reasonably been expected to make such a discovery. The MVB keeps registrations in alphabetical order, and for Queens alone there were 253,000. Not even Detectives Beccone and Ward, fired up as they were in the inquiry, could have been expected to pore through those 253,000 applications by hand.

The task force ran into other problems of a similar nature. For example, Inspector Dowd, who had graduated from City University with a B.A. in English and Latin and received a degree in public administration from Bernard M. Baruch College, found he couldn't get juvenile records. What Dowd was searching for was the recorded itinerary of a man, any man, who may have been arrested three years earlier for molesting girls in a pattern that might even remotely represent the manner in which victims were being singled out now. But the courts—and they were backed by federal and state statutes—said no way.

The inquiry continued relentlessly.

Then in a startling late spring development a letter with the identical slanted hand block-lettering of the previous note left at the scene of Valentina Suriani's murder and her beau's fatal wounding, a second note made its appearance. It was sent to a New York Daily News columnist, Jimmy Breslin.

The note was turned over to police for all the studies they could make to determine who its writer might be. But they failed to come up with a lead. Then they released the note to Breslin with permission to let its contents be known. Here's what the note said:

"Hello from the gutters of N.Y.C. which are filled with dog manure, vomit, stale wine, urine, and blood. Hello from the sewers of N.Y.C. which swallow up these delicacies when they are washed away by the sweeper trucks. Hello from the cracks on the sidewalks of N.Y.C. and from the ants that dwell in these cracks and feed on the dried blood of the dead that has settled into the cracks.

"J.B., I'm just dropping you a line to let you know that I appreciate your interest in those recent and horrendous .44-caliber killings. I also want to tell you that I read your column daily and find it quite informative.

'Tell me, Jim, what will you have for July Twenty-Ninth?

292

You can forget about me if you like because I don't care for publicity. However, you must not forget Donna Lauria and you cannot let the people forget her, either. She was a very sweet girl but Sam's a thirsty lad and he won't let me stop killing until he gets his fill of blood.

"Mr. Breslin, sir, don't think that because you haven't heard from [me] for a while that I went to sleep. No, rather, I am still here. Like a spirit roaming that night. Thirsty, hungry, seldom stopping to rest; anxious to please Sam. I love my work. Now, the void has been filled.

"Perhaps we shall meet face to face someday or perhaps I will be blown away by cops with smoking .38's. Whatever, if I shall be fortunate enough to meet you I will tell you all about Sam if you like and I will introduce you to him. His name is 'Sam the Terrible.'

"Not knowing what the future holds I shall say farewell and I will see you at the next job. Or, should I say you will see my handiwork at the next job? Remember Ms. Lauria. Thank you

In their blood
and
From the gutter
"Sam's Creation" 44

P.S.: J.B., please inform all the detectives working on the slayings to remain.

P.S., J.B. please inform all the detectives working the case that I wish them the best of luck. Keep Em digging, drive on, think positive, get off your butts, knock on coffins, etc.

"Upon my capture I promise to buy all the guys working on the case a new pair of shoes if I can get up the money."

(Signed) Son of Sam

Directly under the signature was a symbol the killer drew. It appeared to be an X-shaped symbolism containing the male and female biological symbols, combined with the letters X and S.

That latest communication, coupled with the repeated

dead ends police were running into, prompted an appeal by the department brass to psychiatrists. Issued through Inspector Dowd, the plea was directed to all who might have had contact with someone of the .44-caliber killer's personality and mentality.

The call went out in flyers distributed to commanding officers of all precincts in the city and suburbs, such as Westchester County, north of the city line, and Nassau and Suffolk Counties, east of the Queens line on Long Island.

Two composite drawings of the killer were sent with each flyer. The latest sketch of the terrorist gunman, now quickly dubbed Son of Sam after having signed his letter with that identity, showed him to be a white male, 20 to 35 years of age, medium to tall in height, with dark modish hair and a build of average dimensions. He appeared clean shaven, clear skinned, pale complexioned, and was depicted with dark piercing eyes.

The message on the flyer itself said:

"There is a strong likelihood that he is a Christian and a probability he had Catholic or Episcopalian schooling. He is a high school graduate, may have attended college.

"He shoots combat style: Two-handed and from a crouch. He carries a .44-caliber bulldog revolver manufactured by the Charter Arms Co. The gun may be carried concealed in a plastic or paper bag or on his person.

"This man is armed and dangerous. He may shoot at police who attempt to stop or arrest him."

That conclusion came to the fore after Dowd, Borelli, and the other investigators studied each of the half dozen times the .44-caliber killer had struck thus far. At none of the gunnings did this triggerman fire more than four bullets. That awareness led the probers to believe that Son of Sam always kept one bullet in reserve in the event that his flight was interrupted by a threat of capture. Authorities reasoned he would then either use that last bullet to wipe out the person menacing his freedom — or to kill himself.

Asked whether cooperation by private psychiatrists was not an unethical approach because it ostensibly violated the confidentiality between doctor and patient, Dowd said:

"We are fully aware of the problems doctors may have with the doctor-patient relationship. But it is our feeling that if a doctor believes he knows who the man is, he should come forth and tell us. We will keep it confidential and we will not ask them to open up their medical records."

The American Psychiatric Association acknowledged that if any of its members was aware that a patient was committing those violent acts, the doctor's cooperation was not unreasonable, or unethical.

But the days and weeks passed and the appeal brought no greater results than the sum total of accomplishments achieved by what was now a full-time 60-man detective force under Inspector Dowd's supervision. Dowd would have been the first to admit on that July 26th night that the investigators were no closer to Son of Sam than they were when the trackdown was launched under a unified command some 10 weeks before . . .

It was 3:20 o'clock on the Sunday morning on June 26th. Exactly 70 days almost to the hour since the .44-caliber killer last struck, which was in the Bronx when he claimed Valentina Suriani and Alexander Esau as the fourth and fifth fatalities on his grim scorecard, which then totaled nine victims when counting the four he had wounded.

The fear that this madman would strike again had not eased anywhere. Especially not since his recent note indicated quite plainly that he wasn't about to let up:

"I . . . I will see you at the next job. Or, should I say you will see my handiwork at the next job?"

When 17-year-old Judy Placido and 20-year-old Salvatore Lupo were seated in their parked car that Sunday morning at the curb in front of a one-family house on 211th Street, Bayside, Queens, they couldn't help but talk about the .44-caliber killer.

That was all they had heard all night long while they were seated in the Elephas discotheque around the corner on Northern Boulevard. Judy herself, who had graduated earlier Saturday from St. Catherine's Academy—the school Valentina Suriani had also attended—was uptight about Son of Sam.

Her fright was lodged in the knowledge that the .44-caliber killer had struck last in her very neighborhood. Judy lived on Wickham Avenue in the Pelham Bay section, which is also not far from where Donna Lauria and Jody Valente became victims of the gunman's initial outrages.

Sal, a mechanic's helper from Maspeth in Queens, had a very real awareness about the .44-caliber killer, too. But he wasn't inclined to be alarmed about him.

How cool Sal was about this dread menace of the night may be seen in his actions. Despite all the talk about Son of Sam, Sal borrowed the disco bouncer's keys to his 1972 Cadillac Coupe de Ville and took his date to the car for an early morning ride.

But no sooner had they sat in the car and Sal, behind the wheel, lit a cigarette for Judy and then himself, than there was a frightening flash of light, the crash of glass and the sting of excruciating pain.

Bullets struck Judy in the right temple, neck and forehead; Lupo was hit once in the right forearm and also the right leg.

The .44-caliber killer had struck again.

Five wounds. Did that mean Son of Sam was getting so bold now that he didn't expect to be stopped or caught—and could expend all five bullets?

No. He still only fired four bullets. The bullet that passed through Lupo's arm was the same one that bore into his leg.

Residents awakened by the shots looked out their windows and saw Judy staggering in the street, shouting "Help me!" Police were summoned and an ambulance took the wounded couple to Flushing Hospital. Judy and Sal were both lucky. Their wounds were not critical and the outlook for recovery was deemed excellent.

Son of Sam had raised the score of wounded from four to six while, fortunately, the toll of dead remained the same.

But for how long would those figures remain static?

The police again were working with threadbare clues.

Descriptions of a mustard colored car were given to investigators but nothing came of that report that the assassin had fled in such a vehicle.

In what was one of the most ironic twists in the case, Inspector Dowd admitted sadly that his detectives had had the Elephas discotheque staked out until about a half hour before the shooting. Then the sleuths slipped off to check out another location where the killer was thought likely to strike.

"I feel we'll be successful," Dowd said. "Unfortunately, we may not catch him until he strikes again. We may have to be very lucky and catch him in the act . . ."

Then Dowd issued a plea to Son of Sam himself:

"Please get in touch with me. You're not solving your problems. We'll give you all the help we can. We know that you are suffering pain and anguish and we understand that you are not in control of yourself.

"You must make that supreme effort to communicate with us, or anyone. We will do what we can to alleviate your problems."

There was no response from the .44-caliber killer and the July 29th anniversary, a Friday, passed without incident. So did the 30th, a Saturday.

If ever the police were ready for Son of Sam to strike it was that weekend. They had the Bronx and Queens blanketed and they had surveillances on more than a dozen possible suspects. If the .44-caliber killer were to try and leave his lethal calling card anywhere in those two boroughs, police felt confident it would be his last outing . . .

There was no thought about danger when blonde Stacy Moskowitz and Robert Violante pulled into the parking lot next to the playground on Shore Road, a service thoroughfare of the Belt Parkway which courses along the Brooklyn shore at this juncture and overlooks Gravesend Bay, which is part of Lower New York Bay.

Stacy and Bob were both 20 and they'd met only a few days earlier, on Thursday, at a restaurant in Sheepshead Bay. Stacy, who'd been working as a secretary-receptionist for a shoe manufacturer in Manhattan, had recently broken off with her fiance and felt free to date other young men.

Violante, who was working as a salesman in a men's clothing store in Brooklyn's Fort Hamilton section, had no attachments either. So he and Stacy had struck it off nicely.

Quickly they decided on a Saturday night date. First it was dinner at a Beefsteak Charlie's restaurant, then to a showing of *New York, New York* at the Highway Theater of Kings Highway and West 7th Street, not very far from where Miss Moskowitz lived with her parents, on East 5th Street.

Afterward it was to the parking lot, a popular spot for young couples and not too far from Violante's home on Bay Ridge Parkway in the Bensonhurst section of Brooklyn, a 10-minute drive from Stacy's home.

Just a few days before she had met her new beau, Stacy had bumped into her ex-fiance. They had remained good friends despite the bustup. On that last get-together, he warned her to beware of the .44-caliber killer.

"Don't worry about me, he doesn't go after girls with blonde hair," Stacy said to her former fiance.

And now Saturday night had come and gone and it was 1:30 o'clock into Sunday morning. Stacy and Bob were at least 20 miles from the nearest locale where Son of Sam had struck. They felt safe and so Stacy and Bob left his brown 1969 Buick in the lot and crossed the foot-bridge which spans the parkway to the seawall. They spent the next several minutes there, then returned to the car.

Moments after they sat inside there was a blinding flash of light and three or four explosions.

Instantly the cry was heard, a man screaming:

"God, I've never done anything! Help me, help me, help me. God, why is this happening? Help me!"

Then followed the incessant sound of the car's horn as Robert Violante, struck by a bullet that entered his temple and exited at the bridge of his nose, collapsed over the steering wheel. Miss Moscowitz was struck by another bullet, one that had first passed through Violante's left hand when

298

he apparently threw it protectively over his date's face. But that slug tore relentlessly into Stacy's skull and lodged in her cerebellum.

The gravely wounded victims were taken by ambulance to Coney Island Hospital but then were transferred to Kings County Hospital where facilities for the delicate surgery each would need are available.

The tragic aftermath of this attack resulted in the loss of Violante's right eye and the possible loss of sight in his left—unless future treatment and possible surgery can save him from total blindness.

For Stacy Moskowitz there could be no hope. The bullet had destroyed her cerebellum, which controls breathing and blood pressure and affects motor coordination. At 5:22 p.m. of Monday, August 2nd, 36 hours after she'd been shot, Stacy became the Son of Sam's sixth murder victim.

The .44-caliber killer had fooled the vaunted New York City Police Department again. While they searched for him and waited to have him strike in his familiar lairs, he brought tragedy and grief to another part of the city.

But this foray was unlike any other the .44-caliber had made. For now instead of just one or two witnesses to the shooting, police had several. There was, for example, the man parked in front of Violante's car who saw the whole thing through his rear view mirror—a man approach the car, crouch into combat stance, and fire away.

Then there was the woman, a middle-aged housewife, walking her dog who saw a bulky young man fleeing in the night. It would take her some four days before she'd get enough courage to go to the police and report what she'd seen.

To be sure, Son of Sam hadn't counted on those visual observations. Those were mistakes he committed that weren't in character for him. But who in wildest flight of fancy would have perceived New York's greatest manhunt for the phantom killer, an investigation that had cost an estimated $20 million, could come down to one of the most stupid of all mistakes—like parking at one o'clock in the morning in front of a fire hydrant?

It was the middle-aged woman, walking her dog and coming almost face-to-face with a man running from the scene of the shooting, who informed Detectives Edward Blasie and Ed O'Sullivan about the ticket.

"Two uniformed officers," she told the sleuths, "had just finished putting a ticket on a light-colored Ford Galaxie. It was parked at the fire hydrant over on Bay 16th Street . . . I saw him get into the car and drive away . . ."

Blasie and O'Sullivan checked the Coney Island precinct and other commands and found that four tickets had been issued during the early morning hours in the vicinity of the killing. But only one had been written out for parking too close to a hydrant. The ticket had been issued at 2:05 a.m.

Checking Motor Vehicle files, the detectives came up with the name of David Berkowitz, aged 24 and residing on Pine Street in Yonkers.

Blasie and O'Sullivan passed the word on and on Wednesday morning, August 10th, Inspector Dowd dispatched Detectives Ed Zigo and John Longo to the city just north of the Bronx line in Westchester.

Zigo and Longo talked to neighbors and learned that their suspect lived in a seventh floor apartment, that he was a loner, a "gun nut," an ex-soldier, worked for the Post Office, and "acted crazy or goofy sometimes."

The detectives nosed around for the Ford Galaxie and found it parked in front of David Berkowitz's apartment building. They had only to peek inside to sense that they apparently were at the end of the long trail.

For on the front seat they saw the butt of a gun (it turned out to be a .45 caliber submachine gun) and an envelope with lettering that looked very much like the notes the .44-caliber killer had dropped at the scene of the Suriani-Esau killings and had mailed to columnist Jimmy Breslin.

The detectives quickly notified Inspector Dowd, who led a team of 15 more sleuths to Yonkers. Meanwhile, Zigo and Longo obtained search warrants for Berkowitz's car.

At 10:15 p.m. as most of Dowd's sleuths were staked out

in their cars and behind lampposts and trees, a bulky young man walked out of the building and went to the Ford Galaxie at the curb. As he turned the key, a voice said softly, "Hello, David."

The man looked around. His eyes opened wide in recognition of a face that had been in the newspapers many times in recent months.

"Inspector Dowd!" the man exclaimed, "you finally got me!"

Then he shook his head and smiled, "I guess this is the end of the trail . . ."

And it was—once police opened the car and found, beside the weapon that could be seen from the window—the .44-caliber revolver that ballistic experts, in subsequent tests, determined was the weapon from which the bullets that claimed five lives and injured eight had been fired from.

David Berkowitz, an adopted child who had grown up in the Bronx, served in the Army in Korea, worked in the post office in the Bronx, and, as authorities charged, terrorized New York City for more than a year as the .44-caliber killer, was out of circulation finally and at last.

The infamous "Son of Sam" pleaded guilty to the murder of Stacy Moskowitz and to five other counts of second-degree murder. He was sentenced to 315 years in prison and is now serving that time at Attica Correctional Facility in upstate New York.

Sex Murder

by Charles Cleveland

Ted Bundy Convicted

TALLAHASSEE, FLA., FEB. 12, 1980

Was that neighborhood marked for murder? Did some sinister magnetism draw that particular man to this particular place, a man law enforcement agencies feared was the most prolific mass murderer in our history?

The neighborhood certainly appeared pleasant and peaceful. If somewhat shabby now, it was a comfortable shabbiness, familiar to most old Southern college towns. The former gentry who once called it home had scattered. Its broad streets, shaded by ancient live oaks, which knew elegant comings and goings, remain. Many of the mansions still stand, their white columns or wide verandahs set back in generous lawns. Elegance, however, has departed with that gracious way of life that built them. Most have been cut up for rooming houses, small rental apartments, or taken over by the fraternities and sororities, for the section fringes the campus of Florida State University. Indeed, it has become almost an appendage to the college.

One would not have imagined that such was a setting for violence.

On Sept. 29, 1970, a woman doctoral student in urban studies was found dead in her bed in her apartment on W.

Lafayette, her nightgown yanked up around her head. She had been beaten to death with a blunt instrument.

One evening in May, 1975, an art student living on St. Augustine St. took her Irish setter walking and disappeared. Both she and the dog were found dead May 17, the dog on the back seat of a car, the partly disrobed body of its mistress in the trunk. She had been shot four times with a .22.

Not far from where the art student's car was discovered in Apalachicola National Forest, another co-ed was left for dead in the spring of 1977. May 1, this girl had told her fraternity date goodnight outside Dorman Hall on Jefferson Street.

"Possibly with a club, conceivably with a stone," according to campus police, she was beaten senseless and dragged unconscious to a campus parking lot students call "the dust bowl."

Her assailant drove down a lonely back road into the Apalachicola Forest and dumped her body. "It was sexual assault," police said.

The co-ed survived, recovered, and returned to her home in the Mid-West. But "she couldn't remember a thing; it was a case of total amnesia," announced police.

While the young girl lay struggling for life in the Tallahassee hospital, one of her closest college friends and sorority sister visited her often, Margaret Bowman from St. Petersburg, Fla.

"Margaret Bowman was so upset emotionally that she couldn't attend classes for three weeks. She took an incomplete. I know it upset her terribly. They were very close," said a professor who taught both girls.

The ravaged co-ed did not return to Florida for the fall and winter semester in 1977-78, but Margaret Bowman did. She moved into the Chi Omega sorority house, which is just one block from where her friend had been attacked, just a few blocks from the W. LaFayette and St. Augustine addresses where the two earlier victims of similar assaults had lived.

Built about 20 years ago, the sorority house is a comparative newcomer among the stately but decaying homes of an earlier era. A brick and white painted building, it looks like a dormitory, and in the winter of 1978 housed about forty girls bent on an education.

Twenty-one year old Margaret, a striking brunet with long black hair, was a junior, majoring in fashion merchandizing, and had been elected to the student senate. Popular, she dated frequently. The daughter of a career Air Force man, she was born in Honolulu. At college, she worked part-time at The Colony, a clothing store.

The second story room right next to Margaret's was occupied by another St. Petersburg co-ed, 20-year old Lisa Levy, a sophomore. Lisa also worked part-time at The Colony and in the Army-Navy surplus store as well to help pay for her education. An attractive, out-going blond, she had been her high school's baton twirling champion. She also was studying fashion merchandizing and was the Chi Omega treasurer.

The room across the hall from the two St. Petersburg co-eds was shared by Karen Conners, a fashion design major, and petite Kathy Dunst of Miami.

Karen, who had been yearbook editor at her Tallahassee high school, took the previous year's sex assault on her sorority sister almost as hard as Margaret Bowman. The Chi Omega pledgemaster, she worried about the safety of the girls living at the house.

Dark-haired Kathy, always sunny and merry, had a delightful gift for pantomime. Active in church affairs, she had met her steady boyfriend at the Methodist Wesley Foundation on campus.

January 14, 1978, was a Saturday night; most of the girls were out on dates or otherwise partying. They straggled back in ones and twos, some of them not getting home until early Sunday morning, January 15. Generally, they entered by the back door which had a push button combination lock, which was supposed to be kept fastened after midnight.

Karen was one of the early ones in. She had had dinner with her parents and got back to her room about 10:30 p.m. After watching television for a while, she went to sleep about midnight. Kathy was already in bed. She had been to a wedding earlier in the day and retired by 11:30 p.m.

Lisa also made it an early evening. After a night cap drink with a sorority sister at a bar next door, the two girls returned

304

to the house about 10:30 p.m.

Lisa went to bed. The other girl sat up talking to Margaret Bowman until about 2:45 a.m. She remembered noting the time on her digital clock as she climbed into bed for a night's sleep.

A co-ed from Altamonte Springs got back from a party at 3 a.m. and found the rear door ajar. Even more strange, the hall lights upstairs were out. Another girl, coming in earlier, was to remember that the lock catch had not been working quite right and that the chandelier over the entry was lighted.

The Altamonte student changed into her night clothes, went to the bathroom, which, as in most dormitories was shared and opened into the common hallway.

While she was brushing her teeth, she heard the closed bathroom door squeak.

"It only does that when someone walks by," she was to explain. "But when I came out, there was no one there." She went on to bed.

Kitty Compton, who by fateful coincidence, had been the roommate of the girl attacked the previous year, came in shortly after. She stepped into the living room to turn off the lights there. She heard a thump.

Wondering if her date had tripped and fallen leaving, she peered out a window. Her boyfriend was getting into his car. As she watched him drive away, she heard footsteps on the second floor above. The footsteps hurried down the stairs.

Kitty turned toward the foyer, then paused. A man was standing by the door. His left hand was under the door knob. In his right hand he grasped a club, holding it in the center so both ends protruded from his fist.

"It looked like a log because of the texture. It was rough, sort of like tree bark. I thought it was either a burglar or one of the girls had got up enough guts to sneak a guy up."

The man appeared "frozen." And she herself in the now darkened living room "three or four yards" away, was motionless. "For a matter of seconds, maybe three," the silent tableau held, then the man was gone through the door.

"I don't think he saw me." His face had been turned the whole time, his profile to her. But, an art major, her eyes had

305

been trained for careful observation. It was a white man, wearing light trousers and dark coat, a knit ski cap pulled far down around his face. He had a sharp triangular blade of a nose, a thin nose but prominent.

He looked somewhat like the sorority houseboy, the only male allowed on the second floor, and then only for maintenance work. But what would he be doing in the house at this hour on a Sunday morning?

Bothered, Kitty ran upstairs to wake her roommate. Shaken awake on a possible burglar scare, Kitty's roommate grabbed her umbrella from the closet, and thus armed, the two girls ventured back down to check the front door. It was locked. They peered out the window. The yard and street were deserted. Still concerned, however, they climbed back upstairs to wake the sorority president.

Down the hallway, they saw Karen stagger out of her room, bent over, her head in her hands as if she were sick. They ran to help her and saw there was blood on her hands.

Through the open room door they saw Kathy sitting up in bed "moaning, not screaming."

Kitty's roommate raced to the telephone at the head of the stairs and dialed 911, the emergency number.

The police arrived at 3:23 a.m. and were admitted by Kitty and her roommate. The first thing Officer Oscar Brannon asked was a description of the intruder, which the art student provided. White male, young, 5-8, 160 pounds, slender build, clean shaven, prominent nose, dark complexion, smooth shaven, toboggan-type cap, and carrying a large stick with a dark cloth or stocking around it. Officer Brannon broadcast it from his small portable sender.

Officer Ray Crew called down from upstairs, "We've got a Signal 7." That changed everything. Signal 7 is a deceased person.

Officer Crew, attached to the university security force, had been only a block away when he received the dispatch call. He had hurried upstairs as Brannon paused to question Kitty and her roommate. He saw Kathy sitting up in bed bleeding profusely, but, fearing her attacker might still be in the building, he rushed past, flinging open doors. The hall now was

306

crowded with anxious girls in bathrobes. The house-mother, looked around worriedly, asked, "Where's Margaret Bowman?"

"Which room?" demanded Crew. He was pointed to the closed door of No. 9. He entered, switching on the lights. The co-ed lay face down on her bed, her yellow nightie hiked up, her arms twisted around and turned palms up on her back. Around her neck was tightly wound a woman's stocking. Her body, her head, bed, walls, and floor, were splattered with blood. On top of the trash can was an empty package that had contained panty hose: Hanes, "Alive," Size D. A pair of panties lay in a heap on the floor by the bed.

Trailed by the housemother, the officers began a room to room search. Crew entered No. 8. A figure lay covered up on the bed.

"That's Lisa Levy," murmured the housemother from the doorway.

"Wake up, Lisa! Wake up!" said Crew, reaching down to shake her. He pulled the cover back from her head. It was battered and bloody.

"Her complexion was pallid, her lips bluish in color, her body temperature way down. She was almost cool to the touch. One of her eyelids was raised and her eyes appeared a little glassy."

On the beds of both victims, on their pillows, in their hair were fragments of bark. Police found similar fragments by the front door.

Down the hall, Officer Henry Newkirk was shaking another girl, a large blond. "Oh my God!" he muttered, "We've got another one." But then, to his relief, the girl stirred. A heavy sleeper, she had just come in about 2 a.m. It was she who had found the punch lock on the back door "strange."

"The door didn't lock. Maybe it just didn't stick."

By this time the emergency rescue squad had arrived. They took over from the girl who was holding a plastic cup under Kathy's chin to catch the flowing blood. The battered co-ed was still sitting up in bed, moaning, and was incoherent when the rescue men eased her into an ambulance. Karen was unconscious.

Don Allen, the emergency squad man, pointed out a puncture type wound near Lisa's right nipple. To Officer Newkirk it looked like a bite mark, "Like I took a bite of an apple and the teeth indentures remained in the skin." The nipple was almost severed.

There was a similar mark on Lisa's left buttock. On Margaret's thigh was an abrasion like a rope burn.

Margaret Bowman was dead at the scene. Lisa Levy was dead on arrival at the hospital. Mercifully, Kathy and Karen would recover and never remember what happened that night.

Meanwhile, at a duplex apartment just a couple of blocks away, the two girls who occupied one unit came home about 2 a.m. Entering they made loud and catty remarks about the volume of their neighbor's TV, hoping to be overheard. It was a bone of contention between the two roommates and the girl from Virginia, a ballet student named Janet Tuffin who was the single occupant of the other unit. The volume was lowered and the roommates went to sleep.

About 4:30 a.m. one of them was wakened by a loud thumping noise, which "sounded as if it was coming from underneath the house, somebody with a hammer banging real loud."

She awakened her roommate.

"We heard Cheryl. She wasn't crying, she was whimpering, more or less. I called a guy I was dating and asked him what I should do. He told me, 'Go see. Go see. Knock on the door.' "

Her roommate, groggy with sleep, was still alert enough to be more cautious. The girls in both units had arranged their own security system: always answer your telephone immediately. Never let it ring on and on.

They dialed Cheryl. "We let it ring five times. And as soon as the phone started ringing, because I was sitting right next to the wall, I heard real wild noises, like running, and I could hear Cheryl a little bit sort of crying or laughing. She didn't answer after five rings and I figured she's not laughing. There's something wrong."

They dialed police. Twelve police cars were there in minutes, while the dispatcher kept the girls on the telephone, soothingly urging them to sit tight.

It was about 4:40 a.m., just a little more than an hour after the first call from the Chi Omega house, only two-tenths of a mile away.

Officer Wilton Dozier found Cheryl Thomas crossways on her bed, a pair of pantyhose tangled in the bedclothes. "She was in a semi-conscious state; she did not respond to any of our commands. There was blood about her body. It was on the bed."

Cheryl did not recover consciousness for nearly a week, and, as Karen and Kathy, she, mercifully, could remember nothing about the attack. She had been severely battered, perhaps with a board she used during the summer to keep her window propped open. She had lost the hearing in one ear, and what was tragically worse, damage to her inner ear threatened permanently to impair her sense of balance and end her chosen career as a dancer. She underwent brain surgery.

Reconstructing the crime, police figured the intruder, whom they presumed to be the same man who invaded Chi Omega, had removed the kitchen screen, bent a curtain rod, and thrust himself into the apartment of the 22-year old dancer. They believe that only the ringing telephone saved her life.

By 5 a.m. all the weeping Chi Omega sisters had been fingerprinted so theirs could be eliminated by technicians processing the house. All available law enforcement personnel were combing the neighborhood. In the next weeks 40 agencies would become involved in the manhunt.

"We have a deranged murderer on our hands, a crazy man," warned horrified officials of the 22,000 student campus. "We don't know where he is, what he will do next. But you must not go out by yourselves. You must not go out." Fraternity men armed with bats volunteered as extra security guards for the residences. Many parents withdrew their daughters. Frightened students walked in groups to classroom.

"Our feelings are mixed with numbness, disbelief and a sense of terror," said the new president of the Panhellenic

Council of all fraternities and sororities. "I won't believe it. I am resentful, but most of all I am overcome by my own sense of helplessness."

A command post was set up near campus. Police checked every acquaintance of the five women victimized and moved house to house questioning, trying to find a trace, any trace of the killer. Was he a student? Did he live in that seemingly fated neighborhood?

There were no suspects, although police began the tedious process of checking more than 100 possibilities. But for the thin prominent nose Kitty had seen, the description was general. In case she had been mistaken in the uncertain light, police widened it to include not just a dark-skinned white man, but also a light-complected black. ID men poured through files. Kitty willingly submitted to hypnosis in a fruitless hope of adding more details to her description. She was kept under heavy police guard.

Inevitably, police explored the possibility of a link between these crimes and the attack on Kitty's Chi Omega roommate the previous year. She, too, would have died, if two boys had not found her in the forest the following day. All of these girls had been bludgeoned, at least two, possibly three of them sexually assaulted.

A few crumbs of information were gathered. Three of the girls, the two that were killed and the ballet dancer had all been at Big Daddy's Lounge the evening of the attack. Other co-eds who were also at the bistro spoke of a young man with a thin sharp nose who had stared at them offensively, "as if he wanted to make me feel uncomfortable." It was vaguely recalled that Margaret Bowman may have made some comment to him as she left the lounge.

Intensive search did not recover the murder weapon, but police decided it must have been an oak branch. There were many old trees in that neighborhood and branches fell in the yards. A pile of such timber was stacked by the Chi Omega back door for use.

All of the girls had been savagely battered. In the opinion of Dr. Thomas Wood, Leon County associate medical examiner, the two who were slain were first knocked unconscious.

This judgement was borne out by the lack of any signs of struggle in their bedrooms.

Lisa Levy had strangulation marks on her neck and "suffered trauma to the anal and genital areas." Police had recovered a hair spray bottle from her floor on which lab technicians found blood and fecal matter, leading lawmen to surmise her assailant had used this to sodomize his victim. She was also bitten on the breast and buttocks.

But, "in all likelihood," according to Dr. Wood, "she was first rendered unconscious by the blows to the head, then bitten, then there was penetration of the anus and vagina and then death by strangulation."

Dr. Wood theorized that the fresh abrasion on Margaret Bowman's left thigh had been caused by forcible removal of her panties. She had been hit so hard on the head that her skull was depressed. Then she had been strangled by a pair of panty hose knotted tightly around her neck so tightly they had to be cut away. They were completely soaked with blood.

The bite marks on Lisa Levy were photographed with a measuring stick placed beside them, and the one on her buttocks was surgically removed for preservation.

A pair of panty hose found on the unoccupied bed in Margaret Bowman's room had had one leg cut off, the other tied, and holes cut for eyes, so that it could be used as a face mask. This was also Hanes "Alives" Size D. Lab technicians found a brown curly hair inside.

Leon County Sheriff Ken Katsaris, who coordinated the investigation, told reporters of his frustration 12 hours after the crimes.

"I think we have a sick individual. He is depraved. So far everything has led to a dead end. We have no information to go on. No leads. The only possible motive we can find at this time is sexual attack."

The Chi Omega killer, according to the sheriff's reconstruction, walked through a recreation room, after entering by the rear door which he found unlatched, then mounted the stairs. At the top was a corridor with doors along both sides.

"He did, in fact, pass over several doors before he entered one. It is entirely possible he looked in the others, possibly he

311

was looking for rooms with just one person," said the sheriff.

Working from Kitty's description of the man whose profile she had glimpsed at the door, artist Francis W. Kenniston, an FSU associate professor, drew a sketch which police released widely.

When she was able to talk, Cheryl Thomas told police that she had returned home that night shortly before 2 a.m. She had heard the girls from the other unit coming in, loudly complaining about her TV and was amused. After fixing herself a snack, she went to bed. Some time later she was awakened by a noise.

"I think during the night I heard a plant being knocked over, but I had a cat that I had just gotten a week before and I thought maybe the cat had knocked over something. I went back to sleep."

She remembers nothing more until she woke up in the hospital several days later.

Despite many hours of overtime and frustration, the case had not advanced after a whole month when, 220 miles west of Tallahassee, Pensacola Police Officer Robert Lee, on routine road patrol, stopped an orange Volkswagen about 1:30 a.m., Wednesday, February 15, 1978. The vehicle had disappeared down an alley and something stirred Lee's suspicions. He radioed to see if it was stolen, then stopped the driver near Oscar Woerner's restaurant, asking for identification.

A young man stepped out from under the wheel and produced ID for a recent FSU student who had been a university track star. At that moment, the car radio crackled back the information: stolen vehicle. The car had been reported missing at Tallahassee the previous Sunday evening.

Officer Lee ordered the young man to lie down on the ground and started to handcuff him. The policeman thought another person was hiding in the Volks. His attention was divided. In a swift surprise movement, his captive kicked the feet from under the officer, slugged him with the handcuffs dangling from one wrist and ran off. Scrambling to his feet, Lee drew his service revolver and gave chase, shooting and calling for his quarry to halt. The man ran on. Lee fired again. The suspect stopped, submitted to handcuffing, muttering.

"I wish you would have killed me!"

As Officer Lee took his prisoner in, the young man commented, "This case ought to help you make sergeant."

Searching the 1972 orange Volkswagen, police found credit cards and other identity papers in 21 names, most of them of FSU students.

The young man continued to insist on the identity originally given Officer Lee. But the real track star himself was quickly located and told police he had lost his ID papers sometime during the Christmas holidays.

The following day, Pensacola Det. Norman Chapman puzzling over the enigma, as all the other credit cards were being checked out, suddenly had a hunch.

The latest FBI "Most Wanted" list had been circulated to law enforcement agencies just the previous Friday. Chapman studied a new name on it: Theodore Robert Bundy.

Det. Chapman phoned FBI. Agents arrived with wanted posters and fingerprints. The identification was positive.

Acting FBI Director James Adams confirmed that Bundy was wanted for questioning in 36 sex assault murders in four western states, dating back to 1969. He had escaped from prison in Colorado while awaiting trial on one of them in which he had been formally accused.

The FBI description read: "College-educated, physical fitness enthusiast. Born Nov. 24, 1946, Burlington, Vermont. Height 5'11" to 6'; 145 to 175 pounds; build, slender; hair, dark brown, collar length; eyes, blue; complexion, pale. Occupations: bellboy, busboy, cook's helper, dishwasher, janitor, law school student, office worker, political campaign worker, psychiatric social worker, salesman, security guard."

There was only one conviction, for a 1974 kidnapping of a 17 year old girl in Salt Lake City, Utah. He received a one-to-15 year sentence. While in prison he was arrested for the 1975 sex-slaying of Caryn Campbell, a Michigan nurse and sister of a Fort Lauderdale, Fla. police officer. Her nude, badly bitten body was found in a Colorado snow bank after she was missed on a skiing vacation. Gasoline credit cards in Bundy's own name placed him in the immediate area at the time of the crime and were among clues leading to his arrest.

On New Year's Eve, 1977, Bundy had squirmed through a ceiling light fixture hole and escaped from prison.

Several of the slayings involved bludgeoning, sex battery, and strangulation. Det. Chapman contacted authorities in Tallahassee investigating the Chi Omega killings.

Among credit cards found in the orange Volks Bundy was accused of stealing was one that might provide leads to another case in the Florida headlines. A 12-year old seventh grader, Kimberly Leach, had disappeared from her school February 9 and was being sought all over North Florida. Investigators in this case as well as those involved in the Tallahassee slayings questioned Bundy Friday, February 17.

At the same time, other detectives in Tallahassee examined the quarters Bundy had rented January 7 in a rooming house four blocks from the Chi Omega house, known as "The Oak" because of the mammoth old tree in its front yard. Fellow roomers were astonished that the young man they knew as "Chris Hagen" was suspect in the monstrous killings.

"He was the silent, nervous type, a little effeminate," said one.

Bundy pulled out of the rooming house Sunday, February 11 without settling his rent. But he left a bag of cookies by the door of one of the girls rooming there. Once he had treated her to a $37 dinner at a posh French restaurant, paying with a credit card, apparently stolen.

In a long rambling all-night interrogation, only part of which was taped, Bundy talked of his personality and his "problem." In later testimony, Det. Chapman said that Bundy complained that "fantasies" were taking over his life.

"He said to keep his fantasies going, he had to do acts against society. He said he was a voyeur.

"He felt like a vampire because he could get by on three hours sleep a night and get in his car and drive many miles."

Asked about the Chi Omega murders, "he dropped his head, and in a very sincere tone, with tears in his eyes, he told us, 'The evidence is there. Go find it,' " Champan said.

While the tape was still running, Bundy spoke freely of his New Year's Eve escape. He made his way to the University of

Michigan and rented a room at the YMCA. But because the Colorado victim was from Michigan, his name was in all the media there. He decided he wanted to go to Florida and look up college catalogues in the library.

He found that the University of Florida was in Gainesville, so he hunted up a map of the state. "Here's Gainesville in the middle of nowhere, you see. And I wanted to be by the ocean, for Christ's sakes. Gainesville on the map didn't look right. Isn't it strange? Didn't look right. If it had been by Tampa Bay, I may have gone there. Who knows? And so I came to the catalogue for Florida State University. All this is almost random in a way. Superstitious."

He got a Trailways bus ticket to Tallahassee. But "I'd made a mistake in choosing FSU. It's not that big, the kind of big major metropolitan campus I was looking for." Nevertheless, he started shopping for an ID.

He wanted a recent graduate. "I figure I had a degree on my own, you know. Wouldn't be terribly deceitful of me to get the identity that had a degree." So he selected the track star.

Resolutions to play it cool and careful faded, and in Tallahassee his "habit of wanting to acquire" resurfaced.

"Little things, things to make life comfortable. I mean not Cadillacs. I started to take shortcuts, see, uh, steal. Towels, you know, some cologne or racquet ball or a pair of tennis shorts. Just like going to the supermarket stuffing my back full of cans of sardines. I'm not a very good job hunter, and uh, I kinda procrastinate. I was losing sight of my plans to just stick with it, get ID, get a job, stay inconspicuous. Stealing a car was a shortcut . . . Stupid old short cut."

He stole a series of cars. But he did have caution to wear leather gloves most of the time, avoiding fingerprints.

Bundy side-stepped questions about a stolen white van which Lake City witnesses had seen the 12-year old school girl enter.

"I really can't talk about it," Bundy said. "We, we, we better not talk about it."

And pressed about the Chi Omega murders, he asked that the tape be turned off and the investigators not take notes. It was then he rambled on about "uncontrollable fantasies" and "vampire feelings," police said. He did not admit to any homicides.

Bundy was ordered by the court to submit to taking of blood and hair samples and teeth impressions.

Although hairs are not as unique as fingerprints and hence do not provide conclusive proof of identity, still by all laboratory tests available, Bundy's hair sample matched the hair found in the pantyhose face mask found at the crime scene.

Dr. Richard R. Souviron, a Coral Gables dentist in private practice who is also consultant to the Dade County Medical Examiner, found that transparent overlays of Bundy's teeth impressions "lined-up exactly" and "fit perfectly" onto police photographic close-up of the bite mark on Lisa Levy's buttock.

Although identification by bite mark has been extremely rare in criminal cases, it can be as conclusive as fingerprints, according to forensic odontologists. Teeth are as individual, they contend. Shapes are unique, relationships of the separate teeth to each other are unique, twisting, tipping, bending are unique. Wearing patterns, fillings and dental work missing or broken teeth add to uniqueness. For these reasons, use of teeth for identification of victims, for example, has long been familiar.

Bite marks however present problems. The soft, yielding, elastic nature of human tissue makes reproduction for comparison difficult. A video-computer technique developed in the NASA program to allow moon photographs to be read for three-dimensional information, however, has solved one major problem by allowing depth of bite marks to be determined by computer analysis.

Dr. Souviron found "30 points of positive comparison" between Bundy's teeth and the bite marks. It was a double bite, he said. Twice the lower teeth sunk into the co-ed's flesh with tremendous force, holding the tissue, "while the upper teeth did the scraping," very sharp upper teeth.

"It is convincing beyond any discussion whatsoever. There is absolutely no way that this can be refuted," declared Dr. Souviron. "I'm not saying that this set of teeth making those marks killed anybody. I am saying that these teeth made those marks."

Dr. Souviron said that in his opinion the bites had occurred "about the time of death" because "of the lack of vital reaction" around wounds of such severity.

Sheriff Katsaris was convinced he had the right man. Prosecutors agreed. In July, 1978, a Leon County Grand Jury indicted Theodore Robert Bundy for the Chi Omega murders. The first act in what was to be a long Bundy drama in Florida was ended.

It was almost a year of judicial maneuvering, frequently prompting headlines, before a Dade Circuit Court Jury in Miami, after seven hours deliberation, found him guilty. Meeting again in advisory session, the same jury recommended death.

Talking with reporters afterward, the foreman, an engineer who had never even heard of Bundy before he was sworn and sequestered for the long trial, said the murders "were too methodical, too clean. This was not passion. It was just a pure criminal act. Our laws are meant to punish such people."

Tuesday, July 31, 1979, Circuit Court Judge Edward D. Cowart sentenced Bundy to the electric chair. He imposed the sentence twice: once for Lisa Levy, 20, and once for Margaret Bowman, 21, both brutally murdered.

State Supreme Court review is automatic under Florida law.

Meanwhile, other Florida law enforcement officers had been assembling evidence linking Bundy to the disappearance of the 12-year old school girl whose battered and ravished body had been found in an abandoned pig sty.

The child had been still missing when Bundy was arrested for speeding in Pensacola. The 21 credit cards in differing names found in the stolen car he was driving provided the first lead in the search for the missing honor student from Lake City Junior High, about 100 miles east of Tallahassee.

Pretty Kimberly Diane Leach, a runner-up for school Valentine queen, had already picked out her party dress for the Saturday night Valentine dance on February 11. Two days earlier, Feb. 9, 1978, was the last day she was seen alive, returning to her homeroom to pick up her purse which she had

317

left there during the first class that morning. A classmate told police she had seen Kimberly getting into a white van.

Stolen credit cards found with Bundy were used in Jacksonville and a Lake City motel the day before the schoolgirl disappeared. The white van had been reported stolen near the FSU campus where the sorority rape-slayings occurred. A man fitting Bundy's general description had signed into the Lake City Holiday Inn on one of the stolen credit cards.

Hundreds joined in the search for the missing youngster, with at least 100 planes and helicopters circling over the swamps and forests of north Florida.

"We fear foul play but until we find the girl or a body, we have no crime," said Columbia County Sheriff Glenn Bailey.

Columbia county with 900 acres of national forest wilderness and almost impenetrable swamp was a tough assignment. Hunters have stumbled on planes crashed there 20 or 30 years earlier.

The man who had checked into the Lake City Holiday Inn February 8 was so "ordinary" nobody remembered much about him. He made no phone calls and checked out February 9 at 7 a.m. Kim was reported missing about 9 a.m. after she did not turn up for her second class that morning. Lake City Police Chief Paul Philpot instituted search, knowing Kim "wasn't the kind to run away."

The Florida Highway Patrol led by Captain Jimmy Love and Lake City investigator Larry Daugherty joined sheriff's deputies in combing a landfall where a white van had been spotted the day of the disappearance, but discovered nothing. Forty agencies coordinated by State Attny. Bob Dekle also joined in. Rain delayed a search along the beautiful Suwannee River, made world famous by Stephen Foster's song, and throughout Suwannee county. But it would be 39 days after the youngster's disappearance that the grim hunt would reach its grisly conclusion.

On the afternoon of Friday, April 7, State Trooper K.W. Robinson, one of about 40 investigators making a second search of an area about 20 miles west of Lake City, lifted the collapsed sheet metal of an old lean-to that had sheltered hogs. Stuffed under a mess of debris was a decomposing body clad in the jeans and T-shirt Kim had been wearing.

Dirt and leaves found in the white van had prompted detectives to return to this remote spot in Suwannee River State Park near Live Oak.

Dr. Peter Lipkovic, who performed the autopsy, reported "an overwhelming, tearing type of injury" to the child's neck, indicating she was strangled or hacked about the neck until she died. There was not enough tissue remaining, however, to establish exactly the cause of the injury. The body had been at the scene about two months and was positively identified through dental charts.

Captain Steve Hooker of the FSU campus police told reporters, "You could see where leaves and debris were caught up under the rear doors of the van and you could see that something heavy was dragged from the vehicle."

Analysis of the leaves indicated they had come from the Suwannee River area. Lake Park Superintendent Clyde Nichols said the spot where the body was found was accessible without going through the main park gate, by a little-traveled but fairly good dirt road less than a mile from the pig sty.

July 20, 1978, the Columbia County Grand Jury returned a sealed indictment in the rape-murder of the seventh grader. It was opened in Lake City Monday, July 31, just hours after Bundy pleaded not guilty in the Chi Omega murders. Trial would have to await resolution of that earlier case.

But after several delays and the grant of a defense motion for change of venue, a jury was finally selected at Orlando in January, 1980. The five-man, seven-woman panel deliberated 7 1/2 hours before finding the 33-year old former law student guilty. Bundy, already facing two death sentences in the sorority slayings, stood expressionless. As in the earlier Florida trial at Miami in July, 1979, he had acted as his own attorney.

A parade of law enforcement officers testified to finding fibres from Bundy's and the girl's clothing in the van; bloodstains on the van carpet; semen on the girl's panties; and two footprints made by Bundy's shoes.

Bundy, in a last minute eloquent plea for acquittal, claimed to have been a victim of circumstances. While the jury was still out, his 32-year old fiancee, a devoted supporter at both trials, bought four red roses and sent them back to her love via a lawyer. When the verdict came in, she raced to phone him comforting words.

At the second session, the penalty phase of the trial, she was the only witness for the defense, and begged for a life sentence, saying, "Ted is a large part of my life."

But the jury was not swayed and recommended the convicted rapist-killer be sent to the electric chair.

Nor were jail officials swayed by love. They refused Bundy's request that he be allowed to marry his faithful sweetheart.

Tuesday, February 12, 1980, Circuit Judge Wallace Jopling imposed a third death sentence on Theodore Robert Bundy.

At 7:16 a.m., on January 24, 1989, Ted Bundy was electrocuted in Florida.

Virginia's Rampaging Serial Rape-Slayer

by Barry Benedict

Neatness was the killer's nemesis.

In the autumn of 1987, a hot-prowl killer was loose on the dark streets of Richmond, Virginia. Called the Southside Slayer, he went about his murderous work with brutal, single-minded professionalism.

His victims were white females. They were assaulted while asleep, helpless and unable to defend themselves against his horrifying onslaught.

The killer knew this, of course. That was how he wanted them—alone, helpless, vulnerable.

The Southside Slayer was not the only serial killer to stalk the history-rich neighborhoods of this old city, which was once the capital of the Old South. In the fall of 1987, however, he was the most feared and the most hunted.

Two dozen highly trained detectives were pulled from other cases to find the Southside Slayer. Their mighty efforts produced a casebook with over 600 clues and testimony of 300 questioned witnesses, over 30 of them possible suspects.

The commonwealth attorney later called it one of the most thorough and exhaustive investigations ever conducted in the county.

The Southside Slayer proved to be a crafty adversary. He

left behind few clues—and no witnesses. He might still be free if it weren't for one detective's long memory and a new identification tool that traced evil to its genetic makeup.

The case began on September 17, 1987, with the report of an abandoned car in front of a South Richmond home. The doors were locked and the engine was still running. Apparently the driver had simply parked the automobile and walked away.

The vehicle was registered to Debbie Dudley Davis, a 35-year-old employee of a local magazine. A police officer went to her first-floor apartment on Devonshire Road to check on the situation. Knocking repeatedly and receiving no answer, he tried the next-door neighbor.

The neighbor said she was a good friend of Debbie's but hadn't seen her since the night before. Nonetheless, she did have a key to Davis' apartment; she gave it to the officer.

Entering the apartment, the detective spotted a broken window in the kitchen and an empty purse on the living room floor. To his keen, unblinking eye, these conditions indicated burglary.

But it was a bit more serious than that, as the police officer discovered upon entering the bedroom. What he saw sprawled on the bed was the limp form of Debbie Davis. She was naked; her hands were tied behind her back and a long pantyhose was wrapped around her neck.

A team of detectives was quickly dispatched to the scene. They soon determined that the pretty, dark-haired woman had slipped into her nightclothes and had been sound asleep when the intruder entered her apartment through the kitchen window.

Ripping the frilly garment from her shoulders, he tied her hands with rope he'd apparently brought along, pushed her onto the bed, and raped and started to strangle her.

Then he tied the pantyhose around her neck, looping it through the rope that bound her hands behind her back in such a manner that her slightest movement caused the makeshift noose to tighten.

After searching her bedroom and purse he left, leaving

322

Debbie Davis to suffer a slow, agonizing death.

Lab technicians combed the tidy, neatly organized apartment and her car, abandoned almost one mile from the murder scene. They came away without a single fingerprint or other incriminating evidence that could be linked to the killer.

Residents told police that Debbie Davis was a good neighbor, always careful whom she let into her apartment and always making sure the doors and windows were locked before she went to bed. No one had heard any screams or other sounds of disturbances the night before. Most of them were long-term tenants of the complex and had experienced little trouble.

Two weeks later, while police were still searching for leads, another woman was raped and murdered. Dr. Susan Hellams was a 32-year-old neurosurgery resident at Medical College of Virginia Hospitals. The pretty blonde physician lived in a two-story home on West 31st Street with her husband, a law student at George Washington University in Washington, D.C.

On October 3rd, her husband came home and found his wife's partly clothed and bound corpse stuffed into the master bedroom closet. He immediately called police.

Patrol officers were the first to arrive, followed by homicide investigators and a deputy coroner. With the crime scene sealed off, the sleuths began a top-to-bottom search of the elegant apartment. They also questioned neighbors, as well as her husband and hospital co-workers.

Detectives learned that Dr. Hellams had left the hospital on Friday evening, October 2nd, and headed home, planning to spend the weekend with her husband.

As far as police could determine, she reached home without incident, cooked dinner and enjoyed a glass of wine before going to bed. Several hours later, she was tied up, brutally raped and strangled.

During their inspection of the scene, the detectives discovered a broken window in the basement. The husband did not remember the window being broken; police as-

323

sumed that it was smashed by the murderer.

Sleuths figured that the killer climbed the stairs to the first floor, where he apparently rifled a purse and stole grocery money stuffed in a kitchen jar. Then he went up a flight of stairs to the second-story bedroom.

An examination of the corpse indicated that the assault had been long and brutal, with the victim being sexually attacked several times before she was strangled.

Sex-crimes detectives quickly noted similarities between the murder of Dr. Susan Hellams and the earlier slaying of Debbie Davis. Both were white women who were attacked while alone in their homes on weekends within two weeks of each other.

Both victims had apparently been asleep in their bedrooms when they were attacked; both had been bound with their hands behind their back and strangled with a garment taken from the house. And the homes of both had been robbed.

As far as police could ascertain, Debbie Davis and Susan Hellams did not know each other or move in the same social circles. Detectives speculated that the victims had been selected at random, perhaps even followed by the rapist in a plan to learn their habits and to be sure they would be alone when he entered their homes. And this made him unusually dangerous.

Hard pressed for leads, detectives turned to the criminal files, searching for crimes that showed similarities to the South Richmond rape-murders.

They had barely begun this procedure when another woman was raped and murdered. Diane Cho was a 15-year-old freshman at Manchester High School in suburban Chesterfield. Dark-haired and pretty, she lived in a comfortable middle-class home on Gavilan Court.

On November 22nd she was found bound and naked in her bedroom. She had been sexually assaulted and strangled.

Though the pretty high school student was much younger and lived 15 miles south of the other victims, it was apparent to detectives that she had been assaulted by the same person.

Aware that a serial killer-rapist was loose and had struck three times within just six weeks, Richmond Police Chief Frank S. Duling formed a task force to work the cases full time. Heading the investigative team of handpicked detectives was Major V. Stuart Cook and Captain Kenneth Jenkins.

The investigators prepared a long list to be checked out; it consisted of criminals who had been convicted of sex offenses or had committed violent crimes and either lived or worked in the neighborhoods where the three women were slain.

The sleuths also contacted the FBI officer in Richmond to request a psychiatric profile of killers whose method of operation matched the man detectives were now calling "The Southside Slayer."

The request was turned over to the agency's crack Psychological Behavioral unit in Washington, D.C. Detectives later received a lengthy form that included detailed questions about the crime scene, victim descriptions and other details learned during the investigations. The form was returned to the FBI. By then, however, police had another murder on their hands.

On January 6, 1988, Rena G. Chapouris was found in her Grove Avenue apartment in South Richmond. The shapely 26-year-old brunette was stripped naked and bound with her hands behind her back. She had also been strangled and bludgeoned. A bloodied claw hammer was found beside the bed.

The police officers first on the scene spotted the telltale signs and were convinced the Southside Slayer had struck again. Task force investigators, who were more familiar with the case, weren't so sure.

For one thing, there was the hammer. The victim had been struck repeatedly in the side of the head, spewing enormous amounts of blood on the bed and walls, cracking her head like an egg-shell.

None of the other victims had been bludgeoned. In fact, those crime scene were almost blood-free.

And, unlike the others, Chapouris, though completely naked, did not appear to have been raped or sexually assaulted.

As detectives searched the small, tastefully decorated apartment and questioned startled, disbelieving neighbors, another corpse was discovered. The victim was Michael St. Hilaire, 29. He was found in his West Main Street basement apartment, nude and hanging from a wire wrapped around his neck and attached to a pipe.

Hilaire lived just a few blocks from Chapouris. According to the coroner's report, he had committed suicide within approximately the same time frame as when Chapouris was murdered.

"It might be a coincidence," a detective told a reporter. "But then, there might be a Santa Claus, too!"

The task-force investigators didn't believe in coincidences or Santa Claus. Searching Hilaire's apartment, they discovered a diary in which Hilaire had hastily scrawled the message, "Need money. Plan to do something dangerous to get it. If not successful, I will kill myself."

That he had done. Police and coroner's investigators both concluded that Hilaire had hanged himself.

The coroner's report also showed that Hilaire was a drug addict who was likely going through withdrawal when he wrapped the wire around his neck.

During the intense search of the tiny basement apartment, investigators found a string of newspaper clippings on the murders of Debbie Davis and Dr. Susan Hellams and the hunt for the Southside Killer. The clips detailed how the women had been found nude with their hands tied behind their backs.

"Looks like we have a copycat killer," one detective remarked.

Physical evidence corroborated that suspicion. Fibers from St. Hilaire's clothing matched fibers found on the sheet where the nude body of Rena Chapouris was discovered. Likewise, fibers from her clothes were found on St. Hilaire's clothing.

Detectives concluded that, desperate for money, Hilaire had broken into Chapouris' apartment looking for cash. Confronted or surprised by the pretty brunette, he smashed her in the head with a hammer, then searched the apartment.

To throw the police off, St. Hilaire had stripped and bound the lifeless body to make the murder appear that it was committed by the Southside Slayer.

What St. Hilaire hadn't counted on was the guilt.

"It appears he couldn't stand to live with what he did, so he killed himself," a detective noted.

Police found nothing linking St. Hilaire to the other rape murders. The official conclusion was that he was just a frantic drug addict driven mad by his habit and who decided to circumvent the judicial system by being his own judge, jury and executioner.

Though one murder case was marked solved, the task-force investigators had been unable to make much headway with the others. The FBI profile hadn't been much help; the questioning of hundreds of witnesses hadn't resulted in an arrest.

Then, in late January 1988, police got a tip. It came from police in Arlington, Virginia, seeking information on a 25-year-old convicted burglar arrested on a rape-murder charge.

The victim was Susan Tucker, 44, an employee with the U.S. Department of Agriculture. On December 2, 1987, a friend contacted police and told them she had not seen Susan since Thanksgiving. She'd called Susan's friends and gone to her home, but was unable to reach her.

Police officers paid a welfare call to Susan Tucker's two-story condominium in the exclusive Fairlington section of suburban Arlington. After finding the woman's car in the underground parking lot, they tried the door. When no one answered, one of the officers climbed through a window.

Susan Tucker was discovered in the master bedroom. Her

nude body lay face down on the bed with a sleeping bag thrown over the upper half of her body. She had been raped and sodomized and had been dead for almost a week.

Entry into the home was apparently made through a bathroom window which had been broken and pushed open. The killer had then made his way to the bedroom, where Susan Tucker had apparently lain asleep.

Police conducted a massive investigation. Neighbors, friends and co-workers were questioned, sex offenders were grilled and the house was searched for the slightest bit of physical evidence.

The clue that broke the case wide open came from an old burglary detective who said the neatness of the crime scene reminded him of a hot-prowl burglar he had once put away.

The burglar was Timothy W. Spencer, 25. A native of Washington, D.C., Spencer had a long rap sheet for burglary and robbery and had just been released to a halfway house.

The detective described Spencer as a "cool, slippery dude" who got a thrill out of breaking into homes while the occupants were asleep. As his record showed, however, not all his attempts were successful.

In June 1981, Spencer began serving a two-year term for breaking and entering. Paroled in December, he was returned to prison on March 4, 1982, after being convicted of trespassing in connection with another residential break-in.

Then, on January 29, 1984, he was arrested and charged with breaking into a home in Alexandria, Virginia. In that incident, a man told police that he woke up and saw a stranger in the bedroom. He later identified Spencer as the hot prowler.

Spencer was convicted of that crime as well as another burglary committed the same evening. He was returned to prison. He was transferred to a halfway house in Richmond on September 7, 1984.

Spencer was black, stood 5 feet 10 inches tall and weighed 160 pounds. When his mugshot was shown to Susan Tucker's neighbors, no one recognized him. His prints were not discovered in the house and he did not have any sex-offense convictions.

Acting on the burglary detective's hunch, investigators decided to question Spencer to see what, if anything, he knew about the murder.

On January 20, 1988, Arlington Police Detective John Horgas drove to Richmond and interviewed Spencer at the halfway house where he was finishing up his parole. Horgas told Spencer only that he was investigating a burglary and wanted Spencer to return with him to Arlington. He said officers wanted to question him and that it might be necessary to give a blood sample.

"Does the blood thing have anything to do with the rape?" Spencer asked.

Surprised, Detective Horgas asked what rape. He had only been talking about a burglary.

Grinning, Spencer said that he had been to prison and knew that police seek blood samples for lab tests in sex-crime cases.

"I suppose it has something to do with that murder," Spencer said.

Again, Horgas was surprised. "What murder is that?"

Spencer shook his head. The murder of that woman in Arlington—he had read about in the papers. Everyone was talking about it.

There had been a small story in the suburban papers. But as far as Detective Horgas knew, no one but the family, police and perhaps the killer were talking about the slaying.

Spencer was returned to the police station and questioned. He told police that he spent most of his time in Richmond but made occasional trips to Arlington to visit relatives.

One of those visits was on Thanksgiving—the last day Susan Tucker was seen alive. Spencer claimed that he spent that holiday taking it easy and watched sports on TV. Except for brief trips to the store, he didn't leave the house.

Relatives confirmed the story. But, during a search of the Richmond halfway house where Spencer was paroled, detectives discovered a camouflage jacket belonging to Spencer which contained small bits of glass that matched the distinctive glass of the broken window in the Tucker home.

The glass fragments were enough to hold Spencer for further questioning. More damaging was the blood sample—it proved to be enough to put him in the electric chair.

The sample was turned over to Life-codes Corp., a New York firm that tested blood and other body fluids for its genetic makeup, or DNA. Preliminary results showed that the genetic material in Spencer's blood sample was identical to that in dried semen scraped from Susan Tucker's thigh. According to lab experts, the chances of two persons having the same genetic makeup was about 135 million to one.

Spencer was charged with the sexual assault and murder of Susan Tucker. His parole was revoked and he was held in county jail without bail.

The hot prowler found himself in more hot water after his "genetic fingerprints" turned up in body fluids discovered at the crime scenes in the Debbie Davis and Susan Hellams cases.

Richmond Commonwealth Attorney Aubrey M. Davis Jr., called a press conference to announce that he would ask a grand jury to indict Spencer on capital murder charges arising from the stranglings of Debbie Davis and Susan Hellams.

Flanked by Police Chief Frank Duling, Major Stuart Cook and Captain Kenneth Jenkins, Aubrey told reporters about the forensic tests and announced, "I am satisfied that the person responsible for the homicides of Dr. Hellams and Ms. Davis is in police custody and is no longer a danger or a threat to the public."

Spencer was also the prime suspect in the murder of 15-year-old Diane Cho, but he would not be charged because not enough semen had been recovered to conduct DNA tests.

Davis expected to handle the prosecution of Spencer himself. He added, "Plea negotiations are out of the question."

He said that he fully expected the grand jury to return

330

indictments and, if Spencer was convicted, he planned to seek the death penalty.

The Richmond grand jury heard the case in April 1988. After two days of testimony, the juror returned indictments against Spencer, charging him with two counts of capital murder and five lesser counts. These included the charges of rape and breaking and entering with intent to commit rape in the death of Ms. Davis, and with rape, breaking and entering with intent to commit rape and sodomy in the death of Dr. Hellams.

After the indictments, Davis met with reporters outside the venerable Richmond courthouse. Asked if he was gratifed with the indictments, the D.A. said, "I won't start dancing in the street yet, because we've got a long way to go. It's a complex case and he has to stand trial first in Arlington before we get a crack at him."

He said he did not expect a trial until September at the earliest. "We aren't in any hurry," Davis said. "He's not going anywhere."

In addition to the criminal charges, Spencer had also been linked to other rapes and assaults committed in Arlington. The crimes were committed in a eight-month period when Spencer was not in prison.

On June 27, 1983, a 23-year old woman was raped at her home, as was another 23-year-old woman on July 16th. In both cases, the rapist entered the homes through an unlocked groundfloor window.

Then, on July 23rd, a man attempted to abduct a woman from the parking lot of her apartment. She escaped, but four days later, a 28-year-old woman was abducted in her car by a man with a knife and raped.

On August 6, a 22-year-old woman was abducted from in front of her apartment and held captive for almost two hours. She was raped and put in the trunk of her car, and the car was set on fire. She escaped.

There were five more rapes and assaults in August, one each in September and October. On December 21st, a woman was raped in her apartment by a man who entered through an unlocked door. A month later, a man burglarized one apartment, then broke into the one next door and raped the occupant, a 32-year-old woman.

Spencer was linked to the crimes because of similar M.O.'s and his physical description.

"The crimes showed a definite pattern," one investigator noted. "It's also significant that the crimes stopped after he was arrested."

Spencer went on trial for the murder of Susan Tucker in July 1988 before Arlington Judge Benjamin Kendrick. Arthur L. Karp was the prosecutor.

The courthouse was jammed with spectators eager to hear not only one of the most sensational murder cases in recent memory, but also the first one in Virginia history to use the so-called DNA "fingerprints" as evidence.

Prosecutor Karp called six scientists to the stand to testify about the reliability of the test and its use in six other states.

Several of these experts emphasized that the DNA test could not yield a false positive result which would incorrectly identify a suspect. "One could get a false negative from not being careful," one scientist said. "But I can't think of a way you can get a false positive from not being careful."

The jury heard that the DNA test was almost as good as fingerprints and that only a sibling could have the same DNA makeup. The panel learned that Susan Tucker was found lying face down and nude on her bed. A cloth found beneath her body, a sleeping bag that partially covered her, and a nightgown lying next to her were taken to a lab for DNA testing.

The items were found to be semen-stained and were tested against a sample of the defendant's blood. The results of that testing were admitted as evidence on July 15th.

A photograph or autorad showing DNA patterns of semen stains next to the DNA patterns of the defendant's blood was enlarged on an overhead projector and shown to the jury on a big screen.

A DNA forensic scientist used a yardstick and pointed three times to corresponding patterns of dots on the screen.

"Nightgown, sleeping bag, defendant's blood," she recited. "Nightgown, sleeping bag, defendant's blood. Nightgown. Sleeping bag, defendant's blood."

The patterns showed exact matches on how Spencer's genes and genes in the semen stains correspond to the three radioactive probes used in the test.

Seated in the darkness, Spencer watched the demonstration impassively.

Defense Attorney Carl Womack did not dispute the lab findings but questioned scientists closely about the chance that blood relatives could have the same DNA patterns.

The he called the defendant's relatives to the witness stand and asked each to list the names of family members.

The defense strategy was to show that relatives living in Arlington had the same genetic makeup as the defendant and any of them would have been capable of committing the murder.

Prosecutor Karp voiced a loud objection. With the jury out of the courtroom, he argued that if the defense was allowed to continue such a strategy, he should be allowed to introduce DNA and other evidence linking Spencer to rapes and murders of Susan Hellams and Debbie Davis.

"We can prove that the Richmond crimes were done with extraordinary likelihood by the same person who did this crime, and that Mr. Spencer had checked himself out of the halfway house and was available to do those crimes," Karp told the judge.

In addition to the DNA testing, Prosecutor Karp said, Spencer had been linked to the crimes by more than a dozen similarities, among them: The victims were white females living alone: each victim's hands were tied behind her back; in two cases, a rope ran from their bound hands to around their necks; each was strangled; each lived within walking distance of where Spencer was staying when the slayings occurred; each was killed at a time when Spencer was signed out from his residence; no money was found in the victims' purses; the blood type belonging to the suspect in all three cases was identical to Spencer's; a window was broken to gain entrance.

Judge Kendrick agreed with the prosecutor. He told Defense Attorney Womack that if he continued with his strategy that suggested a relative could have murdered Susan Tucker, he would allow the prosecutor to introduce evidence from the other murders.

"I think you've opened up the door and no matter what you do, regardless, I don't think you can have your cake and eat it, too," the judge said.

After an hour of discussion, attorneys on both sides agreed to a stipulation that none of Spencer's relatives committed the crime. They also agreed to omit the Richmond evidence from the trial and drop the issue of blood relatives as suspects.

The following day, Spencer himself took the witness stand and declared to the jury that he did not rape or murder Susan Tucker. He asserted that he never came into contact with her and had never heard of her until his arrest.

The jurors found that difficult to believe, however, and on July 17th, they found Spencer guilty of first-degree rape and murder. They also determined that the proper punishment for the crime was life in prison.

It was a victory of sorts for the slight, slow-talking defendant who sat impassively clutching his mother's hand as the verdict was read.

His luck ran out three months later, when a Richmond County jury found him guilty of the rapes and murders of Debbie Davis and Susan Hellams. On September 22, 1988, the jury voted that he should receive the death sentence.

By law, the death penalty verdicts have been appealed to the State Supreme Court. Currently, Spencer resides on Death Row awaiting their ruling.

Did One California Maniac Kill All 11 Victims?

by Bryan Williams

The victims were men, women, children—even a priest slaughtered outside his confession—and for residents of Northern California it was like the Manson Family murder nightmare all over again . . .

It was one of the most curious procedures ever seen in a California court—a man barely adult trying to plead guilty to 10 heinous murders—in fact, begging for the chance to admit guilt.

Santa Cruz Municipal Judge Donald O. May gazed long at the young man in the bright orange coverall country jail uniform. The judge said to the prisoner:

"I do not feel that you are competent to enter such a plea."

The date was March 1, 1973, a cold, rainy day such as had been the winter weather for the coastal community of Santa Cruz, 150 miles south of San Francisco.

The trail of death which had led the young man to Judge May's court had not begun in Santa Cruz. It had started five months before in the beautiful California community of Los Gatos, separated from Santa Cruz by a forested range of coastal mountains.

Los Gatos is a sort of everyman's dream community. It sits on the steep hillside of one of the mountains ringing the southern tip of San Francisco Bay. Its housing conforms to the upper middle-class ethic and the swimming pool is not considered a luxury. The climate is gentle and ideal for cultivation of the surrounding vineyards. Los Gatos is the last place where violence and murder should intrude. Yet both intruded on the afternoon of November 1, 1972.

The intrusion was in one of the community's most pleasant buildings. It was St. Mary's Catholic Church. At 3:50 p.m., Father Henry Tomei, the assistant pastor, told Mrs. Mary Pellitier, secretary-housekeeper in the parish rectory, that he was going next door to the church to see if there were any penitents desiring to have confessions heard. It was All Souls Day, a day of special devotion for Roman Catholics.

Approximately eight minutes later, Mary Anne Crowley, a parishoner, entered the church with its lofty spires. The church appeared empty, except for one person bent over in front of the confessional booth at the rear of the church. The bending person was a male, and he gave the impression of being young, although his back was turned toward Mrs. Crowley.

As Mrs. Crowley was later to tell Los Gatos Detective Sergeant James Shea, the figure straightened from its crouch and began kicking at something on the floor. To her horror, Mrs. Crowley saw that the man was kicking the sprawled figure of a clergyman clad in a black cassock. The clergyman lay in front of the open door of the center cubicle of the confessional booth.

Mrs. Crowley screamed, turned, and ran from the church to the adjoining rectory. When she returned with help from the rectory, the young assistant was gone from the church. The figure on the floor was Father Tomei, partially surrounded by a spreading pool of blood.

The ambulance crew arriving moments later determined that there was no use in moving the priest to a hospital. He was dead.

Sergeant Shea's examination of the body showed the numerous bruises of a vicious beating. It also was determined

336

the clergyman had been stabbed four times in chest and torso.

The detective sergeant sealed off the church, automatically canceling the celebration of the evening Mass. Cancelation of the mass on a Holy Day spread news of the vicious murder throughout Los Gatos. Throughout the city Father Tomei was a person beloved by both Catholic and non-Catholic. The 65-year-old priest had a warm, outgoing personality and scores of friends.

He had been born in France and ordained for the priesthood there. During World War II he had been a member of the Resistance underground. In 1959, however, he had suffered a heart ailment and a climate gentler than his native Marseille was recommended. Father Tomei had selected the San Francisco Bay area because many of his French-born relatives had emigrated there. The clergyman had been a musician of talent and a gifted composer. His hymn, "Virgin of Peace," composed under a military truck during a World War II bombing attack, is still widely sung in his native country.

Despite her brief glimpse, Mrs. Crowley was able to give Sergeant Shea a remarkable description of the slayer.

She described him as young, probably in his 20's, about six feet in height, slender, wearing a black shirt, black trousers and high, laced black boots. She said she had seen no knife used by the killer.

Nor could a thorough search of the silent church turn up such a murder weapon. Sergeant Shea had ruled out robbery as a motive. The small amount of money carried by Father Tomei was found in his clothing. Nor was it credible that Father Tomei had interrupted the burglary of a poor box. The money receptacles for donations to the poor and for votive candles appeared to be undisturbed.

The motive for the slaying of the gentle priest seemed as elusive as the identity of the young man who took the life.

The criminalist fingerprint experts began their chore of dusting the walls of the confessional for their task. It had three separate enclosures, with the center cubicle reserved for the priest to sit and listen to the sins being confessed by kneeling penitents from the two flanking enclosures. Special attention was given to the priest's cubicle, for there were red smudges on its woodwork. It seemed likely the murderer would have touched the woodwork during his vicious attack on the priest.

The following days were spent by police in checking out more than 100 leads on the murderer furnished by Los Gatos residents. None proved to be of any value. But the frustrating work continued throughout November and the later Christmas season. The one positive development was the report of the fingerprint technicians about what had been discovered on the woodwork of the confessional.

The experts reported they had developed highly readable latent prints from the bloodied woodwork. Unfortunately, the technicians were not able to report that they had been able to match the prints with any source of available information pointing to a suspect.

January of the new year had almost passed. It was 10 p.m. on January 23, 1973, when young Fred Winston received a telephone call at his mountain home on the seaward slope of the Santa Cruz mountains. The cabin was 40 miles west of where Father Tomei had died so violently.

The caller was Robert Francis, a neighbor of Fred Winston. Francis asked if his neighbor would deliver a message to his (Francis') wife. The message was that Francis was out of town on business and would be unable to return home that night. He asked that his wife be counseled not to worry.

The call was not an unusual occurrence in the life of Fred Winston. He was the only person in the sparsely populated mountain area who possessed a telephone and he acted as communication center and emergency messenger for his neighbors. Winston's was one of a half-dozen mountain cabins clustered at the end of a twisting lane known as Mystery Spot Road. The road took its name from a commercial tourist attraction located near the cluster of cabins. It was called Mystery Spot for the very good reason that everything in the area appeared to defy the laws of gravity. Water

338

apparently runs uphill and objects soar unexplainably upward at Mystery Spot. Its setting is sylvan and beautiful on the mountain slope.

In the cluster of cabins on Mystery Spot Road, the Francis cabin was one of the most primitive. Not only did it lack a telephone connection, it also had neither plumbing, electricity, nor running water.

Winston drove the less than one mile separating his mountain retreat from that of the Francis family. But he never delivered the message. Instead, he drove hurriedly back to his home and used his telephone to call the office of Santa Cruz County Sheriff Douglas James. Winston informed the Sheriff's Department dispatcher that he had discovered a horrible murder in the cabin at the end of Mystery Spot Road.

Among first arrivals at the Francis Cabin was Sheriff's Lieutenant Ken Pittenger. The veteran investigator found Fred Winston's report of murder to be all too true.

The body of a young woman lay on the floor of the cabin's tiny kitchen. There was a dry stain of blood on the blouse she wore. The blood had spread from a wound in her chest. There was a bullet wound in her head, also ringed with dried blood.

Among furnishings in the small kitchen was a bunk with a mattress. On the mattress, which was smeared with blood, were the bodies of two small boys. The bodies sprawled among an assortment of toys. Each child had been stabbed in the back and shot once in the head.

Fred Winston was able to identify the bodies for Lieutenant Pittenger and the other investigators from the Sheriff's Department. The woman, he said, was Kathy Francis, for whom the telephone message had been intended. The children were her sons, 10 and 3 years of age.

The cabin, with its tarpaper roof and walls of logs made from molded slabs, was a mixed bag. It was untidy but it had warmth. It was no more than 25 feet in length and had been partitioned into three small rooms. The family had lived there approximately nine months before the discovery of the slayings.

The warmth showed in the decorations. The crayon-scrawled pictures by the two murdered children had been pinned on the walls. Christmas stockings still hung from a window ledge. On an exterior wall was hung a picture of Christ the Savior with the inscription, "He is Risen." The bicycle and tricycle of the dead children were in the yard, where they had been abandoned after play by their young owners.

A motive for the violence was impossible to determine from the closest examination of the cabin. There was no sign of a struggle and it appeared the slayer must have been known to his victims.

Nor did a search disclose the firearm and the knife used to inflict the wounds. Robbery never seemed a motive, for the dilapidated appearance of the cabin would probably discourage any criminal bent on quick enrichment.

The tedious process of questioning neighbors in the remote cabins began. Also there began a search for the missing Robert Francis, who had called to say that business kept him from home while a murderer struck.

Fred Winston said he did not know the whereabouts of his caller when he had taken the telephone message. A teletype request was flashed asking all California police departments to be on watch for Robert Francis.

At about the time of the dispatch of the teletype, a woman was making a tragic report to the Santa Cruz Police Department, three and one half miles to the west of the bloody mountain cabin and in the heart of the coastside resort community.

The woman caller told the watch officer in the police headquarters that she was at the northern edge of the community in the home of her daughter and son-in-law. She said she had just discovered her daughter and son-in-law had been murdered.

The address given as the site of these latest homicides was a neat house on Western Drive. It was a study in contrast to the mountain cabin, where murder had been discovered the preceding night.

The Western Drive house was the home of Ralph Gianera, 24, his 21-year-old wife Joan, and their 18-month-old daughter. Where the mountain cabin appeared unkempt, the Gianera home was spotless.

To the investigating officers it was certain that the mother of Joan Gianera had been correct in her report of murder. The body of her daughter lay on the floor of a bathroom, but not quite on the floor. The young wife lay atop the body of her dead husband. She was nude and it appeared she had just finished a bath when her killer struck. She had been shot five times and the wounds indicated a small caliber weapon. The husband had been shot four times, presumably with the same weapon. A trail of blood from a nearby room caused Deputy Police Chief Ernest Marenghi to say it was probable the young husband had been wounded fatally but had crawled to where his wife also was suffering her final agonies.

The mother told Marenghi she had last seen her daughter and son-in-law alive the evening before discovery of the bodies. Her daughter, according to the mother, had asked her to care for the tiny grandchild because the young Gianeras had a social engagement. The grandmother said she agreed to care for the child in her own home and return the granddaughter to her parents at 10 a.m., when the grisly discovery had been made.

Again the motive for murder seemed obscure. There was no sign of struggle and no indication anything had been taken from the home. All signs appeared to point to the slain Gianeras being familiar with their slayer, even to the point of inviting the murderer into the home.

Five homicides discovered in a period of less than 24 hours was cause for close cooperation between the Santa Cruz County Sheriff's Department and the police department of the city. It was becoming apparent that peaceful Santa Cruz was rapidly becoming the murder capital of the West.

Among the first discoveries by the investigators was that

there had been a link between the murder victims. Ralph Gianera and his wife had been known to be friends of murdered Kathy Francis and her missing mate. The couples also had been known to be frequent visitors in one another's dwellings.

And there was current information available to the officers of Chief Pini's department. It was other than social information. The information was that there was reason to suspect that the murdered Ralph Gianera had been on the fringe of the marijuana and barbiturate pill movement in the Santa Cruz area. It was not an unusual suspicion, because Santa Cruz, with its ocean and seaside beauty had early attracted devotees of the hippie population.

To the despair of police, the drug trade had been brisk. There had been, too, the phenomenon of the almost-impossible-to-locate LSD-producing laboratories in the wooded ravines and tree-lined slopes of the mountains.

Exactly 24 hours after the discovery of the murders of Kathy Francis and her sons, a car drove up to the remote cabin on Mystery Spot Road. The occupant was Robert Francis and he said he had been unaware of the tragedy that had taken place in his cabin. Francis was taken immediately to sheriff's headquarters in Santa Cruz.

There he informed Lieutenant Pittenger that he really had not been a husband to the murdered young woman, except in the common-law sense. He was not the father of the slain nine-year old boy. That child had been born to Kathy Francis during her marriage to another man. But he was, explained Francis, the father of the three-year-old victim.

The needs of the family had been simple — $50 a month for rental of the dilapidated cabin, organic foods, and oil for the lamps that served in place of electric illumination. The Francis family had made ends meet on welfare payments and from extra money earned by Francis as a self-employed builder of fiberglass kayaks.

Francis had an explanation for his whereabouts at the time of the three murders in his cabin. But it was not an explanation that Sheriff Douglas James wanted in the public domain. The sheriff has asked that it not be reported until there be a trial of the murderer.

Nevertheless, the sheriff has let it be known that he considers the explanation an iron-clad alibi and has declared that Robert Francis was never a suspect in the triple-slayings in his cabin.

The bullets recovered from autopsies of Kathy Francis, her small sons, and the murdered Gianeras told the investigators there was a conclusive link between the five slayings. The bullets had been turned over to Criminalist Paul Dougherty of the Sheriff's Department of adjacent San Mateo County. Dougherty was the possessor of a well-equipped laboratory and the expertise for precise ballistic examination. The criminalist had reported that the many slugs had all been .22 caliber, and a study of the distinctive rifling marks left by their passage through the barrel of the murder weapon proved that they all had been fired from the same gun. Thus, it was reasonably certain the killer of Kathy Francis and her sons was also the murderer of Ralph and Joan Gianera.

The autopsy which reclaimed the bullets also indicated that the Gianeras and victims in the Mystery Spot Road slayings had been dead approximately the same number of hours. The time of death would have been Thursday, shortly before discovery of the cabin murders by Fred Winston. The fast-moving slayer had struck twice within six hours in separated areas of Santa Cruz County.

Two days after the discovery of the many murders, the attention of investigators in Santa Cruz County was directed to Marysville. Two teenage youths had been gunned down in a parking lot there during a dispute involving narcotics. The weapon that wounded them had been a .22 caliber pistol. Lieutenant Pittenger made the long journey to Marysville to determine whether there was a common denominator between the crimes there and those that had occurred in his own jurisdiction. It was a journey in vain.

The pistol involved in the Marysville shooting was not

the one which had dispatched the Santa Cruz victims. The incident turned out to be nothing more than a local dispute over drugs.

The investigators sought to contact every person who might have had some association with the murdered adults. The search took weeks, and it ranged through all of northern California and as far south as San Diego County and the Mexican border. But it did not produce a slayer.

In Los Gatos, meanwhile, police were experiencing the same frustrations in their search for the killer of Father Tomei.

February 13, 1973, was cold and overcast in Santa Cruz. Fred Perez was busily filling in the rutted driveway of a small house on Gharkey Street, less than one mile from where the bodies of Joan and Ralph Gianera had been discovered the preceding month.

It was heavy work for 72-year-old Fred Perez. His labors were for a tenant who leased the small house with the pocket driveway. The home of Perez was just around a corner from where he tamped earth. It was a substantial structure, for Perez was a member of a family which had been early settlers of Santa Cruz and had been major contributors to its development.

From the window of her own home overlooking the driveway where Fred Perez worked, his young niece watched his labors. She saw an automobile, a sedan, move slowly along the street and halt at the curb approximately 150 feet from where Fred Perez labored. The niece paid only scant attention to the auto until she saw a rod-like object projecting from the window on the driver's side of the vehicle.

To her horror, the niece recognized the object as the barrel of a rifle. The rifle was held by the car's driver and it was aimed at Fred Perez. The niece heard the gunshot and saw her uncle spin violently, clutch at his chest, and fall to the earth.

The rifle was hastily withdrawn into the auto and the auto lurched from the curb, accelerated, and roared away. But not before the niece noted the number on the license plate. She ran to the telephone and gave the description of the auto and its license number to the police dispatcher. In less than 30 seconds, the alert was broadcast to all police and sheriff's patrol vehicles in Santa Cruz County.

Fred Perez was dead by the time his niece reached him.

Patrolman Stan Upton was one of the officers who heard the radio alarm for the sedan with the armed driver. The Santa Cruz officer was patrolling at the eastern edge of the community when he saw the sedan speeding on River Street toward the city limit where the street changed into Highway 9 leading to the rustic mountain towns of Felton and Boulder Creek. Upton swung his patrol car on to River Street, picking up speed as he began the pursuit.

It was a short-lived pursuit and almost an anticlimax considering the desperate situation of the suspect at the wheel of the sedan. Officer Upton flashed on his red light, touched his siren and maneuvered behind the fleeing sedan. The sedan slowed and came to a halt just a few yards short of the city limit.

Officer Upton vaulted from his patrol car and ordered the sedan's driver get out of his vehicle. The suspect was hastily patted, searched and handcuffed, wrists behind his back. The suspect had been unarmed. Officer Upton radioed his report that the suspect in the slaying of Fred Perez was in custody.

At first glance, the arrested man appeared not to fit the role of the desperado. He was slim, slightly below medium height, and his brown hair was close-cropped. A pencil line mustache stretched above his upper lip.

His driver license identified him as Herbert William Mullin, 25, with a home address in Felton, a quaint and pretty mountain community 10 miles east of the point where the sedan had been sirened to a halt. But Herbert Mullin was not talking, immediately, about why he had been at the wheel of an auto from which a witness claimed to have seen the firing of the fatal shot at Fred Perez.

On the front seat of the sedan was a bolt action .22 rifle. Young Herbert Mullin was taken to police headquarters in downtown Santa Cruz. He was booked for investigation of the Perez murder and his fingerprints were routinely rolled on the identification card. Although Herbert Mullin was not talking, his impounded automobile was about to tell a tale.

But first the investigation complied with the letter and spirit of the law. Santa Cruz County District Attorney Peter Chang obtained a search warrant authorizing a complete search of the auto. In the trunk officers found a .22 caliber revolver. It was the inexpensive variety known familiarly in law enforcement circles as the "Saturday Night Special."

The rifle taken at the time of Mullin's arrest and the Saturday Night Special were sent to the laboratory of Criminalist Paul Dougherty in San Mateo County for ballistics examination. The fingerprints of the suspect were circulated to the identification bureau of the California Department of Justice to determine whether their owner possessed a criminal record or was a suspect in any unsolved crime.

The body of Fred Perez was taken to the County Morgue for autopsy. The family of the murdered man said no member had ever known a young man named Herbert Mullin and was fairly certain the senior Perez had known no such person, especially with an intimacy that would produce a motive for the callous slaying in the driveway.

Fred Perez had been owner-proprietor of a prosperous commercial fishing business in Santa Cruz but had retired from active participation in the business. His only contact with his former livelihood was as an amateur angler from the long wharf, which juts into Monterey Bay from the Santa Cruz pleasure boardwalk of roller coasters, carousels, and kewpie doll booths. Fred Perez had been a familiar figure among the hopeful anglers clustered on the long Municipal Pier.

The question facing the officers of the Sheriff's Department and the Santa Cruz Police Department was. Just who was Herbert Mullin, and what was the connection between the young man and the many slaying victims?

The investigators answered the question by moving

quickly from person to person in the Santa Cruz area, seeking anyone who might have known the slim murder suspect. The officers were thorough and accumulated a remarkable amount of information in an amazingly short span of time. This is what the investigators discovered by marathon questionings:

Herbert Mullin had been born in the Monterey Bay area, the son of a Marine Corps officer, who reached the rank of colonel before retirement. The youth's family lived in a pleasant rustic house in the $50,000 price range in the mountain community of Felton. In fact, young Mullin had been headed in the direction of Felton when arrested by Patrolman Upton after the highway pursuit.

Mullin, according to information gathered by the investigators, had been born and raised as a Roman Catholic. He had entered the San Lorenzo Valley High School in Felton in 1961 and one of his high school classmates had been Ralph Gianera. Despite his size — 140 pounds, five feet seven inches — Herbert Mullin had been a varsity football player and outstanding performer in track. One of his teammates in football had been Ralph Gianera, and persons who attended San Lorenzo Valley High School at the time recalled the two young athletes as being very close friends.

Mullin was in the top third of his class scholastically, and when graduated from high school in 1965 he was awarded a scholarship to continue his studies in college. His classmates voted him "most likely to succeed."

Mullin attended Cabrillo Community College near Santa Cruz and completed the two-year course leading to an associate in engineering degree. He declined to be drafted into the military service, but served two years in the job assigned him as essential work and the equivalent of military service.

But at some point, most probably while in college, Herbert Mullin had become deeply involved with narcotics. The strip search of his person after his arrest disclosed Mullin had "Legalize Marijuana" and "Legalize Acid" tattooed on his stomach.

After leaving his assigned job, Mullin sought to enter a monastery of the Catholic Church. The religious superiors, however, informed him that they deemed him ill-suited to the contemplative life of a monk.

Mullin briefly tried college again but dropped out after only a few months. He had become a fanatical reader of tracts on the beliefs of some of the more esoteric religions of the East. And still his experimentation and use of drugs persisted.

He had worked at odd jobs — grocery clerk, bus boy, truck driver — sometimes living at the home of his parents and sometimes in a rundown motel near the Santa Cruz waterfront. He had been living at the motel at the time of his arrest.

A month after his arrest, and despite his earlier conscientious objections to military duty, Mullin tried to enlist in the Marine Corps. But he was rejected when he revealed during his oral interview that he once had been arrested for possessing "narcotics paraphernalia," a charge later dismissed. It was the one police contact Herbert Mullin had before the fatal shooting of Fred Perez. A week later, Army recruiters turned down his request for enlistment for the same reason.

The investigators found where Mullin had purchased his Saturday Night Special revolver. He had simply walked into a general merchandise store in his home community of Felton and designated the blue steel revolver with the three-inch barrel as his choice. The purchase price had been $22.99. Mullin filled in the application to purchase, as required by law. He waited the mandatory five days and returned to the store to pick up the pistol. The check with police for felony convictions had proved negative because Mullin's meager record consisted only of the arrest where charges had been dismissed. There was no legal reason to deny Mullin the handgun. The purchase was made December 16, 1972, more than a month before the murders of Kathy Francis and her children.

Some of the five-day waiting period had been spent by

Mullin at the Santa Cruz Municipal Pier where, police were told, the young man had become a casual acquaintance and sometime angling companion of Fred Perez.

Criminalist Paul Dougherty completed his ballistics examination within 24 hours. He reported to the investigators that it was certain the Saturday Night Special had fired the shots which killed Kathy Francis, her sons, and Ralph and Joan Gianera.

The .22 caliber rifle found in Mullin's car was the weapon which had taken the life of Fred Perez, said Dougherty.

In Los Gatos, the comparison of Mullin's fingerprints with the bloody print left by the murderer of Father Tomei on the wall of the confessional cubicle was complete. The fingerprint examination led Detective Sergeant James Shea to announce the confessional fingerprint impression had been made by Herbert William Mullin.

Mullin was charged immediately in Santa Cruz with the murders of Kathy Francis, her sons, Ralph Gianera, his wife, and elderly Fred Perez. His bail was set at $300,000, a sum Mullin could not possibly post.

To a very weary Sheriff's Lieutenant Pittenger, it appeared nearly certain the one-man reign of terror credited to Herbert Mullin was over and there could be no more grisly discoveries in the already murder-sated Santa Cruz mountains. But the lawman's hopes proved not to be the fact, as was demonstrated when a 22-year-old man left his home in Boulder Creek, another quaint mountain community near Felton, to hike into the woods of Henry Cowell State Park. The date was February 17, 1973, four days after the arrest and jailing of Herbert Mullin.

The young Boulder Creek man had a mission. He was enroute to visit his 19-year-old brother, Brian Card, and three of the brother's young friends, who had been living the lives of woodland recluses among the redwood trees of the State Park. The friends were Robert Michael Spector, 18, David Allan Oliker, 18, and Mark Johnson, 19.

The four campers had been living in the Los Angeles

area before migrating northward seeking the ideal of the hermit's existence in the Santa Cruz Mountains. As a campsite, the four had chosen a knoll above a scenic fishing site on the San Lorenzo River. Because of its natural beauty, the bend in the river was called the Garden of Eden. The four youths lived in a lean-to structure built the preceding winter by young Brian Card. It consisted of a wooden floor, walls and supporting frame fashioned from tree limbs, and the entire structure sheathed in a huge, translucent plastic sheet. It was snug and weatherproof. It also was two miles distant from the home where Herbert Mullin had dwelt periodically with his family.

The stillness was unbroken as Brian Card's brother approached the lean-to campsite. He shouted to the campers but received no reply. Then he saw the reason.

The four campers, including his brother, lay dead and covered with blood! The bodies were sprawled about the new cold and unlit campfire pit in front of the plastic shelter. The campers had been dead for some time, as was indicated by the mold growing on the hand of one corpse.

The young man made his way back through the dense brush to a paved road. There he sought a home with a telephone and called the Santa Cruz County Sheriff's office. And once more Lieutenant Pittenger was informed he was faced with the investigation of another multiple murder.

It was an investigation that began in darkness—it had taken Brian Card's brother until dusk to work his way out of the forest and it took several hours for the sheriff's investigators to make their way back in.

The ascertainable facts were that the four young men had each been killed by a shot in the head fired from extremely close range. The wounds indicated the murder weapon had been a small caliber firearm, most probably a .22. There was no sign of desperate struggle, an all too familiar pattern at this point to Lieutenant Pittenger. The bodies were fully clothed. The young man said he had last seen his brother and fellow campers alive the Saturday preceding the discovery of the murders. The lapse of time would have been seven days. He also said it did not appear anything of value was missing from the campsite.

The bodies were brought from the Garden of Eden with the aid of tractors and a great deal of punishing hand carrying by the officers of Sheriff James' department.

The autopsies brought the removal of the bullets embedded in the skulls of the murder victims. These slugs were turned over to the laboratory of Criminalist Paul Dougherty.

It really came as no surprise to the weary Lieutenant Pittinger when the ciminalist reported that, in his opinion the ballistics examination had shown the fatal shots had been fired from the Saturday Night Special taken from the car of Herbert Mullin.

The following day, Herbert Mullin was charged with the murders of the four young campers in the Garden of Eden. The score against Mullin stood at 11 murder charges in Santa Cruz County.

On that day, parishoners of St. Mary's Church in Los Gatos announced that $15,000 donated by friends of murdered Father Henri Tomei would be used to convert the confessional cubicle into a shrine to the Virgin of Peace.

It would be a memorial to the gentle priest and the plea for sanity he had expressed so many years before in the hymn he composed during the violence of a World War II bombing attack.

Herbert Mullin was given a life sentence.

Oklahoma's Infamous
Osage Murders!

by Charles W. Sasser

The state of Oklahoma has a legacy of badmen extending all the way back to Judge I. Parker, the Hanging Judge, and his marshals who scoured Indian Territory searching for outlaws for the good judge to hang. Criminals like Pretty Boy Floyd, Baby Face Nelson, and Machinegun Kelly, all of whom either lived in the state or hid out in it, helped launch J. Edgar Hoover and his G-men of the FBI to fame. Outlaws were so thick in Oklahoma that FBI agents joined with other lawmen and the Army National Guard in 1923 for an elbow-to-elbow sweep of the notorious Cookson Hills to drive out the badmen.

One of the most famous cases in the FBI's history occurred in Oklahoma. It involved a rich mixture of wealthy Indians, cattle barons, Old West outlaws, and—murder.

"Even lurid fiction," commented the *New York Evening World*, "pales beside the story of these Osage murders."

During the Prohibition era of the 1920s, the million-and-a-half acres that made up Osage County in north-central Oklahoma, the former Osage Indian reservation, was still part Wild West struggling to break into the Twentieth Century. Crime was commonplace in the oil- and cattle-boom environment, outlaws were plentiful. Violent death attracted little attention outside what was known simply as "The Osage."

But inside the Osage, common talk had it that Indians

were being killed for their wealth, an irony, considering that the tribe had been the most poverty-stricken of Indians when it first moved to Indian Territory in 1872. But conditions had changed since the Osage signed a treaty that promised them their Oklahoma land "as long as the water runs and the grass grows." While the land was harsh, desolate, barren, a mosaic of rolling hills, forested draws and ridges, and flats of tall grass prairie, it harbored a secret that promised to make the most impoverished of Native Americans the richest body of people on earth.

And that secret was—oil!

In 1906, the year before statehood, oil was discovered on Osage land. Another monstrous field was located in 1912. The Osage became the richest oil land in the country, if not in the world. Each of the 2,250 Osage Indians received an equal share, or *headright,* in the wealth of the oil land. A headright in 1921 was worth about $100,000—a fortune, a sum to kill for.

Then the bodies of murdered Indians began showing up discarded on the plains and in the canyons of the vast county that stretched more than 100 miles from one corner to another.

There were two of them on the morning of Saturday, May 28, 1921. At 10:00 a.m., Osage County Sheriff Harve M. Frease, a white man, kicked back his wide-brimmed hat and stood looking into a shallow timber-choked canyon located north of Grayhorse, an oil-field camp 25 miles southwest of the county seat at Pawhuska. A youngish full-blooded Indian woman lay face down at the bottom of the canyon. The body's deterioration indicated that it had been there several days exposed to wild animals and the elements.

"The only thing I seen was her and that bottle of whiskey next to her," explained the fence-riding cowhand who found the body. "I figured she was a drunk Indian that fell and killed herself."

The cowhand worked for one of the big ranchers who had bought or leased rich bluestem pastures from the Indians. The rancher was William K. "Bill" Hale. The body had been discarded on property adjacent to the Hale Ranch. It was not on Indian-owned property, which meant local authorities rather than the FBI assumed jurisdiction over it. Federal jurisdiction over crimes committed on Indian land had been rapidly dwindling in recent years as ranchers and other white men wrangled more and more land from the Osages.

The sheriff had no more than identified the dead woman as Anna Brown of Ponca City and determined that she had been executed by a large-caliber bullet fired at close range into the back of her head when an oil-field worker discovered a second corpse in a cluster of brushy timber near an oil derrick just north of Pawhuska. The dead Indian man, like the dead Indian woman 30 miles away, had expired several days earlier. He had been shot twice in the head. A letter in his coat pocket identified him as Charles Whitehorn of Hominy.

Sheriff Frease and his deputies knocked about the Osage in their black Model "T" Fords for several weeks, asking questions. Although the inquiry disclosed that both victims were known to drink illegal "hooch," sometimes to excess, it failed to produce a suspect or a motive for the killings. Apparently, the only thing the two victims had in common was that they were found dead on the same Saturday. Rumors ran wild among the Osages. The Indians accused the sheriff of not doing enough.

"There's a lot of talk," Frease responded, "but you have to have proof, not talk."

That year—1921—was the year Sheriff Harve Frease broke up the Jack Longre gang that had plagued Oklahoma and Kansas banks in recent years. But if he was successful in his war on Longre, he had considerably less luck solving the murders of the Osage Indians. The mystery grew when, in July 1921, an Indian woman called Lizzie Q was found dead in her residence—poisoned.

Lizzie Q was Anna Brown's mother.

"That's a connection for you," Osage Indians harped at Sheriff Frease. "Mother and daughter—both murdered. Who benefits by their deaths?"

354

The answer to that question came easy. Anna Brown's headright went to her mother Lizzie Q upon Anna's death. When Lizzie Q died, both headrights went to Lizzie's surviving daughters, Reta Smith and Mollie Burkhardt, both of Fairfax.

Reta was married to a well-to-do white man, William E. Smith. Mollie's husband was Earnest Burkhardt, nephew of wealthy cattleman William K. Hale, who was also known as "The King of the Osage."

"Those two ladies certainly had nothing to do with murdering their mother and sister," Sheriff Frease allegedly informed nosy reporters.

"Then who did?" the Indians wanted to know.

Authorities could not supply an answer to that question. Weeks and months passed. The authorities repeated what became a well-worn phrase: They didn't have enough evidence to link anyone at all to the unsolved Osage murders.

In early 1923, the murders took up again. By the middle of March the unsolved Osage death toll, the "Rein of Terror" as it was soon known, stood at an even seven. Fear spread among the Osage tribesmen. Many strung electric lights around their homes, bought vicious watch dogs, and stood armed guard at night.

The year's violence began in January, when Henry Roan Horse's wife reported him missing. A week later on a cold Saturday morning, February 6, 1923, two hunters stumbled upon a new Buick abandoned in a lonely spot six miles northwest of Fairfax at the end of a dirt road. An Osage Indian was slumped behind the wheel of the car with his head lolled over into his hat. Like Anna Brown, he had been executed with a single .45 bullet through the back of his head. Sheriff Harve Frease and his deputies soon confirmed that the dead man was Henry Roan Horse, more commonly known as Henry Roan.

A new county prosecutor, Charles L. Roff, joined Sheriff Frease in the investigation. After nearly two weeks of questioning witnesses, the two lawmen turned their attention to a suspect named Ray Bunch, who was reportedly romancing Henry Roan's wife.

"Bunch killed Henry so he could have a clean sweep at Henry's wife," as the general consensus.

There was only one hitch. Bunch had an alibi. A good one.

And then there were three more bodies after a terrific explosion rocked the little town of Fairfax during the pre-dawn hours of Saturday, March 13, 1923. The explosion left the plush eight-room home of William E. and Reta Smith in smoking rubble. It blew clothing and bedding into trees three blocks away and damaged a number of neighboring houses.

When County Attorney Roff arrived, he reported finding Reta Smith and her housekeeper, Nellie Brookshire, a white woman, already dead. William Smith had been blown some distance from the house. He died a short time later.

"Whoever did this," exclaimed expert chemists summoned from the A&M College at Stillwater, "used enough nitroglycerine to make sure it killed everyone in the house."

Outraged, the Osage Indian Council demanded action from the Federal government, since local authorities seemed incapable or unwilling to do anything themselves. This time, Washington could act. Henry Roan Horse, it turned out, had been found dead on the Sol Smith Ranch, but on land that Smith was leasing from its owner, an Osage Indian. That gave the FBI authority.

Scarcely more than a week after the W.E. Smith explosion rained debris all over Fairfax, FBI Agents Tom B. White and Alan Berger showed up in Pawhuska. They confronted County Attorney Roff and advised him that they were taking over the investigation of the so-called Osage Murders.

"I provided them with all the evidence we had obtained," Roff commented, "and that was the last official connection I had with the case."

Agent Alan Berger, later assassinated in another criminal investigation, was the field director of operations. Tom White assumed command of the probe. More than 50 G-men inundated the county at the height of the investigation, some of them posing as cowhands, drifters, and oil roustabouts.

Nothing was sacred. The G-men initiated an extensive background investigation that spared no one in the county, no matter how wealthy or prestigious. It turned out, agents soon concluded, that at least six of the unsolved murders had something very much in common—the rancher William K. Hale.

The connection between Hale and the victims was uncertain in the deaths of Anna Brown, Lizzie, and the Smiths and their housekeeper, since it appeared that Hale did not benefit directly from their demise. Mollie Burkhardt inherited a great deal of wealth due to the murders of her mother and her two sisters and her husband Earnest worked for Hale and was his nephew. Still, this was a poor foundation upon which to build suspicion.

However, the link between Bill Hale and Henry Roan Horse blared out at investigators. Roan Horse had possessed a $25,000 life insurance policy. He listed his beneficiary as William K. Hale.

"I first met Henry Roan about twenty years ago," Hale reportedly responded when FBI agents questioned him. "There were several business dealings with Roan, beginning with small deals and finally terminating into larger ones. Roan owed me several thousand dollars at one time for cattle. He gave me a note for $25,000 which included an insurance policy I had taken out on him, as security for money he owed me.

"We were good friends and he sought my aid when in trouble and needed money. The last time I saw Roan before he was found dead was in the First National Bank at Fairfax, about three weeks before he was found dead. He walked into the bank and asked me for $25 to get liquor. I let him have it."

When Hale was asked if Roan was working, Hale shot back, "Did you ever see an Osage work?"

The FBI composed a profile of the rancher who liked being called "The King of The Osage." That profile revealed that Bill Hale and another cowboy first set boot in the Osage in the early 1880s when they were hired to ramrod a herd of cattle up from Texas. Hale stayed on and he and his wife eventually lived in a tent outside Fairfax while Hale built up his holdings and his influence. Twenty years later, Hale owned several ranches and leased thousands of acres of good bluestem prairie upon which he grazed fine herds of cattle. By his own estimation he was worth more than $150,000 in 1923, the equivalent of a millionaire 50 years later.

Although wealthy and politically influential, Hale appeared to have a penchant for associating with outlaws. His name had been occasionally tied to the Al Spencer gang, whose exploits in robbing banks and trains had earned them a reputation equal to that of Pretty Boy Floyd. One of Hale's best friends was Henry Grammer, a former world champion steer roper and since Prohibition the acknowledged head of bootleg whiskey in the oil-fields of the western Osage. Grammer hired notorious strongarm men like Fred "Wetump" Tindle, Ace Kirby and Johnny Mayo to help run his bootlegging operations.

Hale's intimacy with such men led people to speculate on how it was that a common Texas cowboy managed to wrangle a fortune out of an old tent and a $30 saddle. That speculation, however, rarely found a loud voice. It was said that local law enforcement officers were too indebted to Hale to conduct any impartial inquiry against him. Allegedly, he held an Osage commission as a deputy sheriff, and County attorney Charles Roff himself said he owed his office to Bill Hale.

When Roff started his campaign for County Attorney, a member of the Cattleman's Association reportedly advised him to get Bill Hale active in the race if he wanted to win. With Hale's influence, Roff subsequently carried every precinct in western Osage County. He wrote later how pleased he was when a rancher brought in his precinct's ballot box and informed Roff that he had won every vote except two.

"And we know who cast those two votes," the rancher said. "Our school teacher and his wife—and they won't be there next year."

Against this background and within a climate of open

358

hostility against them, Tom White and his agents continued their probe for clues in the Osage murders. Reportedly, the G-men began recruiting a succession of informants to insinuate themselves into the Osage underworld. On Wednesday, March 11, 1925, the *Tulsa World* reported that it was known that one Blackie Thompson, a bank bandit currently serving life in prison for murder, was released in the custody of FBI agents to act as a "stool pigeon" in Osage County. Although Thompson escaped FBI custody long enough to rob the bank at Avery, Oklahoma, agents were not discouraged. Thompson was reportedly the first man in the Osage to break the curtain of silence that seemed to surround Bill Hale.

According to Thompson's statement, Earnest Burkhardt approached Charles "Curly" Johnson and Blackie Thompson in early 1923 and told them Bill Hale would pay good money to have William and Reta Smith "bumped off." Burkhardt offered the pair a new Buick car and $1,000 cash to do the job.

"I might have done it," Blackie Thompson admitted, "except I was arrested for auto theft first and drew five years."

The break wasn't much, but it was a start. For the first time, someone had explicitly linked Hale to some of the murders.

Blackie Thompson's secondary role as informant was to help grease the pathway between the FBI and the Osage underworld. With Thompson's assistance, agents made contact with such underworld figures as Dick Gregg and Ralph White, both former members of the Al Spencer gang. Henry Grammer's henchman Johnny Mayo, and Dick Gregg's father John, against whom County Attorney Charles Roff had filed bank robbery charges.

It was John Gregg who reportedly made a number of trips to Kansas and Oklahoma prisons to persuade inmates to cooperate and come forward with information on the Osage probe. An air of expectations and nervousness, settled over and across the Osage.

During the summer of 1924, Charles Roff and Bill Hale encountered each other on the long stairway leading from downtown Pawhuska uphill to the courthouse.

"Charlie, I'm glad that we have met this way, accidentally, out in the open," Hale told him, according to Roff. "I have thought of coming to see you, but was afraid it might cause you embarrassment. I know about the talk going around the county about my being implicated in killing Indians. I have never had anything to do with it. Why should I? Osages are worth more to me living than they would be dead. I trade with them and sometimes lend them money. Now, all I ask you to do is, if they have a case, then file charges against me, but I would hate to face a murder charge based on suspicion and rumors."

Both suspicion and rumor grew. So did terror. In 1925 the mystery heightened when Clint Bigheart, a distant relative of Lizzie Q, died of unexplained suspicious causes after he was admitted to an Oklahoma City hospital by Earnest Burkhardt and Bill Hale. Earnest Burkhardt and his wife had reportedly adopted Bigheart's young son, who stood to inherit his blood father's headright after his death.

Contributing to the suspicion surrounding Clint Bigheart's death was the brutal murder of Bigheart's personal attorney, W. W. Vaughn. Vaughn's bullet-riddled body was discovered along the right-of-way of the M.K.& T. Railroad between Oklahoma City and Pawhuska. Detectives theorized that Vaughn had visited his hospitalized client before being kidnapped, killed, and dumped from a sleeping car on the train.

"Could old Clint Bigheart have told him who the Osage killer is?" agents wondered.

Bigheart died without clarifying anything. The death toll attributed to "The King of the Osage" now stood at eight. Still, there was little actual proof that Bill Hale was in any way involved.

Agents turned up the heat. Gradually, bit by bit, information started trickling in. The underworld figures began talking, apparently in an effort to save themselves when the case was finally busted. Their subsequent testimony corroborated statements from underworld informants.

Matt Williams, a Ralston salon owner, secretly approached Agent Tom White. According to official statements and grand jury testimony, Williams claimed that Bill Hale introduced to him a rawboned cowhand named John Ramsey.

"Here's the man I got to do the job (kill Henry Roan Horse)," Hale said.

"I told Hale," said Williams, "to be careful where Roan was killed. He told me he had investigated it and that the (Federal) government did not have jurisdiction."

In fact, however, the Henry Roan murder was the one that finally provided the FBI with the authority they needed to investigate the slayings.

A small-time bootlegger named Billingsley reportedly advised agents that Hale wanted the outlaw Al Spencer to "do the job" early in 1923. Gangmember Ike Ogg arranged a meeting between Hale and Spencer.

"Al met with Hale at Hale's bunkhouse," Ogg later related. "I was there. So were Billingsley and John Gregg. Hale and Spencer walked off from the rest of us to talk. I don't know what they talked about. The only conversation I heard between them was about roping."

John Gregg allegedly told authorities that Spencer contacted him following the bunkhouse meeting and offered to pay him $3,000 to dynamite the William Smith residence.

Gregg said he declined the offer.

Johnny Mayo, Henry Grammer's strongarm man, told detectives that Ace Kirby was the one who finally accepted the job. Henry Grammer was the go-between. Kirby blew up the Smith home with nitroglycerine. Afterward, Mayo saw Grammer slip Kirby a wad of bills.

"Why didn't you tell somebody of the murder?" agents asked Mayo.

"I knew better," Mayo replied. "I'd have been murdered, too, the way the county was then."

Agency reports named John Ramsey as a suspect in the murder of Henry Roan, and Ace Kirby as the likely killer of the Smiths and their housekeeper Nellie Brookshire. Behind them stood Earnest Burkhardt, and behind him Bill Hale.

The slow, painstaking probe gained further momentum

361

when Katherine Cole-Morrison volunteered her statement. The ex-wife of a local hoodlum named Kelsie Morrison, Katherine sad that she, her husband Kelsie, and Earnest Burkhardt's brother Byron were all out drinking with Anna Brown the week before Hale's ranch hand found Anna dead. She said that the four of them drove to Grayhorse and then down a dark road to the lip of a shallow canyon.

"There was a dark-colored car with its curtains up and all its lights off just setting across the canyon from us," she recalled. "Byron and Kelsie took Anna Brown out of the car and helped her walk toward the canyon. She was very drunk. The men returned without Anna. They said they left her near the canyon with some other party."

Who was that other party?

"I don't know," she said.

The case bogged down once more after that. By the end of 1925 the investigation had consumed more than four years. But, then, in October 1925, the G-men in Osage County made their first major move against the murder suspects.

Earnest Burkhardt suddenly disappeared. Testimony later revealed that Agents Tom White and Frank Smith had held him in "protective custody" for two months, hiding him out in various surrounding states to prevent his being assassinated. Rumors spread that he had confessed to his part in the murders of the Smiths and their housekeeper and was implicating Bill Hale as the mastermind behind the Osage murder conspiracy.

Burkhardt released a prepared statement to the Associated Press: "It (is) true that on March 8, 1923, I drove Bill Hale's red Buick roadster from Fairfax to Ripley to tell John Ramsey to tell Ace Kirby to do the job at request of Hale, and before that date Hale had told me that the job was that which Ace Kirby was to do, and before that date Hale had told me he wanted the job done while he and (Henry) Grammer were in Fort Worth . . ."

Hale replied through the press.

"Boy," he told reporters. "I am going to tell you something that I have never mentioned to another living soul . . . (My

362

brother and I) were just kids and we heard that our sister had eloped with a Burkhardt . . . Dad said, 'You boys know that you cannot raise good stock without good breeding animals, and if you boys live to be grown, you will regret that you ever heard the name of Burkhardt.' I have just realized how smart my dad was."

Burkhardt's apparent willingness to turn state's evidence against his boss and uncle Bill Hale prompted others involved in the murder conspiracy to come forward in an effort to avoid the electric chair.

"For almost four years we couldn't get a word out of anyone," an agent said. "And then we found they were lining up in order to confess."

Kelsie Morrison confessed. He testified that Bill Hale paid him $1,000 cash, canceled another $600 debt, and bought him a new car to kill Anna Brown. Hale also furnished the murder weapon.

"Hale said he wanted to get rid of the whole bunch . . . so Earnest would get the money," Morrison stated. "Anna Brown's body was found where I killed her. Byron Burkhardt and I carried her down to the canyon. She was too drunk to walk. My wife (Katherine Cole-Morrison) was with me on the trip . . . Anna Brown was pulled up into a sitting position when I killed her. I told Byron how to hold her up, then I shot her. She fell over. I did not watch her die, but left immediately."

One of the last principals in the case to confess and subsequently testify was the ranch hand John Ramsey, who stated Bill Hale and Henry Grammer wanted the Smiths and Henry Roan Horse killed in order for Earnest Burkhardt to inherit the victims' wealth. Ace Kirby, he said, blew up the Smith residence. He, John Ramsey, killed Henry Roan.

"(Earnest) Burkhardt proposed I give Roan whiskey and then get him out in the pasture where Curly Johnson could kill him."

"It will be a cinch," Burkhardt allegedly remarked. "That Indian would follow a man to hell for a drink and Curly Johnson is rearin' to do the job. Then it will either be blamed on Roy Bunch or Bill Hale, but they both can prove

363

an alibi."

"The chickens," said an agent, "are coming home to roost."

The chickens had already roosted for a number of men involved in the slayings. Curly Johnson was dead. So was Al Spencer, killed by a possse in September 1923. A rural store owner shot and killed a burglar named Ace Kirby in 1924. Henry Grammer died that same year in a one-car automobile accident near Pawhuska.

On January 8, 1926, G-men dethroned the man who for four years had seemed immune to prosecution. William K. Hale joined Earnest and Byron Burkhardt, John Ramsey, and Kelsie Morrison in the Pawhuska jail.

"Let the King of the Osage reign in prison," a G-man quipped.

"They accused me of having many people killed," Hale stated in a press interview, during which he claimed that FBI agents tortured him to make him confess. "I was asked if I was ready to make a confession. I said I was not, that I did not know anything about the case. (Agent Frank) Smith then pulled out some papers and said he had a way of making me sign them, that they had made Burkhardt and Ramsey sign and would make me . . . I never signed."

The Osage Reign of Terror officially ended with a series of state and Federal trials that began in June 1926 and ended in October. Earnest Burkhardt, John Ramsey, Kelsie Morrison, Byron Burkhardt and W.K. "Bill" Hale were all convicted of various roles in five different murders and drew life sentences in prison. The deaths of at least a dozen other Osage Indians, including those of Charles Whitehorn, Lizzie Q, and Clint Bigheart, are still listed on FBI records as being officially unsolved. Many people in the Osage, however, believe that the King of the Osage was responsible for at least 17 murders.

The Boston Strangler!

by Harold Banks & Ed Corsetti

Intimate courtroom revelations about the passion-driven killer of 13 women.

It was a trial within a trial, and the case that wasn't being tried officially was far more dramatic than the one that was.

Formally, the charges against the defendant were—that he talked, forced or broke his way into the apartments of four women—that he flashed a knife or a gun, which happened to be a toy—that he fondled their bodies, committed unnatural and lascivious acts on two of them, compelled one to engage in such an act on him—and that he stole a total of $36 and a diamond ring worth $900.

Ordinarily, such a trial wouldn't have attracted more than a handful of idle spectators to the ancient red-brick courthouse in East Cambridge, Massachusetts, across the Charles River from Boston. But the first-floor courtroom was crowded to capacity and others waited outside in a long line, at times four abreast, in the hope of getting in.

For this was no ordinary trial—because neither the defendant nor the chief defense counsel was ordinary.

The counsel was Attorney F. Lee Bailey, who was flushed with two spectacular courtroom triumphs scored within 29 days. In Cleveland, Ohio, Bailey had won acquittal of Dr. Sam Sheppard in the latter's second trial for the 1954 murder of his wife. In Freehold, New Jersey, Bailey had persuaded another jury to clear Dr. Carl A. Coppolino of the charge that he had murdered his former paramour's husband. And Bailey was confident he would be able to exonerate the doctor of a Florida indictment accusing him of murdering his first wife there.

It was only six years after he passed the bar, yet Bailey had become one of the country's most astute trial lawyers.

His client, sitting quietly within the bar enclosure in the East Cambridge courtroom, was as infamous as Bailey was famous.

His name was Albert Henry DeSalvo, he was 35 years old, he was tastefully clad in a well-cut, shadow-striped black suit, black socks, black shoes, white shirt with a button-down collar and a gray Windsor-knotted tie — and he was the self professed Boston Strangler who had slain and sexually abused 13 women within an 18-month period that began June 14, 1962, and ended January 4, 1964.

Though DeSalvo says he is The Strangler — and his counsel says so, too — the Commonwealth of Massachusetts has not yet accused him of any of the homicides. First, Massachusetts refused to proceed against De Salvo because he was diagnosed as mentally incompetent by state psychiatrists. And now, after DeSalvo has been ruled competent, the State hesitates to prosecute him for those murders because of lack of "usable" evidence against him.

Actually, the State has DeSalvo's full and voluminous "confession" on tape and in transcripts, but it was obtained on the strength of an agreement with Attorney Bailey that it could not be used against DeSalvo in a trial for the stranglings — except under certain conditions. One such condition, for instance, is that the State would not ask for the death penalty and would not object to the seating of jurors who are against capital punishment.

It had been two years now, since Bailey first listened to DeSalvo's story in early March, 1965, in the so-called but misnamed State Hospital at Bridgewater, Massachusetts, where DeSalvo was confined as mentally ill. Bailey had been fighting to have him confined for the rest of his life, not in a prison, but in some institution where he could be studied by psychiatrists.

What they might learn from him, Bailey has said again and again, might help all psychiatrists to recognize danger symptoms in other patients before such individuals get out of control and become multiple sex-slayers.

The fight that Bailey had been carrying on publicly became a judicial matter with the opening of DeSalvo's trial on the lesser charges at 10 a.m., Tuesday, January 10, 1967, in the East Cambridge courtroom. Tuesday and part of Wednesday were consumed by a preliminary hearing to re-establish DeSalvo's competence to stand trial and to impanel a 14-man jury of which two members were alternates who would eventually be eliminated by lot when the time came to reach a verdict.

That time arrived at 12:32 p.m., Wednesday, January 18th, when Superior Court Judge Cornelius J. Moynihan, tall, learned, austere and dry-humored, finished his charge to the jurors and directed them to retire to deliberate.

To guide them to the 10 verdicts they had to return on as many indictments, the State, represented by Assistant District Attorney Donald L. Conn, of Middlesex County as prosecutor, had offered the testimony of 17 witnesses, three of them being psychiatrists. Defense Attorney Bailey, locking horns with his Boston University Law School classmate, Conn had to rely on only two witnesses, both of them psychiatrists.

". . . The only defense here raised," Bailey had said during the preliminary hearing, "will be to confess and avoid the charges by declaring insanity and, thus, no responsibility for admitted acts . . . DeSalvo has told counsel and doctors that he does not have a desire to be free . . ."

Bailey and his co-counsel, Attorney Jon A. Asgeirsson, who had first represented DeSalvo on the sex offenses and related charges, called to the stand two witnesses other than the psychiatrists, but they were heard by the judge alone, with the jury out of the courtroom, to determine whether their testimony was relevant to the indictments for which DeSalvo was being tried.

These two witnesses were former Assistant Attorney General John S. Bottomly of Massachusetts and Boston Police Detective Phillip J. DiNatale. Bottomly had headed the unique Strangler Bureau, which had been established in the office of the Attorney General. DiNatale, a 20-year veteran with a highly commendable record, was one of the Bureau's indefatigable workers.

Through Bottomly and DiNatale, Counselor Bailey intended to present to the jury some evidence that DeSalvo's "confession" of the stranglings was, in their opinion, true. Bailey got his message through to the judge, to the press and to the public—but not to the jury.

The judge ruled that the jury, which was locked up for the duration of the trial, could not hear testimony from DiNatale or Bottomly, who had resigned as much because United States Senator Edward W. Brooke, who was the Massachusetts Attorney General at the time, refused to proceed against DeSalvo on Bailey's terms, as for any other reason.

So, without the testimony of Bottomly and DiNatale, the jury withdrew to its deliberation room to sort out the conflicting opinions of five psychiatrists, to consider the straightforward accounts the four women victims gave of the offensive acts to which DeSalvo had subjected them, to correlate the statements made by other witnesses—to weigh it all and, at last, to arrive at verdicts "beyond reasonable doubt."

The issue was not whether DeSalvo had committed the "transactions," as the legal term goes, charged to him, because he admitted them—but whether he should be found *not* guilty by reason of insanity. Thus, 12 laymen were burdened with deciding which of the psychiatrists was more nearly right than the others.

They had the opinions drawn from Dr. James A. Brussel, Dr. Robert Ross Mezer, Dr. Ames Robey, Dr. Samuel Allen and Dr. Samuel Tartakoff.

The two called as witnesses by Bailey were Dr. Mezer, a private practitioner in Boston and Dr. Brussel, associate commissioner of the New York State Department of Mental

Hygiene and called "America's Sherlock Holmes" by Manhattan police for his deductive powers which helped them solve the case of the "Mad Bomber" in 1956 and other crimes.

In his opening statement to the jury, Defense Counsel Bailey spoke of DeSalvo's sordid youth, described him as subject to "one of the most crushing sex drives that psychiatric science has ever encountered," referred to the 11 months of a two-year sentence he served for breaking and entering and taking measurements of women, clad and unclad, on the pretense that he was a photographer's agent offering modeling jobs paying as much as $40 an hour for nude poses; and declared that DeSalvo's ex-wife, now in West Germany with their two children, had rejected him sexually after his release from the House of Correction in Billerica on the ground that he had to "prove himself all over again."

"And," Bailey continued, "Albert DeSalvo was on the loose with no controls and immediately reverted to the conduct which caused him to be incarcerated, only by this time, so much had been pent up that there were not only indecent assaults — but for a period of 18 months, 13 acts of homicide by a completely uncontrollable vegetable walking around in a human body."

Now Bailey had it on the record that DeSalvo was the Boston Strangler, and he called Dr. Brussel to the stand.

Dr. Brussel traced DeSalvo's sexual activities that began at the age of 6 or 7 and increased to the point where he sometimes spent whole days with two women at the same time. Brussel pointed out that in regimented situations such as public school, the army, jail or a hospital, DeSalvo's behavior was good. He seemed to thrive in institutions. Then the learned doctor mentioned the stranglings. He said he had read the "confession" in those murders. He described DeSalvo's sensations before each killing, quoted DeSalvo was saying he felt he was "burning up inside . . . like little fires, like little explosions . . . feeling hungry, yet he could not eat."

Sexually, Dr. Brussel said, DeSalvo has an abnormal capacity, extreme . . . insatiable . . . irresistible."

369

"I believe," the doctor said, "that he is suffering and has been suffering for many years from schizophrenia, which might be called an undifferentiated type, because he does show predominantly paranoid features, and my diagnosis is schizophrenia of the paranoid type. Schizophrenia is a major mental illness, the commonest one known to psychiatry . . . a split mind.

"It is characterized by a withdrawal from the general flow of society with its demands, its restrictions, its taboos, its regulations. It is a withdrawal from and an indifference to certain precepts that are commonly accepted, whether they be in the law or in religion or in social customs. It leads to dwelling within the self. And in creating this more pleasant world of his own, the schizophrenic becomes all-powerful, omnipotent is the word, where he's not only the only inhabitant of that world, he is the god of that world, and the only authority in it."

And that, the doctor made clear, was the kind of creature DeSalvo was and is. "The schizophrenic is not in the world of reality as we know it at any time," he said. DeSalvo, he went on, is "quite shrewd, innately shrewd . . . and will do anything to avoid detection." That, the doctor said, accounted for DeSalvo's use of gloves and rubbers so he would leave no clues behind him after each of the stranglings.

Under cross-examination, Dr. Brussel remained unshaken by a diagnosis at Westborough State Hospital, where DeSalvo was sent for mental observation before he was sentenced to the Billerica jail, that he was suffering merely from a "sociopathic personality disorder."

Even if a policeman were at his elbow, the doctor said, DeSalvo would pursue the immediate gratification of his sexual desires, but would try to cover his tracks before and after the commission of his crime.

"He can tell the difference between right and wrong," the doctor continued, "as it is prescribed by law and religion and custom, but it means absolutely nothing to his personality structure . . . What he does and feels . . . has to be right because he is the sole judge."

In redirect examination by Bailey, Dr. Brussel was asked,

"Is there, in your opinion, any hope of cure in his case?"

"Very little," Dr. Brussel replied.

And then Bailey called Dr. Mezer to the stand to strengthen the defense's contention that DeSalvo was and is suffering from a serious mental illness.

Dr. Mezer, characterizing DeSalvo as a sexual phenomenon capable of multiple climaxes even "without the usual stimulation which most men require," said, among other things, that "he told me he was The Strangler, that he had strangled thirteen women."

"It had to do with his relationship with his wife," Dr. Mezer said, "who told him that he would have to prove himself as a man before she could take him back sexually."

His diagnosis was that DeSalvo was a case of chronic, undifferentiated schizophrenia—but he narrowed DeSalvo's irresistible impulses down to the sex act itself. Before and after it, Dr. Mezer declared, DeSalvo's impulses were resistible. He even knew that the sex acts were legally and morally wrong, the doctor said, "but he felt that they were his entitlement."

"The schizophrenia was still in him," the doctor added, "and the irresistible impulse was still in him (before and after the sex act), but it was not irresistible. It's just like a person with a temperature. It goes up and down, but the germ is still there."

With Dr. Mezer on the stand, defense Attorney Bailey was permitted to put a question which, for the first time in Massachusetts jurisprudence, set squarely before the court the Model Penal Code test that broadens the limits of the legal definition of insanity.

"Do you have an opinion as to whether or not, at the time he committed the acts which are charged in the several indictments on trial, Albert DeSalvo, as a result of mental disease or defect, lacked substantial capacity either to appreciate the wrongfulness of his conduct or to conform his conduct to the requirements of the law?" Bailey asked.

"He lacked that capacity," said Dr. Mezer.

That was the main thrust of the defense's case—and to offset it, Prosecutor Conn sent a string of rebuttal witnesses to the stand; a man who had been with DeSalvo at the Bridgewater State Hospital as an inmate for 118 days, the deputy master of the Billerica jail and a senior officer there; C. Russell Blomerth, a small Malden building contractor; Charles Berry, vice president of Highland Contracting Company of Wakefield; its foreman, David Johnson, Mr. and Mrs. Harold Orent of Malden, and then, the three psychiatrists, Dr. Robey, Dr. Allen and Dr. Tartakoff.

Blomerth, Berry and Johnson were men with whom and for whom DeSalvo had worked as a semi-skilled laborer. Mr. and Mrs. Orent were a couple for whom DeSalvo had done repair work on their home privately. All of them—including Deputy Master John A. Keriakos and Senior Officer Adam Kozlowski—testified that they never observed anything strange in DeSalvo's behavior, dress or speech.

The battle of the psychiatrists began with Dr. Robey, who resigned as medical director of the Bridgewater institution in July, 1966, approximately 20 months after DeSalvo was first sent there early in November, 1964. That was 10 months after the last strangling and ten days after DeSalvo had committed the last of the four "transactions" for which he was being tried.

Dramatically, Dr. Robey abandoned his earlier diagnoses that DeSalvo was a case of either acute or chronic undifferentiated schizophrenia and classified him as suffering a "sociopathic personality disorder, anti-social type, with sexual deviation and schizoid features." In other words, Dr. Robey said, to him, DeSalvo was not mentally ill at all.

DeSalvo could distinguish between right and wrong, knew his conduct was legally and morally unacceptable and was not laboring under an irresistible impulse—he merely didn't want to control it, Dr. Robey said.

He had changed his mind as late as the middle of the trial itself, he explained, in the light of all he learned about DeSalvo since July, 1966, some of the testimony he had heard from Dr. Brussel and Dr. Mezer, and DeSalvo's perfect control in the courtroom.

"You felt that you had been taken in up to now, is that it?" Bailey asked him in cross-examination.

"Yes, I did," Dr. Robey replied.

"Are you trying to tell us that Albert conned you?" Bailey asked.

"Much as I hate to admit it," the doctor responded, "I'm afraid that is exactly what I am trying to tell you."

Three times—on February 4, 1965, on April 12, 1966, and on June 30, 1966, less than seven months before the trial—the doctor had testified at court hearings that De-Salvo was not mentally competent to stand the trial.

"Did Albert manipulate you, Doctor?" Bailey asked.

"I suspect he did," was the answer.

Later on in the cross-examination, Dr. Robey, although he admitted he once told DeSalvo he would treat him without compensation and testify for him under the proper circumstances, said, "I will not accept blindly the fact that anyone who could commit thirteen homicides must, by definition, be psychotic."

"This is indeed an individual," he said of DeSalvo, "who has a great deal of very severe sociopathic sexual deviation, and faced with a rejection by his wife and with the typical inability to displace or put off his demands, his own inner sexual demands, he would immediately go and seek gratification. That he chose the ways he did to achieve it is certainly indicative of the extent of his sexual deviation. It could also be indicative of some much deeper process. Certainly, I will have to allow this. I just don't feel that this is true at this time."

"By that I assume you mean possible schizophrenia?" Bailey asked.

"Yes, sir," the doctor replied.

"So you don't rule that out, really, do you, doctor?"

"Oh, no, I cannot rule it out," the doctor answered.

Dr. Samuel Allen, acting medical director of the Bridgewater institution since Dr. Robey's resignation, said indirect examination by Prosecutor Conn that DeSalvo knew right from wrong, legally and morally, and that he was not suffering from an irresistible impulse in his offenses against the four women.

Cross-examination of Dr. Allen by Bailey went this way:

373

"Is Albert DeSalvo insane?"

"In my opinion, yes."

"And the mental illness is schizophrenia?"

"That's correct."

"And sufficiently severe so that you deem him committable to an institution?"

"That's correct."

"He's sick and dangerous?"

"That is correct."

"That's it. That's all," Bailey said.

Dr. Allen had last seen DeSalvo as a patient only a week before the trial began.

Bailey appeared to have brought out a difference of opinion between two of the prosecutor's expert witnesses. The best that the prosecutor could elicit from Dr. Allen to mend the breach was a concession that DeSalvo's schizophrenia was "mild."

The prosecution's last rebuttal witness was Dr. Tartakoff, director of the division of legal medicine in the Massachusetts Department of Mental Health.

He, too, classified DeSalvo as suffering from a sociopathic personality disorder, "a defect of character, but not a mental disorder in the terms of psychosis." DeSalvo, he said, as Dr. Robey and Dr. Allen did before him, knew the normal and legal difference between right and wrong and was not subject to irresistible impulses.

Still, under cross-examination by Bailey, Dr. Tartakoff admitted the DeSalvo "has a partial or complete inability to cope with the rules that society has laid down."

Though DeSalvo was *not* mentally ill in his opinion, the doctor said, he was committable as "sexually dangerous."

"Do you have an opinion of what the prognosis (future outlook) is for Albert DeSalvo?" Bailey asked.

"Not good," the doctor replied.

"Mr. DeSalvo's case," the doctor stated moments later, "is unique. I have not seen any identical with it."

So, Bailey had two of the prosecution's experts saying that DeSalvo belonged properly in an institution where he could be treated. And the prosecution rested its case.

There followed Bailey's unsuccessful attempt to have former Assistant Attorney General Bottomly and Detective DiNatale testify about the stranglings only to bolster the defense's contention that DeSalvo was and is hopelessly insane.

In a "voir dire" hearing, as it is legally called, before the judge without the jury present, Bottomly testified he talked with DeSalvo. "The purpose," he said, "was to determine his knowledge of certain homicides which were being investigated, to then investigate his assertions to determine whether they were accurate or not on the basis of the information available to us . . . I brought things for him to see and identify, if he could."

That was as far as the judge permitted Bottomly to go. In an "offer of proof," another perfectly legal stratagem, Bailey said that if Bottomly were permitted to continue his testimony, he would say that DeSalvo's "confession" was tape-recorded and transcribed, that Detective DiNatale checked out the details and that DeSalvo provided extraordinary "proof" that he committed one particular strangling.

Out of 70 or more photographs spread before DeSalvo at the Bridgewater institution, Bailey said, Bottomley would testify that DeSalvo picked out Mrs. Nina Nichols, a 68-year-old divorcee, who lived at 1940 Commonwealth Avenue in Boston's Brighton section. Mrs. Nichols was The Boston Strangler's fourth victim—and no photo of her had ever been published, but DeSalvo recognized her.

Balked in his attempted to have Detective DiNatale testify, Bailey made another "offer of proof"—that the detective, acting on information provided to him from DeSalvo through Bottomly, discovered that DeSalvo knew more than police did about the death of 83-year-old Mary Mullen in her apartment at 1435 Commonwealth Avenue. Her demise had been listed as due to natural causes, but DeSalvo said he was instrumental in hastening her death and that she was, in effect, the second of his 13 victims.

"DiNatale would say, as would others who did detective work with him," Bailey informed the judge, "that at the conclusion of the investigation conducted pursuant to the instructions of Mr. Bottomly, the detectives and the division of the Attorney General's office, which had been assigned to the task, did advise the psychiatrists at Bridgewater that the history of the defendant was accurate."

Then the time came for final summations to the jury and Bailey said, in part, "I suggest to you that Albert DeSalvo is very sick . . . an animal walking around without human restraint . . . The only way in which you can, in good conscience, say that the defendant is guilty is if you satisfy yourselves that you have figured him out — that you have the answers, something none of the psychiatrists had, and unless you have those answers, you cannot be satisfied of anything . . . Albert DeSalvo is a sick man, whether you call it schizophrenia, character disorder or a rose by any other name . . . The temptation may be to say it is our job as jurors to . . . make sure that this guy stays in the lock-up, and so we are going to find him guilty and worry about reasonable doubt as to sanity later.

"Every person like Albert DeSalvo who is found guilty by men who should pause and recognize the unknown — that is what we ask you to push aside. It puts us one step farther back from ever finding out what makes them tick, what they are made up of and finding them at the age of fifteen, when they can be pulled off the street and treated or cured or, at least, kept apart . . . Sociopath or schizophrenic . . . I say to you either one is a defect or mental disease. Hopefully, we are somewhat more enlightened than our forebears, who thought that the way to cut evil out of society was to burn witches or stone them to death.

"If you will make your judgment not only for the benefit of the defendant, but for the benefit of society, honestly and conscientiously, and simply report that . . . the defendant is insane, perhaps another jury sitting here ten years hence will be furnished with some answers, instead of only naked questions in the fantasy area that we cannot see into and certainly do not see out of at the present time."

And the prosecutor said, in part:

"Criminal conduct? Of course. The conduct of a sick man? I respectfully suggest no . . . His ultimate motive,

like any other criminal, was to gain entrance and to take
jewelry . . . and money . . . This manipulative, cunning
man knew the difference between right and wrong . . . He
certainly did not lack the capacity to conform his conduct
when he wanted to . . . Clever. Cunning. Cute. Vicious.
Manipulative . . . Are you going to sit and acquit this
man?. . . You have a duty. It is a duty to every citizen in
this Commonwealth, to your wife, to my wife, to everyone
who could conceivably be the subject of an attack of this
type."

Judge Moynihan's charge was simple, clear and short.
And so, at 12:32 p.m., Wednesday, January 18th, 12 of the
14 jurors retired to reach their verdicts.

What may have been etched most deeply in the minds of
the jurors was the stories the four women victims told on
the witness stand.

After their appearances, there was some corroborative
testimony from patrolman James R. O'Connor of Melrose
concerning the woman who had been compelled to perform
an unnatural act on DeSalvo—and testimony from Detective Sergeant Duncan S. McNeill of the Cambridge Police
Department concerning DeSalvo's arrest, among other matters of identification of the suspect by another of his victims.
A member of DeSalvo's family, the detective sergeant testified, said, in his presence, "Al, tell them everything. Don't
hold anything back." And DeSalvo had told him a number
of things thereafter, the detective sergeant said. Then De-
Salvo had been arrested, arraigned, sent to the Bridgewater
institution and eventually indicted by the grand jury.

But it was probably the stories of the women, whose real
names will not be given here to spare them embarrassment,
that flared most clearly in the memories of the jurors.

There was, for instance, this account from young Mrs.
Barbara Doe, who has moved from Cambridge to a Mid-
western city, of what befell her the morning of October 27,
1964.

"I awoke at a quarter of ten and there was a man standing
in my bedroom doorway. I asked him what he was doing
there and he said he knew me. He said, 'You know me.' I

said, 'No, I don't.' He said, 'I am a police detective' and he wanted to ask a few questions.

"I said, 'Please go outside until I get dressed.' He was dressed in dark slacks and a zipper jacket, navy blue, I believe, and green sunglasses. I was wearing a nightgown. He started walking toward the bed and I asked him please to leave again and he said he was running away from the police and that they were surrounding the building and I told him he should leave out the back door.

"As he approached the bed, I got up and I screamed, and he pulled out a knife. It looked very old, very worn, very thick. He told me not to look at him and he wouldn't hurt me. He turned me on my stomach and got my husband's pajamas on the chair and tied my feet and my hands behind my back and blindfolded and gagged me. Then he turned me over on my back and pulled up my nightgown and . . ."

Here, she graphically told how DeSalvo kissed her body and performed an unnatural act on her.

"Then," she went on, "he asked me to stand up. After I stood up, he again pulled up my nightgown and . . ." He kissed her body again and then put her back on the bed, she said. "After he started to leave," she continued, "he asked me please to forgive him and not to tell his mother. He started to leave and, through the gag, I asked him please not to leave me tied up so tightly. He said he would send his friends back to untie me later, but then he came back and loosened the ties and left."

And there was this story from Mrs. Frances Roe, whose daughter was 8 months old then, of what occurred to her in her Wakefield apartment the morning of May 29, 1964:

"I woke up at 9:15 a.m. and there was a man in the bedroom. He pulled the blankets down and lifted my nightgown and just started . . ." He fondled her body, she explained. "Then he said he had known my husband and that he just got out of the service and he was—if I was looking for a modeling job, he said. He heard that I was, through my husband or something like that, he said. I said we talked about it but I never would model, and then he went over to the baby, took the baby from the crib, and she started to cry.

"I looked at the phone a couple of times, but I was afraid for the baby. I just stayed calm until after he left. I took the baby from him and walked out to the kitchen. He followed me. He said something about — I don't know — and then he picked up my nightgown and just started . . ." Again, she explained that he fondled her body.

"I had put the baby back," she went on. "I looked at the clock and I said, 'Gee, it's late. I didn't realize it was so late!' And that Jean, the photographer, was coming to take pictures. And then he said, 'Oh, you wear glasses. We couldn't use you. I have the wrong woman.' And he ran out the door."

This, as Mrs. Ruth Boe of Arlington told it, is the story of her harrowing experience in her apartment at 9 a.m., September 29, 1964:

"The first thing I remember was that I heard someone knocking on doors and whoever it was came up and eventually knocked at my door. I had on my underclothes, a housecoat and black slippers. I went to the door, but I didn't open it. I stood there and this person was knocking and I asked who it was and a man said, 'There's a terrible leak in the basement. It's half full of water and I have to get in and shut off all the water pipes.'

"I told him to go away, that there was no leak in my place. He continued knocking on the door. He was very persistent. I asked who he was. He said he was Dave. I was suspicious of the voice. Dave was the custodian of the building. I opened the door to look out to see who it was. The door opens out. As I opened it, it was pulled open out of my hand and he slipped in with a gun in his hand. He raised his arm and put it right at my forehead. (She had no way of knowing the gun was actually a toy.)

"He said, 'This is a holdup, lady. I want your money.' He stepped in and I said, 'Take it.' He shut the door behind him. He asked me where the money was and I told him it was in the wallet in the pocketbook on the chair. Then he told me to go and sit on the couch. And there was a click.

"And all of a sudden there was a sharp feeling here on my

379

throat and I remember thinking it was a needle. He said, 'That's a knife at your throat, lady.' And the gun was there and I got the gun somewhere else on my head and then, eventually, in the back of the head. And he was sort of behind me, holding the knife to me. He said, 'Don't make a sound or yell, because if you do, I'll cut your throat from ear to ear.' He went on telling me that if I thought he didn't mean it, not to kid myself. He said if I thought he wouldn't cut my throat because he might go to prison, not to kid myself, because he had already been in jail, and, besides, the police were looking for him. They had been looking for him for two or three years, he said.

"I said, 'Don't worry. I won't yell.' He picked up a pair of pajamas belonging to my husband and he tied my ankles with one half and he put the other half on my head. It fell this way and I could see him. Then he went over to the bureau and he found a scarf belonging to my husband. He came back and tied my hands behind my back.

"I said to him, 'Why are you doing these terrible things?' He said, 'What terrible—what things? What things?' I said, 'Coming in here like this and robbing me and tying me up. What would your mother say if she could see you now? She wouldn't like it.'

"He started unbuttoning my housecoat and he said something about kissing me and I didn't want him to kiss me. Just as he was about to kiss me, I turned my head, and he kissed me on the neck."

But she wasn't able to avoid his caresses of the upper part of her body, she said.

"I said to him, 'I'm an old woman and don't want you bothering me,' or something of that order," she went on, "and he came at me to touch my bosom. He went over and searched the bureau drawers and he turned around and said, 'Where do you keep your silk stockings around here?' I said, 'I don't have any,' and he said, 'Why not?' I said, 'I don't wear them this time of the year.'"

He crossed the room in front of her gaze, she said, and as he did so, he engaged in an act of self-pollution.

"When I saw him doing that to himself, I turned my head

away. I didn't want to look at him. I remember that he went in the bathroom and I heard him go into the kitchen and I could hear the cupboard doors opening and closing in the kitchen. Then he came out of the kitchen and walked in front of me. He came up to me and he had the gun in my ear and he said, 'Where do you keep the rent money around here?' I said, 'There isn't any.' He said, 'There has to be because it's the end of the month.' "

DeSalvo searched the premises, she said, found a $900 diamond ring in her jewelry box and put it in his pocket. After he finally left, she said, she freed herself, discovered that he had taken $11 from her wallet, as well, and that he had cut the phone wire.

"I was never so scared in my life," she said finally.

And, lastly, there was the testimony of Mrs. Helen Coe, who was living alone in a Melrose apartment the morning of June 8, 1964:

At 7:45 a.m., she said, she was awakened by a knock at her door and, through it, a man told her there was a leak in her apartment. She put a dressing gown over her shorty pajamas and opened the door, she said. DeSalvo came in, she said, and went to her bathroom. On his way there she quoted him as saying, "Are you tired, Helen?"

"I said, 'Yes. What time is it?' " she testified. "He said, 'A quarter to 8.' He put his hand on my shoulder, just barely touched it, and I didn't think anything of it. He went into the bathroom and he said, 'I guess it isn't here. I think it must be in the bedroom.' So we went into the bedroom and over to the windows. He grabbed my arm, the left arm, behind my back and put the other arm around my face and he said to get down on the bed. I said, 'All right. All right. I will.'

"He got the bottom of my shorty pajamas off and he blindfolded me right away with kerchiefs from a drawer and put a gag in my mouth. I pulled it out. He said, 'Don't do that again. Leave it in.' "

Then he pushed her down on the bed, she said, kissed her body and committed an unnatural act on her. He asked her for $20 and he'd leave, she said, but she told him she had only one dollar and he wanted to know where it was. She told him it was on the coffee table in the living room and he directed her to lead him out of the bedroom and show him where the dollar-bill was.

"So I did," she went on. "On the way out, the kerchief fell off my eyes down around my neck and I heard a snap. So I looked down and there was a knife. He had it right at my side and he said, 'Turn around and go back to the bedroom. Get down on the bed.' He told me he would kill me if I screamed. He said, 'I have killed before and I will do it again. I even got an old lady, but they don't know about it. I don't want to hurt you.' Then he tied my feet with kerchiefs. I was blindfolded again. I asked him please to take the blindfold off. He pulled me forward. I was sitting on the edge of the bed . . ."

It was then, she said, that he ordered her to commit an unnatural act on him.

"I did," she said simply — and the silence in the crowded courtroom, jammed with teenagers as well as with men and women, some of them obviously there only for the sensational testimony that would titillate their prurience, was almost as shattering as an unexpected explosion.

And then, at last, after tying her ankles together and her hands behind her back, putting the gag back in her mouth and telling her to give him five minutes before she moved, DeSalvo was gone. She waited a few minutes, she said, then rolled off the bed to the floor, managed to get to her telephone and contrived, somehow, to dial for the operator and tell her to send the police. Within five minutes, she said, eight police officers were in her apartment. Her ankles were so loosely tied that she was able to walk to the door and, turning her back to it, she opened it with her tightly-bound hands.

Those were the stories the jurors couldn't possibly forget. From the courtroom, after the judge delivered the case into their hands at 12:32 p.m. that Wednesday, January 18th, they were driven, as usual, in a chartered bus to their quarters in the Hotel Commander in Cambridge to have lunch. Then they were driven back to their deliberation room on the second floor of the courthouse.

In the first-floor corridor, among others, stood a handsome woman clad in a bright green dress. She had come up for the trial from New Jersey.

"I had to see this animal," she said. "I had to see what he looks like."

Once this attractive woman with the sad eyes had a lovely, young daughter named Sophie, who had been studying at a Boston school to become a laboratory technician. On December 5, 1962, less than six weeks after her 19th birthday, Sophie Clark was found dead in the apartment she shared with two girls at 315 Huntington Avenue. She had become the Boston Strangler's seventh victim.

"There is no doubt in my mind or in my heart," the slain girl's mother said in the corridor, "that this man, DeSalvo, killed Sophie and the others. I can only pray that they find him guilty. That's what he deserves."

Elsewhere in the courthouse, Defense Attorney F. Lee Bailey paced a floor as the time passed, slowly, slowly, slowly, until it was 6:09 p.m. — and the jury signified it had reached its verdict.

Ten times the court clerk put to the jurors the ancient question, "How do you find, gentlemen of the jury?" — and 10 times, in steady voice, the foreman answered, "Guilty!"

Prosecutor Conn moved for sentence. Before that was done, Bailey obtained a stay of execution and an agreement that DeSalvo be sent back to the Bridgewater institution pending an appeal that would be made for him in the Superior Court first for a new trial, and failing that, in the Massachusetts Supreme Judicial Court for the same purpose.

"Do you wish to be heard on the matter of sentence, Mr. Bailey?" Judge Moynihan asked.

"No, Your Honor," Bailey replied. "My petition is that this defendant must be incarcerated for so long as he shall live, unless and until psychiatric science can tell us a lot more about him than it presently knows, as demonstrated by the evidence. I think the evidence has made clear the defendant's desire to remain in a situation where society is protected from him. I think that if I were sitting in your

383

position, I would give a sentence in this case that would incarcerate him for the rest of his natural life — and I have no further remarks to make."

Albert DeSalvo did receive a life sentence; however, on November 26, 1973 another inmate at the Walpole State Prison in Massachusetts murdered him by stabbing him in the heart.

6 Pretty Victims in Texas' "Killing Fields"

by Turk Ryder

Is a latter-day Jack the Ripper on the loose in the Southwest? That's what Lone Star detectives wonder as they try to solve the mystery.

Slinking along the twlight-lit street in mid-August 1987, the pixie-faced woman was not alarmed when the beige Ford pickup pulled beside her. Dressed provocatively and pretty to boot, she had her share of wolf-whistling admirers, whether on foot or cruising Texas' sizzling El Paso streets in cowboy pickups or low-slung imports.

The tall, dark-haired dude in the pick-up fit this category of admirer. "Lift?" he drawled.

The young beauty narrowed her dark, heavily-mascaraed eyes and flashed a coquettish smile. Yes, she said, a ride. That would be nice.

The buck-toothed cowboy grinned wolfishly. He wanted to give her a ride. He also wanted to take her into the desert, tie her up and, according to police, rape and kill her.

As it turned out, he didn't get his wish. But this chance meeting did result in an investigation that took a dangerous sex offender off the streets and, in the minds of a few detectives, ended a series of abductions and murders that struck terror into the hearts of El Paso residents.

The victims, all girls and young women, ranged in age

385

from 13 to 24. A few were troubled and rebellious; most were happily living conventional lives.

They disappeared mysteriously—often after short trips to the neighborhood store or walks around the neighborhood.

Three are still missing. Six others—and police have not discounted the possibility that there could be many others— have been found in a barren stretch of desert in northwest El Paso, dubbed the "Killing Fields." It is as barren and lifeless a place as the name implies.

"The place sends a chill up your spine," said a recent visitor to El Paso's notorious unlicensed graveyard. "I swear, you go out there at night, and you can almost hear the dead speak."

The dead weren't speaking—or at least no one could hear them—when Marjorie Knox, 14, of Chaparral, disappeared. The pretty eighth-grader left her Byrum Street home on September 14, 1987, to buy a soda pop at the neighborhood store.

She stopped to talk to some friends, police learned later, then continued on her way. She never made it to the store. No one has seen her since.

Melissa Alaniz, 13, of northwest El Paso, met a similar fate. On March 7th, she left her Orpheus Street home to go play with some kids down the block. She didn't return home for dinner, and she, too, is still missing.

Marjorie and Melissa didn't know each other, but a common thread in their lives was that the parents of both kids worked for Rockwell International near El Paso.

Desiree Wheatley, 15, was the third victim. On June 2nd, the pixie-faced eighth-grader at H.E. Charles Junior High left her Tiber Street apartment to buy a sugar cone at the store.

When she didn't return, police were called. They learned that after buying the sugar cone, Desiree had stopped to talk with a bunch of kids who hung out in front of the store. One girl saw Desiree talk to a dark-haired man who had pulled up in a pickup. Nobody knew who he was, though several said they had seen him before.

No one saw Desiree get into the pick-up. One minute she

was there, the next, she was gone.

Three days later, 20-year-old Karen Baker of Arlen Street in El Paso disappeared after leaving home on foot to go to see friends.

Cheryl Lynn Vasquez-Dismukes, 19, lived in northwest El Paso, where she worked for a plastics firm. On June 28th, she left her apartment and walked three blocks to buy cigarettes. She was reported missing early the next morning.

Later retracing her probable route to the market, detectives could find no witnesses who had seen the girl or had heard screams or other disturbances indicating foul play.

Cheryl's boyfriend didn't have any clues to what happened to her. "I doubt she ran away," he said. "She would have told me."

The disappearance did not go unnoticed. Alarm rippled through the communities of northwest El Paso and Chaparral, New Mexico, wherever girls lived. Residents blamed an evil, modern-day Pied Piper for luring their youngsters from the safety of their neighborhoods to an unknown fate.

Worried and terrified, the citizenry held a demonstration in downtown El Paso to call attention to the missing children. They demanded that police make an all-out effort to find the kids—or their bodies.

Investigators had little to go on. Although parents of several missing children worked for Rockwell International, detectives could find no evidence that any employee at the giant aerospace company was responsible for these disappearances. They pursued the theory that since no one reported screams or foul play, the girls must have known or trusted the abductor and had gone willing with him.

Despite exhaustive background work, probers were unable to come up with a suspect.

Of course, rumors were rampant. One theory was that the girls had been lured from their neighborhood and then brainwashed into joining a religious cult. Another was that the young Anglo females had been abducted and taken across the border to be drugged and forced into prostitution.

Yet another was that a serial killer was cruising the suburban streets for likely victims, then gleefully killing them and burying their bodies in the desert.

On September 4, 1987, the missing became the dead when two men reported finding a body. Investigators sped to the desert off McCombs Street in northwest El Paso where they were greeted by two workers from the county water district.

The men took the officers to a spot about 200 yards into the desert. In a shallow grave lay the remains of a young woman. She was about 5 feet 6 inches tall, of medium weight, with dark hair that curled to neck-length. Her slacks and panties were pulled to her knees, her blouse was open and her bra pulled down.

She was identified as Maria Casio, a 24-year-old resident of Addison, Texas, who had been vacationing in El Paso. She was last seen on August 20th leaving a friend's home to buy cigarettes.

Investigators combed the area for clues. During the search, which unearthed everything from snake skins to beer cans, searchers turned up another corpse.

The victim was a young woman, about 5 feet 4 inches tall, who'd worn a sleeveless blouse and blue jeans. Animals had ravaged the shallow gravesite and exposure had reduced the corpse to little more than dried skin and bones. No identification was on the body, but dental charts identified her as Karen Baker, 20, of the 4500 block of Arlen Street, El Paso. She had been missing since June 5th.

The bodies were enclosed in plastic body bags and taken to the coroner's office. The autopsies did not show knife or bullet wounds or skull fractures that might indicate bludgeoning. Body tissue samples showed no presence of poisons.

In his preliminary report, the El Paso medical examiner gave his opinion that the victims had been either choked or strangled to death.

The apparent motive was sex. Neither woman was known to carry much money, and their clothing was arranged in such a manner as to indicate sexual assault.

Three weeks later, another phone call sent investigators

back to the Killing Fields. Two hikers had been searching for rock formations in a wash area off McCombs Street. One of them discovered a mound in the otherwise flat terrain. It was about six feet long and three feet wide and, in the hiker's words, it looked "like a grave."

He scraped away some sand. It was.

Underneath the sandy shroud; still dressed in shorts and halter top, was Desire Wheatley, the 15-year-old reported missing on June 2nd. Nearby was Dawn Smith, a 14-year-old runaway reported missing on September 10th. Both bodies were badly decomposed and had to be identified by dental charts.

On November 3rd, a fifth victim — Angelica Frausto, 17, of El Paso — was added to the list. The pretty brunette had been reported missing on September 6th.

El Paso police detectives headed by Lieutenant J. R. Grijalva were assigned to the string of desert deaths.

Using guidelines on serial killers established by the FBI and the Los Angeles Police Department, the investigators compiled lengthy biographies on the seven girls who were missing and dead. The cross-indexed data sheets were stored in a computer for easy access.

The story of the seven missing and dead girls was front-page news in this Old Western town of 600,000 that sits on the banks of the Rio Grande. It reminded some of a string of unsolved murders in El Paso's sister city, Juarez, Mexico. Six girls in their early teens to early 20s were found floating in or on the banks of the Rio Grande. Three were wearing only bras, and all were nude from the waist down.

The first victim was found on February 22, 1986, on the Mexican side of the Rio Grande near the Stanton Street Bridge. The last turned up on April 18th on the Mexican side of the river near the Zaragosa Bridge. Police believed that the girls were from the interior of Mexico and had been raped and strangled while trying to cross illegally into the United States.

Because the girls were either completely nude or clad only in bras, investigators initially concluded that the killer was a sex maniac. After more investigation, however, they believed it was also possible that the women were simply stripped in order to make identification more difficult.

If that was the intention, it was successful. Of the six, police were able to identify only two, both local women who were reported missing.

In an effort to zero in on the killer, police conducted sweeps of downtown Juarez and along the banks of the Rio Grande, arresting dozens of known criminals and drug addicts. They questioned all these individuals at headquarters extensively. In spite of the large numbers of suspects rounded up, though, the investigators could not focus on any single person as a prime candidate for arrest and lodging of charges. The Rio Grande murders remain unsolved as this issue went to print.

El Paso detectives assisted Juarez lawmen in that case. Their participation in the probe helped them determine that those slayings of the naked and bra-clad women were not related to the disappearances and slayings in El Paso a year later.

Serial killers, they knew, can be the most methodical of criminals, selecting victims that fit a certain type and then torturing, killing and disposing of them in a manner that rarely varies.

Ted Bundy, perhaps the most infamous of serial killers, is a good example. He selected as victims women in their late teens or early 20s who had long, dark-brown hair parted in the middle. William Bonin, the so-called Freeway Killer, selected only young women whom he picked up hitchhiking.

The victims in the desert and Rio Grande murders were young women and girls. The girls found in the desert were clothed and found buried in shallow graves, while the Juarez victims were nude or wearing only bras and were tossed in the river. So the two series were not connected — except by the grim facts that young women were brutally murdered and their killers were still free.

In compiling background information on the seven girls in El Paso, detectives had come up with several common threads. One was that the parents of three girls — Desiree Wheatley, Marjorie Knox and Melissa Alaniz — all worked for Rockwell International.

Another thread was that Melissa Alaniz, Cheryl Lynn Vasquez-Dismukes and Desiree Wheatley had gone to the same junior high school, though at different times.

A third thread was that Karen Baker, Desiree Wheatley and Marjorie Knox had lived in the same small community of Chaparral, New Mexico, and that Wheatley and Knox had known each other.

Police did not have enough information to determine if these were normal coincidences due simply to living in the same community, or if they formed a pattern that somehow linked the girls to a single killer.

And if the killer selected his victims according to the pattern, how did Maria Casio, Angelica Frausto and Dawn Smith fit in? Nothing connected them to the other girls.

On the theory that on some level the crimes were sex-related, investigators searched files of known sex offenders who had been recently paroled and whose behavior pattern fit the desert killer.

For a clean-living, Bible-thumping town like El Paso, the list turned out to be surprisingly long and detailed.

Police also checked out tips that were phoned in or collected during routine police work. Often the calls were pointless—for example, a crank airing his lungs at police expense. Occasionally they were self-serving—the anonymous tipster wanting to know if a reward had been set up, or an amateur psychic whose late-night reverie might crack the case that would win national exposure.

There were also the calls from well-meaning citizens who believed they had information that might solve the case.

A lead developed when two women, ages 19 and 24, contacted police with information that a man had abducted one and raped the other in separate incidents. Both women had been arrested for prostitution and narcotics. They insisted, however, that they were telling the truth about being attacked.

The 19-year-old said she was standing on a street corner in downtown El Paso late one night when a man in a beige pickup stopped and asked if she wanted a lift. She said yes and got into the pickup.

Suddenly, the guy pulled a knife and then drove north into the desert. "I asked him to stop but he wouldn't," the teenager said. They went past the old brick plant in northwest El Paso and continued into the desert. Terrified that he might kill her, she grabbed the wheel with two hands and then managed to jump out of the pickup while it was still moving.

The driver made a U-turn, but instead of chasing her, he drove back toward town. She eventually caught a ride back to her house.

The next day, she ran into her friend and told her about the midnight ride into the desert. The friend said she'd had a similar experience in July. A man in a beige pickup had picked her up hitchhiking on Dyer Street, pulled a gun and drove her into the desert off McCombs Street, not far from the old brick factory. After making several right and left turns, he stopped and told her to get out.

He threw her a shovel and ordered her to dig, she told police. She started to dig but stopped when she heard voices coming out of the darkness. He forced her back into the pickup and they drove for about a half mile. Then she said, he raped her and drove her back to town.

The woman told detectives that she didn't report the rape because she had a police record. She was only reporting it now because her friend had been abducted.

From her description of the pickup, a police artist was able to create a composite. It showed a Caucasian in his mid-to-late 20s, with long black hair and dark eyes.

The women said he was about six feet tall, weighted 170 pounds, and had tattoos on both arms and his chest. One tattoo on his left shoulder showed a human skull that gazed up toward his neck, its hair tangled into a snake hanging down to his triceps.

The rape victim and her friend said they would be able to identify the man if they saw him.

They got their chance sooner than expected. The description fit 30-year-old David Wood, a suspect in the desert murders.

Wood had an extensive rap sheet for sex offenses. In 1976 he pleaded guilty to a charge involving an offense against a child. The victim, a 12-year-old girl, was riding a bicycle with a friend when Wood asked her to help him find a lost dog. According to the record, Wood lured her into a schoolyard and attempted to rape her in the playground.

Released in January 1980 after spending three years in prison, Wood was arrested three months later for the rape of a 13-year-old girl. The girl told detectives that Wood came up behind her, forced her under a bridge and raped her.

Wood was also charged with the rape of a 19-year-old he'd once dated. The girl had not seen Wood for eight years when he called her up and asked her out. She said that they went to several night clubs, but when she asked to go home, he took her into the desert and raped her. Then he took her home.

Wood pleaded guilty to both rapes and was sentenced to 20 years for each, the sentences to run concurrently. He served seven years and was paroled in January 1987.

Police put Wood's picture in a photo lineup and showed it to the two recent victims. They identified him as the driver of the beige pickup who took them into the desert.

Brought to the police station, Wood denied the charges. He claimed that since his release, he had kept his nose clean. "I am not proud of what I have done," he declared. "But, hey, it's over. I am a new man."

"Then you don't have any problems appearing in a lineup," one of the detectives suggested.

Agreeable or not, Wood appeared in a live lineup on November 5th. That's him!" the 24-year-old rape victim said, pointing to Wood. "That's the man who raped me."

Wood was charged with suspicion of kidnapping and rape. His parole was revoked and he was held in the county jail without bail.

The 30-year-old sex offender became a media sensation after word leaked out that he was a prime suspect in the so-called desert murders. Reporters didn't spare the purple prose. One who was granted an interview wrote: "David

Leonard Wood has this nervous laugh. And these soft blue eyes that look out of place on a worn, sunken-cheeked face.

"He rolls his smokes methodically, pinching tobacco from an old plastic peanut butter tub onto white, gummed Bugler cigarette paper. Then he puffs, facing intently ahead, and his eyes are the only thing soft about him.

"His skin looks tough, beaten, much older than his 30 years. His upper lip stretches thinly over a thick, pouty lower lip.

"His right forearm sports a butterfly tattoo. Above it is a likeness of Jesus. The left forearm features a knife wrapped in ribbon.

"He said he also has tattoos of a cobra circling his belly and a Harley-Davidson bike on his back. Another skull, this one with a knife, is on his chest."

Wood declared to reporters that he wasn't guilty. "Take my word for it," he said. "I'm not the guy. And I'm going to do everything I can to fight, just to prove that fact."

He said that police "have no evidence, no suspects, no leads. There's nothing that ties me in. No clothes. No hair. No fingerprints. No tire tracks. No nothing. How can they tie you to something you didn't do?"

Wood denied the abduction and rape charges. Though his record spoke otherwise, he scoffed at the notion that he had to rape a girl to get sex. He claimed that it would take 15 or 16 pages to list the names of girls he knew socially who would eagerly have sex with him. "Talk to them," he suggested.

One reported did—and found staunch supporters. A 16-year-old with a doll face described Wood as "kind, generous and understanding. He's the kind of guy you can really talk to." She said she met Wood in June. On their dates they did "fun stuff"—going to the amusement park, watching fireworks shows or playing video games at the pizza parlor.

"He is so trusting and caring," she said. "I know he didn't do it."

Wood went on trial on the rape and abduction charges in March 1988. Jurors heard from the rape victim who told of being driven into the desert.

"What happened then?" the prosecutor asked.

"He raped me," she replied.

"Did he say or ask you anything before he raped you?"

"Yes," the witness said. "He told me to say I was thirteen years old."

The defense attorney pointed out that the victim waited almost a month before she reported the alleged rape. He also said that the witness was an admitted heroin addict with a long rap sheet for narcotics busts.

"Isn't it true that the heroin ruined your memory?" the defendant's lawyer asked.

"No," the witness responded. "Heroin didn't do anything to my memory. I know what happened and who did it."

The trial ran smoothly and without incident until March 15th, when the judge suddenly ordered the jury to be sequestered.

No reason was given, but courtroom watchers immediately learned why—another body had been discovered. A couple scavenging for tin cans at about 12:30 a.m. came across what they believed to be a grave. Further investigation revealed a badly decomposed corpse.

It was too far gone to determine the sex, but clothing found nearby indicated that the remains were that of a young girl. The discovery was made in the Northeast El Paso desert near the burial sites of the other victims.

According to the county medical examiner, Dr. Juan Continin, the corpse appeared to be of a tall, thin woman who was wearing braces. She was the sixth victim pulled from the desert.

Meanwhile, the jury spent just three hours and 40 minutes in deliberations before reaching a verdict. They found David Wood guilty of sexual assault.

Wood, who had expressed confidence that he would be acquitted, appeared ashen-faced and stunned as he listened to the verdict. He was quickly led from the courtroom.

Wood appeared for sentencing on March 24th. His defense attorney argued that Wood ought to receive no more than a 20-year sentence. Acknowledging his client's prior record of sexual offenses the attorney said simply, "I must live with that. Most of all, my client must live with that."

Judge Jose Baca could *not* live with that and sentenced Wood to 50 years in prison, the maximum sentence the law allows.

Wood remains a suspect in the desert murders. Though not charged in those crimes, he has been linked to four of the murder victims and one of the missing girls.

Witnesses have told police that Wood was the man in the pickup who talked to Cheryl Lynn Vasquez-Dismukes shortly before she disappeared on June 28th. Police have also determined that Wood knew Karen Baker and went motorcycling with her five months before her body was found on September 4th.

One witness told police that murder victim Mario Casio looked like a girl he and Wood met at a topless bar. Other witnesses have stated that they saw Wood with Desiree Wheatley, whose body was found on October 20th, and that Wood once dated Dawn Smith, found dead the same day.

Wood maintains that he is innocent. He says he knew or talked to some of the girls, but that was understandable since he dated every night and had a busy social life. "I am a lover," he declared, "not a killer."

Wood has not been charged with the murders or the disappearances. Police say that he is a suspect, but he is only one of several and the investigation is continuing.

David Wood is currently serving his term for rape in the Texas prison system. He has not been charged with any other crimes as of this writing.

Chained Beauties For The Prowling Sex Monster!

by Howard and Mary Stevens

Indiana's ten-year reign of terror.

A hard-nosed Indiana police chief who launched his own fight against crime with a brassy bumper sticker: "Fight crime, shoot back!" faced a close-to-home challenge in 1987 — a string of vicious rapes dating back a decade.

Terre Haute's top gun, Police Chief Gerald Loudermilk, was at a loss to explain why his community, situated along the historic Wabash River, consistently won a running battle against overall crime evils but lost a frustrating war against a series of brutal rapes of young women. Loudermilk was particularly alarmed when two teenaged girls were reported missing near the end of 1986, both dropping out of sight mysteriously in the middle of the night.

The veteran police officer, appointed to the department in 1961, felt he knew most of the rapist's moves. After all, Loudermilk's investigators, headed by Sergeant Joe Newport, had painted a familiar picture of the man who stalked the city's streets, picking his young victims from a two-mile-square area on the east side of town. Studying their quarry from all angles, Newport and his fellow police officers were convinced that the man they sought chose his targets with care and deliberation, staging his forays with a studied, but bold execution.

397

Newport, working closely with Loudermilk, suspected that the rapist operated near his residence, since he was known to be able to disappear quickly, melting into the darkness. From observations gleaned from the rapist's victims, detectives learned that the man they wanted to talk to was red-haired, short and stocky and smart. Detectives also learned that he often laughed or giggled as he ran from the scene of his crimes, the eerie sound trailing off into the night.

Newport and other investigators also noted that their quarry exhibited a strange fetish. He shaved the pubic hair off his prey and he often trimmed the hair on their heads, chopping away at it with a pocket knife. They also found it unusual that the rapist often placated his victims by some seeming act of kindness: turning out a light, closing a door or leaving with a warm embrace.

At one point in the probe, Newport made a mental note that the rapist nearly always used electrical cord to bind his victim's hands and feet and a handgun to terrify and threaten them.

On occasion, investigators reported, the rapist left the scene of his crimes in an old, dark-colored van that sputtered and coughed but managed to carry its occupant to safety. Officers agreed that they must find their adversary before he killed one of his victims.

"His method of operation is simple, but highly effective," Newport told fellow officers. "We do not underestimate his ability to hide from us. It is apparent to us that he enjoys the cat-and-mouse game he plays with us. I worry that he may carry his encounters one step further and kill."

The rapist, investigators agreed, was an expert at his trade — breaking into and entering dwellings to get at his prey. They suspected he was also an arsonist, setting fires to cover his tracks. A collector of precious metals, the rapist was also a strong suspect in a number of burglaries involving dental offices where he stole large quantities of gold and silver.

One of the women assaulted told Newport that her attacker bragged to her about his finesse at entering dwellings.

She said he seemed to enjoy sharing tales of his criminal exploits with his victims.

Other women told investigators that the assailant admitted to them that he used police scanners to monitor law enforcement activities and that he robbed only when he needed money. The man made it clear that he was selective in stalking his prey, frequently checking addresses of possible victims in the telephone book and municipal directories. He also claimed to be an avid newspaper reader, checking funeral notices, sporting events and wedding announcements in order to get a line on potential future victims.

Although few of the women attacked got a good look at the rapist, one described him as having "flaming red hair." At one encounter, the assailant took off his ski mask, revealing "sleepy, half-closed eyes and a dreamy expression." She told officers she would always remember "that face."

Newport, who coordinated all the information assembled in the investigation, observed that the suspect made use of heavy metallic tape to bind his victims and glue to seal their eyes shut. In one outing, he used common window putty to blind one of his first targets, a librarian. She told police that the attacker waited until her escort pulled his car away from her residence before striking her, forcing her into her home and raping her repeatedly. She told investigators that the masked man was deliberate in his actions and took a number of valuables with him when he left by the back door.

Police patrols of his suspected lair were increased and officers alerted to keep a sharp lookout for the dark-colored van, probably blue. They also were instructed to report house burglaries involving the theft of silverware, gold watches and coin collections. The suspect had told one victim that he watched the precious metal market to get the best value on his gold and silver holdings.

In conferences with officers involved in the case, Newport stressed the fact that their quarry was no pushover and had enjoyed nearly a decade of evading detection. He was described as "wily, sly and extremely clever." The detective also sought to impress investigators with a sense of urgency, suggesting that the rapist might escalate his attacks to a more dangerous level and kill one of his victims.

Newport also warned the lawmen in the case to be especially careful about their radio transmissions. "I am convinced that he watches and listens to our comments," he cautioned the men.

Both Newport and Loudermilk agreed that the man sought by authorities generated at least a dozen rape complaints and twice as many burglary reports. The two officers acknowledged that their quarry was not an impulse pursuer of women, but a careful, thoughtful stalker. "He has unbelievable smarts, street smarts," they both believed.

A break, a lead or a tip was needed to solve the baffling series of assaults on young women. Police knew the rapist did not select his victims at random, but carefully picked the most vulnerable. His success at avoiding detection suggested that he did not strike at the spur of a moment; rather, he picked his objects with care and a great deal of detailed planning.

The break in the case arrived unexpectedly during the second week of February 1987 when police received a telephone tip that a 17-year-old girl was being held against her will in an attic of an eastside residence.

Armed with search warrants, Newport and Detective Grey McCoy found the Terre Haute teen, Alice Fox, in an attic of a home located just blocks from her own home. The young girl was taken to Union Hospital for observation, then released to her parents. An ordeal that began four months earlier when she was abducted while walking near her home was over.

Seized on criminal confinement and theft charges was Bill Benefiel, 30, a man who had never been arrested but a man police suspected was involved in as many as a dozen rapes. Benefiel's house, police found, was guarded by a number of large dogs, tightly screened behind wooden fences and protected by a compound-type wire fence rising 12 feet in height at several spots.

Inside the dwelling and two adjacent houses and garages, Newport and uniformed police officers recovered loot valued at "thousands of dollars," including silverware, gold and silver antiques and boxes of gold dental pieces and fillings. The houses also contained an assortment of tools, appliances — some still in their original boxes — radios, television sets, watches, rings and rare coins.

Newport estimated that the material recovered represented Benefiel's decade of burglarizing homes and businesses. Some of the material in his three homes, such as plumbing and furnace material, was also stolen, the detective suspected.

The attractive young girl, a high school senior, told authorities an incredible story of torture and criminal deviate conduct on the part of Benefiel. She said he repeatedly threatened her with a gun, slashed her with a knife and raped her more than 60 times. The teen said she lost count of the number of rapes, although she tried to remember in order to tell police if and when she was released.

One time, the young girl said, Benefiel stuck a gun in her vagina, cut her on the neck and chest and forced her to submit to deviate sexual conduct. She told Newport that her assailant fed her a potato and a glass of water daily, kept her chained by her neck and often took pictures of her in a disrobed state. Her captor, Fox said, frequently tortured her by placing a gun to her head and pulling the trigger. She was chained continually she said, and handcuffed most of the time she was confined.

Telling officers that she was "scared to death" of her captor, the young teenager described how the man cut her on the back with a knife, cut off her fingernails and took a part of her hair for a scrapbook which he said contained samples of hair taken from earlier rape victims.

In the first month of 1987, the prisoner learned that her abductor had taken another victim, Delores Wells, 18, whom she happened to know. Fox told Newport that Wells, a baby-faced mother, was also mistreated, beaten brutally with his fists and lashed with electrical cords wielded by Benefiel. "There were large welts over most of her body and her face was black and blue when I saw her," Fox told officers.

During one torture encounter witnessed by the first girl to

be taken captive, Wells, her body marked by cuts and abrasions, was given a shower by Benefiel. He wore a gorilla mask to conceal his identity but he frequently slapped at Wells' nude body, the girl recalled.

At the time she was kidnapped, Fox told detectives that she was threatened with death on more than a dozen occasions. She said Benefiel forced her into his van as she walked along the street near her home, thrusting a gun into her face. He wore a purple stocking over his face, she remembered.

Days before police rescued her, the young girl said Benefiel mellowed somewhat, apparently centering his sexual assaults on Wells, the latest addition to his personal harem. She also said that Wells "knew too much to release" (in Benefiel's words) and he warned her that she was "going to go, too."

Meanwhile, police intensified their search for Wells when they learned from Fox that Benefiel confided in her that he had killed Wells by wrapping duct tape around her face and burying her body in a shallow grave. Wells' family members and friends continued a search for the young mother in isolated sections of the community.

After weeks of searching by Wells' family, friends and as many as 100 volunteers, the young mother's nude body was found buried on February 22nd southeast of Terre Haute in an isolated area near an abandoned mine shaft. Wells' hands and feet were bound and she had been raped and sodomized before being killed, an autopsy revealed. She had been struck in the head and traces of duct tape were found around her mouth. Her long blond hair had been cut short but not shaved, investigators reported.

Dr. John Pless, an Indianapolis pathologist, said the young woman's arms were bruised, indicating that she had struggled with her attacker. He told police that Wells probably died before she was buried. Cause of death was listed as asphyxiation. Finding of the body ended a month of anguish for the Wells' family and gave police additional evidence to prove Benefiel's involvement in her disappearance.

On the first day of March, silent and solemn family members and friends said goodbye to Delores Wells at Woodlawn Cemetery. Her portrait and a blanket of red roses rested on top of the white and copper casket. The minister offered words of comfort and hope to the family: "God is our refuge and strength."

As police continued to collect evidence linking Benefiel to the Wells' torture-slaying, the jailed defendant attempted to take his own life at the Vigo County Jail. A jailer found him lying on his bunk, a pool of blood darkening the floor. He was treated at the hospital for a cut on his wrist and returned to his jail cell.

Sheriff Jim Jenkins told reporters that Benefiel had chewed the eraser from a pencil and dug at his left wrist with the pencil's metal band. The defendant, held under $800,000 bond, would be watched more closely in the future, the lawman said.

Publication of Benefiel's photograph in Terre Haute's newspaper brought a traumatic reaction from a woman who told police she recognized Benefiel as the man who'd abducted and raped her a decade ago. The woman told detectives that she was taken from her home to a dungeon on the city's east side, chained to a mattress and raped. Her head and body were shaved and she was taken, nude, to a rural region where she was tied to a tree and left unattended. She said she finally freed herself, made her way to a nearby home and eventually to safety.

In the spring of 1988, accused murderer Bill Benefiel was judged competent to stand trial by Judge Michael Eldred. The trial date was set for September 12th. During the hearing, the defendant claimed that he would kill himself and he wanted "to die as soon as I can." He also told the magistrate that he didn't intend to help his defense attorneys, Christopher Gambill and Daniel Weber.

Prosecutor Phillip Adler asked Benefiel why he didn't simply plead guilty. The defendant told Adler that he "refused to answer that." Benefiel was charged with murder and other crimes against Wells and sex crimes against the teenager.

The judge indicated that he felt the opinions of two mental health experts who examined Benefiel were correct in finding the defendant competent to stand trial. They told the court that the accused appeared not to be able to act rationally in the normal sense, but rather to further his own goals.

One of the psychiatrists, who has both medical and law degrees, suggested that Benefiel has two personalities: "Billy," the good guy, and "Bill," the bad guy. He told the court that Billy wants to die as a means of controlling Bill, who hates women. At the conclusion of the hearing before the magistrate, both defense attorneys complained that their client had not been discussing the case with them.

Sparring between defense attorneys and the prosecuting attorney began in earnest a week before jury selection was scheduled to begin at Evansville. To avoid prejudice generated against the defendant in his immediate home area, the judge ruled that jurors had to be selected elsewhere. Selected jurors would be returned to Terre Haute to hear evidence in the case. The trial was expected to take at least a month.

The court asked each side to prepare briefs outlining their views of the law covering an insanity defense. The defense requested individual questioning on sensitive and potentially embarrassing matters, including religious beliefs and questions regarding alleged sexual offenses. If convicted, Benefiel would face a possible death sentence.

During further legal proceedings, defense counsel maintained that their client was not responsible for his actions because he was insane at the time of the crime. They indicated that they had new evidence in the form of mental health records not previously available to counsel or the court.

The court reminded counsel that a 1984 change in the law narrowed the scope of an insanity defense. Attorneys for the defense countered that the law provides broader scope during insanity proceedings. They also argued that their client did not understand the charges against him nor was he able to help them in his defense.

At about the same time, Benefiel for the second time slashed his arm with a razor, a disposable one which he had managed to hide from jailers. The jail commander said a cellmate of the accused slayer alerted guards to Benefiel's profuse bleeding and the subject was rushed to the hospital where seven stitches were taken in his forearm. He was also given a pint of blood.

Less than 24 hours later, Benefiel's mother died at the same hospital. The pair, police report, frequently clashed during Benefiel's childhood.

In the first week of February 1988, Benefiel surprised nearly everyone connected with the case and requested successfully to be allowed to marry a woman with whom he had lived for almost 11 years. The couple, who professed their love for each other, were married at ceremonies conducted in the outer lobby of the county jail.

The groom, father of the couple's three children, wore a bright orange jump suit, standard attire for jail inmates. His bride was clad in a purple and pink flowered dress. They told reporters they loved each other.

In an interview with reporters prior to the wedding, the woman told newspeople that she and Benefiel had always planned to marry but never got around to it. She also explained that she was not marrying Benefiel to avoid giving testimony at his trial, scheduled for the second week in September. Conducting the ceremony, which took about five minutes to perform, was the county clerk. It was witnessed by workers in the sheriff's office.

On June 14th, a third suicide attempt by Benefiel was thwarted by Vigo County jail personnel. This time the defendant cut both wrists by using a small piece of cell mirror made of stainless steel. Once again, Benefiel was treated at the hospital, then returned to his jail cell. Despite the three attempts on his own life, the short, stocky inmate was generally regarded as a good prisoner who caused little trouble, jail officials said. Guards, who checked Benefiel at 15-minute intervals, removed the mirror from his cell.

The long-awaited trial of the accused torture-slayer opened the second week of September with instructions to jury members delivered by the judge. Opening statements by the state and defense followed and it was announced that the actual trial would be moved to Vigo Circuit Court where a larger courtroom would accommodate a greater number of expected spectators.

Seven women and five men were selected to hear the capital case with two additional women chosen as alternates. Jurors were sequestered at a nearby motel and warned not to discuss the case with anyone. Prosecutor Adler said he planned to summon 20 witnesses and introduce 70 to 90 exhibits. He told the court that his phase of the case would consume about six days.

Defense attorneys said they would offer evidence of the defendant's long-term mental illness and his difficult childhood. They also argued that their client led a "tortured, deprived, brutal, chaotic life, and that he had been abused physically, emotionally and sexually throughout most of his formative years."

In his opening statement, Adler maintained that a person claiming to have more than one personality should not necessarily escape justice. The prosecutor, who had never lost a murder case, told jurors that Benefiel's fist victim, a 17-year-old, was chained to a bed, assaulted daily and never saw the light of day for 60 days. Police finally rescued the young woman from an attic where the defendant had hidden her, "huddled in a fetal position, mumbling like a baby," he told the court.

"Our appeal is not for mercy or sympathy. We are asking you to make civilized decision. I invite you to go with us on a journey through hell," Defense Counsel Daniel Weber told jurors.

Fox, the state's star witness, led off the state's presentation of evidence in what the prosecution termed a "tale of terror at Benefiel's hands." The young girl told the court that she was handcuffed and chained almost continually and raped so many times, she lost count.

When she began to bleed, she told the jury, Benefiel slipped her out of the house, placed her in the van and drove her to Vincennes for treatment. The young woman said her captor warned her if she tried anything, he would kill her and everyone else. Despite the doctor's advice, they returned to Terre Haute where he started raping her again.

After Benefiel brought Wells to the house, he gave her the same treatment the young woman told the court. He once asked Wells: "Do you want to die fast or do you want to die slow?" She responded that she wanted to die fast but Benefiel told her she would die slowly, Fox, now 19, told jurors. "He didn't lie," Alder added.

A surprise witness for the defense was the defendant's wife, who admitted that she was the person who tipped off police to the whereabouts of the Fox girl. Wearing the same dress she wore when she married Benefiel at the jail earlier, the woman testified that Benefiel beat and terrified her during the year they lived together. She told the court that she left Benefiel on many occasions but returned home because she loved him.

The 31-year-old woman testified that her husband often became excited while watching television, particularly during violent movies. "When someone was killed, he would clap his hands," she told the court.

Before she left the witness chair, the tearful wife, who was later convicted of a charge of welfare fraud, told jurors that Benefiel also attacked her after tying her to their bed. "He slapped me, ripped off my clothes and raped me at least seven times." She said he also shaved off her pubic hair, but later told her that she had done it herself.

During cross examination, she conceded that she had once seen the younger woman with Benefiel and that it had made her "boiling mad." She had no idea that the young woman was not there of her own free will, she told the court. At that time, the defendant had moved into his own home and was doing his own cooking.

While his wife testified, Benefiel appeared aloof to her testimony and turned his chair away from the witness stand. He appeared not to notice her and gave his attention, instead, to members of the jury. As his wife told her story to the jury, the defendant rocked in his chair and his eyes moved quickly around the courtroom. He eyed spectators and seemed, at one point, to be counting the house.

Testifying for the state, Dr. John Pless, Indianapolis forensic pathologist, told the jurors that his examination

407

showed Wells had sustained recent injuries to her face and forehead caused by moderate to severe force. Pless testified that he found a hard, glue-like substance in Wells' eyes and nostrils and that her nose had been compressed together. He said her death was caused by asphyxia due to smothering.

Pless informed the court that when he examined the victim's body, Wells' hands were tied behind her back, her ankles were secured with rope and a loop of rope was tied around her neck, pulling the body into a fetal position. Pless testified that Wells had been raped both vaginally and anally a few hours before she succumbed to death.

In earlier testimony by a state serologist, hair found stuck to trash bags taken from the home occupied by the defendant and his victims sufficiently matched hair belonging to Wells and Fox. Defense attorneys posed no questions to either the pathologist or the serologist.

A clinical psychologist testified that Benefiel could have known what he did was wrong. In addition to having primarily a schizotypal personality disorder, Benefiel was also viewed as anti-social and sadistic. Offering strong support for the state's position, a psychologist testified that he was certain the defendant could have known what he did was wrong. He told the court that the accused was a person who pulled back from normal interaction with other people and developed "oddness and peculiarities because no one ever stepped in to correct the situation."

Before the state rested its case, a videotape of the exhumation of Wells' body was shown the jury. Defense counsel strongly protested the presentation, arguing that the tape served the purpose of inflaming the passions of the jury. The judge rejected defense objections and jurors intently watched the tape. Benefiel watched from his chair beside counsel, leaning back in his chair with his fingers laced together over his stomach.

Testifying in his own behalf, Benefiel, speaking in a soft, almost gentle voice, told the jury that the woman who raised him would often hit him on the head with a broom or belt. He also recalled how he was sexually molested as a child and he said he feared he never had any friends.

"I was often made fun of," he told the court.

Benefiel told the court that he often experienced unusual dreams. He said he would go to sleep in one place and wake up in a different place. He described his confining, raping and abusing Fox as a "dream."

After a court recess, Benefiel refused to retake the witness stand. One of his lawyers informed the court that talking about his childhood misfortunes and the charges filed against him caused their client to suffer a nervous breakdown. The state suggested that the defendant "just didn't want to get back in the case."

Judge Michael Eldred summoned the jury and told them that the defendant need not be present at his trial. He explained that the law allows a defendant to be present or not present and that the trial would continue. He advised the counsel and jury that he had explained the defendant's constitutional rights to him and told him that the trial would continue.

Counsel for the defense argued that Benefiel's breakdown was evident to them. They described how the defendant's features became contorted, he began to shake and sobbed uncontrollably. "He believes that everyone is laughing at him," one of his attorneys advised the court.

During the furor over Benefiel's decision to walk out of the courtroom, a bomb threat was received at three courthouse offices. The building was evacuated and the jury returned to their motel. No devices were found and the trial continued under tighter security.

As the torture-slaying trial entered its third week, the prosecution labeled Benefiel as "the Mount Everest of criminals." Prosecutor Adler called the whole subject of Benefiel's supposed split personality "a red herring." "A sad childhood does not mean that you are going to forgive him rape and murder. If that is justice, I am in the wrong business," he informed the court.

On October 2nd, the jury found Benefiel guilty in the torturing and murder of Delores Wells. The defendant told reporters that he was happy with the jury's decision and wanted to die. One of the defendant's attorneys, Weber, said he was not sure about his client's death wish. Benefiel was insane and suffered from a severe mental illness, said Weber. "I see it, I believe it and I know it."

Twenty-four hours after the jury found Benefiel guilty of murder, rape, confinement and deviate sexual conduct in the death of Wells, members of the jury recommended that the defendant should die. However, whether or not the death sentence would be imposed rested with Judge Eldred.

After a month of deliberating, on November 3rd Judge Eldred ruled that Benefiel must die in Indiana's electric chair. Benefiel commented that he got what he wanted and he grinned at his defense attorneys. Eldred said evidence presented showed that the defendant killed Wells in "a savage, barbaric and cruel manner."

No specific date was set for Benefiel's execution; the judge said he would do that after review by the Indiana Supreme Court. State law requires review in a case involving the death penalty. Members of the Wells family said the death sentence was too good; they felt he should suffer as Delores Wells had.

Weber, one of Benefiel's defense attorneys, told reporters that he was not sure his client really wanted to die. His colleague, Christopher Gambill, was bitter about the death sentence. "I just cannot accept a society that kills mentally ill persons."

The foreman of the jury which found Benefiel guilty and later recommended the death penalty described the sentence as "fitting the crimes." He said there was no doubt in his mind about either of the jury's decisions. The jury foreman drove to Terre Haute from Evansville to hear the Judge's decision. "It was worth the hundred-mile drive," the man said.

Ironically, an Evansville man sentenced to death in the same courtroom five years ago remains on death row at Michigan City following repeated appeals. The inmate, Donald Ray Wallace, received the death sentence after he was convicted of killing a family of four at Evansville in 1980.

The last man to die in Indiana in the electric chair was Steven Judy on March 9, 1981. Judy, like Benefiel, insisted on the death penalty and asked his defense counsel not to appeal his sentence. He was convicted of slaying a woman and her three children south of Indianapolis.

Six years ago, Indiana authorities spent $5,000 refurbishing the state-owned electric chair. It is located 13 steps from the death row cells.

EDITOR'S NOTE

Alice Fox is not the real name of the person so named in the foregoing story. A fictitious name has been used because there is no reason for public interest in the identity of this person.

Stop The Brutal Beast Who Stalks Young Innocents!

by Brian Marriner

The epidemic of child abductions and sex killings has prompted police in the United Kingdom to launch "Operation Stranger"

Susan Maxwell, a pretty 11-year-old schoolgirl, was enjoying the sunshine of a July heat wave. The freckle-faced youngster was playing near her farm home outside Coldstream, at Cornhill-On-Tweed in Northumberland. This is a part of the Scottish Borders area of Britain. Like any farmer's daughter, Susan had been brought up strictly; and living in a remote rural area, she had been repeatedly warned never to talk to strangers, never to accept a lift in a stranger's car.

Yet on the evening of July 30, 1982, Susan Maxwell disappeared. It was as if she vanished off the face of the earth. Despite massive newspaper publicity, with her portrait prominently displayed everywhere, nobody came forward who had seen her or knew of her whereabouts. Her parents clung to the hope that Susan had somehow wandered off, that one day she would turn up unharmed.

Two weeks later, senior police officers called at the farm to see Mrs. Maxwell. They brought grim news. It is perhaps the most terrible aspect of a policeman's work, having to tell parents the stark news: "Your child is dead."

The stunned mother listened in disbelief as a detective told her, as gently as he could, that the badly-decomposed body of her daughter had been found 260 miles away in Uttoxeter, in Staffordshire. On August 12th, a hiker had come across the body callously dumped in a wood beside a motorway. The motive for the killing had been sex. It was every mother's nightmare come true — a stranger came out of nowhere to snatch her child and then, after satisfying his perverted lust, killed his innocent victim. What kind of man could do such a terrible thing?

Despite massive police investment in time and officers, no clue to the killer of Susan Maxwell was ever found. Forensic evidence uncovered during the post-mortem was of no use. The Murder Incident Room, set up by the police after any homicide, continued to function, the Murder Log being updated daily, but day by day its activities grew less urgent as the trail went cold.

Little blonde-haired Caroline Hogg was just five years old. She was last seen alive in a "funfair" near her home in Edinburgh's Portobello district on the evening of July 8, 1983. Witnesses turned up who had seen her being led away from the funfair by a furtive-looking stranger holding her hand. Ten days later, on July 18th, her decomposed remains were found in a ditch near a layby close to Twycross in Leicestershire. It was close to a motorway.

At first, police did not link the two killings, yet gradually they were forced to face the fact that they were most likely hunting the most dangerous rogue male in any society — the sexual serial killer.

The following March, Caroline's parents took part in a police video appeal shown on national television. For the first time, the parents were able to express their anguish publicly. It was hoped that the reconstruction of Caroline's abduction, depicted on television by actors, would jog someone's memory and lead to the capture of the vicious abductor-killer.

Thousands of man-hours of painstaking detective work went into the hunt for the killer of Caroline Hogg. As of today, he has not been found.

In the police video, Caroline's father expressed his fear of the possibility of a carbon-copy killing. "You think it can never happen to you," he said, "but it has been proved time and time again that it can, and it could once more, if this man is not caught in the near future."

His grim prophecy came bitterly true in March 1986. Sarah Jayne Harper, a bright 10-year-old schoolgirl who was a member of the local Salvation Army choir, was sent by her mother to run an errand to the corner shop, less than 100 yards from her modest terraced home in Brunswick Place, Morley, West Yorkshire. The date was March 26, 1986, and it was about 7:30 in the evening when Sarah went on the errand to fetch bread.

She never completed that errand. She arrived at the shop and bought the provisions—the shopkeeper remembered serving her—but she never reached her home again. Somewhere along that short route a killer waited. He abducted Sarah—and life came to an end, both for her and, in a sense, for her mother. Despite an extensive neighborhood search by police, she was not found—nor was the loaf of bread. It could have provided vital forensic clues.

By April 3rd, the girl's mother appeared at an emotional press conference and tearfully told journalists that she feared her daughter was dead. In a faltering voice and staring straight into the TV camera, she said, "I just want her back—even if she's dead. If someone would just pick up the phone and tell us where the body is . . ." She revealed that the worst torment of all was the waiting—to hear that Sarah's body had been found. As she left the press conference, held at Leeds' Holbeck police station, she collapsed and had to be helped by her mother and police officers to a chair.

The body of Sarah Jayne Harper was found three and a half weeks later, on April 19th, in the swollen waters of the River Trent in Nottingham, over 70 miles away. She had been badly battered and sexually abused.

The pattern was now becoming clear: This was a killer who snatched girls in the North of England and dumped their ravished and desecrated bodies in the Midlands. Men with occupations which took them along that route, from the Midlands to the North, men like truck-drivers, commercial travelers or taxi drivers, were among the prime suspect group.

The police began the usual routine things — checking on all men with convictions for sexual molestation and all sex-offenders recently released from prison, and eliminating them from the inquiry.

But first the ritual of burying the latest victim, Sarah Harper, had to be observed. The entire town of Morley came to a standstill when Sarah was finally laid to rest. More than 200 people crammed the tiny Salvation Army citadel in the town, with hundreds more standing outside, joining in the singing of Sarah's favorite hymn, "Jesus Loves Me, This I Know."

The Morley Salvation Army leader addressed the congregation and described Sarah as having been a "friendly, motherly, confident young girl." He went on: "Society must be protected — young people and the elderly must have their freedom — they must not be prisoners in their own homes."

Police stopped all traffic to allow the cortege a free route through Morley to the cemetery, where on July 1st, Sarah was laid decently to rest. Among the wreaths was one from Nottinghamshire Police, and another from the West Yorkshire Police.

Three police officers stood apart, watching. They were Detective Superintendent John Stainthorpe, who led the search for Sarah; Detective Chief Superintendent Tom Newton, heading the hunt for her killer, and Detective Superintendent Ron Tough of Nottinghamshire Police. They were there both to express their own private grief, and to remind the public that they were ever-vigilant, determined to see the case to an end and the killer behind bars.

By the time of the funeral, much investigative work had already been done. Immediately police were notified of Sarah's disappearance, Morley was sealed off by police roadblocks and hundreds of drivers were stopped and questioned. As a result of door-to-door inquiries, Detective Superintendent Stainthorpe was able to issue a description of a mystery man seen in the alley between two houses on the route Sarah would have had to take on her errand to the corner shop. The man was described as being in his twenties, 5 feet 7 inches to 5 feet 9 inches tall, of medium build with collar-length hair, and wearing a fawn casual jacket. Several witnesses saw him between 7:15 p.m. and 7:30 p.m.

Studying a map of the area made it immediately apparent that the man could have parked his car in adjoining Peel Street, then gone along the alley to Brunswick Place and stood waiting for his victim. He would then have had to snatch Sarah, take her back along the alley, and bundle her into his car. Yet nobody had seen anything, or heard a child's desperate cry.

The atmosphere in the town of Morley was oppressive as if a deadly, dark cloud had descended on it. One neighbor living close to the Harper family described the atmosphere as being terrible. She added: "After finding out what happened to Sarah I found myself looking at everyone, wondering whether they had done anything to the girl." Mothers were frightened to let their children out; they had indeed become prisoners in their own homes.

The belief that the killer must be local to Morley was to plague the investigation. Because the town is such a small, intimate place, full of back-streets and alleys, it was reasoned that the killer would have had to know the area well. This simply wasn't true. The killer didn't even have to know that Sarah had gone to the shop. He could have just been waiting for the first young girl who happened along. Morley, it must be remembered, lies alongside a major motorway leading from the North to the South. The killer could have driven into the town from the motorway and picked his victim at random.

Meanwhile, police had the witnesses who had seen the mystery man lurking in the alley work closely with a police artist to produce a composite sketch of the man. In early June 1986, a large plain brown envelope without a stamp was delivered to the head office of the Yorkshire Post newspaper in Leeds. Inside it was a head and shoulders portrait of a man, executed in an oil painting. On the back of the canvas was scrawled: "22nd April 1986. Portrait of Sarah Harper's killer." The newspaper immediately handed the painting over to West Yorkshire Police.

After detailed examination by forensic and art experts, the police established that the painting had been done *before* the police sketch of the wanted man had been published in newspapers, yet it bore an uncanny likeness to him. Both men had thinning red hair, steel-rimmed spectacles, narrow lips and the same shape of nose and eyes. The eyes themselves were a significant clue. Because of the way they had been drawn art experts thought that it could well be a poor self-portrait by a tormented or tormenting killer. Painted on a good-quality cotton canvas, neither the painting nor the envelope it had arrived in bore fingerprints.

Detective Chief Superintendent Tony Newton said of the painting: "This may well be the face of the murderer." He said the police were treating the painting "very seriously indeed," adding, "This painting does bear a striking likeness to the man who had been drawn in our artist's impression, and it does look as though there could be a link." He asked anyone who recognized the man in the painting to come forward. But if the painting was indeed a clue, like all the others, it petered out into a dead end.

At this stage in the investigation, over 200 officers had interviewed 10,144 people, had taken 1,114 statements. Yet the tremendous police effort drew a blank. And it should be noted that the inquiry into the murder of Susan Maxwell, which was still running, had led to 30,000 statements being taken, 18,000 vehicles traced, and 75,000 people interviewed. It was tremendously labor-intensive and expensive, and it produced no result.

Now the police had to come to terms with what faced them. Almost certainly the killer of Sarah Harper did not live in or anywhere near Morley. The forensic evidence and other clues linked the three murders as being indisputably the work of one killer. Susan Maxwell, Caroline Hogg, and now Sarah Harper, had all been murdered by a fiend who struck at random. The victims had all been female, had been sexually assaulted, had been abducted in the North and their bodies dumped in the South.

In the case of Caroline Hogg and Susan Maxwell, the link was strongest of all. Their homes had not been many miles distant, and their bodies were found less than 40 miles apart in Leicestershire and Staffordshire. In addition, both girls had vanished on a Friday night during a July heat wave.

Whoever the killer was, it was apparent that a personality profile could be easily drawn up of him. His mentality had to be that of a beast; he must have viewed the world as being his own private chicken-coop, and he was the fox.

There was initially and inevitably much bureaucratic wrangling over the three murders. It was obviously inefficient to allow three separate police forces to pursue three separate inquiries. Yet which force should have overall command? The decision was eventually made to place the investigation in the hands of the deputy chief constable of the Lothian and Border Police, Hector Clark, 53. He had led the initial inquiry into the murder of the first victim.

Clark set up the headquarters for his detective team in Wakefield, halfway between where the children had been abducted and where their bodies had been found. He had to act as liaison between six different police forces—those of Nottingham, Northumbria, Leicestershire, West Yorkshire and Staffordshire, and his own force based in Edinburgh.

A secret meeting of top police chiefs was held at Leeds just two weeks after Clark was put in overall charge of what had now become Britain's biggest-ever murder investigation, even though some detectives were still not sure if there was any link between the three murders. High on the agenda of the meeting were the murders of Caroline Hogg, Susan Maxwell and Sarah Harper. Among the officers present were Colin Sampson, Chief Constable of West Yorkshire; Charles McLachlan, the Chief Constable of

Nottinghamshire, the deputy chief constables of both Lothian and Borders; and the heads of C.I.D.'s from six police forces.

A start had been made on using a computer to collate the mass of information on the three cases, and a report was leaked to the press that the computer had identified a couple who could be linked to all three murders. Constable Clark refused to confirm this. By now the inquiry had cost well over one million pounds, and it was still only February 1987. The various chief constables agreed to put pressure on the central government to meet the cost of a super-computer.

The murder team also had to take on board other cases of missing children which might be linked to the three child-murders under investigation. Similar cases included the baffling disappearance of Genette Tate, 13, who vanished while delivering newspapers in the village of Aylesbeare, next to Exeter, in August 1978. She had apparently been knocked off her bicycle by a vehicle. The bike was found, she was not. Even today, posters bearing Genette's photograph are still displayed in police stations throughout Britain.

At one stage, more than 7,000 people turned out to help police carry out a search for the youngster's body, but despite a nationwide hunt, Genette has never been found. Her father published a book about the case.

There was also the case of Christopher Laverack, age 9. Christopher, who lived with his mother and stepfather at Anlaby, Hull, vanished from his home on March 9, 1984. It was a Friday night. His body was recovered two days later from a local stream. It was badly beaten and wrapped in a plastic carpet bag.

Two years later — on Mother's Day — police renewed their appeal for information about Christopher's disappearance. The file remains open on this case, as it does on all the other cases, and it will not be closed until the killer is apprehended and convicted.

By late 1987, a "summit" meeting at Scotland Yard was

called by Metropolitan Police Commander Philip Corbett, head of the Yard's CII Criminal Intelligence branch, and coordinator of "Operation Stranger," the hunt for the killer of schoolboys Barry Lewis and Jason Swift. There were some links between these two cases and those of the three murdered girls. The links included a red car seen in the case of Barry Lewis, 6, from North London, whose body was found buried in a field in Essex after he went missing in September 1986. Red cars had been mentioned by witnesses in the cases of Susan Maxwell, Caroline Hogg, Sarah Harper and Genette Tate.

The summit involved officers from 16 forces who met to discuss a total of 19 unsolved child murders. Among cases being studied were those of Martin Allen, 15, last seen at King's Cross tube station on November 5, 1979. His body has never been found. Marion Croits, 14, was knocked off her bicycle deliberately by a car near her home at Fleet, Hampshire, in July 1981. Her body was found about a mile from a fairground. She had been raped and beaten to death. Colette Aram, 16, was found strangled and sexually assaulted in Keyworth, Nottinghamshire, in October 1983. Mark Tildesley, 7, was abducted on his way home from a funfair near his home in Wokingham, Berkshire, in June 1984. He has not been seen again.

Jason Swift, 14, and Barry Lewis, 6, were found buried six miles apart in the Essex countryside. Police believe that both were murdered by the same man, believed to be a homosexual child-killer. There was even discussion of a ring of pedophiles who might have been jointly responsible for both murders. Jason Swift had written to his mother to say that he was with a fair in Southend.

Red cars, fairgrounds and funfairs—such clues litter these cases. Or are they just red herrings? They were to cause police a serious distraction and lead them far away. One of those fairs had been an American one touring Britain. That had to be checked out.

British police had had their share of long and protracted nationwide hunts for sex-killers. The hunt for the Yorkshire

Ripper, killer of 13 women, took five years and millions of pounds before Peter Sutcliffe was finally apprehended. More important, that long hunt revealed the true cost of such a huge police inquiry. It could not be measured simply in cash terms. There was the cost of human resources. Detectives on the case worked themselves into the ground. Senior officers broke under the strain; one had a heart attack, another had to take sick leave. Marriages broke up. Officers started drinking too much and ended up becoming bitter and disillusioned. It is impossible to sustain police morale at a high level for such a protracted length of time. That was one true message of the case.

Bad mistakes were made during the hunt for the Ripper, frankly admitted by the Home Secretary of the day and senior police chiefs. At least six books on the case criticize specific police blunders, but it is always easy to be wise after the fact, as hindsight is always 100 percent accurate.

For officers on the ground, the problem became one of sheer paperwork. The numbers of people questioned, statements taken soared into the hundreds of thousands, creating an empire of paper which clogged up the system.

In the new hunt for the killer of Susan Maxwell, Caroline Hogg and Sarah Harper, it was decided at a very early stage that every technological advance would be used. Priority was given to getting all the relevant information on computer.

By March 1987, Deputy Chief Constable Hector Clark said the case was like "looking for a tiny needle in a huge haystack." He revealed that a government computer dubbed "HOLMES" was being used to collate and cross-check all data coming into the police Murder Incident Room. HOLMES, which is an acronym for "Home Office Major Enquiry System," was being used to link investigators from six forces into the cases of the three murdered girls. More than 40,000 names were held in its database, and among the facilities it offered was "free text retrieval." For example, if one single piece of information was being sought — say the number of times witnesses had mentioned a leather jacket —

then all the databases could be merged to seek out all references to a leather jacket. Clark said that the half-million-pound machine, based at police headquarters in Yorkshire, would be used "to determine whether or not the girls were killed by one man."

Deputy Chief Constable Clark was still being very cautious. Awarded the Queen's Police Medal to mark his 32-year career, he travels from Edinburgh to spend three days a week on the computer operation. At a press conference held in Wakefield in January 1987, he said that it was still not clear if there was any definite link between the murders of Sarah Harper, Caroline Hogg and Susan Maxwell. Nor was it clear if more than one person was involved.

He did reveal that in only one case—Caroline Hogg's—did the police have a satisfactory description of the suspect to work from. A man had been seen walking hand-in-hand with the little toddler from the fair near Edinburgh. He was described as being between 25 and 45, about 5 feet 10 inches tall, of shabby appearance and wearing spectacles. Another clue—spectacles.

Clark also revealed that three new lines of inquiry were being followed. Detectives would go to Amsterdam to investigate one new murder lead, while inquiries would also be launched in Scotland and the Midlands. He would not reveal details of the inquiry, but he said the decision to travel to Amsterdam had been made on the basis of fresh clues.

The constable would not disclose if the suspect was a man or a woman and would say nothing of a document leaked from inside police headquarters to the effect that police were searching for a couple. He told reporters: "My own view is that the person we are looking for is probably a man between the ages of twenty-five and forty-five who travels a lot in Britain and possibly abroad, and has previous convictions of a similar nature involving female children."

On the eve of the anniversary of the second year of her daughter's disappearance, on March 25, 1988, the mother of the Harper girl made a public plea to the sex fiend who had killed her daughter. She urged him on television: "Give

422

yourself up. You have a terrible weight on your conscience, which must haunt you constantly." Detective Superintendent Stainthorpe, who appeared with her, urged anyone with information about the murder to come forward.

At this point, I feel that I should mention my own personal involvement with the case, one which—if it did not give me a unique insight into the investigation—at least enables me to have a particular empathy with the victims.

In late November 1986, I was invited to take part in a television program about the case. Called simply *MISSING KIDS*, it was a late-night discussion show by Central Television, the TV company which covers the Midlands and is sometimes networked nationally.

As one who has been writing professionally on the subject of murder for many years, I had been invited to join the panel and contribute my personal ideas as an "expert." Also present and taking part in the discussion were the parents of Susan Maxwell, Caroline Hogg and Sarah Harper; Detective Superintendent John Stainthorpe; a lady who had written a play on a similar theme; a newspaper reporter who had been covering the case; and a psychiatrist from Broadmoor Hospital for the Criminally Insane, which houses some of Britain's most notorious killers.

Many in the studio audience were parents who had suffered losses of their own. The format of the show was simple enough. A presenter related the facts of each case while photographs of the children were flashed on the screen. Then, one by one, we were used to bounce ideas off one another.

Before the program, in the hospitality room, I was able to meet and talk with all three sets of parents. I was enormously impressed by them, touched by their stories, and moved by their courage. The parents of Susan Maxwell in particular had a profound influence on me. They were well-educated and middle class, and it was impossible to believe that they would have brought up a child in such a way that it would willingly go off with a stranger.

All the parents had similar stories to tell. From the moment they lost their child, after tragedy had hit them out of a clear blue sky, they became pariahs in their communities, shunned as if they carried some contagious disease. Even old friends crossed the road to avoid them. People simply did not know how to cope with their grief, and so avoided them. As a result, the bereaved parents felt alone; they tended to stay inside their homes, unwilling to go out, because if they did, people stared at them as if they were freaks. No form of counseling was available, and for this reason the parents had founded their own society — *Parents of Murdered Children* — to provide group support and even to agitate for political reform, such as the restoration of the death penalty.

The psychiatrist on the program talked of the many different types of sex-killers. Some were very controlled personalities, other disorganized. He thought this particular killer was extremely controlled, to the extent that his own wife or family would not suspect his perverse mania for young girls. Some indication of sadistic behavior might be visible in early childhood. Unfortunately, such traits are not observed until after the killer has been apprehended, and comes under analysis.

The program host tried to draw out Superintendent Stainthorpe on whether police had any definite suspects, if all these killings were linked, and on the leaked report that a couple might be involved. Like any responsible police officer in the midst of an ongoing investigation, he tersely replied, "No comment."

My own contribution to the discussion was based on a number of things, anger not the least of them. I could not believe that it was possible for the killer to lure the children into his car without someone hearing their cries for help or seeing something amiss. If he simply grabbed them off the street, he would have to stop his car, get out. Go around it. Snatch the child and drag her back to his car. It seemed an insane risk to take. Superintendent Stainthorpe told me privately afterwards that he believed the killer simply punched the children in the face with great force, rendering them unconscious or dazed, and then bundled them into his car.

I was also motivated by a desire to spare the parents' feelings. If they could believe that it was not their fault, that their children had not disobeyed them, but had been tricked into going with the killer, then it would make it much easier for them to come to terms with the situation.

I argued that traditional police methods, valuable as they are, were not enough. It is not good enough to wait for the killer to strike again, and then hope he will make a mistake. What was needed is a radical kind of policeman: One who can use unorthodox methods to get inside the mind of the killer.

I was firmly on the side of the "couple" theory, on the basis that a child would more willingly enter a car occupied by a man and woman, especially if, for example, they told her that her mother had been involved in an accident. And the mere fact of being a couple confers a kind of respectability, which a single man alone in a car does not have.

I pointed out that there was a long list of precedents of couples acting in concert to carry out their deadly fantasies, the classic *folie a deux* of criminology. Literally "the madness of two," it is a clinical condition in which a couple, one of whom is dominant, act out their joint madness. From Leopold and Loeb, to Fernandez and Beck, the Moors Murderers Brady and Hindley, Bianchi and his cousin Buono, the Hillside Stranglers, to cases in the pipeline which include an Australian husband and wife who are alleged to have kept teenage girls prisoner for sexual thrills, killing them when they got bored, to Gary Heidnik, accused with his partner of keeping women prisoners, and killing them, at his home in Philadelphia.

All these cases illustrate *folie a deux* in action — a situation in which two individuals who, separately, are harmless, come together and infect each other with their madness. The result is explosive, like mixing nitric acid with glycerine.

My suggestion was that police should concentrate on wife-swapping "contact" magazines which circulate in Britain. Many of the advertisers not only offer to swap their wife or husband, but their children, too. There is an extensive pedophile underground network which should be penetrated.

My own personal theories may be well wide of the mark. I cannot know what lines of inquiry the police are following in secret and for good reason. But I was angry enough at the thought of this monster preying on children in our society to stick my neck out. Only time will tell if I am in any way close to the truth, because I am convinced that one day the killer *will* be caught.

My anger led me to be perhaps unfair to British police. They are very experienced professionals with extensive knowledge of their field. At one time, Scotland Yard's famed Murder Squad used to be called in as a matter of routine to investigate any homicide in the nation which local police could not solve. The Squad was disbanded years ago, and now each force has its own Serious Crimes Unit.

Use is being made of computers, which can provide officers with such information as parameters of age of the likely killer, in percentage terms whether it is likely to be a close relative or a stranger, the most likely area in which the body will be found—from the last sighting of the child—all of which produces a statistical profile of the offender. Long gone are the days when a chief officer would put 100 to 200 officers into an investigation. Now he is looking for the best use of his resources, and computers can be of great assistance.

And Britain has had its "firsts." It was a British scientist, Dr. Alec Jeffreys at Leicester University, who discovered "genetic fingerprinting" in September 1984. It is a byproduct of research on DNA, the building blocks of life which contains a unique code that determines whether we are born with red or brown hair, an aquiline or snub nose, blue or brown eyes. The DNA code was cracked by Crick and Watson in the early 1950s. This code can be compared to the bar-code used on supermarket groceries. Each individual has his own code; it is unique to him, and no other individual in the world has exactly the same code. The test devised by Dr. Jeffreys can match a tiny sample of blood or semen to a suspect. Perhaps one valuable aspect of it is that not only can it prove a person's guilt, but it can also establish that person's innocence.

The first criminal case in which the Jeffreys test was used was in a rape case in November 1987. The rapist was sentenced to eight years in jail after it had been proved that semen stains on the victim's clothing were identical to the suspect's DNA code. But the case which attracted worldwide attention was known as the Enderby murders. In November 1983, Lynda Mann, 15, was found raped and strangled near her village Enderby in Leicestershire. Police failed to apprehend the killer, but his semen stains were preserved.

Three years later, in July 1986, Dawn Ashworth, 15, was found raped and strangled at Enderby. The unknown killer had struck again. The police initially arrested and charged a 17-year-old youth. But after his blood sample was taken to Leicester University and tested by Dr. Alec Jeffreys, it was established that he was totally innocent. He was released; police had to restart their investigation. There was intense press interest in the murders, and police were under pressure to come up with the killer quickly.

Since it seemed probable that the killer was local, police arranged to have all males in the area give blood samples. Of all the hundreds of samples, not one matched the DNA code of the unknown killer. Then someone heard a man in a Leicester pub boasting of how he had helped out his pal by offering his own blood sample in place of that of his friend. He showed police his friend's driving license as proof of identity.

The stand-in was arrested after the overheard conversation came to police attention. The man said he had been paid 50 pounds by a fellow worker at a bakery to stand in for him, as the man had a police record for sex offenses. That man was Colin Pitchfork. His DNA code matched the preserved semen stains exactly. On January 22, 1987, Pitchfork was found guilty of both murders at Leicester Crown Court and sentenced to life. His stand-in got 18 months.

Despite this enormous advance in forensic science — at the time of writing over 40 rape cases in Britain have been solved by "DNA fingerprinting" — the fact is that in the detection of the sexual serial killer, the USA is years ahead of Britain.

The VICAP program in the USA was pioneered by the FBI. VICAP — "Violent Criminal Apprehension Program" — is now part of the National Center for the analysis of violent crimes. Details of all homicides in the USA — there were 19,000 in 1987 — are gathered at the FBI headquarters. At the FBI Academy in Virginia, teams of officers look for psychological clues in the cases. From scene of crime clues, they are able to predict the likely murderer, his age, the car he is most likely to drive, and the probable area where he lives.

Sounds impossible? Yet it works. These FBI officers have become "mind-hunters." By going into prisons and talking to such notorious serial killers as Richard Speck, Emil Kemper, Charles Manson, Juan Corona, and David "Son of Sam" Berkowitz, they have gained a unique insight into the mind of the killer. They discovered that all these killers had one thing in common: all are intelligent, but all were abused and rejected as children, and so had retreated into a world of fantasy. The result of the VICAP Program is that we now have cops who can think like killers and by getting inside their heads, predict their next move.

Roger Dupue, head of the Behavioral Science Unit, categorizes killers into various types according to methods used. Most crime is committed by the young — the 15-to-24 year bracket — but they are inept and quickly caught. Serial organized criminals he categorizes as the "best" and they contradict conventional criminology which states that the psychopath does not learn from his mistakes. Roger Dupue tells us that these "best" serial killers *do* learn, and become more proficient and more cunning with each killing. "Their level of sophistication increases the longer they are killing."

He goes on to warn us: "They modify and refine their processes and techniques."

The officers in the VICAP Program have come to learn that rape is not committed for sexual gratification, but for *control* for *power* over another individual. "Sexual assault does not service sexual needs, but power needs." It is necessary for the "mind-hunters" to understand the perverse fantasies which fuel the sexual serial-killer. The repetitiveness of their crimes becomes a pattern that makes it easier for them to commit their crimes as they commit more.

Given the background of the murders, the "mind-hunters" can predict which sadistic fantasy is being enacted, predict where and when the killer will strike next, get into his mind and think like him, figure out his fantasy and discover why he does what he does, and then try to imagine what his post-crime behavior is like. Will he be boastful or remorseful? Either way, the killer's own fantasy can be used against him to trap him.

The profiles of killers which VICAP officers have developed have been shown to be remarkably accurate when matched with the apprehended killer.

The latest news in the cases of Caroline Hogg, Susan Maxwell and Sarah Harper is that all the details have been sent to the FBI "mind-hunters" in the hope that they can help trap the killer. It is the fervent hope of all that this proves to be the case, because until this monster is caught, every mother's nightmare will continue to exert its malevolent influence night after night over England's green and pleasant land.

The Demon Brothers Of L.A.

by Turk Ryder

Nine murders and 100 rapes linked these demonic brothers.

Pretty Jodi Samuel, a spunky 15-year-old freshman at St. Mary's Academy in Los Angeles, was a bright and popular student who took special pleasure in making people happy. When she learned that the church choir director's birthday was coming up, she convinced other students to throw him a surprise party, complete with a three-layer chocolate cake, 42 candles on top.

The cake was completely unexpected and was a big hit. The choir director thanked the students and, with tears in his eyes, said that it was one of the nicest things anyone had done for him.

No one at the Catholic school in the mid-Wilshire district was happier than Jodi. Called Sammy or Simply Sam-Jo by her friends, she loved nothing more than making people happy.

On May 18, 1984, Sam-Jo darted out of her Longwood Street home. Wearing her school uniform and with her books tucked under one arm, she raced to the corner of 23rd Street to catch the school bus.

As she ran, a red Mustang suddenly pulled onto Longstreet and followed her slowly before pulling to the curb.

The driver stuck his head out the window and yelled at the running girl.

Sam-Jo looked at the driver, turned and kept running. Moments later, shots rang out.

The shooting was reported to the Los Angeles Police Mid-Wilshire Division at 8:15 a.m. When the first officer arrived, a small crowd had already gathered. Crumpled on the sidewalk was a small, dark-haired girl dressed in a Catholic school uniform. Next to her lay the school books she had clutched in her hands.

"It's Sam-Jo," a voice from the crowd said softly.

The officer crouched beside the wounded girl. Blood trickled from a gunshot wound in the side of her head. She was unconscious, but still alive.

Moments later, an ambulance pulled to the curb. The little girl was loaded on a stretcher and rushed to Cedars-Sinai Medical Center.

Then the investigators arrived. One witness told Detective Sherman Oakes that he was walking down Longwood Avenue on the way to the market when he heard a shot and saw a red Mustang pull away from the curb and race toward 23rd Street.

"He was really smoking," the witness said. "I turned and saw the little girl. She was just lying there on the sidewalk and I went to see how she was."

Investigators contacted the girl's mother. She was absolutely stunned and raced to the hospital to be with her daughter. She told the probers that she could think of no reason why anyone would want to shoot her daughter.

Detectives were still searching for clues when they got word from the station of another shooting in Crescent Heights.

"It matches the M.O. in your shooting," the detective told Sherman Oakes. "She took five slugs but is still alive."

Forty-three-year-old Lisa Virden had left her home and was jogging along Whitworth Drive near Crescent Heights Boulevard when a man in a car pulled up and ordered her to get in. She took off running and the man pursued her on foot. He closed the gap and shot her five times in the back and hips; then he ran back to his car and sped away.

The victim was taken to Cedars Sinai, the same hospital where Sam-Jo lay unconscious, fighting for her life.

Seriously wounded, but expected to recover, Lisa talked to police. She said she was completely stunned by what happened: "There was no warning. He just appeared out of nowhere and told me to get into the car. When I didn't, he started shooting."

She described the car as a red Mustang and the driver as a black man in his late teens or early twenties, about 5 feet 10 inches tall, 180 pounds with a thin mustache and wearing blue jeans and a white muscle T-shirt.

She helped police create a composite of the gunman and said she was certain she would be able to identify him.

As detectives searched for the gunman, Jodi "Sam-Jo" Samuel lay unconscious on the fourth floor of Cedar Sinai, struggling to survive.

The senseless shooting of the fun-loving 15-year-old freshman stunned her classmates. The halls of St. Mary's usually resonated with the chatter of excited young girls. Now the girls were hushed, solemn-faced, as they hurried to class.

"They walked into school Friday and there was complete silence," a history teacher remarked. "They were all in shock and they couldn't grasp the senselessness of it."

The girls at the school prayed for Sam-Jo's recovery and were buoyed by reports that their friend had moved an arm and showed signs she might be coming out of the coma. That evening, some friends stopped by the hospital and gathered around their school chum. For a moment, there was silence, and then the group spontaneously broke into "Amazing Grace"—a song Sam-Jo had wanted to sing at a Eucharist celebration two weeks earlier.

Sam-Jo never recovered consciousness, however. Five days later, she was dead.

A reporter who went to St. Mary's found a school rocked by grief, yet filled with persons eager to talk about Sam-Jo.

"Make sure you tell how much fun she was, how she liked to make people happy," one person said.

So the reporter wrote down the fun things as well as the sad. The fun things included how Sam-Jo was always ready to get into mischief, how she once shed her socks and shoes and jumped into the fountain at Inglewood City Hall, how she did a handstand against an alley wall while her blue school uniform skirt hung around her face.

He wrote how she constantly wrote letters and poems to friends, poking fun at her teachers, making up corny jokes and trying to cheer up her friends. To some good chums she'd written: "Roses are read, violets are blue, nobody loves you as much as I do."

"Jodi always had a sparkle in her eyes, even when she was down," recalled a friend. "Don't forget that in your story."

The reporter didn't forget. Neither did the police, who wanted very much to find the gunman who in an instant of madness had silenced a life filled with so much joy and promise.

Clues were scarce. Except for the composite, the description of the red Mustang, and the slug taken from the wounded runner and the murdered Catholic school freshman, detectives didn't have much.

A few days after the slaying, police arrested a man who was driving a stolen red Mustang. He roughly matched the age and description of the gunman, but he was later dropped as a suspect when his alibi for the morning of the shooting checked out.

Crime reports turned up a few more leads, none of which went anywhere.

Then, on June 26th, police were called to investigate another murder. The victim was Laverne Stolzy. She was found by a friend bludgeoned to death in her mid-Wilshire apartment.

The friend told detectives that she and Stolzy were secretaries at the same insurance company. Laverne Stolzy had agreed to give her a lift to work, but when she did not arrive, the friend became concerned and went to her co-worker's apartment.

Walking up to the front door, the friend saw an open purse lying on the grass and the front door ajar. Worried, she went next door and asked a neighbor to help her search for Laverne.

They got no further than the living room. The 56-year-old insurance secretary was sprawled naked on the floor. Her face was battered and a small pool of blood soaked the carpet in front of her open mouth.

They immediately called the police.

Detectives searched the crime scene. Laverne's body lay 10 feet from a chair which faced a television. Her clothing was a few feet away. The apartment had been completely ransacked, top to bottom, and jewelry, cash and other valuable items had been removed.

The autopsy revealed that the middle-aged single woman had died as a result of a brutal beating that had crushed the side of her head like an eggshell. Before the beating she had been raped and sodomized.

The evidence suggested to investigators a likely scenario of what happened.

Laverne Stolzy must have eaten dinner and was watching television when the intruder crept or forced his way into her small but tidy one-bedroom apartment.

The attack came violently and quietly—no one in the neighborhood reported hearing screams or sounds of a scuffle. The killer dragged her to the floor, ripped off her clothes and assaulted her before leaving her to die.

Then he methodically ransacked the home, apparently taking only easily concealed items, like jewelry, before leaving.

It was a cold, brutal crime with few clues and little physical evidence. The sole good lead came from the next-door neighbor, Clifford Barnes.

Barnes said that he and the victim were friends who often did favors for each other.

He'd been standing at the curb the night before chatting with a girl he had just met, he said, when a black man walked past him and disappeared down a narrow cement walkway that led to Laverne's apartment. "That seemed kind of odd," he said.

"Why?" the detective asked.

"You should have seen this guy," the neighbor said. "He had a flat-top haircut that was shaved on the sides and wore leather top to bottom. He looked like that punk rocker, Grace Jones."

After the leather-clad man passed, Barnes said, he resumed his conversation with the pretty girl. He had almost lined up a date when, 30 minutes later, the flat-top guy walked back down the alley, got into a car and drove away.

"You can identify the car?" a detective asked.

"Sure," Barnes responded. "It was Miss Stolzy's car."

The car was found two days later, abandoned in a supermarket parking lot. It had been wiped clean of prints and nobody at the market reported seeing the driver.

Reasoning that Laverne Stolzy's killer did not have a car and had been on foot, detectives went through crime reports of men who had been stopped in the mid-Wilshire district on suspicion of burglary or robbery and who roughly matched the suspect's description.

But the lead that would crack the case did not materialize until four months later. By then, there had been another murder.

On September 26th, Detectives Woody Parks and Jim McCann were called to an apartment complex on Dunsmuir Avenue to investigate a "possible 187"—homicide.

The victim was Dolores Clement, a 55-year-old linotype operator. Her body was discovered that morning by the apartment manager.

As he sat in the back of a police cruiser, the manager's benign, round features twitched with apprehension. He had been inspecting the exterior of the apartments that morning, he said, when he discovered a screen from Dolores Clement's window lying on the ground. Alarmed, he looked in the open window and saw the woman's body sprawled on the bed.

"I knew right away she was dead," he said, and he'd called police.

The one-bedroom apartment was clean and neat and filled with mementos of Dolores' childhood in Canada. The 55-year-old attractive linotype operator lay naked on the bed, her face covered with blood.

The autopsy revealed that she had been strangled. She had also been raped, sodomized and penetrated with a foreign object—a corncob—found lying next to the corpse.

Detectives determined that the woman had been asleep when the intruder removed the screen and slipped through the open window. A witness upstairs heard a loud, piercing scream about midnight. "Then it stopped," she told police. "If there had been more, I probably would have called police, but there wasn't."

It was an appalling crime with few clues. But one bright spot surfaced when a crime-lab technician lifted a partial palmprint from inside the bedroom closet. "We can match the print if you get a suspect," the technician told Investigator Parks.

As days passed, that seemed less and less likely.

In mid-October, Detective Parks looked at a beat report brought to his attention by Patrol Officer Elliot Rada. On October 9th, two officers were cruising the mid-Wilshire district when they noticed a man standing by an apartment complex looking at an open window. Spotting the cruiser, the man jammed his hands in his pants pocket and scurried away.

The apartment was in the neighborhood that had reported several recent hot-prowl burglaries.

Suspicious, one officer turned to his partner and said, "Let's take a look." They caught up to the scurrying man and told him to stop. "Identification?" one of the cops asked.

Lip curling, he produced a driver's license. "Why are you stopping me?" he asked.

"We'll ask the questions," the second officers said.

The driver's license identified him as Kevin Bernard Haley, 20, of South Bronson Avenue.

"What were you doing back there?" one of the officers inquired.

"Back where?" Haley asked.

"Back where you saw us and took off."

"Just walking. I like to walk at night."

"And looking in apartment windows?"

"Hey!" Haley exclaimed. "What are you talking about?"

The patrol officer ran a crime check. There were no outstanding warrants. Haley was clean.

"We had nothing to arrest him on," Officer Rada told Detective Parks. "But something wasn't right. The guy was a long way from his apartment, it was past midnight and he was looking in that apartment window."

The officers decided to bring Haley in and fingerprint him. Afterward, he was allowed to leave.

The prints were sent back to the crime lab for comparison with the partials lifted from the Clement home. The report came back that the prints were a match. Kevin Haley had definitely been inside the Clement home.

That proved to be just the tip of the iceberg, however. Detectives went back to mid-Wilshire and showed a photographic "laydown" to Clifford Barnes. He was able to identify Haley as the Grace Jones look-alike he'd seen walking up to Laverne Stolzy's house and later leaving in her car.

Lisa Virden, the 43-year-old runner, also identified Haley as the man who'd ordered her into the red Mustang and later shot her five times. This identification not only made Haley a prime suspect in the shooting of the jogger, but also in the shooting-murder of Jodi Samuel, who was shot the same day by a man driving a red Mustang.

Kevin Haley and his older brother, Reginald, 23, were arrested at their South Bronson Avenue apartment. They were booked on suspicion of burglary.

Kevin Haley was brought to an interrogation room. A professional dog-groomer, he admitted to leading a double life — clipping pooches by day, hot-prowling by night. He said he'd started burglarizing and robbing homes about five years earlier, after developing a cocaine habit. He and his brother, he said, began as weekend "snorters" but quickly developed $100-a-day habits.

"I couldn't work, couldn't do nothing without coke," Haley said. They broke into businesses. They broke into homes. It was easy — maybe too easy."

Kevin Haley was the mastermind. As detectives later learned, he selected as his victims elderly single women because they were the most vulnerable and the easiest of targets. Haley would follow a woman to her home, check it out, and return at a later time.

One of Haley's favorite tricks was to break into the home and hide in the closet. When the victim walked in, he leaped out — stripped from the waist down.

Haley talked easily about burglary.

"How many did you commit, Kevin?" Detective Parks asked.

"Lots," he said. "At least fifty. Maybe a lot more. One hundred. I don't know. We were doing them two, three times a week."

He was asked if he knew Dolores Clement, who'd lived on Dunsmuir Avenue. Haley said he had never heard of her. Detective Parks explained that she had been sexually assaulted and strangled.

"I don't know nothing about murder," the suspect declared.

"Your prints are in her house," the detective said.

"Bull!" Haley exclaimed.

"Suit yourself," Parks said. "We found them in the closet."

Haley's sensuous lips turned at the corners. He

438

shrugged. "I didn't know her name," he said softly.

Haley was again advised of his constitutional rights. Out of self-interest, he probably should have stopped—California has the death penalty—but Haley was one of those criminals whose mouth was almost as big as his sizable ego.

He was a big-time criminal—he was compelled to talk. Haley jabbered like a magpie. He confessed to the murder. He confessed to eight rapes—five never reported.

Before he finished, police linked the dog-groomer to nine more murders, and enough violent crimes to keep mid-Wilshire detectives buried under paperwork for a month.

The victims ranged from 35 to 90 years old. They were attacked in their homes, usually late at night or early morning. Without exception, they were completely defenseless.

That was okay with Haley. "I liked it," he admitted. It turned me on."

In the Clement case, Haley told detectives, he'd surprised the woman in the bedroom and struggled with her to keep her quiet. During the struggle, he said, "I became aroused," and he started ripping at her clothes. That caused the terrified woman to struggle, which only increased his excitement.

He raped her. He sodomized her. Then he killed her.

Kevin Haley was booked into county jail for the murder of Dolores Clement. He and his brother Reginald were also charged with multiple counts of rape, robbery and burglary.

At a press conference, Police Chief Daryl Gates said that the Haley brothers were responsible for one of the worst crime waves ever to hit the City of the Angels: "We have linked them to possibly hundreds of violent crimes and there are probably a lot more we don't know about."

For this reason, Chief Gates said, Haley's picture was being released for publication in the hope that victims of other unreported rapes and assaults might come forward.

439

Veteran Prosecutor Steven Barshop was assigned to the Haley case. "We had a single purpose in mind, and that was to get the death sentence," Barshop said.

The prosecutor was confident that a jury would find Haley guilty of the Clement murder. In the dozens of murder cases he had prosecuted, he said, this was perhaps the strongest.

Haley had confessed to the crime. His prints were in the house. Haley had drawn a diagram of the house and the bedroom where Clement was attacked.

If there was such a thing as an air-tight, conviction-guaranteed murder case, this was it.

Barshop said that just in case a jury, for some insane reason, found him not guilty, he was prepared to go with one of the other murder cases. The State would continue until Haley was convicted.

And how does the defense combat an airtight case?

"They stall," Barshop said. "They age the case. Time is always on the side of the defense."

It took four years of appeals and continuances before the Haley brothers went on trial.

Reginald Haley was first. After a three-week trial, he was convicted, in April 1988, of a string of rapes, kidnappings, burglaries and robberies, and he was sentenced to 60 years in state prison, plus a life term. Under California law, he must serve at least 45 years before he is considered eligible for parole.

Kevin Haley went on trial in May. On June 6, 1988, he was convicted of the murder and sexual assault of Dolores Clement. But the jurors deadlocked on whether Haley had murdered Laverne Stolzy, and on the attempted rape and oral copulation charges involving a third victim, who was unable to testify because of health problems. Mistrials were declared on those charges.

During the penalty phase, the jurors heard evidence linking the dog-groomer to the shooting of jogger Lisa Virden and the shooting death of Jodi Samuel. They also heard testimony linking him to other murders and rapes.

During the trial, the defense chose not to present evidence that might persuade the jury to spare their client's life. Had they done so, Prosecutor Barshop said that he was prepared to present rebuttal evidence of approximately 50 burglaries committed by Kevin Haley, and of Haley's botched attempt to escape from the county jail.

That evidence — which included character-witness testimony from relatives and a family minister — was presented to the judge in written form on July 5th, after jurors voted that Haley should receive the death penalty for his crimes.

Haley was returned to the courtroom on October 4th. Before sentencing him, Judge Judith C. Chirlin said that Haley had preyed on some of the community's most vulnerable members to satisfy his lust for drugs, for power, for money and for sex. Those crimes evinced a "depravity which is unspeakable."

Judge Chirlin said that she had read the mitigating evidence presented by defense attorneys, but she agreed with the jury that the death sentence verdict "is supported overwhelmingly by the weight of the evidence.

"I am satisifed beyond a reasonable doubt that Kevin Haley had murdered two other women, attempted to murder a third and raped a fourth."

Calling Haley a "serious danger to society," Judge Chirlin sentenced him to die in the electric chair at San Quentin. By law, the verdict must be automatically appealed to the state supreme court. Until a ruling is reached, Kevin Haley remains confined on San Quentin's Death Row.

EDITOR'S NOTE:

Lisa Virden and Clifford Barnes are not the real names of the persons so named in the foregoing story. Fictitious names have been used because there is no reason for public interest in the identities of these persons.

El Bandito —
The Mad Dog Of
Five Nations!

by John Dunning

Rogue, robber, rapist, remorseless killer.

It was 3:15 in the morning of February 18, 1983, and the lobby of the three-star Bristol Hotel facing the railway station in Lyon, France, was empty except for two men. One was a hotel guest who was waiting for his girlfriend, a waitress in a nightclub, to get off work. The other was 61-year-old Angelo Perret, the night porter, watchman, and desk clerk.

The door to the elevator slid open, a young man stepped out, made a circle of the lobby, and reentered the elevator.

"That's the gentleman in three-oh-six," remarked Perret. The elevator door opened again and the young man reappeared, carrying a small suitcase. Advancing to the desk, he opened the case, produced a sawed-off shotgun, pointed it at the two startled men and snapped out a string of orders in barely intelligible French.

Possessing sharp reflexes, the hotel guest dived behind the nearest table from which, peering over the top, he saw the gentleman from Room 306 drop his gun, pull out a large dagger, and stab Perret in the groin.

Groaning, Perret staggered toward the door to the hotel linen room, while the young man turned and bent over

442

his suitcase.

The guest bolted from behind the table, ran for the stairs, leaped them three at a time, reached his room, and locked himself in. He snatched up the telephone to call the police, but he suddenly realized that he could not. To obtain an outside line, he had to be connected over the hotel switchboard — and Perret was not there to do it!

For a quarter of an hour, the guest remained barricaded in his room, afraid to come out. Then, the telephone rang.

It was his girlfriend, finished with work and at the hotel to meet him. There was no one in the lobby, she said.

Now the police were summoned and Angelo Perret was found in the laundry room. The stab wound had severed the femoral artery. He had bled to death.

The hotel guest was able to provide a detailed description of the murderer. The assailant was young, under 30, dark, rather frail-looking, and he had a thin, black mustache. His hair was combed down over his forehead and he spoke French with an almost unintelligible, Spanish accent.

According to the hotel register, room 306 had been occupied by a Mr. Fernando Dome. Not surprisingly, this proved to be an alias and untraceable.

At 5:15 a.m. that same day, only two hours after the murder of Angelo Perret, 23-year-old Alain Cardot, night porter at the Hotel Ibis in Valence, 60 miles south of Lyon, was setting out the breakfast dishes for the guests in the company of 53-year-old waitress Yvonne Fischer.

Suddenly, a young man with a black mustache appeared in the breakfast room and demanded a cup of coffee.

Before Cardot or Fischer had time to react, the man produced a sawed-off shotgun, tied the two employees to chairs, and gagged them with napkins.

His attempt to open the cash register failed, however, because it was electronic and, because he did not know how to operate it, the mechanism became blocked. To solve this problem, he pressed an awl deeper and deeper into the flesh of Cardot's chest until the porter told him what to do.

There were only 300 francs in the cash register, a sum worth less than $50, and this so annoyed the robber that he struck Cardot and Miss Fischer several violent blows in the face with the stock of the sawed-off shotgun before departing.

On February 23rd, according to the reconstruction of the crime by the police, the robber entered the underground parking garage of the Solhotel in Cannes on the Cote d'Azur, 200 miles southeast of Valence. Taking the elevator to the roof, he jumped down onto a balcony and entered the room where Dutch tourists Jan and Katarina Smid were sleeping. He rudely woke them and made his demands.

Jan tried to resist and was stabbed in the foot. The robber collected a small amount of jewelry, but only 700 francs. This made him so angry that he tore the couple's passports to shreds and trampled Mr. Smid's glasses into junk. He then left through the door.

The following night, he hit the Hotel Palma in Cannes. The victim this time was 56-year-old Robert Bergel, who refused to hand over the contents of the cash register. The robber responded by tying him to a chair and stabbing him in the thigh and the hand.

Convinced by the knife point which was being forced deeper and deeper into his flesh, Bergel explained how to open the cash register and the robber made off with 5,000 francs.

The Cannes police had been notified in both cases and, having detailed descriptions that corresponded closely, they had a sketch prepared by the police artist and distributed nationwide.

Responses were promptly received from Lyon and Valence. A special commission was formed, headed by Chief Inspector Jules Grandin of the Cannes Police Department of Criminal Investigations.

Immediately it was presented with a new case. On the morning of March 1st, the chambermaid coming to tidy room Number 7 of the Hotel Brice in Nice, 20 miles further east along the Cote d'Azur, found the bathroom literally a sea of blood.

Lying in the middle of it was 57-year-old Nicolas Defeo, married, father of two children, and the night-desk clerk at the hotel.

The occupant of Room 7 had been a Mr. Antonio Arrete, described as young, dark, frail, and wearing a thin, black mustache. He had spoken French, as in the French slang expression "comme une vache espagnole (which means 'like a Spanish cow')."

"What we have here," said Chief Inspector Grandin, "is not a cow but a mad dog. He is not even bothering to disguise his appearance and he is striking at incredibly short intervals. I want every police force along The Cote d'Azur on full alert until he has been apprehended."

A tall, well-built man in his late fifties, with a grave, deliberate manner and penetrating, light-brown eyes, the chief inspector had summoned the key members of his commission together for briefing and discussion.

"Is there any reason to believe that he'll confine his activities to the Cote d'Azur?" asked Inspector Paul Serreau, who had been appointed Grandin's second-in-command.

"None," said the chief inspector. "However, he started in Lyon, came south to Valence, and then to Cannes and Nice. Criminals of this type usually dislike retracing their steps, possibly because they think someone may recognize them."

"Are we going to run the sketch in the newspapers?" asked the identifications officer.

"It could scare him out of the area," said Inspector Serreau. "We don't want that."

"I think we'll have to chance it," said Inspector Grandin. "He doesn't appear to be concerned about showing his face, and he may be recognized when he checks into a hotel."

445

That afternoon, in all the hundreds of communities along the Cote d'Asur, from Menton on the Italian border to the great city of Marseille, police forces went on alert.

By good fortune, it was the off-season and the number of residents was a fraction of what it would be in July and August. The lovely stretch of Mediterranean coastline known as the Cote d'Azur (literally the "Blue Coast") is still the most popular vacation place in Europe.

However, when, on March 8th, the "Night Clerk Killer," as he was labeled in the press, struck again, it was in the city of Grenoble, 150 miles to the north.

The scene was the Savoie Hotel. The victim was 28-year-old Brahim Mrabet, the night porter.

This time, the killer used a machine pistol instead of the sawed-off shotgun. Binding Mr. Mrabet hand and foot, he locked him in the telephone booth in the lobby and made off with 2,000 francs from the till.

Police all over the southern half of the country were now equipped with copies of the sketch of the killer and details of his modus operandi. Grenoble police immediately recognized the man being sought by the Cannes commission and, when they showed Mr. Mrabet the sketch, so did he.

Chief Inspector Grandin was informed and a squad was dispatched to Grenoble. They arrived at 8:30 in the evening; at 9:30, a Mr. Rene Foucher was shot in the leg in the basement parking garage of the large apartment building in which he was residing.

Mr. Foucher had heard suspicious sounds coming from the basement and had thought that someone might be stealing his car. He had gone to investigate and had found himself confronted by a slender young man with a thin, black mustache, who brusquely ordered him out of the basement in a mixture of French and Spanish.

Mr. Foucher prudently withdrew, but then imprudently returned. Whereupon the man shot him in the leg and left.

The Grenoble force went on full alert, off-duty officers

were called in, and the exit roads from the town were blocked off. Details were sent to cover the railway station and the bus terminal. Forty persons were taken into custody, but before they could be checked out, they were proved innocent when the Night Clerk Killer struck in Toulon, the French naval base on the Cote d'Azur, 20 miles east of Marseille.

Now, the killer added kidnapping and rape to his crimes. It was seven o'clock in the evening of March 9th and Marie-Christine Artus, a ravishing young blonde salesgirl at a large department store, was returning to her apartment at 30 Boulevard de Strasbourg.

As she entered the building elevator, a young man with a thin black mustache got in after her. He was wearing jeans and a marine-blue sweatshirt.

No sooner had the elevator door closed than he pulled out a gun, pointed it at her head and informed her in very broken French that she was taking him home with her.

Frightened nearly out of her wits, Marie-Christine had no choice but to obey. Once inside the apartment, though, she tried to scare him off by telling him, "My fiance is coming very soon."

"Good," said the man, smiling. "We'll wait for him."

Marie-Christine had been telling the truth. After a short time, her fiance, Philippe Herr, arrived and found himself looking down the barrel of the killer's gun.

"We're expected at friends," he said, trying, in his turn, to frighten off the intruder. "They'll be suspicious if we don't turn up and we don't have a telephone here."

"No problem," said the killer. "I'll go to a pay phone and telephone them that you can't come. I'm taking the girl with me. You keep quiet. Or else . . ."

Fearful for his fiancee's life, Herr could only remain helplessly in the apartment while the man and Marie-Christine left.

The killer did take her to a telephone booth from which she was forced to call the friends and cancel the visit.

Then instead of bringing her back to the apartment, he searched her handbag, found the keys to her Ford Escort, forced her into the passenger seat and taking the wheel, set off in the direction of Cavaillon, a town located 70 miles to the north.

"Where are you taking me? Who are you?" groaned the terrified girl.

"You'll see," said the man "You can call me El Bandito."

It was the first mention of a title that would eventually become very well known in the south of France.

At the time, it meant nothing to Marie-Christine, who assumed that, sooner or later, she was going to be raped. Although the prospect chilled her, she was determined at least to survive.

The only hope for that lay in cooperation. She had already noted that the man talked a great deal, as if he were grateful for the opportunity to confide in someone. Therefore, she became a good and sympathetic listener.

"I came from Uruguay," said El Bandito, opening his shirt to the waist to reveal a hideous scar crossing his chest. "I was a political dissident, a fighter for freedom, and I was captured. They tortured me, beat me with a whip made of barbed wire. Finally, I managed to escape. Your friend was lucky. If he had tried anything, I would have cut his throat."

"No one is going to try anything," said Marie-Christine hurriedly.

Upon their arrival in Cavaillon, El Bandito took a double room at the Pergola Hotel. There, having remarked that he had not made love for a long time, he raped Marie-Christine four or five times; she lost count after the third time.

The experience seemed to have a calming effect on him. Early the following morning, he set off in good spirits for Saint Raphael, again on the Cote d'Azur and 10 miles west of Cannes, where he accepted Marie-Christine's suggestion that he go into the cathedral and offer up a few prayers.

His prayers completed, he drove to the railway station, released his prisoner, gave her 200 francs to pay for her gasoline, said, "Please don't denounce me!" and disappeared.

Marie-Christine assured him that she would not. Then she hurried straight into the nearest cafe to telephone the police. Scant minutes later, she found herself surrounded by most of the Saint Raphael police force. She did not suspect that the man who had abducted and raped her was the Night Clerk Killer, but the police did.

Having had a more extended and intimate contact with El Bandito, as he now became known, than had any of his previous victims, she was able to provide several new details concerning his appearance — in particular, the scars on his chest and one on his right thumb.

Despite the very prompt response of the Saint Raphael police, El Bandito eluded arrest. The railway station was a busy one and trains were departing constantly. After an exhaustive check of railway personnel and such passengers as could be located with not a single witness report of a sighting, Chief Inspector Grandin came to the conclusion that driving to the railway station had been no more than a ruse. El Bandito had not taken a train. He had simply remained in Saint Raphael.

By March 12th, however, he was in Marseille, where he tried to gain entrance to the apartment of a pretty schoolteacher, Miss Maryse Blanc, in the same manner he'd employed with Marie-Christine. But Miss Blanc was quicker on her feet and managed to get inside and slam the door in his face. Attracted by her screams, two of her neighbors pursued El Bandito down the street, one of them emptying the magazine of a blank cartridge pistol after him.

The experience failed to discourage El Bandito. That same afternoon, he attacked, handled in an intimate manner, and robbed a Mrs. Paule Lecornu in the basement garage of an apartment building only a few blocks from where he'd made the unsuccessful attempt on Maryse

449

Blanc.

With the perpetrator of both attacks identified as El Bandito, Marseille was swarming with police and the Cannes commission was on the way down.

As far as El Bandito was concerned, they might as well have been ballet dancers. Employing one of his favorite techniques of climbing over the roof, he gained entry to a luxury apartment building at 9 rue de la Visitation; by eight o'clock in the evening, he had taken captive Jean Coguillot, a retired army colonel, and his wife Yvette.

The Coguillots were slow to cooperate, so El Bandito shot the colonel in the hip and his wife in the shoulder with a .22-caliber rifle, of which the stock and barrel had been sawed off.

The Coguillots' daughter, Therese, who heard the sound of the shots, rushed from upstairs to investigate. She was forced to hand over 2,000 francs in cash. El Bandito also took Mrs. Coguillot's rings, some other jewelry, and several watches.

Following a telephone call to the police, the flying squad from the Cannes commission arrived in a matter of minutes, but El Bandito was gone.

Chief Inspector Grandin was deeply perturbed. "This is incredible!" he exclaimed. "The man robs, rapes, murders right under our noses. We have excellent descriptions of him. We have his fingerprints. We even have samples of his semen. And he goes about his business as if the police did not exist!"

"On top of that, he speaks such bad French that he's conspicuous the moment he opens his mouth," added Inspector Serreau gloomily. "The man must be completely insane."

"Not in my opinion," said Dr. Yves Desmoines, the slender, elegant medical expert assigned to the commission. "His actions are rational, purposeful, and, you must admit, efficient. It's merely that he operates on a totally self-centered basis. He's not handicapped by any moral principles, any feelings of pity, any reservations. What he

450

wants, he takes. If anyone stands in the way of it, he eliminates them."

"It's partly because he's a foreigner," said the chief inspector. "Wherever he comes from, he probably has a police record, but we have none here and he's not registered anywhere. Fernando Dome, Antonio Atrete, and Antonio Pietro are definitely all false names."

"Uruguay reported no record on the fingerprints," said Inspector Serreau. "Maybe we should try other Spanish-speaking countries. All the witnesses agree that he speaks with a strong Spanish accent."

"Yes," said the chief inspector. "Try them. Try them all—and Spain too. Although, as he apparently never uses it, I don't know what good it would do us to know his real name."

As if to add insult to injury, the elusive criminal now transferred his operations to Cannes, the commission's own bailiwick, where on the night of March 17th, St. Patrick's Day, and El Bandito's 35th birthday—he clambered over the roof of an apartment building at 8 rue de General Ferrie and entered the bedroom of Pierre and Paulette Cohen.

He was armed with a pistol and a dagger and he immediately obtained the elderly couple's full cooperation, because sleeping in another room of the apartment was their little granddaughter.

He demanded money and was quickly given 3,000 francs from the drawer of the night table. Then he took Mrs. Cohen's valuable collection of jewelry from her dressing table and searched the apartment, finding a wall safe containing another 5,000 francs, 200,000 Italian lire, and a checkbook.

After forcing Cohen to sign a check for 20,000 francs, he announced that he was staying the night—he intended to accompany the Cohens to the bank in the morning so that there would not be any problem with cashing the check.

He indicated that he would not be averse to a little hospitality. Having partaken of a light collation, served by the Cohens from their own kitchen, he suggested that Mrs. Cohen might like to kill the time by washing his hair.

Mrs. Cohen gave him a shampoo. The following morning, she and her husband accompanied him to the bank, where he collected the 20,000 francs from the check. He brought them back to their apartment, thanked them for their hospitality, assured them that they were as good as dead if they breathed a word, and he disappeared.

The Cohens rushed to report the robbery to the police and the crime commission sealed off Cannes.

With—as usual—no results. By noon of that same day, El Bandito was back in Saint Raphael in the rue Gounod, where he visited a jewelry store owned by Mr. and Mrs. Claude Veron-Roque and asked for an appraisal of Mrs. Cohen's jewelry.

Mr. Veron-Roque was not present and his wife suggested that El Bandito return later. She did not suspect that he was the famous Night Clerk Killer. Not many jewel thieves bring their booty into a prominent jewelry store and ask for an appraisal.

While waiting, El Bandito took Room 41 at the nearby Hotel de Geneve, which was owned by Mr. Maurice Chenaud. He had lunch at the hotel and struck up an acquaintanceship with a chambermaid of whom he took some pictures and who, at his request, took some pictures of him. He then returned to the jewelry store.

Mr. Veron-Roque had returned. He assessed the value of two rings set with rubies as 40,000 francs. An emerald ring and two with diamonds were worth somewhat more.

"I'll send them to a friend of mine in Marseille," said El Bandito. "Right now I have a train to catch."

The following morning, Mr. Veron-Roque and Mr. Chenaud opened their newspapers almost simultaneously and, almost simultaneously, leaped out of their chairs. Plastered across the front page of the Saint Raphael newspaper, as it was across the front page of every newspaper

452

along the Cote d'Azur, was a remarkably accurate police sketch of El Bandito.

Both men rushed to telephone the police. A heavily armed detachment of detectives soon stormed Room 41 at the Hotel de Geneve.

El Bandito was not home, but he obviously planned to return, because he had left his professional equipment there. This included two 12-gauge shot-guns and a .22-caliber long-rifle carbine, all three with sawed-off stocks and barrels, a dagger with brass knuckles on the hilt, various burglary tools, most of Mrs. Cohen's jewelry, and 50,000 francs.

There was no indication of where he had gone, but he had mentioned Marseille and a train to Mr. Veron-Roque, and it was known that he often traveled by train.

The Saint Raphael highway station was immediately staked out with dozens of plainclothes officers, while another large detachment remained at the hotel. The Cannes commission had arrived by this time, and there was no shortage of manpower.

At a little before eight o'clock that evening, a plainclothes police inspector watching the passengers disembark from the train that had just arrived from Marseille saw a young man with thin black mustache raise his arm to look at his watch. The sleuth recognized the scar on the thumb as described by Marie-Christine Artus.

Signalling his men, he closed in. El Bandito suddenly found himself surrounded by detectives who seized his arms while the inspector held his service pistol within six inches of his nose.

"Que pasa?" cried El Bandito, limp with astonishment. The question meant, "What's going on?" What went on first was a body search of the suspect.

This produced a P38 pistol with a round in the chamber. As the inspector opened the suspect's shirt, the terrible scar reported by Marie-Christine became visible.

El Bandito had been taken at last!

Brought to police headquarters in Nice, El Bandito

promptly confessed and gave his name as Pedro He-chauge. He had been born in Uruguay, he said, and was married to a Maria Fernandez who lived in Spain.

None of these personal details were true. El Bandito's real name was Fernando Alonso de Celeda and he had been born in Buenos Aires, Argentina rather than Uruguay.

Little was known of his parents, but he had already established a criminal record by the age of 13. From that time on, he had been continually in and out of detention centers and prisons.

On February 13, 1979, he had contracted a marriage with a woman known simply as Azbiga, whose whereabouts were currently unknown. He had continued his career of arrest, imprisonment and release until 1980, when he had fled Argentina to pursue his profession in Brazil, the Canary Islands, Spain, and, finally, in January of 1983, France.

Brought to trial on November 2, 1987, El Bandito confessed readily to all the charges against him, but said that the victims had been consenting. Marie-Christine had almost forced him to have sex with her, he said, and her claims of rape were merely to prevent her fiance from finding out the truth. The Cohens had been so taken with him that they had cooked him a meal and Mrs. Cohen had washed his hair. They had given him the money and jewels voluntarily, he told police.

Whether this novel defense would have succeeded is doubtful. On November 4th, Celada became weary of the game and confessed in court to the murders of Angelo Perret and Nicholas Defeo.

The court listened to testimony by psychologists who'd had Celada under observation for over a year and who described him as the most dangerous violent offender they had ever seen.

He was then sentenced to life imprisonment.

Did Alligators Eat The Pretty Texas Waitresses?

by Alan Hynd

> Hardbitten homicide detectives, faced with what was
> probably the state's most hideous crime, had to find
> the answer to an unbelievable question . . .

There were two attractions at Joe Ball's drinkery of
U.S. Highway 181 outside of Elmendorf, Texas besides the
booze—the waitresses and the alligators. But the drinkers
who knew what was best for their health didn't get too
close to either the dolls or the reptiles. The girls, who
came and went with great frequency, had come to be
known as Ball's babes. The alligators—five of them in a
cement pool out back—were always hungry, being particularly fond of live dogs and cats. Nor, as it was to turn
out, were dogs and cats the only special nourishment the
reptiles gulped down—not after they had developed a
fondness for something sweeter and, shall we say, more
civilized.

The proprietor of Social Inn, as Joe Ball called his
place, was a towering, square-jawed, leathery-skinned man
with a bluish beard who had once had a cheery word and
a friendly backslap for everybody. Joe sprang from a
wealthy and respected family of ranchers with German
blood in its ancestry and after graduating from the University of Texas, he joined the family enterprise. Then

along came the first world war and Joe dropped everything to enlist at age 26.

Joe was a changed man when he came back from the war — a hero with decorations. "Screw the medals," was his way of commenting on his citations for heroism at the Western Front. Sullen and morose, Joe didn't seem to have any of his previous ambition left, either. He wanted no part of resuming work on the great family ranch. All he seemed to care about now, as he shacked up in a couple of rooms in the centre of Elmendorf, was all the booze and babes he could handle.

Joe took his time in looking for work and when he did decide on gainful employment it wasn't exactly legal: it was bootlegging. Joe zoomed around in a big truck filled with prohibition-era varnish remover, supplying speakeasies in quite a radius from Elmendorf. He drank up quite a bit of his own inventory as the years passed and seemed to grow more sullen — and sex crazy — as the time went on.

Then, in 1933, when good liquor became legal again, Ball, now 42, opened Sociable Inn. It caught on at once. It drew not only the red necks but the smarter trade from San Antonio, not far to the north. There was a nice, long bar, at which Joe himself presided, and a few tables at which three waitresses — each of them prettier than the other — served, in addition to booze, not-too-bad food. Ladies weren't barred but they weren't encouraged. The waitresses slept in quarters adjacent to the Sociable Inn.

The big attraction at Sociable Inn — the thing that drew customers from distant points of the Lone Star State — were Joe's alligators. He had used quite a lump of his bootlegging profits for an enormous pool for the reptiles. He fed the alligators — in the beginning, anyway — great chunks of raw beef, principally horse meat. One edge of the pool was only about 30 feet from the rear of the Inn but could be reached only through a rear door of the Inn. So curious people on Highway 181 didn't have access to it. If a drinker hung in with the proprietor of Sociable Inn—and one way to get in right with Joe was to take on a load—he was taken out back and shown the alligators.

One thing quickly became apparent to several of the regular drinkers at Joe's place. And that was that Ball changed waitresses awful fast. They were all so pretty that they were immediately given double takes by the drinkers when they put in their first appearances at The Inn. Thus it became obvious, to several of the smarter customers that some of the dolls simply disappeared after a night or two, to be replaced by newcomers. Where Ball was getting all the girls, and how, was something of a puzzle to the wonderers—then anyway.

One night, about a year after Joe had opened the Inn, a drinker well along the road to a terrible morning was alternately studying Joe, hustling the drinks, and the three waitresses who were hustling fried chicken, the specialty of the house.

"Joe," said the drinker, loud enough for a couple of other customers to hear, "you sure as hell change waitresses awful fast."

Joe, drawing a beer, seemed not to hear. A second drinker got into the act. "Joe," he said, "Charley here says you sure change waitresses awful fast."

Ball looked up. "Yeah," he said. "Waitresses don't stay in one place very long."

"Maybe," said the first questioner. "But I've seen an awful lot of them here today and gone tomorrow in the year you've had this place."

Ball, his bluish face growing bluer, glowered at the drinker and had one word to ask: "So?"

"So," came the reply, "I've been wonderin'."

"Wonderin' what?"

"Wonderin' if you're throwin' the waitresses to the alligators."

There was a dreadful moment or two. Ball's face became a darker blue. The drinker, and the fellow who had got into the act, started to break up at the crack—funny as all hell.

The drinker was still laughing at his own joke when Ball came around from the other side of the bar, grabbed the man, and tossed him out on Highway 181. When he came back for the second laugher the man had slipped away. "Some jokes," Joe muttered to other drinkers who had been caught up in the episode, "just ain't funny a-t-a-l-l."

It wasn't long after that episode, in the early hours of one morning after Sociable Inn had closed for the night, that a little Mexican who worked on a ranch that adjoined the Sociable Inn property was out on horseback checking fences. A full Texas moon was very brilliant this particular night and the Mexican, suddenly finding himself close to Joe's alligator pool, pulled up short.

There, in the moonlight, was Joe Ball, tossing the contents of a burlap bag, piece by piece, to his alligators.

Ball, as if out of the corner of his eye, suddenly became aware of the man on horseback looking at him in the bright moonlight. "Oh, hello there," Joe said to the Mexican.

"What was that," asked the Mexican, not bothering to say Hello, "I just saw you throwin' in the pool?"

"A cat," answered Joe.

"It didn't look like a cat to me," said the Mexican.

"What'd it look like?"

"*It looked like somebody's leg.*"

"You're nuts," said Joe. "It was a cat."

"*And before the leg,*" continued the Mexican, who sure as hell didn't know which side his bread was buttered on, "*it looked like somebody's arm.*"

"No," said Joe, "it was another cat."

Now the Mexican, with a sudden rush of intelligence, gave his horse the business and got to hell out of sight.

Next night the owner of the ranch next to Joe's place dropped into Sociable Inn for a word with the proprietor. "Joe," he said, "lemme know if you hear of a good general worker I can get to keep tabs on my fences."

"How come you need one all of a sudden?" asked Joe, as if he didn't know.

"I had a good man—a little Mexican—but he suddenly up and disappeared without sayin' a word," came the answer. "Here one day and gone the next. Damned queer."

As time passed the rapid change in Ball's waitresses came to be taken for granted among the regular patrons. Sometimes fierce jealousies would develop among the girls over Joe's affection; sometimes, on the other hand, friendships would spring up between two or all three of the girls. But jealousies and friendships never lasted long; rather, the girls didn't.

It was in the summer of 1937, after our boy had entered his fifth year as the proprietor of Sociable Inn, that things began to come to a climax in more ways than one. A tall blonde named Minnie Mae Goddhardt stepped off a bus in front of Sociable Inn carrying a newspaper ad in which Joe had asked for a waitress. Minnie Mae specialized in low-necked dresses and when she stooped she conquered.

The trouble with Minnie Mae's appearance was that there was another girl on the serving staff—a red-haired doll named Maggie Carter—who was not only nuts about Joe but who had but one intention in life—to become his wife.

So there they were, Minnie and Maggie, vying for Joe's personal services, pouring out their passion to him, spewing their venom at one another. A third girl on the serving staff at this time—known only as Stella—wasn't in on the fight for Joe. Stella had served her purpose with the proprietor, it seemed, and was being kept on simply because she was such a good waitress and so popular with the patrons.

It sure was a hot summer in 1937, around Sociable Inn, in more ways than one. Then one day in August Minnie Mae told Stella that the boss was going to take her on a picnic at Corpus Christi, more than a hundred miles to the Southeast. "I think he's going to propose marriage to me," she spouted to Stella in a voice loud enough for two drinkers to hear.

"That's great," the drinkers—who were one day to be found by the law—heard Stella replying to Minnie Mae. "I hope you beat out that red-headed bitch."

She was laughing, Minnie Mae was, when she ended her little talk with Stella. Next morning, at dawn, she set out for Corpus Christi with Ball for what she apparently thought was going to be a ball. And that was to be the end of Minnie Mae.

Late that night, when our boy got back to Sociable Inn, Stella asked him where Minnie Mae was. "I drove her to Corpus Christi to catch a train," Joe replied. "She got tired of it here."

That didn't quite make sense to Stella in view of what Minnie Mae had told her prior to leaving. Stella began to wonder.

A few days later, Joe and Maggie Carter, the vanished Minnie Mae's rival, drove to San Diego, California, to become man and wife.

During the absence of the newly-weds, Stella fell into dark talk with a young dishwasher at the inn called Charlie. It so happened that Charlie had been sweet on the now-missing Minnie Mae and had hoped that she would lose out in her fight with Maggie Carter for Joe's affections.

Damned curious, if not yet outright suspicious, Stella and Charlie went into the room Minnie Mae had occupied and poked around. They weren't in the room very long when they became downright suspicious. Minnie Mae hadn't taken any of her clothes or other possessions with her. Her quarters gave the impression of a girl who had gone away for the day, as Minnie Mae had said she was going, not for good.

During the days that were still to elapse before Joe and

his red-headed bride returned to the Inn, Stella and Charlie started speculating. Stella told patron friends about her puzzlement at Minnie Mae's vanishment. Charlie, in sessions at the bar, told everybody who would listen that he considered Minnie Mae's disappearance nothing short of a mystery.

When Joe Ball returned from his honeymoon with his bride he quickly heard what had been going on during his absence. If the fur didn't fly, something else sure as hell must have. A couple of nights later—again in the moonlight—Joe was seen in the pre-dawn hours tossing stuff to the alligators. And it was Charlie who saw him.

Next day, Charlie wanted to tell Stella about having seen Joe tossing stuff to the alligators in the pre-dawn hours. The trouble was he couldn't find Stella because there was no Stella. She had disappeared.

Now Charlie began spouting his feelings, which he couldn't exactly describe, to some of the drinkers. Not that Charlie had too long to spout. For Charlie, too, vanished, quite suddenly, from Sociable Inn, like a figure rubbed from a blackboard.

The waitresses continued to come and they continued to go. Joe's marriage to Maggie Carter was quickly on the rocks. Then, in April of 1938, little more than half a year after she had snared the blue-faced proprietor of Sociable Inn, Mrs. Ball dropped from sight.

It was immediately after his bride vanished that Joe, now at the end of his fifth year at the Inn, widened his staff. Up to now Joe had employed only two or three girls but now he had four or five. And why? You'd never guess.

It had become something of a Texas joke around the general region of San Antonio that Joe had need for so many girls because he fed them to the alligators. Not that the joke was taken or meant seriously; it was just some Texas humor. Joe of course heard the story. But he didn't object to it—publicly, anyway. It was the big reason, re-

461

ally—the grim publicity it created—why business at Sociable Inn was booming.

Up to now, Joe had, so nearly as was one day to be determined by the Sheriff of Bexar County, in which Elmendorf is located, employed at least a hundred dolls during his first five years near the alligator pool. He drew the dames by inserting ads in papers all over Texas and in sheets as far away as California, promising good pay and big tips and pleasant surroundings. The dolls had to send not one but several photographs of themselves when applying for work at Joe's.

But Joe was not through. Other victims were yet to come to Joe's. Stepping up, like batters in a baseball game, most of them were quickly to have three balls and two strikes on them with the big one coming up.

It was along about now that a sort of an umpire got into the game—Deputy Sheriff Elton Cude of Baxter County. It was in later years that Cude, then a San Antonio undertaker, filled me in on much of the Joe Ball story.

Deputy Cude received a visit in his San Antonio Office one day from a strong-jawed, glint-eyed man who operated the ranch that adjoined Ball's place. This was the ranch where the little Mexican hand had seen Joe tossing what looked like an arm and a leg to the alligators in the moonlight—and then dropped from sight, "There's somethin' damned funny goin' on at the place of Ball's—the place with them damned alligators," the rancher said to Deputy Cude.

"Like what?" asked Cude.

"First, lemme tell you why I think what's funny is funny."

"You mean strange."

"Call it funny or strange. It's damned suspicious."

The rancher told Cude about his ranch hand who had, not long after Ball had opened up Sociable Inn, claimed to have seen Ball feeding an arm and a leg to the reptiles. "He told me about it," the rancher now told Cude, "and I

462

paid no attention, figuring my man had been drinking, and I never said nothin' about it til now. I guess I should have, though, because my man dropped from sight a couple of hours after he told me the story."

"So how does that tie in with your visit today?" Cude asked the rancher.

"It's the stink," said the rancher.

"What kind of a stink?"

"A stink that's like nothin' I ever smelled—except one time when they found a dead man who'd been rotting for a while."

"And this stink comes from Ball's place?"

"From no place else."

"Have you spoken to Ball about it?"

"I'm afraid to."

"Why?"

"It's the way Ball looks at people. When I drop into his place for a drink he's lookin' at everybody like he's ready to cut their throats—and maybe throw them to the alligators."

The deputy who was later to become an undertaker told me that there was something about the rancher—and his story—that sent a sort of a shiver through him. He said he got another shiver—a bigger one—when he dropped out to see Joe Ball about the stink.

"It's nothing, Sheriff," said Joe, forcing a smile but with unadulterated hatred flashing from his eyes. "The smell's just dead meat that I keep for my alligators. Sometimes it does get a little strong. I'll see that a cover is put on the barrel it's kept in."

Depute Sheriff Cude started to wake up in the middle of the night and not be able to get back to sleep again after that visit to Ball's—and that tale that the hired hand's boss had kept to himself all these years.

Deputy Cude was still waking up in the watches of the night, and not being able to do anything about it, when, in the summer of 1938, a piquent little brunette named

463

Hazel Brown appeared as a waitress at Ball's. Hazel, who was just nineteen, had lived with her parents in McDade, up near Austin, and had answered one of Ball's ads in an Austin newspaper. Hazel was quite different from the others. For one thing, she was a virgin. For another, she was a little go-getting hound for efficiency.

It wasn't long after she had checked into Sociable Inn before Hazel, chaste while being chased, stopped running. She seemed to have, despite her lack of experience, precisely what it took to keep Ball under control. The truth of the matter seems to be that Hazel was a little plotter — a great one for pointing out the bad features in others. There were three other waitresses when she checked in. Then there were but two others. Then but one. Then none.

Hazel was a great one for slashing expenses — a true corner cutter. She altered the menus for greater profit and sold Joe on getting glasses with high bottoms that paid for themselves and showed profits in no time at all. Ball was simply nuts about Hazel — either horizontally or perpendicularly.

Then Hazel began to over-extend herself, according to tales eavesdropping drinkers were one day to pass on to the law. She found fault with Joe's habit of feeding live dogs and cats to the alligators. "It's cruel, loved one," one boozer heard her telling Joe.

So what happened? Joe, weighing things in bed against the appetites of his reptile friends, quit feeding them live dogs and cats.

Then Hazel Brown made, it was later to be suspected, a fatal mistake. She was talking at the bar with Joe one night, within earshot of the ever-present eavesdroppers, when she was heard to say: *"Joe, I think it's time we got rid of the alligators."* That was all; nothing more, nothing less. And what did our boy do? How did he react to brazen Hazel's suggestion? He simply measured Hazel with narrowed eyes and never said a word. Not a single word.

But Joe must have thought plenty about that terrible remark. Hazel made the suggestion along toward closing time one morning and next day Joe didn't have his lone waitress and was waiting on the tables himself.

Three weeks after Hazel Brown had been seen for the last time at Sociable Inn, or anywhere else, her old man, Harry Brown, walked into the office of the Sheriff of Bexar County. He was turned over to a Deputy named Jack Klevenhagen. Deputy Klevenhagen had a desk right next to that of Deputy Cude.

"And how can I be of help?" Deputy Klevenhagen asked the father of Hazel Brown.

"It's about my daughter," said Brown. "My daughter Hazel. She's disappeared."

"Disappeared? From where?"

"She came down to this vicinity—to Elmendorf—from our home in McDade to work at an Inn—a place called Sociable Inn." It was at this point of the visitor's tale that Deputy Cude, sitting at the next desk, pricked up his ears. "We haven't heard a word from her in three weeks and she never fails to write twice a week."

"Do you know positively," asked Deputy Klevenhagen, "that your daughter actually went to work at Sociable Inn?"

"Oh, yes," replied the girl's old man. "She wrote to us twice a week saying how much she liked it and how very fond she was of Mr. Ball, the proprietor. Then her letters just stopped coming."

Deputy Cude gave Deputy Klevenhagen the high sign at this point and the two got together in the men's room. "I know what's on your mind," Klevenhagen said to Cude. "This is more of that same business you told me about some time ago—the business of that ranch-hand thinking he'd seen this man Ball throwing somebody's arm and leg to the alligators."

"Exactly," said Cude. "Ever since I heard that story I've been waking up in the middle of the night thinking about

465

it."

The trouble with the story the rancher had told Cude was that it had been five years old by the time he told it. Now, though, here was a distraught father from another part of the Lone Star State with something very recent.

Returning to Harry Brown, Klevenhagen asked him why he hadn't been in touch with Joe Ball about information relating to his daughter. Brown said he had written to Ball but had received no answer.

Questions put to Brown by Deputy Klevenhagen disclosed that the missing girl had saved her tips in an account she had opened in a San Antonio bank. When the father and the Deputy went to the bank and found that Hazel's account was intact they began to fear the worst.

Harry Brown hung around San Antonio while Deputy Klevenhgen popped out to Sociable Inn. It was early afternoon and the three waitresses that Ball had hired to take Hazel's place were on duty and Ball was tending bar. Klevenhagen got right to the point: he wanted to know where Hazel Brown was.

"Who?" asked Joe, trying to throw the word away.

"Hazel Brown."

Joe pretended to be searching his mind. "Oh," he said, snapping his fingers, "you must mean that little girl who did all the work around here before she left."

"Left? Left for where?"

"California. She was nuts about California." Joe poured himself a drink and gulped it in one gulp. "Something wrong about Hazel?" he asked the Deputy.

"No," answered Klevenhagen, playing it smart. "Nothing at all. Our office merely got a letter from Hazel's father saying he hadn't heard from her lately and was wondering."

"Tell the old man not to worry," said Ball. "Hazel's probably too busy getting settled in California to have written." Now, during a period of silence, Joe poured himself another drink and gave it the one-gulp treatment. "She was

466

a nice kid, Hazel was," he said, looking at Deputy Klevenhagen with a black glare that sent a shiver through the officer. "I'm sorry, in a way, she had to go . . ."

It was now — too late, to be sure — that letters that had for a few years been coming into the Sheriff's Office and the San Antonio Office of the Texas Rangers from all parts of the country made a grim sort of sense. These letters had been from parents, brothers and sisters of girls who had gone to "the vicinity of San Antonio" to seek employment. The girls had gone, written once or twice, then lapsed into eternal silence.

It was quite obvious to Deputies Klevenhagen and Cude that at least some of the girls had disappeared after going to work for Joe Ball. Curiously, though, not a single one of the letters had contained a morsel of information upon which the Sheriff's Office could have started some sort of a probe. Not a letter had mentioned the town of Elmendorf and, of course, Joe Ball's name had never been mentioned. If ever an arch-killer was hung with horseshoes it was our Ball.

But now Hazel Brown's old man had come out of the woodwork to put a different slant on things. Klevenhagen and Cude had, of course, known about Ball's rapid turnover of waitresses and they had heard the joke about the drinkers accusing Joe of feeding the girls to the alligators. Now, though, the joke was far from funny.

Yet, assuming Joe was one of the great arch-fiends of modern criminal history, what was the law going to do? A man can't be given the legal business for murder unless the law produces a corpus delicti. And how could so much as one corpus delicti ever be established when the body had long since been chopped up, fed to the alligators?

Klevenhagen and Cude shadowed Sociable Inn, tailed some drinkers after they left, and questioned them. Since most of the drinkers were steady customers and had been going to Joe's place for quite a while, they remembered

467

things they had picked up. There had been snatches of conversation participated in not only by the missing Hazel Brown and Joe but between Minnie Mae Goddhardt and the waitress Stella—dolls who had both now vanished. Stella and Charlie, the dishwasher, had leaked at the mouth about Minnie Mae, who had lost out in her love fight with Maggie Carter and left all her clothes behind when she dropped from sight. And where, Klevenhagen's and Cude's informants were wondering, was Mrs. Ball?

One piece of data that the two deputies picked up, and which made a deep and dark impression on them, was the way Joe Ball had reacted, almost five years previously, when the joking drinker had asked him if he was feeding the waitresses to the alligators. "Nobody," the Deputies' informant told them, "could possibly have been so enraged at that crack if there hadn't, without the man who made the crack realizing it, been something to it."

It was time, Deputy Klevenhagen decided, to have another talk with Joe Ball. Klevenhagen didn't want to know very much—just about what had become of Hazel Brown, Mrs. Ball, Minnie Mae, Stella and Charlie—and perhaps half a hundred pretty waitresses.

So Klevenhagen pulled up to Sociable Inn on the night of September 24, 1938. Joe was busy at the bar, and didn't notice him, when he walked in and he kept going, out the back door, to the alligator pool. He was just curious as he stood there, looking at all five of the reptiles coming up to the edge where he was standing, their jaws wide open. "What a shame," he muttered to himself as he studied the hungry reptiles, "that you can't talk . . ."

Returning to the Inn, Klevenhagen soon caught the eye of Joe, busy at the busy bar. Joe, recognizing the Deputy, approached him with a smile that seemed forced. "Yes," Joe said. "What can I do for you *this* time?"

"To begin with," said the Deputy, "I want the truth about Hazel Brown."

"That business is a damned mess," said Joe. "But I'll

468

help out all I can. Stick around for a little while til my relief bartender shows up."

With that Joe wasted no time. He simply went to the cash register, rang up a No Sale, pulled an automatic out of the drawer and brained himself.

Now the Texas Rangers stepped into the case—five years too late, as one citizen put it. It was the Rangers, digging back among the steady drinkers at Sociable Inn, who learned that Minnie Mae Goddhardt had said she was going on a picnic with Joe to Corpus Christi. Poking around Corpus Christi, the Rangers found a couple of teen-age girls who had, about a year previously, seen a man doing some strange digging and burying along the sand dunes.

Was it possible, the Rangers wondered, that Joe had cut Minnie Mae into pieces and buried her in the sand instead of feeding her to the alligators? Widespread digging did nothing else but turn up enough of Minnie Mae, including her teeth, to affect identification.

One day, about a month after Joe Ball had brained himself, Ranger Lee Miller received a collect telephone call from San Francisco. And who was it from, but the little Mexican who had dropped from sight after having seen Joe throw to the alligators what the Mexican insisted had been an arm and a leg.

Ball, the Mexican now told Ranger Miller, had hunted him down late the following afternoon—after the Mexican had told his employer about what he had seen—the tale the employer didn't believe at the time.

"Have you told anybody about what you saw?" Joe had asked the Mexican.

"No, sir," lied the Mexican.

"It's a good thing," said Joe. "Breathe one word of what you saw and you'll wind up with the alligators." Now Joe handed the Mexican five hundred dollars in cash. "Get going," Joe instructed the terrified Mexican, "as fast as you can and as far as you can get and don't ever come back. And remember, if you ever open your trap I'll kill you. Anyway, what the hell could you prove after my alligators have eaten something?"

And so the Mexican had taken a paid-for powder and continued to be so fearful of Ball that he never opened his mouth—until after Joe had checked out for another dimension. Why Joe didn't kill the Mexican at the time he had been caught in the aftermath of the murder act is an enigma. It's possible, Ranger Miller later told me when he had become a special agent for Alamo Express, Inc., that Joe feared murdering the Mexican might arouse suspicion. True, the Mexican left the scene, but Joe knew that the man was still alive—and could, in a pinch, always be found and produced.

Such qualified students of the case of Joe Ball as Lee Miller always felt that there was no question that Minnie Mae's friend Stella, Charlie the dishwasher and countless girls who had vanished after going to work for Ball had, purely and simply, been fed to the reptiles. Hazel Brown had missed the pool, though. She had been chopped up and her remains—which were to be identified through teeth—were found along the banks of the San Antonio River.

EDITOR'S NOTE:

Maggie Carter is not the real name of the person so named in the foregoing story. Because there is no reason for public interest in the identity of this person, a fictitious name has been used.

470

BLOCKBUSTER FICTION FROM PINNACLE BOOKS!